W9-BZA-724

ADOBE®
Illustrator® CS
Hands-On Training

lynda.com/books

Jeff Van West | with **Lynda Weinman**

Adobe Illustrator CS | H·O·T
Hands-On Training

By Jeff Van West
Developed with Lynda Weinman

lynda.com/books | Peachpit Press
1249 Eighth Street • Berkeley, CA • 94710
510.524.2178
510.524.2221 (fax)
http://www.lynda.com/books
http://www.peachpit.com

lynda.com/books is published
in association with Peachpit Press,
a division of Pearson Education
Copyright ©2004 by lynda.com

ISBN: 0-321-20303-8

0 9 8 7 6 5 4 3 2

Printed and bound in the
United States of America

H•O•T | Credits

Original Design: Ali Karp, Alink Newmedia *(alink@earthlink.net)*

Editor: Jake McFarland

Copyeditor: Darren Meiss

Compositors: Rick Gordon, Deborah Roberti

Beta Testers: Marla Rebenschied, Crystal Waters

Cover Illustration: Bruce Heavin *(bruce@stink.com)*

Indexer: Lisa Stumpf

H•O•T | Colophon

The original design for *Adobe Illustrator CS HOT* was sketched on paper. The layout was heavily influenced by online communication—merging a traditional book format with a modern Web aesthetic.

The text in *Adobe Illustrator CS HOT* was set in Akzidenz Grotesk from Adobe and Triplex from Emigré. The cover illustration was painted in Adobe Photoshop and Adobe Illustrator.

This book was created using QuarkXPress, Adobe Illustrator, Adobe Photoshop, Microsoft Office, Microsoft Windows, and OS X Panther on both PC and Macintosh machines. It was printed on 50 lb. Utopia Filmcoat at Phoenix Book Tech.

Adobe Illustrator CS | H•O•T _____ Table of Contents

Bonus Chapter on H·O·T CD-ROM

I.

Introduction

| A Note from Lynda | About the Author | Acknowledgments |
| How to Use This Book | Macintosh and Windows System Differences |
| Macintosh and Windows Screen Captures |
| Illustrator CS Systems Requirements | What's on the CD-ROM? |
| What Makes Vector-Based Illustration Different? |
| Varied Uses of Illustrator |

no exercise files

Illustrator CS H•O•T

A Note from Lynda

In my opinion, most people buy computer books to learn, yet it is amazing how few of these books are actually written by teachers. In our Hands-On Training series, we intentionally work with experienced classroom teachers, who not only know how to show you the way do something, but explain why and when you would choose to do so! In this book, you will find carefully developed lessons and exercises to help you learn Illustrator CS—one of the most powerful digital illustration tools on the planet.

The premise of the hands-on exercise approach is to get you up to speed quickly with Illustrator CS while actively working through the lessons in the book. It's one thing to read about a product, and another experience entirely to try the product and get measurable results. The Hands-On Training series motto is, "read the book, follow the exercises, and you'll learn the product." We have received countless testimonials to this fact, and it is our goal to make sure it remains true for all of our hands-on training books.

Many exercise-based books take a paint-by-numbers approach to teaching. While this approach works, it's often difficult to figure out how to apply those lessons to a real-world situation, or to understand why or when you would use the technique again. What sets this book apart is that the lessons contain lots of background information and insights into each given subject, which are designed to help you understand the process as well as the exercise.

At times, pictures are worth a lot more than words. When necessary, we have also included short QuickTime movies to show any process that's difficult to explain with words. These files are located on the **H•O•T CD-ROM** inside a folder called **movies**. This book also refers you to the lynda.com Web site, where you'll find additional bonus movies created by the author that help you learn even more! It's our style to approach teaching from many different angles, since we know some people are visual learners, others like to read, and still others like to get out there and try things. This book combines a lot of teaching approaches so you can learn Illustrator CS as thoroughly as you want to.

We welcome your comments at **illcshot@lynda.com**. Please visit our Web site at **http://www.lynda.com**. The support URL for this book is **http://www.lynda.com/products/books/hot/illcs/**.

Jeff and I hope this book will improve your skills to create exciting print and Web graphics using Illustrator CS. If it does, we will have accomplished the job we set out to do!

About Jeff Van West

Jeff Van West started working with computers on his middle-school's Apple II with 24 KB of RAM and no disk drive. He opened and saved his programs by attaching a cassette tape recorder borrowed from the math teacher. Over the years, he taught himself the ins and outs of various Apple, MS-DOS, Macintosh, Windows, and UNIX systems, as well as basic new software packages whenever he needed to use them. Jeff has always had a passion for teaching and spent several years applying his technical and design skills developing science curricula for elementary and middle-school teachers. He also developed a program linking teachers and students over the Internet in the early days of the Web.

Jeff now has over a decade of experience as an instructional designer, freelance writer, and corporate trainer. He has worked internationally to facilitate collaborative projects in numerous fields, including information technology and the aviation industry. His books and multimedia technical training programs have been used in North America, Europe, Japan, and Australia.

When he's not writing, teaching, playing with his children, or cooking dinner (what he refers to as "satisfying his inner Jewish grandmother"), Jeff can often be found at the controls of an airplane. In 1998, Jeff added flight instruction to his teaching repertoire and has loved sharing the freedom of flight with students ever since.

Jeff Van West with his wife Jenny and their two sons Charlie (2) and Baxter (8 mo).

Acknowledgments

This book would not have been possible without the assistance, support, creative input, and patience of many people. A book may have only one person's name on the cover, but it is the product of a team's sweat, attention, and love.

My deepest thanks and appreciation to:

My wife, **Jenny**, for her unwavering confidence and support, patience with my moods and stress, typographic critiques, use of her computer when needed, and help proofing all those pages!

My boys, **Charlie and Bax**, for letting Daddy work even though he was right there in a home office, leaving enough toys on my office floor so I wouldn't miss them, and playing chase at the end of the day.

Garo Green for giving me the opportunity to write this book, volunteering assistance whenever possible, remaining patient when a Class 3 hurricane disrupted the production schedule, and showing me where to get a good Reuben in L.A.

Lynda Weinman for her assistance with this book's style and content, providing such encouraging feedback with each successive chapter, and for creating such a great series of training titles in the first place.

My beta testers, **Scott Cuzzo** and **Crystal Waters,** for their detailed critique of the text and the exercises. They often saw the intent behind a awkward sentence or step and offered an excellent alternative to make it better. Thanks to Scott as well for teaching me to capitalize "Web."

Domenique Sillett for her brilliant artwork and patience with my often cryptic and last-minute requests. You can see more of her work online at **http://www.littleigloo.com.**

The folks at Adobe for consistently making such phenomenal software. Special thanks to **Mordy Golding** and **Teri Pettit** for their assistance to me personally, their support of the Illustrator Beta-testers and for their devotion to the Illustrator community at large. Thanks to Teri as well for sending me her beautiful and well-documented example files.

The staff of Lynda.com, especially **Susan Rogers-Sasher** and **Auriga Bork**, for making my visit and video recording sessions a success.

My copyeditor, **Darren Meiss,** and the staff of Peachpit Press for editing my work and turning it into such a great-looking book.

The community of Adobe Illustrator users. These folks are the real experts and the people to ask when you have a question. For their assistance and input, I especially thank **John Damm, Wade Zimmerman, Gary Newman,** and **Jean-Claude Tremblay.**

John D. Berry for clarifying a number of questions about OpenType.

You, the reader, for joining me in an exploration of one of the coolest pieces of software you'll ever see. Let's get going!

How to Use This Book

This book, and the accompanying CD-ROM, has several components, including step-by-step exercises, commentary, notes, warnings, and movies. Step-by-step exercises are numbered, and file names and menu commands are bolded for clarity. Commentary is set in separate paragraphs and italicized. Wherever we would have pointed out an item on your screen in a classroom, we have circled or otherwise highlighted that item in a screen shot.

The book is organized generally sequentially in that each exercise builds on previous work, and over the course of the book a couple complete illustrations are produced. Items that are explained in detail in earlier chapters are not repeated in later chapters. The exercise files folder for each chapter, however, contains the completed work up to that point, so if you want to jump directly to Chapter 12, the **chap_12** folder contains all the files and artwork you need to complete the Chapter 12 exercises without going back to earlier chapters.

Macintosh and Windows System Differences

Adobe does an amazing job of minimizing the differences between the Macintosh and Windows versions of Illustrator CS. This job is made easier by the floating palette nature of the software design. The Mac OS and Windows versions look very different stylistically, but the location of buttons, menus, and whatnot is generally the same on both platforms. Differences usually occur where Illustrator interacts with the operating system, such as when printing. Where significant differences exist between the Macintosh and Windows versions, we include examples from both. If an extra step or concern exists only on one system, it appears as a note or warning.

Macintosh and Windows Screen Captures

Most of the screen captures in this book were taken on a PC using Windows XP. The only time we used Macintosh captures was when the interface differed from the PC under Windows XP. We made this decision because Jeff writes primarily on the PC and would have to continually interrupt his wife to use their Macintosh for screen shots. We noted important differences when they occurred and took screen captures accordingly.

Illustrator CS Systems Requirements

Illustrator CS will operate on a variety of system configurations, but the faster your CPU and the more memory you have available, the better your Illustrator experience will be. Here are the requirements as specified by Adobe:

The Official Requirements
Macintosh
PowerPC G3, G4, or G4 dual processor
Mac OS software 10.2.4 (version 10.2.6 recommended)
192 MB of RAM installed
450 MB of available hard-disk space for installation
Windows
Intel Pentium III, 4, or 5 processor
Microsoft Windows 2000 with service pack 2 or Windows XP
192 MB of RAM installed
470 MB of available hard-disk space
Printers
If using Adobe PostScript printers: Adobe PostScript Level 2 or Adobe PostScript 3

The reality is that 192 MB of RAM is not enough to open complex Illustrator files. If you are working in Illustrator regularly, consider 384 MB a minimum. Mac OS X, Windows 2000, and Windows XP all allocate memory dynamically—meaning several programs can "share" the same memory—but it definitely slows things down if you rely on this feature too heavily. If you have several other programs open at the same time as Illustrator or you expect to create complex files, you may need between 512 MB and 1 GB of RAM to get excellent performance.

Illustrator CS runs well under "older" processors such as the G3 and the Pentium III, but you may have to wait while the computer renders complex or multi-layered effects. If the waiting is tedious for you, it makes a great excuse to get that new Macintosh G5 you are itching to buy, but if you must choose between a faster machine with less RAM and a slightly slower one with more RAM—get the RAM.

What's on the CD-ROM?

Exercise Files

Your course files are located inside a folder called **exercise_files** on the **H•O•T CD-ROM**. Each chapter has a separate subfolder containing both Illustrator files and other documents used in the book exercises. In order to save your work as you conduct the exercises, you will be instructed to copy these files from the **H•O•T CD-ROM** to your hard drive. Windows 2000 users may find that files copied from the **H•O•T CD-ROM** are still read-only on their hard drives. If you are using Windows 2000, please read the section "A Note to Windows 2000 Users" in this chapter for instructions on changing them to read and write formatting.

Movies and Bonus Movies

In addition to the exercise files, we have included numerous movies on the accompanying **H•O•T CD-ROM**. The movies demonstrate step-by-step some of the more complex exercises in the book. Sometimes actually watching someone else move through the steps makes the process clearer. The movies also allow us to utilize the dynamic nature of so many of the Illustrator tools more easily than we can do in print.

You'll also find over 20 bonus movies on the lynda.com Web site. The bonus movies demonstrate additional Illustrator CS features or techniques that we couldn't fit in the book as exercises but had to share with you. Each bonus movie has an exercise file that goes with it so you can try out the feature yourself, following the steps you see in the bonus movie. The bonus movie exercise files are in the appropriate folder for each chapter, so the exercise file for a bonus movie in Chapter 5 would be in the **chap_05** folder. The bonus movies are available online at **http://www.lynda.com/books/ hot/illcs/movies/**.

File Naming Conventions

In both Windows and the Mac OS, files have extensions attached to their names. For example, Illustrator files have the extension ".ai" (for **Adobe Illustrator**) after the file name. These extensions may not appear on your screen when you open and close files depending on how your system is configured. Mac OS X shows them by default; Windows XP hides them. Throughout this book, we will refer to the files with their extensions, but you can open them whether or not you see the extensions. The file **blank grid.ai** and **blank grid** are the same file.

A Note to Windows 2000 Users

If you use Windows 2000 and Illustrator CS for the exercises in this book, you may need to unlock the exercise files after you copy them from the **H•O•T CD-ROM**. By default, Windows 2000 sets files copied from a CD-ROM to read-only. This means you will not be able to save your changes to any the exercise files copied from the **H•O•T CD-ROM**. Macintosh and Windows XP users will not have this problem.

To change copied files to read and write under Windows 2000:

1. Open the **exercise_files** folder on the **H•O•T CD-ROM** and copy the folder for the exercises you want to your hard drive. For example, to use the exercises for Chapter 4, copy the **chap_04** folder to your hard drive.

2. Open the copied folder and choose **Edit > Select All**.

3. Right-click on one of the selected files and choose **Properties** from the pop-up menu. Make sure the other files stay selected when you right-click. If not, click anywhere outside the pop-up menu and select all the files again.

4. On the **General** tab of the **Properties** dialog box, uncheck **Read-only**. This unlocks all the selected files and makes them read and write. You must do this every time you copy a folder from the **H•O•T CD-ROM** to save any of your work.

Illustrator Help Files

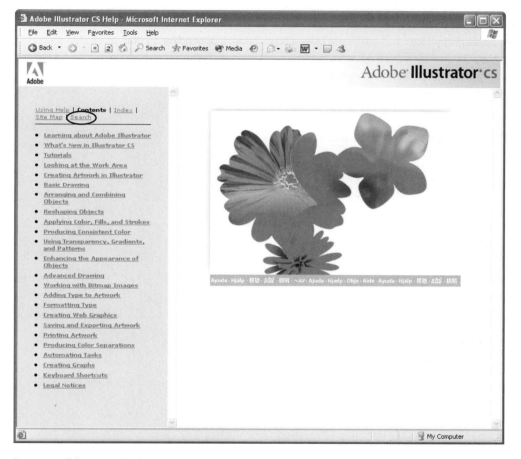

Illustrator CS uses a Web browser help system, so when you choose **Help > Illustrator Help** in Illustrator CS, your favorite Web browser opens and provides an interface to the Help system. These Help files are located on your hard drive so you do not need an Internet connection to use the help. The search function on the Help is an excellent way to get more information on particular Illustrator features or functions.

What Makes Vector-Based Illustration Different?

All computer-generated graphics can be loosely categorized into two categories: raster graphics and vector graphics. The difference lies in how the image is defined. A raster graphic defines the image in terms of pixels. Each pixel can be thought of as a point of color sitting next to other pixels like tiles in a mosaic. When viewed as a whole, the complete image is seen. When you manipulate a raster image, you are changing each affected pixel. Raster-based graphics programs such as Adobe Photoshop provide amazing control over the look of raster graphics, but there is a limit to how much you can manipulate the look of an image before image quality suffers.

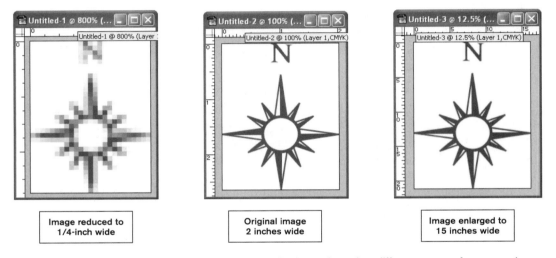

| Image reduced to 1/4-inch wide | Original image 2 inches wide | Image enlarged to 15 inches wide |

Reduced and enlarged raster images showing quality loss, viewed at different zooms for comparison.

Raster graphics also do not scale very well. If you shrink them down, pixels must be removed and others changed to mask the loss of resolution. If the image is shrunk too much, it becomes unrecognizable. If you magnify a raster image, the pixels grow larger, and the image looks muddy. In the example above, the compass rose was reduced and enlarged by eight times in Photoshop.

Vector graphics programs like Illustrator use a completely different philosophy to define an image. Rather than specify each dot of color on the screen or spot of ink on a page, Illustrator lets you precisely design the desired final look—the position, shape, and width of each line, the mix of different colors and effects, and much more—without locking yourself into a specific pattern of colored points on the screen or the page. You will explore the details of how Illustrator does this in the following chapters, but regardless of how vector graphics work, they provide the artist with two very powerful benefits. First, they allow complete freedom to manipulate image shape, color, size, and design. Second, images can be scaled up or down with zero loss in quality as long as there is a printer that can print at the desired size. Because the same vector image file looks as good on a billboard as it does on a business card, a single Illustrator file works well across a variety of media.

Varied Uses of Illustrator

Print

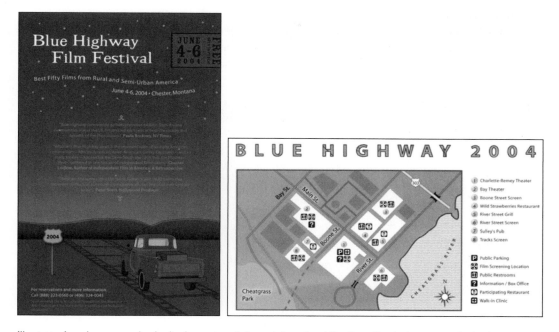

Illustrator's primary use is designing artwork for print and publication. Illustrator-generated art appears on the covers of major magazines, on posters, on maps, in books, on packaging—you name it. While strolling through your local supermarket or mall, you are probably surrounded by literally hundreds of images created in Illustrator.

Web

Illustrator is also a favorite tool for artists creating artwork for the Web. The lynda.com logo was created in Illustrator.

Multimedia, Video, and Film

Graphics used in Macromedia Flash movies, CD-ROM training titles, and even graphics added to video and film are sometimes created using Illustrator. As with Web graphics, the artwork is usually exported from Illustrator and edited into the final product using other tools.

Presentation

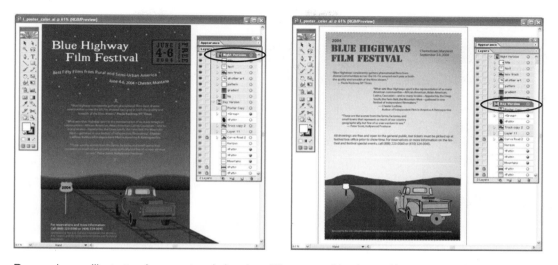

By opening an Illustrator document and showing different combinations of layers, you can present a variety of design variations to your colleagues or clients. If you don't want to present using Illustrator itself, the files can be output into pages of an Abode Acrobat document (PDF) or images for Microsoft PowerPoint or Word documents. Illustrator also allows for data variables. This means you can link graphs in Illustrator to databases or spreadsheets and dynamically update graphs that you can export to presentation software, print, or the Web.

Now that you have a good idea what makes Illustrator unique, it's time to see how Illustrator works. Let's get going!

2.

Interface

The Welcome Screen	The Illustrator Workspace
The Toolbox	Keyboard Shortcuts
Palette Control	Setting Preferences

no exercise files

Illustrator CS H•O•T

Illustrator has been around since the late '80s, so it is a mature application with a large number of features and functions and dozens of shortcuts. Finding your way around the Illustrator interface, navigating around your document, and managing your screen real estate are all critical factors in your satisfaction using Illustrator. This chapter will familiarize you with how Illustrator differs from other drawing programs you may have used and how the Illustrator workspace is organized. If you already use Illustrator, many items in this chapter will be review, but take a few moments to read through it. You may find some features or functions you didn't know existed even if you have been using Illustrator for years.

The Welcome Screen

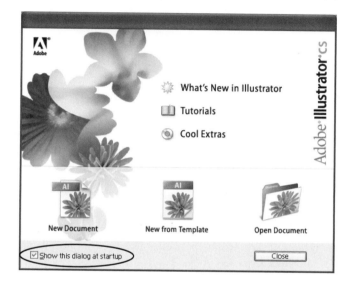

When you open Illustrator CS for the first time, a **Welcome Screen** appears with links to the new features document, tutorials, and CD extras. There are also buttons to open documents or templates. These are handy buttons since you will certainly open something when you launch Illustrator; but if you don't want this screen to appear in the future, uncheck the **Show this dialog at startup** box. You can still open the Welcome Screen whenever you want from the Help menu.

Just for Mac Users

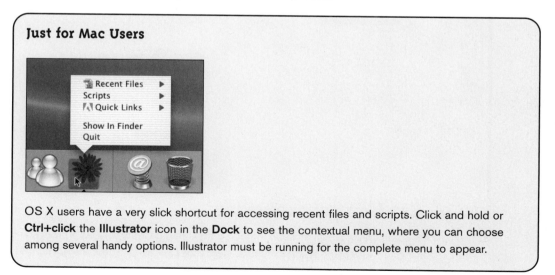

OS X users have a very slick shortcut for accessing recent files and scripts. Click and hold or **Ctrl+click** the **Illustrator** icon in the **Dock** to see the contextual menu, where you can choose among several handy options. Illustrator must be running for the complete menu to appear.

I. ——————————The Illustrator Workspace

Throughout the book, the various parts of the Illustrator workspace are referenced by name. This exercise will acquaint you with the different features of an Illustrator file and their uses.

1. Launch **Illustrator CS** and choose **New Document** from the **Welcome Screen**.

2. When the **New Document** dialog box appears, ensure that **Letter** (**8.5** by **11** inches) is set for the **Size** and **Inches** are set for the **Units**. Click **OK**.

3. The new file opens at a magnification so that it fills the screen. Choose **View > Zoom Out** to see the entire page with some space around it. Next choose **View > Show Page Tiling** to see some of the border of the imageable area.

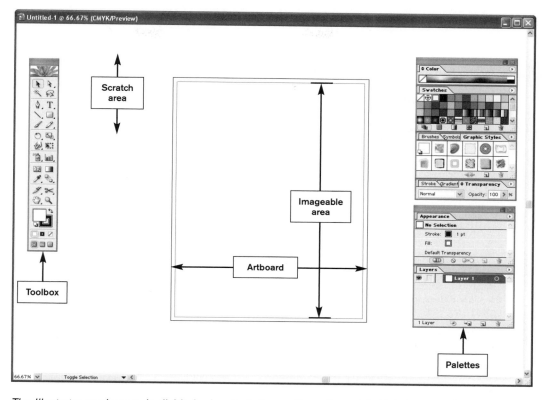

The Illustrator workspace is divided primarily between the **artboard** (which is most often the page size you have selected) and the **scratch area**. The scratch area is available to create and edit artwork, but anything in the scratch area will not print. This is a great place to place a copy of part of your illustration while you experiment with the original on the artboard. If you "manipulate" the art beyond salvaging, you can simply take your copy off the scratch area and try again. The entire scratch area is square and quite large at 227 inches per side.

The Artboard is further divided into the **imageable** and **non-imageable** area by a light dotted line. The imageable area is the area your selected printer can actually print on. Most printers can't print to the very edge of the page. If you change your printer in the **Print** dialog box, the imageable area may change.

You can set up an Illustrator document so that it prints a single artboard over several pages. This is useful if your artwork is too large to print on your printer, or if you want to print several pages from a single Illustrator document. This technique is called **tiling** and is discussed in Appendix C, "Print Issues."

4. Leave this file open for further exploration in Exercise 2.

The Toolbox

The Illustrator **Toolbox** is similar to other Adobe software in that tools are organized into groups with flyout menus. For example, all the basic shape tools that create rectangles, ellipses, polygons, and so on, all share one spot on the Toolbox. To see the flyout menu with all the tools, click and hold on the tool icon.

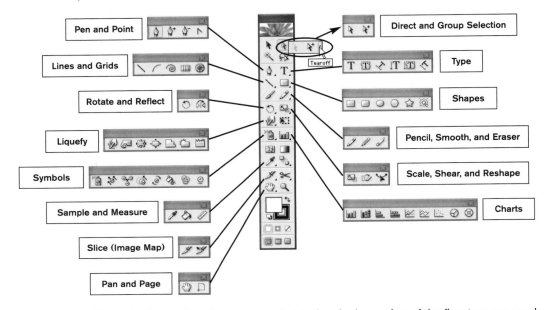

To select a tool from the flyout, drag the cursor to that tool and release. Any of the flyout menus can be "torn off" so all that the tools are always visible by extending the menu of tools, dragging to the far end of the menu, and then releasing on the tear-off icon. This figure shows the Toolbox with all the flyout menus torn off.

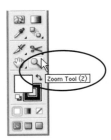

Tip: Holding your mouse over a tool on the Toolbox for a moment makes the tooltip appear, which shows the name of the tool and its keyboard shortcut in parentheses. If you commonly use two tools on the same flyout menu, find out what their keyboard shortcuts are and use the keyboard to switch between tools.

Keyboard Shortcuts

Most tools in Illustrator have default keyboard shortcuts. These shortcuts save your time and your wrist by preventing unnecessary trips up to the Toolbox to switch tools. There are actually so many keyboard commands that some of them may conflict with other shortcuts you are used to. For example, **Cmd+H** is used by OS X to hide the active program. This prevents Illustrator's default of **Cmd+H**, which shows and hides points and handles on a path, from working. If you want to change a keyboard shortcut, you can customize any of the shortcuts by choosing **Edit > Keyboard Shortcuts**.

Just to get you going, here is a short list of the killer shortcuts you will find handy. If you are familiar with other Adobe products, you will notice that many of these are the same or similar to shortcuts you already know. The word "temporary" before a tool name means that the tool appears as long as you hold down the key(s) but switches back to the last selected tool as soon as you lift your fingers from the keyboard.

Crucial Keyboard Shortcuts in Illustrator		
Command	**Windows**	**Mac**
Show/Hide all palettes	Tab	Tab
Show/Hide all palettes except tools	Shift+Tab	Shift+Tab
Fit to page	Ctrl+0	Cmd+0
Zoom in	Ctrl++ (plus sign)	Cmd++ (plus sign)
Zoom out	Ctrl+− (minus sign)	Cmd+− (minus sign)
Selection tool	V	V
Direct Selection tool	A	A
Temporary Selection tool*	Ctrl	Cmd
Temporary Zoom In tool	Ctrl+spacebar	Cmd+spacebar
Temporary Zoom Out tool	Alt+Ctrl+spacebar	Option+Cmd+spacebar
Temporary Hand tool	Spacebar	Spacebar
Constrain tool motion	Shift+drag	Shift+drag
Duplicate a selection with a Selection tool	Alt+drag	Option+drag
Toggle selection and direct selection	Ctrl+Tab	No default setting
Toggle fill or stroke on top	X	X
Set fill or stroke to none	/	/

*The Selection tool used, normal or direct, is whichever one you had chosen most recently.

2. _____ Palette Control

Illustrator makes extensive use of floating palettes—there are 31 main palettes and several more containing libraries of brushes and styles. Thirty-one palettes would clog even the largest monitor, so understanding how to manipulate your palettes is essential to working smoothly in Illustrator.

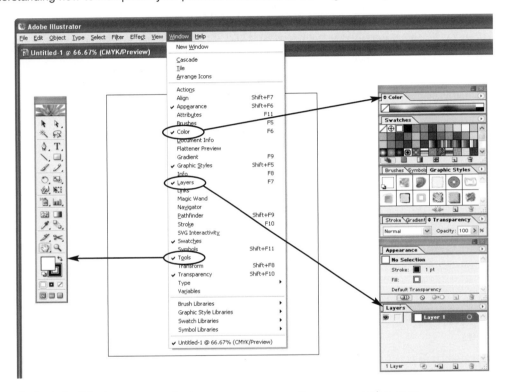

1. Click the **Window** menu and release your mouse so the menu remains open.

The Window menu lists most of the palettes and the Toolbox, shown as the Tools palette, and indicates which are visible with a checkmark. Some palettes appear as unchecked in the list even though their tabs appear visible in palette groupings. For example, the Brushes palette tab is visible behind the Graphic Styles tab even though Brushes is not checked in the Windows menu list.

2. Click the **Window** menu to make it disappear. Now press the **Tab** key. All the palettes disappear from view. Using the **Tab** shortcut key is very handy to see your work unencumbered by tools. It's also great for presenting work to clients who might be overwhelmed by seeing all the tools next to your artwork. Press the **Tab** key again to show all the palettes and then press **Shift+Tab**. All the palettes except the **Toolbox** hide. This shortcut is great to keep your main tools available while creating a less cluttered screen.

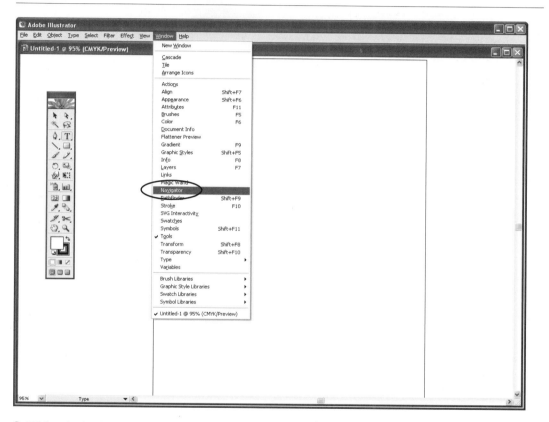

3. With only the **Toolbox** visible, choose **Window > Navigator**. The **Navigator** palette appears. Now press **Shift+Tab** and see that the other palettes reappear. Once you have added the **Navigator** palette, it will show and hide with the other palettes.

Palette position and visibility is stored in your Illustrator preferences. So when you close Illustrator and reopen it later, the palettes will remain exactly where you left them. This is a plus once you arrange your workspace the way you like it, but a drag if you want different arrangements for different kinds of work. Currently, there is no capability to save a specific workspace, as is possible in some other Adobe products.

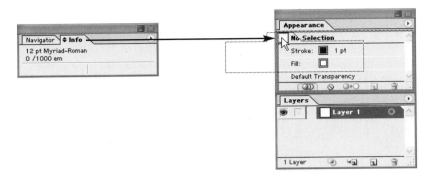

4. Many palettes are grouped by default according to similar function, but you can customize these groupings however you like. Click the **Info** palette tab behind the **Navigator** palette to bring the **Info** palette to the front. Next, drag the **Info** palette tab to a spot next to the **Appearance** palette to group it with that palette.

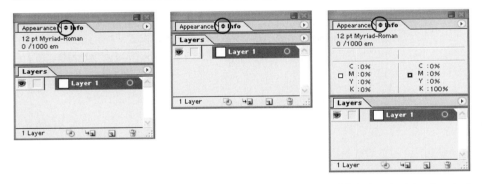

5. The **Info** palette contains a double triangle next to its name. Click the double triangle three times to cycle the palette through its three possible views: most commonly needed information, collapsed, and all information. Even palettes that do not have the triangle will collapse and expand with a double-click on their tabs.

The Appearance, Info, and Layers palettes are also grouped in a window with Minimize and Close buttons on their top bars. These are a small line and an x in Windows and a green and red ball on the Mac. These buttons will collapse or close the entire window and all its palettes. If you close one of these windows, click the Window menu and choose any palette that appeared in that window to open the window again (with all the same palettes showing).

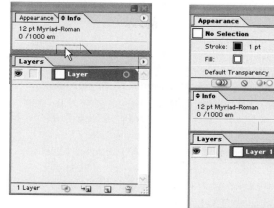

6. If you don't want two palettes sharing space, you can drag one of them to a new location. For example, drag the **Info** palette off to a part of the screen where no palettes exist and release the mouse. Illustrator creates a new window just for the Info palette. Or, you can drag the **Info** palette by its tab between the **Appearance** and **Layers** palettes so a thick, gray line appears. Release the mouse. The **Info** palette now has its own area in the window with the other two palettes. Just to set things back to right, drag the **Info** palette back into the same window with the **Navigator** palette.

NOTE | No Palette Reset

Once you start customizing palette position, there is no command to reset the palettes to their default positions. The default grouping of palettes is the result of years of experience working with Illustrator and is a good place to start as you learn the program.

---

7. Close the file without saving.

NOTE | Something Is Missing

Those of you familiar with Illustrator may discover that some tools present in Illustrator 10 and earlier are missing in Illustrator CS. The Illustrator 10 Lasso tool doesn't exist any longer because the Direct Lasso tool made it largely unnecessary. The Ink Pen is gone with much of its functionality replaced by the new Scribble effect. The Twirl tool is gone. The Multiple Master palette is gone in favor of the new Open Type standard—which you will learn about in Chapter 8, "*Adding Text.*" Illustrator CS still supports Multiple Master fonts, but you cannot manipulate their weight and other factors as before. There was actually a movement to remove the entire Filter menu because it overlaps in function with the Effects menu, but that didn't make it to this version of Illustrator. Don't be surprised if the next iteration of Illustrator has some significantly different menus, however. And last, but not least, Botticelli's Venus is gone in favor of the coordinated look of the Adobe Creative Suite. If you miss Venus, hold down the **Alt** key and choose **Help > About Illustrator** (Windows) or hold down the **Option** key and choose **Illustrator > About Illustrator** (Mac). You will get a secret Venus splash screen from now on. To put Venus back on the Toolbox, type **VENUS** when the **Type** tool is not active.

Setting Preferences

There are quite a few preferences for Illustrator, and in most cases, the default values are the best bet until you have a good reason to change them. There are a few preferences you should be aware of as you get to know Illustrator.

The location of **Preferences** is one of the few menu items that is different between the Windows and Mac versions of Illustrator.

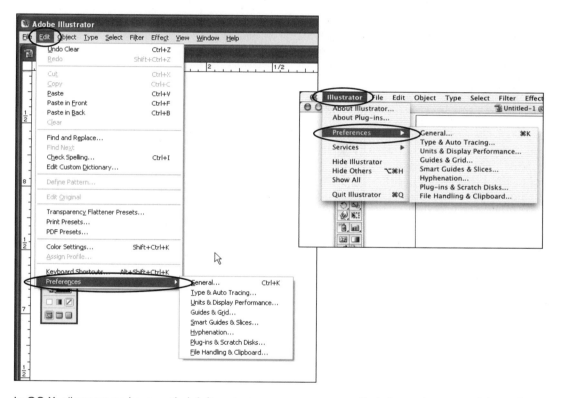

In OS X, all programs have as their leftmost menu a program menu that shows the name of the active application. The menu contains details about the software and, usually, program preferences, so the preferences appear under this **Illustrator** menu on the Mac. There is no Illustrator menu in Windows. In Windows, Illustrator preferences are found under the **Edit** menu. In both operating systems, the preferences appear on a submenu. Opening any of the items on the submenu will open a dialog box with all the preferences accessible from a drop-down menu.

Preferences

General

Keyboard Increment: (0.1 pt)

Constrain Angle: 0 °

Corner Radius: 12 pt

OK

Cancel

Previous

Next

☐ Object Selection by Path Only
☐ Use Precise Cursors
☑ Show Tool Tips
☑ Anti-aliased Artwork
☐ Select Same Tint %
☑ Append [Converted] Upon Opening Legacy Files

☐ Disable Auto Add/Delete
☐ Use Japanese Crop Marks
☐ Transform Pattern Tiles
☐ Scale Strokes & Effects
☐ Use Preview Bounds

Reset All Warning Dialogs

When you move objects about on the Illustrator artboard, it is very difficult to move them less than 2 points (about 1/36 of an inch) with the mouse because the object has "snap-to priority" within 2 points of its original location. This means it will stay put unless you move it more than 2 points with the mouse. The four keyboard arrow keys are great for nudging an object in any direction, but the default keyboard increment is 1 point. This is often too much for super-exact nudging. If you find this true in your work, try .1 point. When you need to nudge something a larger distance, hold down the **Shift** key while you press the arrow key and it will move ten times as far.

Preferences

Units & Display Performance

Units

General: Inches

Stroke: Points

Type: Points

Asian Type: Points

☐ Numbers Without Units Are Points

Identify Objects By: ⊙ Object Name ○ XML ID

OK

Cancel

Previous

Next

Display Performance

Hand Tool:

Full Quality   Faster Updates

The **Units** preference determines the default measurement for new documents. If you are working on Web graphics most of the time, you might want your default setting to be **Pixels** rather than **Points** or **Inches**. This setting is only the default. You can still set individual documents to whatever setting you like from **File > Document Setup**.

Guides & Grid preferences let you specify the look and position of your guidelines. The default guides are cyan, which is very faint on most screens. If you change them to a more noticeable color, such as red, they are much easier to see.

If you have more than one physical hard drive on your computer (not a single hard drive that is partitioned), you can get a performance increase by setting the hard drive that *does not* contain the operating system as the **Primary Scratch Disk**. The scratch disk is an area of your hard drive where Illustrator writes and reads data temporarily while it manipulates your files. If you have only one hard drive in your computer that is partitioned into two logical drives, ignore this setting. Setting a partitioned drive as a scratch disk may actually slow down performance.

That's enough to get you going with Illustrator's overall organization. It's now time to start editing some artwork.

3.

Selecting and Arranging

| Selecting and Arranging Shapes |
| Basic Stroke and Fill | Aligning and Distributing |
| Grouping and Group Selections |

chap_03

Illustrator CS
H•O•T CD-ROM

A fundamental concept in using Illustrator is arranging and stacking simple shapes to create more complex ones. In this chapter, you will use Illustrator's selection tools, the Toolbox, and the Align palette to arrange objects and adjust their appearance. Illustrator provides three selection tools for selecting and arranging objects on the screen: the Selection tool, the Group Selection tool, and the Direct Selection tool. This may seem a bit excessive, but each one has its use. You can do a surprising amount of editing using nothing but these tools.

I. —————————Selecting and Arranging Shapes

Illustrator artwork is created by assembling basic shapes into more complex ones. In this exercise, you will learn how to select, resize, and rotate shapes as you assemble a more complex piece of art. This exercise demonstrates several features of Illustrator at once, so it has an accompanying movie in the **movies** folder to help you out.

1. Copy the **chap_03** folder from the **H·O·T CD-ROM** to your hard drive. For clarity, it's best to keep the folder name as **chap_03**.

Throughout this book, each chapter starts with copying the chapter exercise folder to your hard drive. These folders contain Illustrator files and other images used in the exercises for the chapter.

2. Open the file **reel_parts.ai** from the **chap_03** folder. The file includes a graphic of a film reel that is the shape you will create over the next two exercises, four small circles, and a rectangle.

*As mentioned in Chapter 1, "Introduction," the file name may appear as **reel_parts.ai** or **reel_parts**, depending on how your system is configured. It is the same file with or without the .ai extension.*

3. Choose **View > Show Rulers**, **View > Show Grid**, and **View > Snap to Grid**.

The rulers and gridlines are very helpful to see the size of objects and provide a background so that black and white artwork stands out against the artboard, but they do not affect your drawing tools. Snap to Grid will constrain your drawing and moving tools so they will only draw on the gridlines.

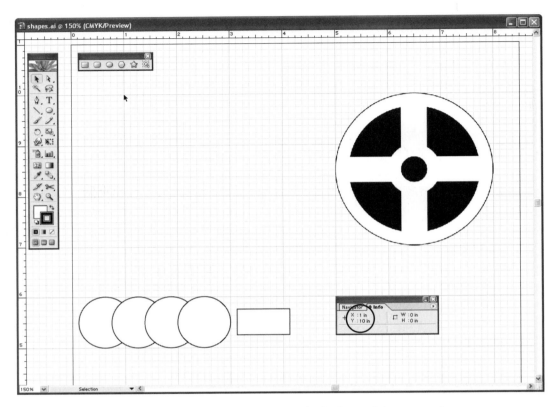

4. Choose **Window > Info** and position the **Info** palette in the lower-right corner of your screen.

The Info palette is another way to control, or at least see, the exact position and size of the shapes you create. As you move your cursor around the screen, its x and y coordinates are constantly updated. The vertical Illustrator ruler puts zero at the bottom of the page by default so that this y value is a positive number. In this example, the cursor is one inch in from the left of the page and 10 inches up from the bottom (one inch down from the top). As you draw shapes, the position where you began the drag is held as the x and y coordinates and width and height of the shape appear.

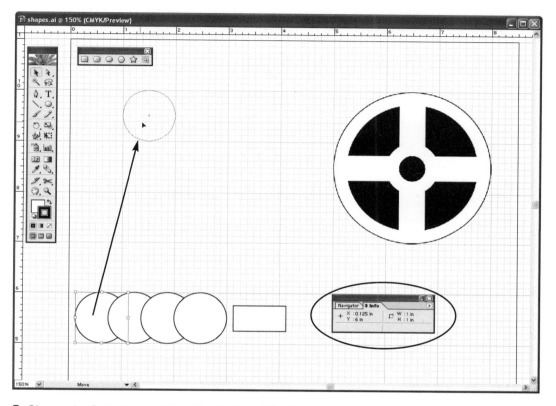

5. Choose the **Selection** tool from the **Toolbox**. Click the leftmost small circle at the bottom of the page to select the circle. Once selected, it is outlined in a blue bounding box, and its size appears in the **Info** palette. Using the **Selection** tool, drag this circle up to the gridline one inch down and one inch right of the top of the page.

A key feature to notice here is that the four circles are stacked on top of one another. Each new shape you create in Illustrator is a separate object, much as if you were cutting them out of paper and stacking them on a drafting table in front of you. Illustrator remembers the exact order that each object is stacked with the most recently drawn object on top. In this case, the leftmost circle was made first and the rightmost made last. As you build a shape, you may need to adjust which shape is on top, as you will see in this exercise.

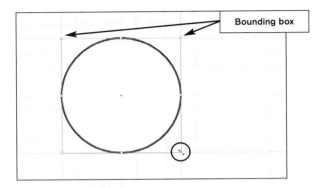

6. Now that the circle does not have another object on top of it, you can see the entire **bounding box**. This box displays the outer dimensions of the selected shape, the position of its center (as a blue dot), and provides handles to resize and rotate the shape. Position the cursor on the lower-right handle and it changes to a resize cursor.

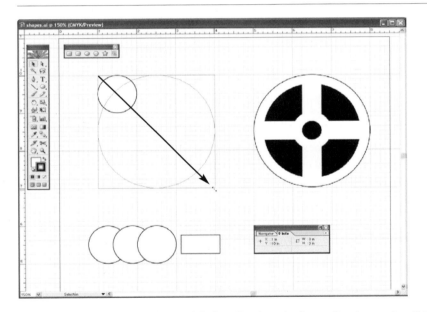

7. With your cursor on the lower-right handle, drag the **bounding box** out until the circle is three large gridlines wide. The **Info** palette shows this is a 3-inch circle. Hold down the **Shift** key as you drag to keep the height and width of the circle proportional.

Normally you must hold down the Shift key to maintain perfect proportionality as you resize, but since Snap to Grid is active, your cursor will stop only on large gridlines. Therefore you can maintain a perfect circle without the Shift key.

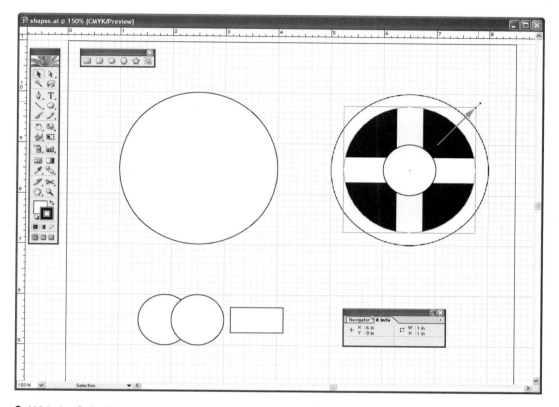

8. With the **Selection** tool, select the second circle from the bottom of the page and center it over the image of the film reel on the right side of the page. Hold down the **Alt** key (Windows) or the **Option** key (Mac) and drag any corner handle of the bounding box until the circle is the same size as the black circle of the film reel.

The Alt or Option keys will resize the object from the center. Holding down Shift and Alt or Option will resize proportionally and from center. If you didn't get the circle exactly centered at first, you can adjust it after you resize to get it just right.

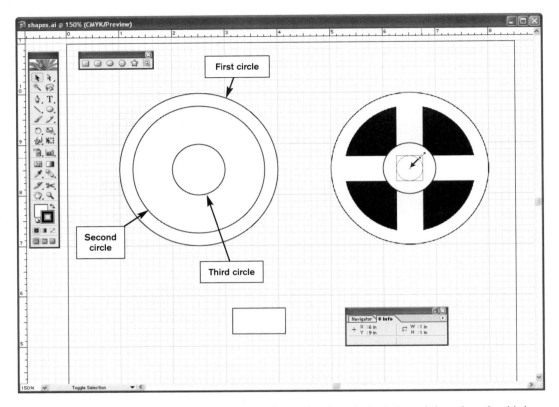

9. Drag the second resized circle so it is centered over the three-inch circle and then drag the third circle up from the bottom of the page to the center of the reel you are building on the left. (It's already the perfect size—what a coincidence!) Next, drag the fourth circle over the image on the right and resize it smaller to match the small, black inner circle.

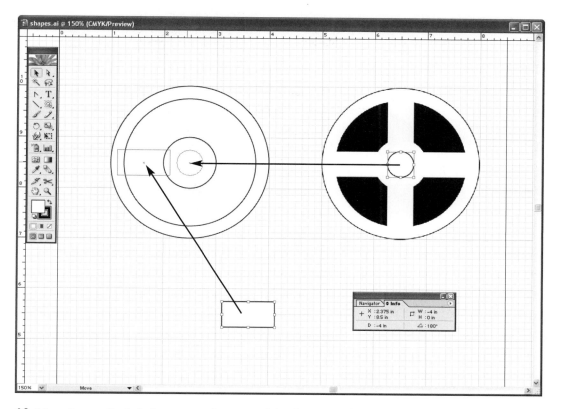

10. Move the smallest circle to center it on top of the first three. Select the rectangle with the **Selection** tool and drag it up so that it overlaps the middle two circles in the 9-o'clock position. This rectangle will become one of the spokes of the film reel.

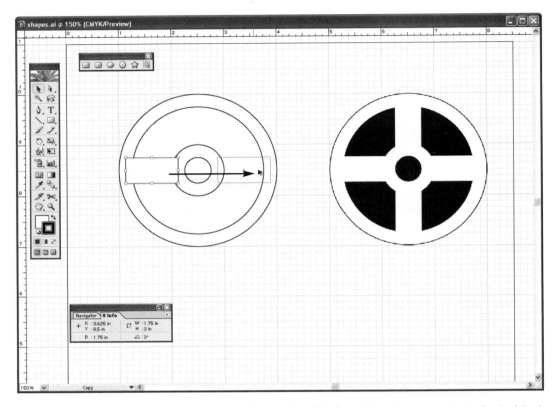

11. Hold down the **Alt** key (Windows) or the **Option** key (Mac) and drag the rectangle to the 3-o'clock position. Instead of moving the rectangle, a copy is created and moved, leaving the original untouched.

*The **Alt+drag** or **Option+drag** shortcut to copy a shape is possibly the most useful shortcut in all of Illustrator.*

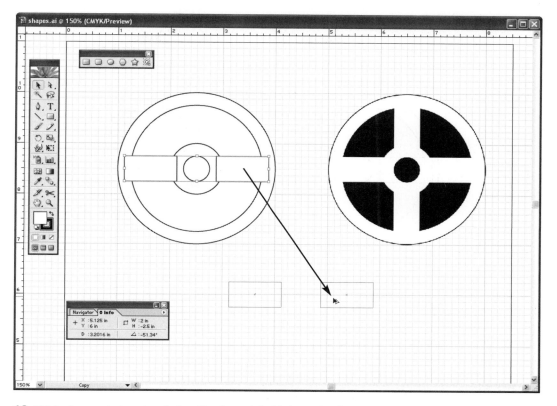

12. While the copied rectangle is still selected, hold down the **Shift** key and click the first rectangle. Both rectangles are now selected, and they are encompassed by a single bounding box. Hold down the **Alt** key (Windows) or the **Option** key (Mac) and drag the selected rectangles down to a blank area of the artboard.

No matter how many objects you select on the artboard, there will be only one bounding box that shows the outer boundaries of the entire group of objects. Any movement, resizing, or rotation of the bounding box affects all the objects within it. Note that some objects may appear inside the borders of the bounding box, but they are not selected so they will not be changed. In the example shown here, the small circle appears inside the bounding box, but since it isn't selected, it will remain unaffected by actions performed on the rectangles.

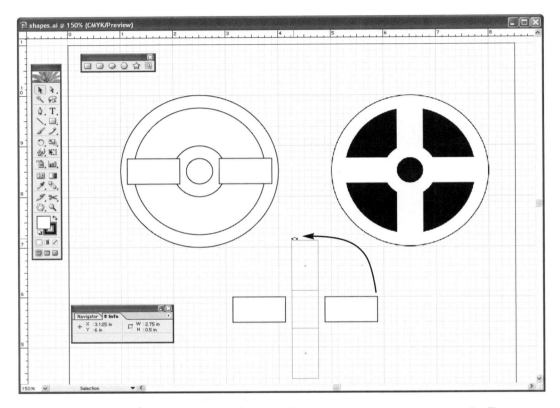

13. Position the cursor near any corner of the bounding box but not actually on the handle. The cursor will change to a curved rotation cursor. Drag the cursor in an arc to rotate both rectangles 90 degrees. Once you have rotated the rectangles, drag them both up to the 12-o'clock and 6-o'clock positions on the artwork.

*To rotate the rectangles a perfect 90 degrees with Snap to Grid active, you must keep the cursor very close to the edge of the bounding box (because the cursor snaps to the grid rather than the box). If you have trouble rotating exactly 90 degrees, temporarily turn off Snap to Grid by choosing **View > Snap to Grid**, and rotate the rectangles while holding down the **Shift** key to constrain the rotation to 90 degrees.*

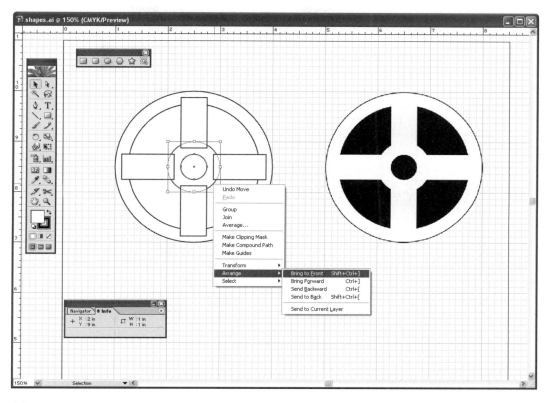

14. Congratulations, you now have all the pieces of the film reel in place. It would look a bit better if the center two circles were on top of the rectangles, however. Select both inner circles by clicking and then **Shift+clicking** with the **Selection** tool. Next choose **Object > Arrange > Bring to Front**. Alternately, you can right-click (or Ctrl+click on one-button Macs) the selected items and choose **Arrange > Bring to Front** from the contextual menu.

15. Choose **File > Save**.

MOVIE | arrange.mov

To view the complex steps of this exercise and the next one performed, watch **arrange.mov** located in the **movies** folder on the **H•O•T CD-ROM**.

2. ———————————Basic Stroke and Fill

Every Illustrator shape has a basic stroke (outline) color and fill color assigned to it. Sometimes the assignment is "none," meaning the shape is not stroked with a color or its inside area is not filled. In this exercise, you will adjust the stroke and fill of the shapes you arranged in Exercise 1 to visually blend one shape into another and get the final effect of a black-and-white film reel.

1. Open **reel_parts.ai**, or continue from Exercise 1.

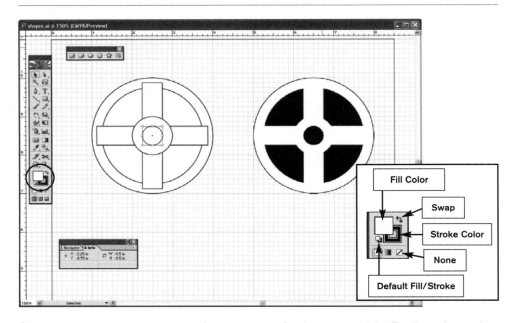

2. Select the center circle with the **Selection** tool. On the bottom of the **Toolbox**, the stroke and fill of the current selection appears. In this case, it is the default of a 1 pt black stroke, indicated by the black hollow square, and a white fill, indicated by the white solid square.

*The white Fill square appearing on top of the black Stroke square means that any color changes you make apply to the fill and leave the stroke untouched. To change the stroke color, click the hollow **Stroke** square or press **X** on the keyboard. Clicking either the **Fill** or the **Stroke** squares will automatically open the Color palette if it is not open. This exercise will not use the Color palette since an entire chapter (Chapter 5) is dedicated to strokes, fills, and color. Feel free to play with colors as you do the exercise, though.*

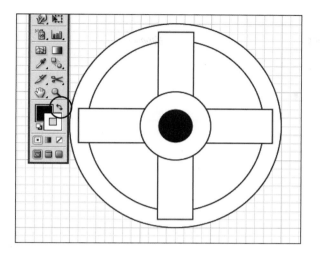

3. Click the **Swap** arrow to the upper-right corner of the **Stroke** and **Fill** squares. This will change the selected circle so the stroke is white and the fill is black.

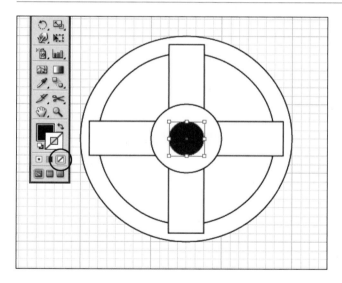

4. You could leave the stroke as white, and no one would know it was there because it blends into the white fill of the circle behind it. The white stroke does overlap the black fill inside the circle, however, and does not need to be there. Make sure the **Stroke** square is on top. If it is not, click the square or press **X** on the keyboard. Next, click the **None** icon or press **/** (slash) on the keyboard. The stroke disappears and the inner circle will look slightly bigger. Toggle the stroke between white and none a few times using **Edit > Undo** and **Edit > Redo** if you can't see the slight difference right away.

> ## TIP | Secret Strokes
>
> If all you want is a filled shape, it's a good habit to set the stroke to none, even if you can't see it. "Secret" strokes sometimes get in the way, making two objects that should look the same look a bit different because one is stroked and the other is not.

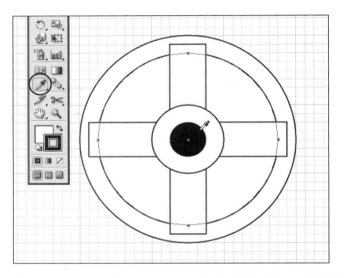

5. Select the second largest circle with the **Selection** tool. Click the **Eyedropper** tool on the **Toolbox** or press I (lowercase L) on the keyboard. Click the eyedropper inside the no-stroke black-fill circle. The larger circle will switch to no stroke and black fill as well.

The eyedropper will take all the attributes from one object and apply it to others. In this case, the attributes are very simple: no stroke and black fill. When you use the eyedropper in later chapters, you will see it is capable of copying all the attributes, including special effects, from one object to another.

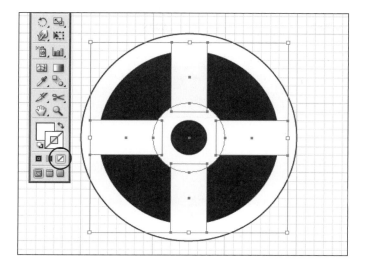

6. Switch back to the **Selection** tool and select the third-largest circle and four spokes by clicking each one while holding down the **Shift** key. Make sure the **Stroke** square is on top in the **Toolbox**. If it is not, press **X** on the keyboard. Next, click the **None** icon or press **/** (slash) on the keyboard. To see the full effect of changing the stroke, deselect all the items on the artboard by choosing **Select > Deselect** or by clicking with the **Selection** tool anywhere on the artboard that does not contain artwork.

7. Save the file and close it.

Take a moment to look back and see how you built up a complex shape, the film reel, by stacking simple shapes and adjusting the way Illustrator traced (stroked) and filled them. The process of building illustrations by creating layers of simple lines, shapes, and text is fundamental to how Illustrator works. Sometime today take a look at something flat in your home or office, like a window or the front of a file cabinet, and think about how you would build that image as a stack of simple shapes.

Preview Versus Outline View

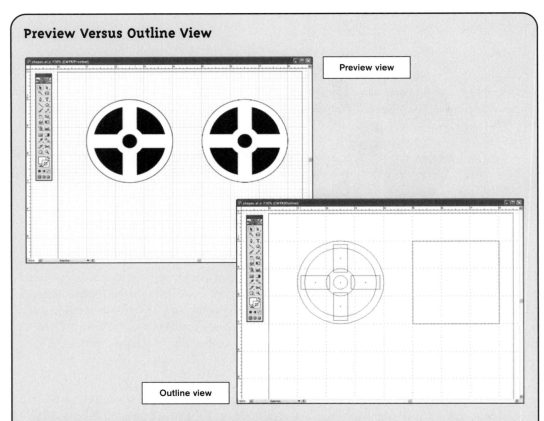

Preview view

Outline view

When shapes overlap and have the same or similar fill colors, such as the spokes of the film reel, it can be very difficult to see where one shape ends and the other begins. It is sometime difficult or impossible to select the shape you want to edit or move. To help with this, Illustrator provides two primary modes for viewing your artwork. So far you have been working in **Preview** view, which shows what the artwork will look like when printed or opened in another program.

Outline view shows the same artwork, but it shows only the paths that make up the artwork. You can still draw, select, move, or use any Illustrator command while in Outline view, but you will not see its effect on the fill and stroke until you switch back to Preview view. When selecting objects in Preview view, you can click any part of the stroked path or the filled area inside the path. In Outline view, clicking on a path selects that shape but clicking inside a shape has no effect. (You can make Preview view behave this way, too, by checking **Object selection by path only** in the **General** preferences.) Note that the raster image of the film reel on the left contains no paths but shows up as a box to mark its place.

3. ————————Aligning and Distributing

As you learn each of Illustrator's major functions, you will discover there is often a tool palette devoted to that feature. Since you are working with arranging shapes, now is a good time to look at Illustrator's **Align** palette. These functions can be huge timesavers and provide far greater accuracy than you could accomplish by sight. The **Align** and **Distribute** commands often work well in conjunction, as you will see in this exercise.

1. Open the file **map key.ai** from the **chap_03** folder. Choose **Window > Align** to see the **Align** palette.

2. Using the **Selection** tool, drag a box (marquee) around the map symbols to select all of them. Click the **Horizontal Align Center** button on the **Align** palette. As you might expect, the symbols are now vertically aligned.

You need not be perfect when dragging the marquee around shapes in Illustrator. All objects with at least part of their shape inside the box you drag are selected.

3. While the symbols are still selected, click the **Vertical Distribute Center** button on the **Align** palette to evenly space out the symbols.

*Distribute uses the bounding box in determining the area over which it distributes the objects. In this case, the parking symbol is at the top of the box and the first aid symbol at the bottom. These two symbols do not move, but the remaining three are evenly distributed in the space between them. To spread them out a bit, drag the parking symbol up slightly and click the **Vertical Distribute Center** button again. To bring them closer together, drag the parking symbol down slightly and click **Vertical Distribute Center** again.*

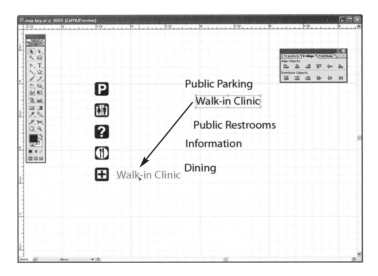

4. Select and drag the text "Walk-in Clinic" down to its desired position near the first aid symbol.

5. Select the "Walk-in Clinic" text. Hold down the **Shift** key and click the first aid symbol. Now both are selected so you can align them vertically. Before you align the objects, click once on the first aid symbol. Next, click the **Vertical Align Bottom** button. Note that the bottom of the text box is lower than the bottom of the text, so there will still be some space below the text.

*The click before alignment sets the first aid symbol as a **key object**. The key object will not move, so rather than the two objects aligning to each other, the text moves to align with the symbol.*

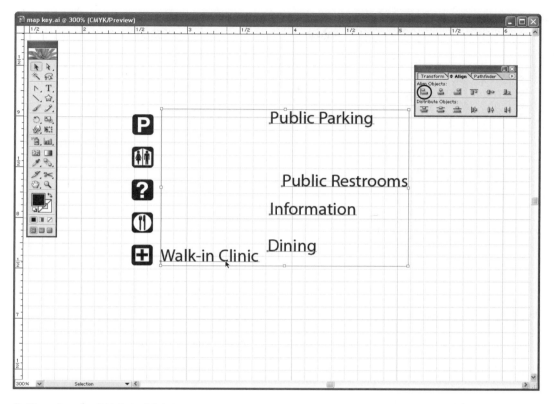

6. Now that the "Walk-in Clinic" text is in position, you can use the set key object trick again. Select all the text by dragging a box (marquee) around the text with the **Selection** tool. Click once on the "Walk-in Clinic" text to set it as key. Next click the **Horizontal Align Left** button to align the left margins of all the text with "Walk-in Clinic."

7. Repeat Step 5 for the parking symbol and the "Public Parking" text with the symbol as the key object so it doesn't move but the text does.

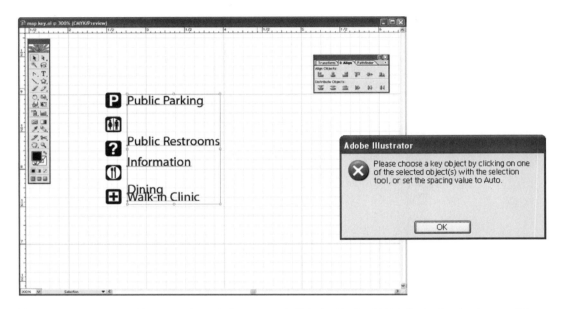

8. The final move should be to select all the text and click the **Vertical Distribute Center** button. Since the top and bottom text (Parking and Clinic) are in position, drag a rectangular marquee around all the type and click the **Vertical Distribute Bottom** button. You will get an error.

9. To fix the problem, click the flyout menu on the **Align** palette and choose **Show Options**. Click the drop-down menu on the **Distribute Spacing** row and choose **Auto**.

When you aligned the first aid symbol with a key object, you unknowingly changed the space Illustrator uses for aligning and distributing from Auto—which will use all the space in the bounding box—to zero inches. If the options had been visible while you worked, you would have seen it change. This setting exists so you can specify exactly how much space you want between objects. For example, if you wanted to distribute objects vertically with exactly .25 inches between them, you would enter .25 inches in the drop-down menu box and click the Distribute Vertical Space button, which sits to the left of the drop-down menu.

TIP | Align to Artboard

The **Align to Artboard** option on the flyout menu essentially makes the page the key object and aligns or distributes objects relative to the entire page. You can toggle this function on and off from the flyout menu.

10. Once the spacing is back to **Auto**, click the **Vertical Distribute Bottom** button to distribute the text so it aligns perfectly with the symbols.

11. Save the file.

MOVIE | align.mov

To view the complex steps of this exercise performed, watch **align.mov** located in the **movies** folder on the **H•O•T CD-ROM**.

4. ——————————Grouping and Group Selection

This is a quick exercise to demonstrate a simple but key concept in Illustrator: **grouping**. As your artwork gets more complex, selecting all the parts of an object individually is a pain. Grouping allows you to treat a bunch of objects as a single larger object but still access and edit the individual members of the group when needed.

1. Open the file **map key.ai**, or continue from Exercise 3.

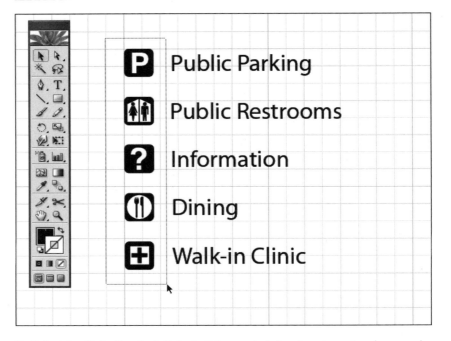

2. Select the **Selection** tool. Select all the symbols by dragging a box (marquee) around them.

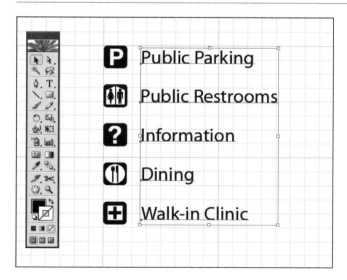

3. Choose **Object > Group** or press **Ctrl+G** (Windows) or **Cmd+G** (Mac) on your keyboard.

4. Select all the text by dragging a box (marquee) around them. Choose **Object > Group**.

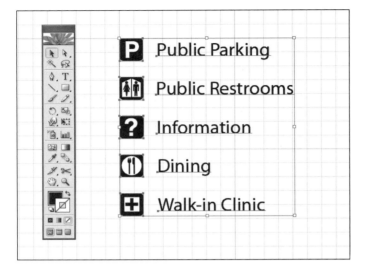

5. Click the parking symbol. Because it is grouped with all the other symbols, all the symbols are selected. Hold down the **Shift** key and click the text "Public Parking." Now you have two groups selected, each one containing five objects. Choose **Object > Group** again.

*You now have a group containing two objects, each of which is itself a group containing five objects. You can nest groups as many levels deep as you wish. You can ungroup objects at any time by selecting the group and choosing **Object > Ungroup**.*

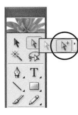

6. Choose **Select > Deselect** to unselect everything. On the **Toolbox**, click and hold the **Direct Selection** tool until the flyout menu appears. Move your cursor over and click the **Group Selection** tool (which looks like the **Direct Selection** tool with a plus sign above it).

You will use learn about Direct Selection tool in the next chapter. We promise.

| One click | Two clicks | Three clicks |

7. Click once on the parking symbol with the **Group Selection** tool. Only the parking symbol is selected even though it is part of a group. Click the parking symbol a second time. Now all the symbols are selected because they are grouped with the parking symbol. Click the parking symbol a third time. Now the symbols and the text are selected.

The Group Selection tool lets you select the object or any group the object is part of. Each click selects the next larger group. There is also no bounding box around the selected objects when you select objects with the Group Selection tool.

8. Save the file and close it.

Now that you know how to select and move objects, it's time to start drawing!

4.

Basic Shapes

| What Are Shapes? | Rectangles and Ellipses |
| Polygons and Stars | Editing Points on a Shape |
| Editing Points with Direction Handles |

chap_04

Illustrator CS
H•O•T CD-ROM

A great place to start your exploration of Illustrator is with the shape tools. These tools let you make basic shapes—rectangles, ellipses, triangles, polygons, and even stars—quickly and easily. As you saw in Chapter 2, "*Interface*," by doing nothing more than combining and stacking these shapes on top of one another you can build some fairly complex artwork. Add to that the ability to edit the basic shapes and you're on your way to understanding Illustrator.

The most important part of these exercises is an opportunity to play with the tools. As you move through the chapter, feel free to try things beyond what is spelled out in the steps. That is one of the best ways to really understand how the tools work. Before you launch into using the tools, Here are short explanations of what Illustrator does to create a shape that will help you understand why the tools work the way they do.

What Are Shapes?

All Illustrator shapes have three basic characteristics that define how the basic shape will look: path, stroke, and fill. In addition to these basic characteristics, there may be several layers of other effects that influence the final look, but these basic characteristics are always there.

Path

A **path** is defined as a series of straight or curved lines that run between **points** in a connect-the-dots fashion. The simplest path you could see on screen is a straight line.

A rectangle needs four points.

That works great for straight lines, but if all you used to define shapes was a series of points, you would need an infinite number to create a curve. Instead, Illustrator allows you to add **direction handles** to the points. (The math behind this is referred to as a **Bézier curve**.) Think of these handles as a way to bend the path as it moves from one point to the next. Using direction handles, you can define a circle with only four points, each of which has two direction handles.

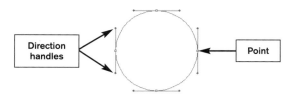

Direction handles bend the path in the direction of the handle points. The longer the handle, the more it bends the path.

When you use the shape tools, Illustrator takes care of selecting the placement of points and handles so you don't have to. By adjusting various points and handles yourself, you can create any shape you want. You'll have a chance to manipulate handles firsthand in Exercise 4, and you will use several different handle and point editing tools in Chapter 10, "*Pen and Point Tools*."

Stroke and Fill

A path defines a shape, but a path alone doesn't result in an image on the screen or page. Paths must be assigned a **stroke** and/or a **fill**. A stroke is a color, gradient, or pattern that traces the path; a fill is a color, gradient, or pattern that fills the area inside a path. Paths normally have one stroke and one fill, but they can have multiple strokes and fills that can be applied in any order. The following six circles are all the same path, with different combinations of stroke and fill applied.

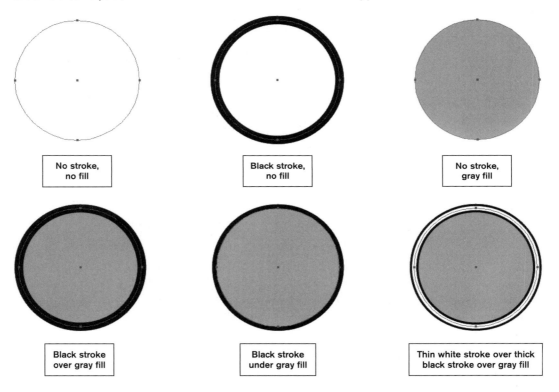

| No stroke, no fill | Black stroke, no fill | No stroke, gray fill |

| Black stroke over gray fill | Black stroke under gray fill | Thin white stroke over thick black stroke over gray fill |

When you draw shapes in a new Illustrator document, they appear with the default setting of a 1pt black stroke over a white fill until you specify otherwise.

I. ——————Rectangles and Ellipses

Rectangles and ellipses, which include squares and circles, are building blocks you will use over and over in your work. The **Rectangle** and **Ellipse** tools are very intuitive and can be used successfully with no training at all. These tools have a number of "hidden" features and capabilities, which you will learn about in this exercise.

1. Copy the **chap_04** folder from the **H•O•T CD-ROM** to your hard drive. For clarity, it's best to keep the folder name as **chap_04**.

Throughout this book, each chapter starts with copying the chapter exercise folder to your hard drive. These folders contain Illustrator files and other images used in the exercises for the chapter.

2. Open Illustrator CS and choose **Open Document** from the welcome screen or choose **File > Open**. Open the file **blank grid.ai** from the **chap_04** folder on your hard drive.

3. Press **Shift+Tab** on your keyboard to hide all palettes except the **Toolbox**. If you want the artboard to fill more of the screen, zoom in with the **Zoom** tool or by pressing **Ctrl-+** (Windows) or **Cmd-+** (Mac). These screen shots were zoomed in to 150%.

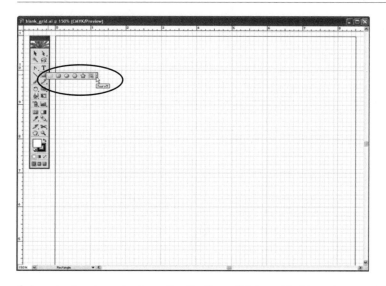

4. Locate the shape tools on the **Toolbox**. Click and hold on the currently visible shape tool (probably the **Rectangle** tool) until the flyout menu appears showing all the shape tools. Drag your mouse to the **tear-off triangle** at the end of the menu and release the mouse. All the shape tools are now visible on their own floating palette. Drag the **Shape Tools** palette away from the **Toolbox**.

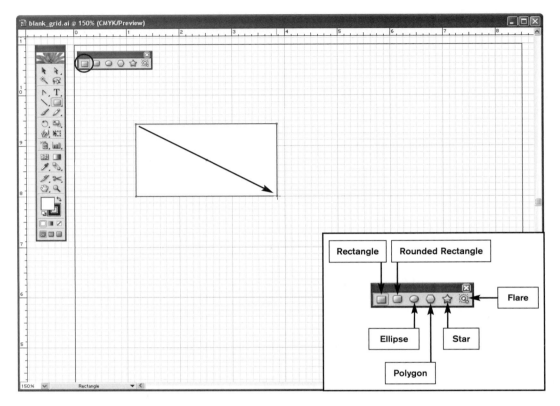

5. Select the **Rectangle** tool by clicking on it in the tear-off palette if it is not already selected. With the tool selected, move your cursor over the artboard, and click and drag to create a rectangle any size or shape you desire. Release the mouse button to have Illustrator draw the rectangle. The rectangle will appear stroked with a black line and filled white.

While the mouse button is held down, a blue-lined box appears showing the size of the rectangle you are about to make. A small blue x shows you the location of the rectangle's center. Once you release the mouse, Illustrator records the locations of the four corners of the rectangle on the page. Next it connects those four corners to create a path. Finally it traces, or strokes, that path with a black line and then fills the area inside the path with a white fill. The white fill prevents you from seeing the grid behind the rectangle.

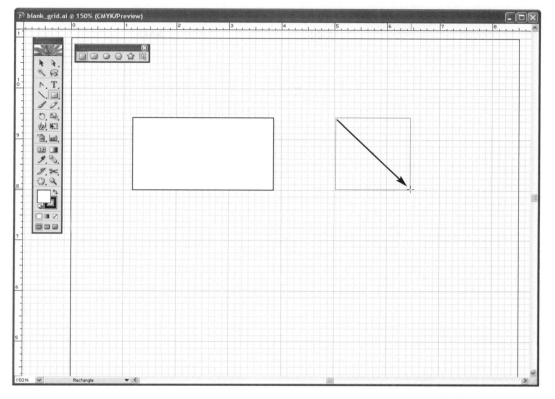

6. Create a square next to your rectangle by holding down the **Shift** key as you drag with the **Rectangle** tool.

The Shift key constrains the Rectangle, Rounded Rectangle, and Ellipse tools so they make squares, rounded squares, and circles, respectively. Pressing and releasing the Shift key while you are drag-ging toggles back and forth between square and rectangle modes. Illustrator draws whichever shape is shown when you release the mouse button.

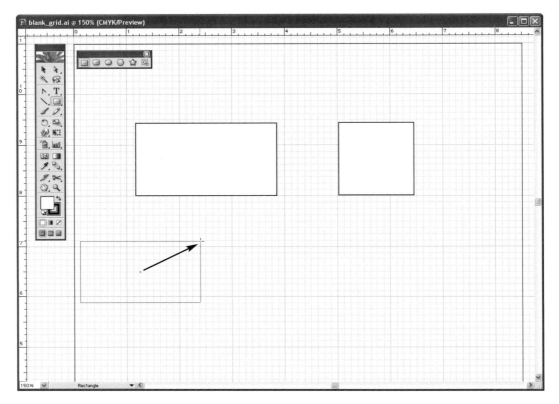

7. Below the first rectangle, create a rectangle drawn from the center rather than the corner by dragging while holding down the **Alt** key (Windows) or the **Option** key (Mac).

Holding the Alt or Option key also causes the Rounded Rectangle and Ellipse tools to draw from the center. Holding down both the Shift key and the Alt or Option key while drawing the rectangle creates a square that is drawn from the center.

Rectangle

Options
Width: 2.5986 in
Height: 1.8817 in

OK
Cancel

8. When precision is important, the shape tools can create exactly measured shapes. With the **Rectangle** tool still selected, click and release the mouse in the area below your square. The **Rectangle** dialog box appears with the dimensions of the last rectangle you created as a default. Enter a **Width** of **2** inches and a **Height** of **1.5** inches and click **OK**. The rectangle appears with its upper-left corner positioned where you clicked with the mouse. Want the rectangle positioned so that its center is where you click rather than the corner? Hold down the **Alt** or **Option** keys and click with the **Rectangle** tool. The same dialog box appears, but the rectangle will be drawn from the center after you click **OK**.

If you have the rulers visible, as you do in this file, you can see the location of your cursor at all times as a small dotted line on both rulers. This provides another way to make a more precise shape. If you note where the cursor is on the ruler when you begin to drag with the tool, you can see how far each side of the shape extends. You can do this even more accurately using the Info palette.

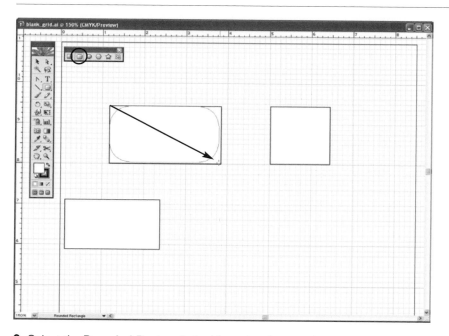

9. Select the **Rounded Rectangle** tool from the shape tools tear-off palette. Position the cursor on the upper-left corner of the first rectangle you drew and drag the cursor to the lower-right corner. A new rectangle will appear on top of the original one, but with rounded-off corners. The corners of the original one will be visible for comparison.

Rounded Rectangle

Options

Width: 2 in

Height: 1.5 in

Corner Radius: .5 in

OK

Cancel

10. Click once with the **Rounded Rectangle** tool in an open area of the artboard. The **Rounded Rectangle** dialog box has one extra field for the radius of the rounded corner. Enter **2** inches for the **Width**, **1.5** for the **Height**, and **.5** inches for the **Corner Radius**. Click **OK**.

The larger the corner radius, the more rounded the corner. The corner radius can be any number from zero, which makes a normal rectangle, up to half the length of the shortest side of the rectangle. In this example the largest radius would be about .75 inches (half of 1.5). At half the length of the shortest side, the rounded sides form a half-circle, and the tool makes a shape resembling a vitamin. If you enter a corner radius that is too large, it is reduced to the max value rather than returning an error. Try it and see for yourself.

TIP | Adjusting the Corner Radius

Drag the rounded rectangle to the size you want and before you release the mouse, use the up and down arrow keys to increase or decrease the corner radius. The left and right arrow keys toggle between a normal rectangle and a rounded one.

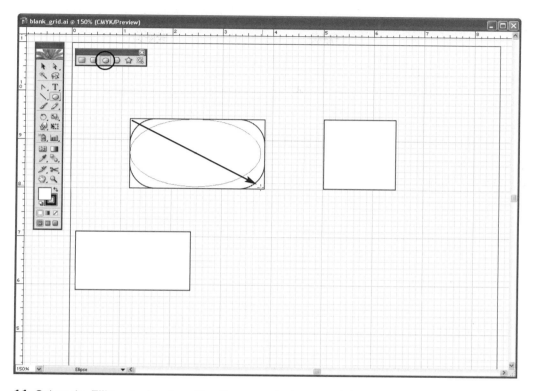

11. Select the **Ellipse** tool and position the cursor in the upper-left corner of the first rectangle you drew. Drag to the lower right and release the mouse. This resulting ellipse is drawn on top of the rounded rectangle such that the curve of the ellipse is tangent (just touches at one point) to each of the four sides of the rectangle.

*As with the rectangle tools, holding down the **Shift** or **Alt** keys constrains the drawing tool and clicking rather than dragging opens the **Ellipse** dialog box.*

12. Choose **Select > All** and press the **Backspace** or **Delete** key to clear the artwork off the artboard.

TIP | Moving While Drawing

If you start drawing a shape and decide you want it draw in a different location, hold down the spacebar *before* you let go of the mouse button. While holding down the spacebar, you can drag the shape around the screen. After you release the spacebar, you can continue drawing the shape in the new location.

2. ——————————Polygons and Stars

Polygons and stars follow the same logic as the Rectangle and Ellipse tools. In some aspects, they are actually more simple to use.

1. Start with a blank artboard from the previous exercise or open a new copy of **blank grid.ai**.

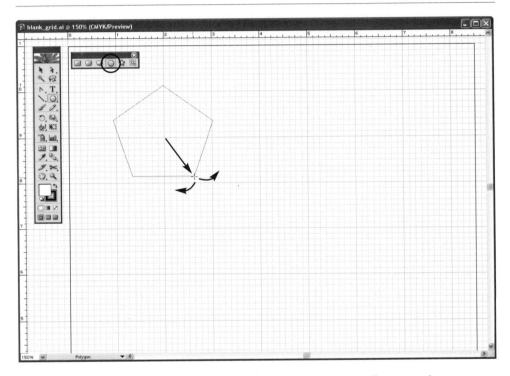

2. Select the **Polygon** tool. Starting in the center of where you want the new polygon to appear, click and drag the tool outward in any direction. The polygon (a hexagon if this is the first time you have used the tool) appears in blue lines. Before releasing the mouse button, rotate the polygon by moving your mouse up and down or left and right across the page. When you like the look of your polygon, release the mouse button.

*Holding down the **Shift** key will constrain the polygon so the bottom surface (odd-sided polygons) or bottom point (even-sided polygons) is always parallel to the bottom of the page. All polygons are drawn from the center, so the **Alt** or **Option** keys have no effect.*

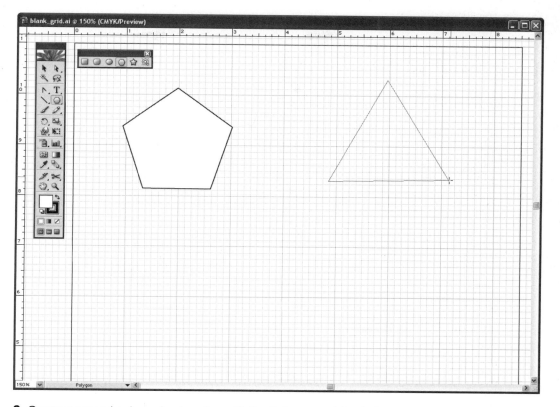

3. Create a second polygon by dragging with the **Polygon** tool, but before you release the mouse button, use the up and down arrow keys to change the number of sides to the polygon. Reducing the number to four creates a square; reducing the number to three (the minimum) creates a triangle.

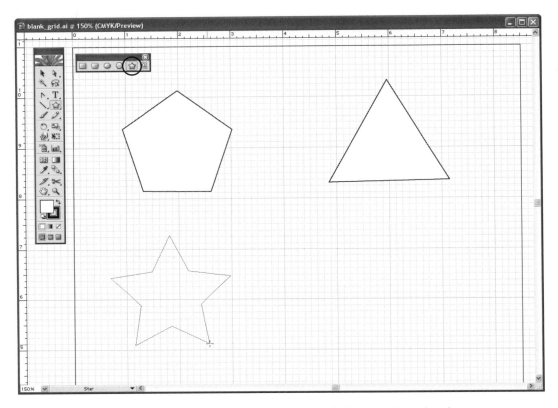

4. Select the **Star** tool and drag to create a star. As with the **Polygon** tool, moving the cursor away from the center increases the size of the star; moving the cursor up, down, right, or left rotates the star; and using the up and down arrow keys changes the number of points on the star. When you like the results, release the mouse button.

5. Play with the **Star** and **Polygon** tools until you have the feel for them. When you are finished, close the document without saving it.

Polygon and Star Dialog Boxes

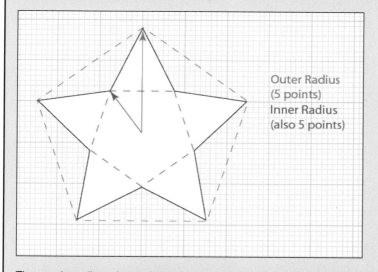

The Polygon and Star tools relate to each other similarly to the Rectangle and Rounded Rectangle tools. A polygon is created by a radius distance from the center of the polygon to each point (vertex) and the number of points total. A star is defined by an outer and an inner radius and the number of points.

Outer Radius
(5 points)
Inner Radius
(also 5 points)

The star is really a shape defined by connecting the dots between the points of two polygons. The outer radius forms a large polygon, and the inner radius forms the smaller one. When you drag with the Star tool, the inner polygon has a default radius half that of the outer one. If you want a different setting, you can use the **Star** dialog box, or you can hold down the **Ctrl** key (Windows) or the **Cmd** key (Mac) while you are dragging with the **Star** tool. Holding down this key temporarily freezes the inner radius while still letting you adjust the outer radius and see your results.

Warning: Changing the inner to outer radius with the dialog box does not change the setting when you drag with the Star tool to make your next star. Changing the relationship with the **Ctrl** or **Cmd** key affects all subsequent stars you make.

3. ————————Editing Points on a Shape

Illustrator's basic shape tools are great, but very soon you will need a shape that is not so basic and can't be built directly with the shape tools. You can still use these tools as a start and then use the **Direct Selection** tool to customize individual points on the path and create the exact shape you need.

1. Open the file **stars.ai** from the **chap_04** folder.

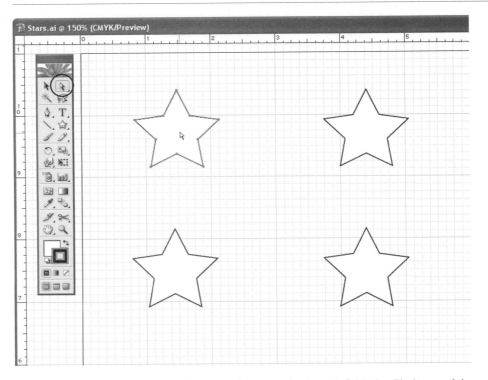

2. Click the **Direct Selection** tool or press **A** on your keyboard. Click the filled area of the upper-left star with the **Direct Selection** tool. Instead of a bounding box, all ten points that define the star are highlighted with blue dots, and all the path segments that connect them are highlighted with blue lines.

Instead of seeing a bounding box, you see all the points that define the star. Since there is no bounding box, you cannot resize or rotate the selected star with the Direct Selection tool. Clicking in the filled area does select all the points that define the star, so dragging the star around would move the entire star just as if you had used the Selection tool.

TIP | Selection Tool Toggle

You can toggle between the Selection tool and the Direct Selection tool by pressing **Ctrl+Tab** in Windows. In Mac OS X, **Cmd+Tab** is used to switch programs between active programs, so it will not switch your Selection tool. You can redefine the command if you want by choosing **Edit > Keyboard Shortcuts**, choosing **Menu Commands** from the drop-down menu, and then choosing **Other Select > Switch Selection Tools**. Since this is a menu command, it must contain the **Cmd** key. Using **Cmd+Option+Tab** is a good substitute since you can still do it one-handed fairly easily.

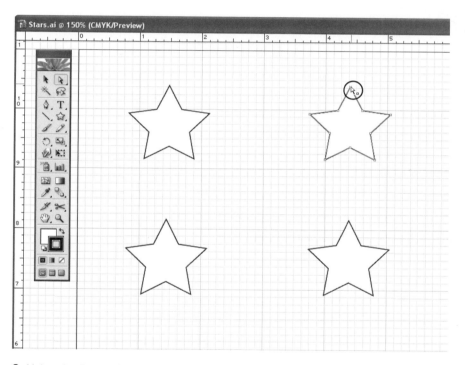

3. Using the **Direct Selection** tool, bring your cursor over the top point of the upper-right star. When you are over the top point, the cursor icon changes to show a small box below the arrow. **Click on the top point**. That point is now selected and is highlighted with a solid dot. The other nine points that define the star are highlighted with hollow dots, but they are not selected.

The difference between selecting a single point, as you are in this step, and selecting all the points in the star, as you did in Step 2, is subtle but absolutely critical to using Illustrator! When you select a single point or points with the Direct Selection tool, you can move those points separately from the rest of the points in the shape. If you move only some of the points in a shape, you will change the shape itself.

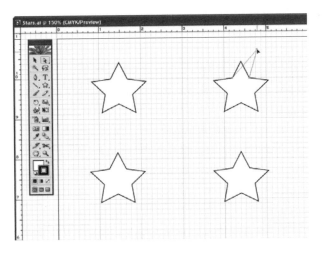

4. Drag the selected point away from the star. As you do, you will see blue lines showing the new path segments connecting the point you are moving to the two points on either side. When you like the new position of the point, release the mouse button.

You moved only one point in the star shape, so the shape is now different. This is the key difference between the Selection tool and the Direct Selection tool. The Direct Selection tool selects individual points within an object. It also ignores groups, so you can select objects or parts of objects that are grouped without selecting the rest of the group. For more information on groups, see Chapter 2, "Interface."

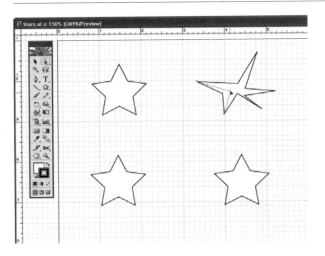

5. Repeat the process for other points on the star as you like by clicking on a point with the **Direct Selection** tool and dragging only that point to a new location.

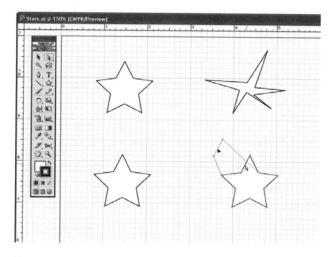

6. With the **Direct Selection** tool, drag the path segment between two points on the lower-right star. Note that the path segment you are dragging does not change, but the two segments on either side of it do.

Dragging the segment is identical to selecting and dragging the two points that define that segment.

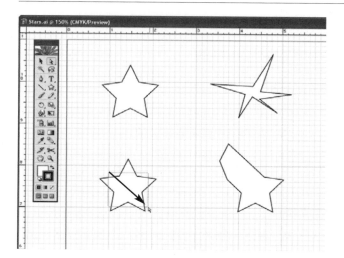

7. Position the **Direct Selection** tool to the upper left of the third star so that when you drag with the **Direct Selection** tool, it forms a box around the middle five points of the star. Drag to create the box and release the mouse button. The five middle points are now selected.

*An alternative to selecting several points is to hold down the **Shift** key as you select the desired points on the star.*

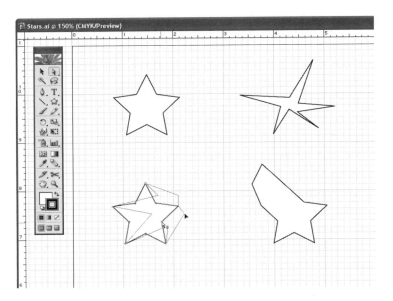

8. Click and drag any of the five selected points. These five points move together, but their positions relative to each other remain unchanged. The reshaped segments appear in blue. Release the mouse button to see the result of the move.

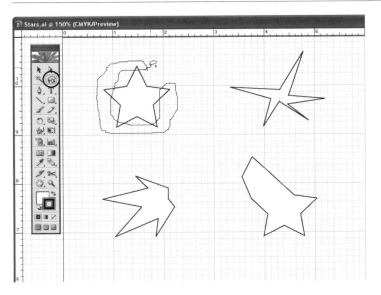

9. Select the **Lasso** tool from the **Toolbox**. Use it to drag a path that encircles all the outer points of the star but leaves the inner ones unselected.

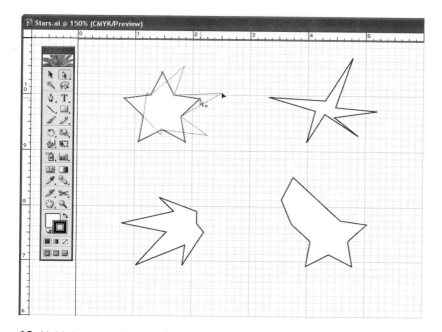

10. Hold down the **Ctrl** key (Windows) or the **Cmd** key (Mac) to switch the cursor temporarily to the last used selection tool. In this case, that is the **Direct Selection** tool. While holding down the modifier key (**Ctrl** or **Cmd**), drag any of the selected points and view the result.

Notice how selecting and moving the outer ring achieved essentially the same result as the one shown in Step 8 by moving the inner ring of points, albeit in opposite directions. This is another example of how you can achieve the same result through different methods in Illustrator.

11. If you like your reshaped stars, save the file and close it. Otherwise, close it without saving.

4. —————Editing Points with Direction Handles

Points with direction handles create curved lines. Using the Direct Selection tool, you can edit these curved lines and create a nearly infinite variety of curved and twisted shapes. In this exercise, you will see that even a few key changes to the points and direction handles have a big effect on the final shape.

1. Open **moon.ai** from the **chap_04** folder. Choose **View > Snap to Grid**.

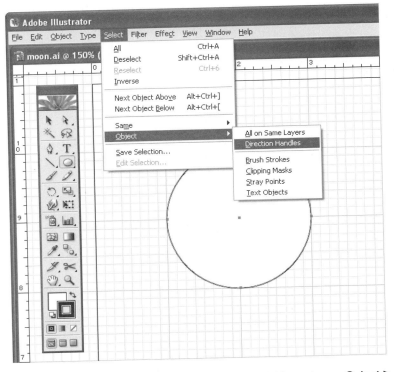

2. Select the moon with the **Direct Selection** tool. Next, choose **Select > Object > Direction Handles**. All the direction handles appear.

*Clicking on any point with the **Direct Selection** tool automatically shows the handles for that point. The **Select > Object > Direction Handles** command shows all the direction handles in the entire object. Because the circle contains curved path segments, all the points have direction handles. Without the handles, the four points of the circle would be connected with straight lines and form a diamond.*

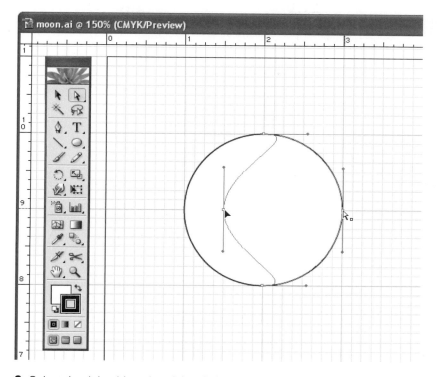

3. Select the right-side point of the circle and drag it left to form a crescent moon shape. Because Snap to Grid is active, you will be able to easily drag it directly to the left. As you drag, the selected point and its direction handles remain visible as well as the unselected points on either side and one of their direction handles.

The resulting moon shape after you move the right-side point is an interesting example of how direction handles work. Imagine a straight path connecting the top point to the point you just moved. The top direction handle is almost perpendicular to the straight path between the points so its effect on the paths is very pronounced, it bends the path a great deal, but its effect is over a short distance. The middle point's handle that points up is nearly parallel to a straight line between the points, so its effect is more subtle, but it affects the path over a greater distance.

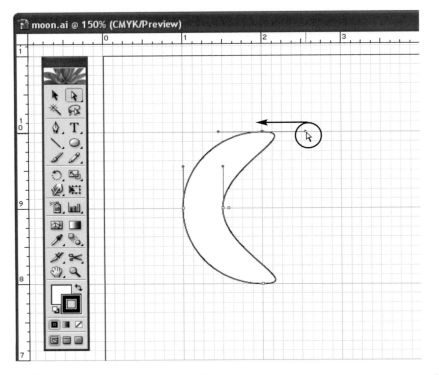

4. All four points in this circle are still smooth points that create rounded shapes. To make sharp corners on the moon, you must convert the top and bottom points into corner points. You can do this by removing one of the direction handles. With the **Direct Selection** tool, drag the right handle of the top point to the left until it collapses into the top point.

Collapsing a point with the Direct Selection tool is easy to do with Snap to Point or Snap to Grid active, but can be quite a challenge without them. As you bring the direction handle close to the point, it's almost impossible not to mess up the other direction handle. Another, more versatile, way to change smooth points into corner points is with the Convert Anchor tool covered in Chapter 10, "Pen and Point Tools." Once you collapse the handle completely, you cannot get it back without the undo command or the Convert Anchor tool.

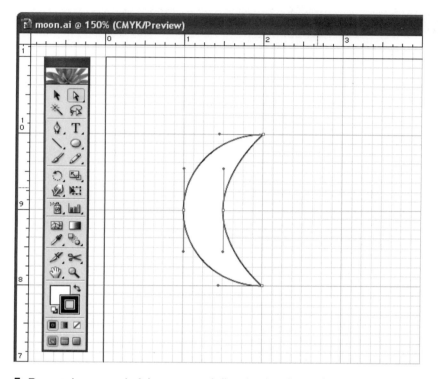

5. Repeat the removal of the unwanted direction handle on the bottom point. Select the entire moon by clicking inside the filled area. Choose **Select > Object > Direction Handles** to see that the moon now contains two smooth points and two one-handle corner points.

6. Save the file and close it.

Deleting with the Direct Selection Tool

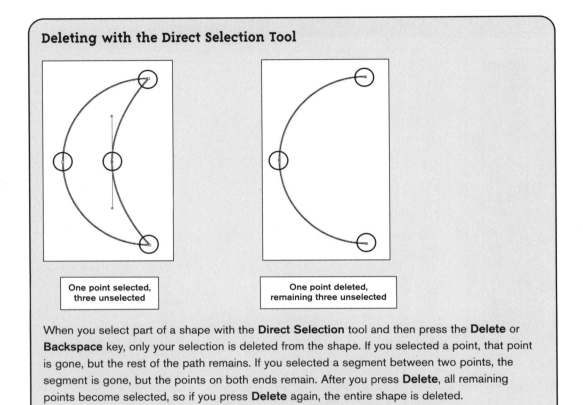

One point selected,
three unselected

One point deleted,
remaining three unselected

When you select part of a shape with the **Direct Selection** tool and then press the **Delete** or **Backspace** key, only your selection is deleted from the shape. If you selected a point, that point is gone, but the rest of the path remains. If you selected a segment between two points, the segment is gone, but the points on both ends remain. After you press **Delete**, all remaining points become selected, so if you press **Delete** again, the entire shape is deleted.

The Flare Tool

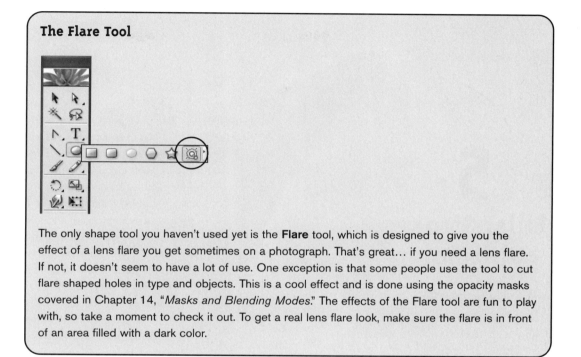

The only shape tool you haven't used yet is the **Flare** tool, which is designed to give you the effect of a lens flare you get sometimes on a photograph. That's great... if you need a lens flare. If not, it doesn't seem to have a lot of use. One exception is that some people use the tool to cut flare shaped holes in type and objects. This is a cool effect and is done using the opacity masks covered in Chapter 14, "*Masks and Blending Modes*." The effects of the Flare tool are fun to play with, so take a moment to check it out. To get a real lens flare look, make sure the flare is in front of an area filled with a dark color.

Whew! That was a lot of work for just "the basics," but the techniques you learned in this chapter will serve you well as you employ the more advanced features of Illustrator.

5.

Fills, Strokes, and Color

Color Models	Color and Color Swatches
Patterns and Pattern Swatches	Swatch Libraries
Strokes and Dashes	Caps and Joins
Linear Gradients	Radial Gradients	Multiple Strokes

chap_05

Illustrator CS H·O·T CD-ROM

In Chapter 4, "*Basic Shapes*," you adjusted the basic fill and stroke of objects to create the film reel. In this chapter, you will explore fill and stroke much further to bring color into the picture. You already know that in Illustrator you create your art by layering object upon object and that each of these objects is assigned a fill and a stroke. As Illustrator grew over the years from a black-and-white-only drawing tool to the powerful design tool it is today, the number of techniques for adding and adjusting fills and strokes grew. Part of what you will see in these exercises is that you can edit fills and strokes several ways. As you gain experience, you will find certain tools work best for you, and you will use them regularly. If there is one key to avoiding frustration as you learn, it's knowing what an object's fill and stroke is currently and how to make changes to only the parts you want.

What Are Color Models?

This chapter is also about color, so it's worth taking a moment to discuss the various models Illustrator uses to define colors.

Without going into the details of color theory (which would require a book of its own), color models offer different ways of representing the colors you choose. The **R**ed-**G**reen-**B**lue (RGB) color model is typically used for artwork that is destined for projection. This includes anything viewed on a computer monitor, such as Web graphics, TV footage, or film clips. The **C**yan-**M**agenta-**Y**ellow-**Blac**K (CMYK) color model is for artwork destined for printing. In practice, you can often get away with using either color model. There are some RGB colors that cannot be reproduced on paper without using custom inks, however, and sending a RGB file out to a print service center might cause problems.

The practical result of this is that you must choose the appropriate color model when you create a new Illustrator document. You set the color mode in the New Document dialog box, but you can change it at any time by choosing **File > Document Color Mode** and selecting the other mode. You can set only one color model per document.

While working on an illustration, you can define colors using any color mode you like no matter what the document color mode is, and Illustrator will convert the colors to the right mode automatically. This is helpful if, for example, you know the CMYK color from a brochure and want to reproduce it in RGB for a Web graphic. See the section titled "More About Colors" at the end of Exercise 1 for more information.

I. ——————————Color and Color Swatches

Here's a chance, finally, to add some color to your work! Adding and adjusting the color of your fills and strokes can be done many ways, depending on exactly what you need. In fact, a bigger challenge than adding color is managing your color palette for the artwork. In this exercise, you will adjust colors using several different methods and manage those colors using the **Swatches** palette.

1. Copy the **chap_05** folder from the **H•O•T CD-ROM** to your hard drive. Open the file **map_05.ai** from that folder.

2. Choose **Window > Color** and **Window > Appearance**. This opens the **Color** and **Appearance** palettes, as well as several other palettes that share the same palette windows.

The Color palette is all you need to edit strokes in your document, but the Appearance palette provides some key information that can prevent quite a bit of frustration once you know what to look for. The Color palette is attached to eight palettes: Color, Graphic Styles, Swatches, Brushes, Symbols, Stroke, Gradient, and Transparency, so quite a bit will open into view when you open the Color palette.

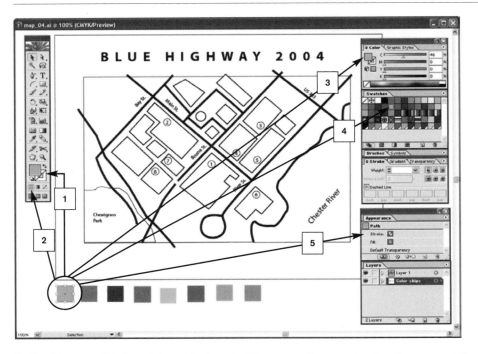

3. The file **map_05.ai** contains a black-and-white map, with several colored squares at the bottom. Using the **Selection** tool, click the **light blue square**.

While the square is selected, color information appears in five places (see the screen shot):

1 The color of both the fill and the stroke of the selected object appear in the Toolbox, with one square on top of the other. In this case, the Fill square is over the Stroke square. As you saw in Chapter 4, "Basic Shapes," clicking the Stroke square would put it on top. When the Fill square is on top, you can edit the object's fill. When the Stroke square is on top, you can edit the object's stroke.

*2 The color of the object fill or stroke that is on top appears near the bottom of the Toolbox. This is the **selected color**. This color remains until an object with another color is selected. If you choose a different fill type, such as a gradient or a pattern, this last selected solid color remains visible. If you click this small square of solid color, it replaces the current fill or stroke, depending on whether the Fill square or Stroke square is on top.*

3 The same fill and stroke information shown on the Toolbox appears on the Color palette. You can control fill and stroke color from either location.

4 If the selected color is one of the colors on the Swatches palette, that swatch will highlight, too.

5 The fill and stroke, or in some cases multiple fills and strokes, of the selected object appear in the Appearance palette.

Yikes! That's a lot of options for controlling color. Part of the reason is historical. The color options on the Toolbox appeared as features before there was a Color palette. It really doesn't matter which control you use for color, but I recommend using the Color palette (3) and Swatches palette (4) for your primary color control. They probably offer the best blend of convenience and options.

NOTE | Selection Tools Versus the Layers Palette

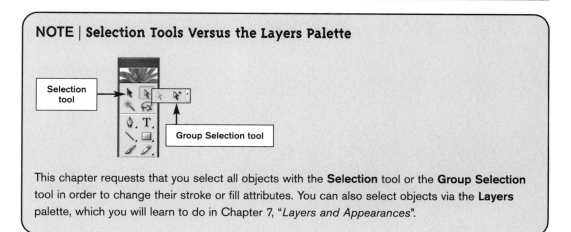

This chapter requests that you select all objects with the **Selection** tool or the **Group Selection** tool in order to change their stroke or fill attributes. You can also select objects via the **Layers** palette, which you will learn to do in Chapter 7, "*Layers and Appearances*".

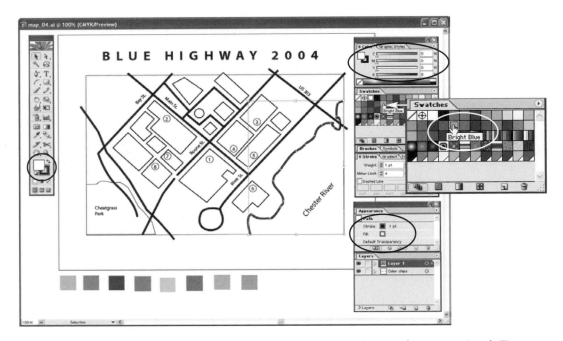

4. With the **Selection** tool, click anywhere inside the river area on the map (as you see here). The color information will change with the new selection. Make sure the white fill is the selected color by ensuring the white **Fill** square is on top of the black **Stroke** square. If it is not, click the **Fill** square on either the **Toolbox** or the **Color** palette or press **X** on your keyboard. Next, click the swatch shown here in the **Swatches** palette for **Bright Blue**. This process will fill the river area of the map with the color bright blue.

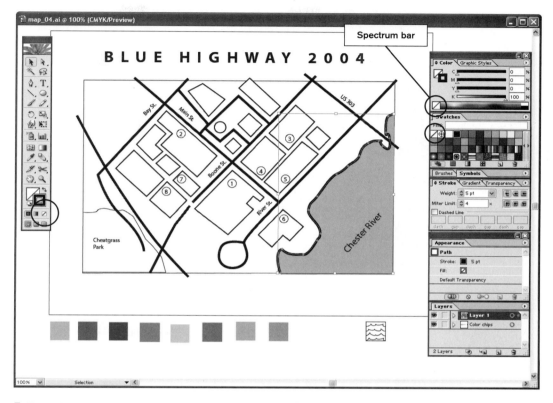

5. Press **X** on your keyboard again to put the **Stroke** square on top. The **X** key is a toggle between stroke and fill. Set the stroke of the river area to none by clicking by the **None** icon on the **Toolbox**, the **None** color area on the **spectrum** bar, or the **None** swatch.

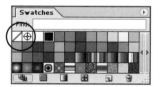

*There are two special swatches on the Swatches palette. The **None** swatch has the same effect as clicking None on the Toolbox. The **Registration** swatch is specifically for setting registration colors and is discussed in Appendix C, "Print Issues."*

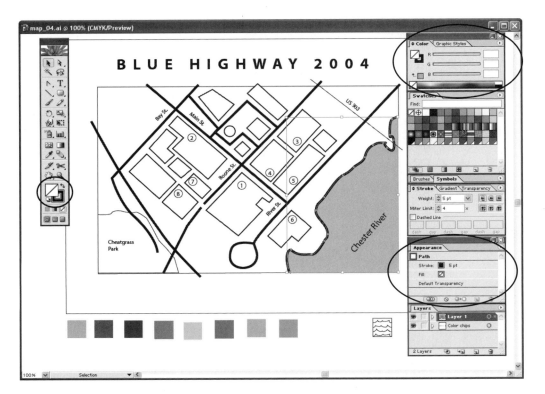

6. Click the shoreline along the edge of the river. The fill and stroke info for the shoreline appears on the **Color** and **Appearance** palettes. The shoreline of the river is marked with a 5 pt black line.

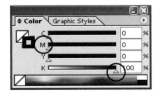 

7. Click the **Stroke** square on the **Color** palette to make it come to the front, if it is not already there. Drag the **Black (K)** slider down from **100%** to **0%**. The color is now white, both on the **Stroke** square and on the shoreline path on the map. Drag the **Cyan (C)** slider to **100%** and the **Magenta (M)** slider to **50%**. You can enter the percent value in the fields to the right of the sliders instead of sliding them if you prefer.

The color updates on the map as soon as you stop sliding, but it changes on the Color palette as you slide so you can see the effects immediately. As you move the sliders, the colors of each bar change as well. In the previous image, the far left side of the Cyan bar is pink. If you moved the Cyan slider to the far left, the selected color would become that shade of pink.

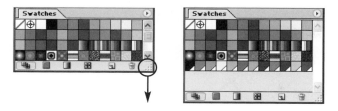

8. You can save custom colors on your **Swatches** palette for later use, but first you should make sure you can easily see them. If your Swatches palette does not show an empty area (as shown here on the right), drag the lower-right corner of the palette down until the empty area appears.

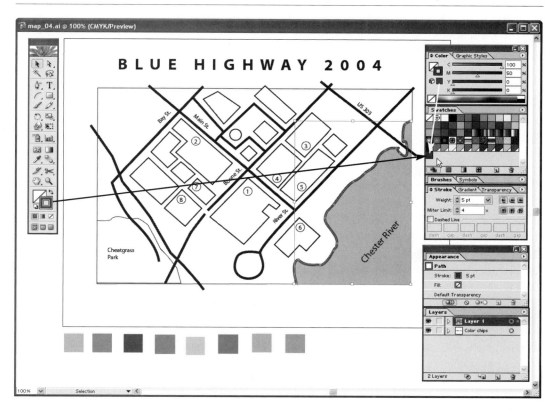

9. Drag the **Stroke** square from either the **Color** palette or the **Toolbox** down to an empty area of the **Swatches** palette. A new swatch appears in the **Swatches** palette for the color you just created.

Swatches are a great way to keep a palette of all the colors in your document. Next time you need this color, you can simply select the stroke or fill you want colored and click the appropriate swatch. As you'll see in this and subsequent exercises, swatches can hold patterns and gradients as well.

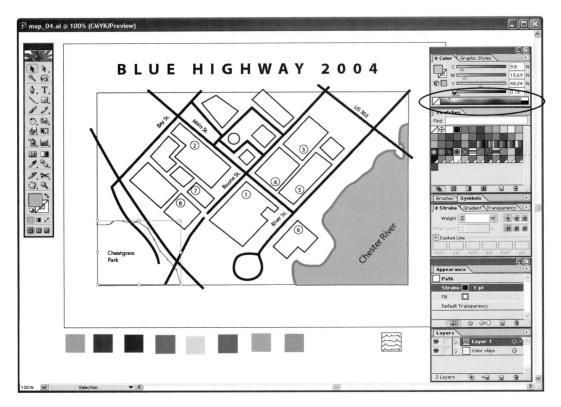

10. Click with the **Selection** tool anywhere inside the area of the park (as shown here). Using the **Color** palette, set the **stroke** to **None** and then press **X** on your keyboard to put the **Fill** square on top. Move your cursor over the **spectrum** bar. As you do, it will change to an eyedropper icon. Try to sample a color on the spectrum bar matching the **light brown** square below the map.

Tip: When you use the spectrum bar, hold down the mouse button as you drag over the spectrum bar. The selected color changes as you drag. To change the hue of the color, drag left or right. To make the selected color lighter, drag up. To make it darker, drag down.

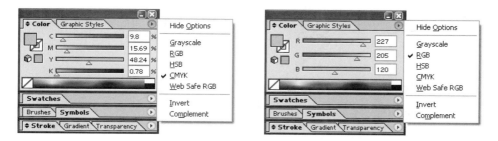

11. The exact color is **9.8% Cyan**, **15.69% Magenta**, **48.24% Yellow**, and **.78% Black**. Rather than enter the numbers as CMYK, open the flyout menu on the **Color** palette and choose **RGB**. The same brown is **227 Red**, **205 Green**, and **120 Blue**. You can change these numbers with the sliders or by typing the number in the fields to the right of each slider and pressing **Enter** (Windows) or **Return** (Mac) after each one.

If you have the color information you want but using a different color model, such as RGB, its fine to switch to the RGB model to enter the color. Because this document uses CMYK color, the color you choose is converted to it's CMYK equivalent as long as it is within the CMYK gamut (see the "More About Colors" section later in this chapter).

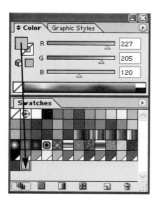

12. Drag the new color down to the **Swatches** palette so you can use it later.

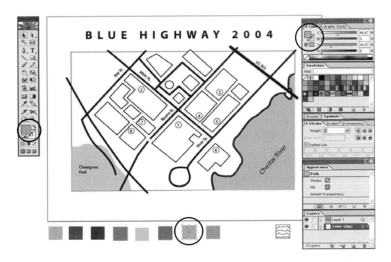

13. Select the **Selection** tool and click the **light green** color square. Make sure the **Fill** square is on top in the **Toolbox** or the **Color** palette.

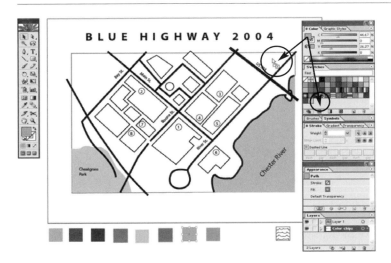

14. Drag the color from the **Color** palette to the land area of the map. The map will fill with green. Drag the green color to your **Swatches** palette to add it to your swatches as well.

You can also drag a swatch onto an object in your illustration to apply that color. This applies to either the stroke or the fill, depending on which is on top in the Color palette or Toolbox. This is why you made sure the Fill square was on top in Step 12.

15. Save the file.

More About Colors

That was a lot of information for one exercise, but it only begins the potential exploration of working with color. Many of the decisions about color have more to do with artistic choice than using Illustrator. Here is some more information about how Illustrator handles color.

Uses for Color Models

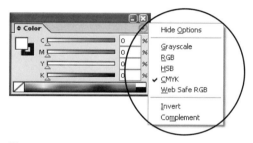

There are only two color models for your document overall—RGB and CMYK—but there are several color models you can use for individual colors in the artwork. You would access these additional color models, described in the following chart, through the flyout menu on the Color palette.

Additional Color Models		
Color Model	**Color Range**	**Use**
CMYK	All colors that can print using a standard four-color process	Full-color print
RGB	Almost all colors a human can see	Projection (film, video, TV)
HSB	Another way of representing RGB colors	Projection (film, video, TV)
Grayscale	Pure white to pure black	Print or projection
Spot Color	Varies	Exact color reproduction in print

A good use for the HSB color model is if you like a color (hue), but want it slightly brighter or darker (adjusted brightness) or more or less intense (adjusted saturation). To do this, select the color in your document. Switch to HSB on the Color palette and adjust the color as you wish.

Process Colors Versus Spot Colors

The terms "process color" and "spot color" refer to how color is put on a page using ink. Full-color printing is done by mixing four colors of ink: Cyan, Magenta, Yellow, and Black. The advantage of process color is that most colors can be put on the page with a single pass through a four-color printing press. The disadvantage is it is difficult or impossible to create certain colors with this system. A spot color is an ink mixed to an exact color before printing. With spot colors, you can create almost any color, including metallic and other special colors that cannot be achieved through the four-color process. You can also see a sample of the ink on paper and know exactly how the color appears when printed. The disadvantage to spot colors is that the press must be able to use the spot color—you can't print all four process inks and a spot color ink if the press holds only four inks—and the print service must have that ink color in stock.

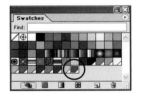 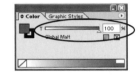

The Swatches palette denotes spot color swatches with the small white triangle in the corner. When you look at the color in the Color palette, there is a slider for how dark (tint) you want the color printed. Many of the swatches in the swatch libraries are commonly used spot colors. The use of spot colors is covered in Appendix C, "*Print Issues*," as well.

Out of Gamut

With certain colors, the Color palette displays **Out of Gamut** warnings. The **Out of Print Gamut** warning, a triangle with an exclamation point, says that the selected color cannot be printed using the CMYK color process. You can still use that color in your document, but if you print it, any out of gamut colors will shift. Usually out of print gamut colors are too bright to print and are very pure red, green, or blue. Often a slight change of the color will bring it back within range. There are two simple ways to do this. You cannot create an out of print gamut color using the CMYK sliders, so you could only use that color model. Alternately, you could define the color using the RGB or HSB sliders and then click the color that appears in a square to the right of the warning icon. This replaces the out of gamut color with the closest in gamut color.

The **Out of Web Gamut** warning, a cube, indicates the selected color is outside of the Web-safe color palette. This is only a concern if you are creating a Web graphic and want 100-percent certainty the colors do not shift on older computers. With so many computers supporting thousands or millions of colors, Web-safe color is becoming a thing of the past, unless you are designing for PDAs, Smartphones, or similar device that have very limited color palettes.

The Color Picker

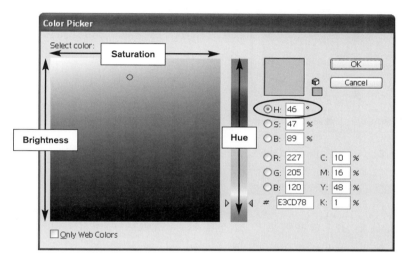

If you double-click a fill or stroke color in the Toolbox, you open the **Color Picker**. This window works similarly to the spectrum bar on the Color palette, except that one component of the color model, in this case hue, has a dedicated slider and the other two, saturation and brightness here, are mapped on a large square. The larger area makes it easier to find exactly the right color. Click any radio button to change which part of the color model is on the slider and which parts are shown in the large square. The Color Picker does not provide CMYK sliders, but you can enter CMYK values and immediately see the nearest equivalent values on the other two color models.

2. ——————————Patterns and Pattern Swatches

Fills can consist of tiled patterns instead of solid colors. These patterns are created in Illustrator and then stored on the Swatches palette for use in your document. In this exercise, you will create a custom pattern fill for use on the map.

1. Open **map_05.ai** or simply continue from Exercise 1 if the file is still open.

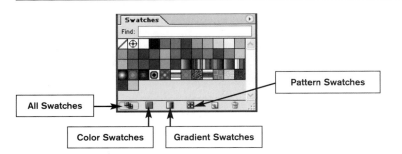

2. Click the **Pattern Swatches** button on the bottom of the **Swatches** palette.

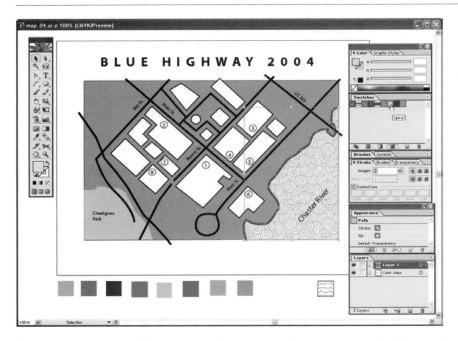

3. Click the water area (shown selected above) with the **Selection** tool. With only the pattern swatches visible, click one to fill the water with that pattern. Try a few for fun.

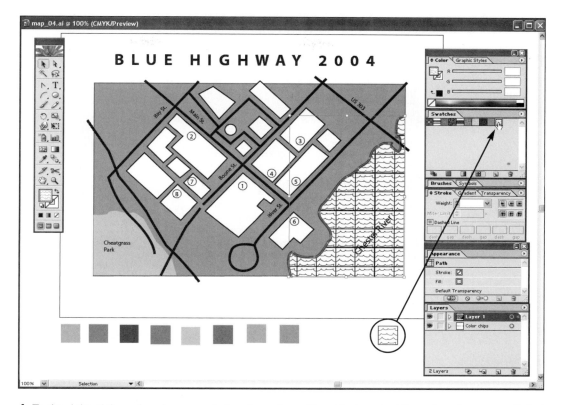

4. To the right of the colored squares below the artboard is a black-and-white pattern for waves. Select the patterned square (circled above) and drag it to the **Swatches** palette. Select the water area again and click the new pattern swatch to fill the water area.

The pattern filling the river consists of the square you dragged to the Swatches palette repeated, or tiled, many times. There are several problems with the tiled pattern however. The black border on the square makes the tiling very obvious, so we'll remove it. Also, the white background should be blue. The size of the waves is large enough that you can easily see the repeating pattern, so the pattern needs to be scaled down. In Chapter 6, "Transformations," you will see how to scale down a pattern after using it to fill an object, but for now you can reduce the size of the original square.

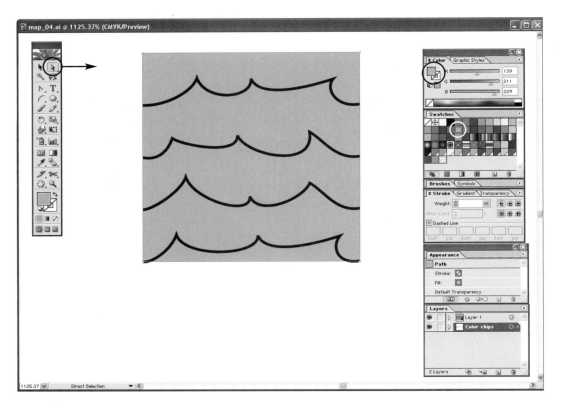

5. Using the **Zoom** tool, drag a square (marquee) around the wave pattern to zoom in on it. Choose the **Group Selection** tool. Click the the outer box to select it and change the fill to **Bright Blue** and stroke to **None**.

You must use the Group Selection tool to select the square because it is grouped with the wavy lines. Using the Selection tool will select the square and the lines.

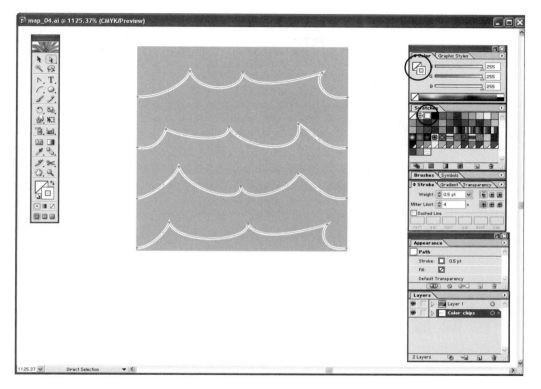

6. With the **Group Selection** tool, click the top wavy line twice. The first click selects the line and the second selects the other three lines it is grouped with. Change the waves to a stroke of **White** and fill **of None**.

Note that for each of the four wave lines the height of the line is the same on the left and right sides of the square. This ensures that when the waves repeat (this process is called tile) over an area the line will appear continuous.

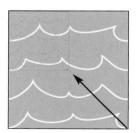

7. Switch to the **Selection** tool and click anywhere in the blue fill. This selects the square and the wavy lines since they are all grouped. Drag the lower-right corner of the bounding box until the pattern is about one-quarter of the original size. Double-click the **Hand** tool to zoom out and see the whole page.

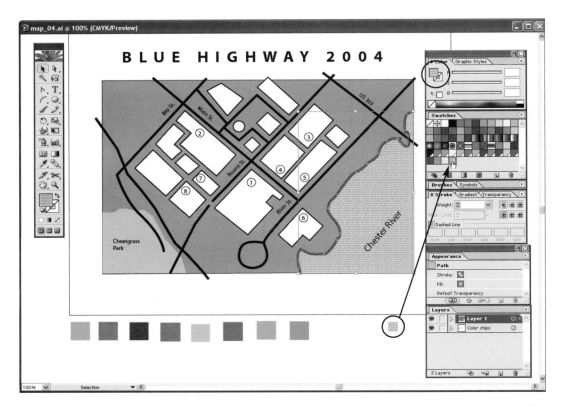

8. Drag the newly colored and resized square to the **Swatches** palette. Select the water area and click the **Fill** square so it is on top. Click the new pattern swatch to fill with the new pattern.

9. Save the file.

▶ MOVIE | pattern.mov

To view the complex steps of this exercise performed, watch **pattern.mov** located in the **movies** folder on the **H•O•T CD-ROM**.

3. —————————Swatch Libraries

As you add swatches to the Swatches palette, they become part of the Illustrator document. When you open the document later, your swatches will be exactly as you left them. If you send the document to someone else, they will see your custom swatches. Swatches can also be saved separately into their own libraries for use on later documents or for viewing on multiple swatch palettes.

1. Open **map_05.ai** or continue from Exercise 2.

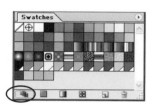

2. Click the **Show All Swatches** button on the **Swatches** palette to see all types of swatches.

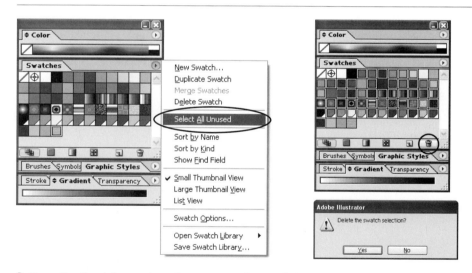

3. From the **Swatches** palette flyout menu, choose **Select All Unused**. Click the **Trash** icon on the **Swatches** palette to delete the unused swatches. Click **Yes** when asked to confirm the deletion.

Saving a swatch library saves all the swatches in the Swatch palette—even ones you have not used in your illustration. By selecting all the unused swatches and deleting them, the Swatches palette contains only the swatches you are using. If you are using a color that you didn't add to the Swatches palette, however, it won't be saved in the swatch library.

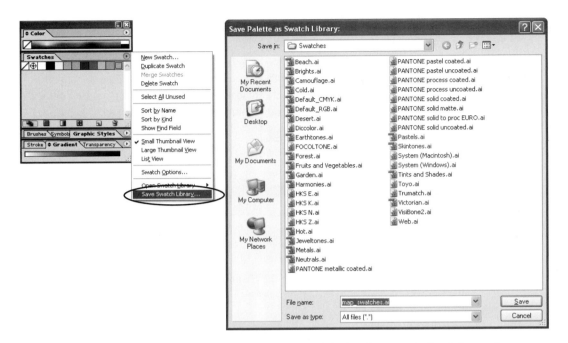

4. Now that you have only the swatches used in the artwork in the document's **Swatches** palette, choose **Save Swatch Library** from the **Swatches** palette flyout menu. Enter the name **map_swatches** and click **Save**.

The Illustrator Swatches folder opens as the default for saving a new swatch library. You can actually save the library anywhere you like, but if you save it in this folder, it will appear in the flyout menu of swatches the next time you start up Illustrator.

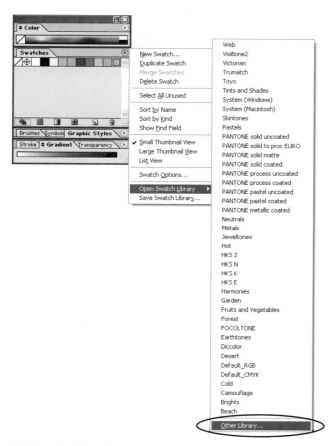

5. From the **Swatches** palette flyout menu, choose **Open Swatch Library > Other Library**. Find the name **map_swatches.ai** in the **chap_05** folder and open it.

Swatch libraries open on their own palette. You can use them here the same way you can with the Swatches palette, but you cannot add or delete swatches. Swatch library palettes are not saved with the document either. If you want the swatches in the library to become part of the Illustrator document, you must add them to the document's Swatches palette.

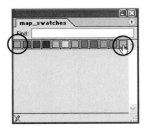

6. Click the first swatch on **map_swatches**. Hold down the **Shift** key and click the last swatch on **map_swatches**. This selects all the custom swatches.

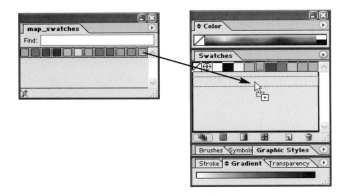

7. Drag the swatches from the **map_swatches** palette to the **Swatches** palette. Now all the custom colors are part of the document.

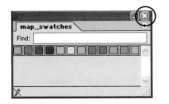

8. Once the custom colors are on the document's **Swatches** palette, there is no need for the swatch library palette. Close the **map_swatches** palette.

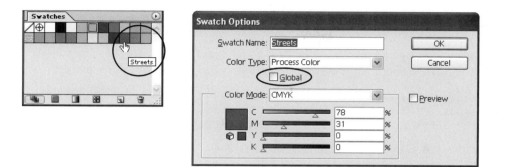

9. On the **Swatches** palette, bring your cursor over the new swatches. As you pause over each one, a tooltip will pop up with the name of the custom swatch. Find and double-click the blue **Streets** swatch. The **Swatch Options** dialog box will open.

The Swatch Options dialog box lets you do much more than name swatches. You can change the Color Type, Color Mode, and color itself. If you leave Global unchecked, any changes you make here will change the swatch and any selected objects in your Illustrator document, but will not affect previous uses of that swatch. With Global checked, all instances of that swatch color will change in your document.

10. Click **OK** to close the **Swatch Options** dialog box. Save the file.

TIP | Swatch Libraries

Swatch libraries are just Illustrator files with no objects and a customized Swatches palette. This fact lets you do a slick trick. If you have an old file with swatches you want to copy to a new file, open the new file and then choose **Open Swatch Library** from the **Swatches** palette flyout menu. Next, open the old file containing the swatches you want to copy as if it were a swatch library. All the swatches from the old file appear on their own palette in the new file.

4. _____Strokes and Dashes

In Exercises 1 through 3, you added color to the fills and strokes of the map. In this exercise, you will edit both the color and appearance of strokes to improve the look of the map and add information to it.

1. Open **map_05.ai** or continue from Exercise 3.

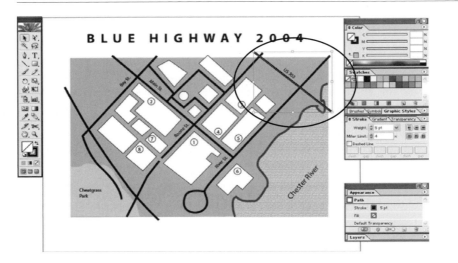

2. Select the **Selection** tool and click the road under the words "US 303."

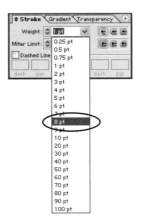

3. The **Stroke** palette is grouped with the **Color** palette you already opened. On the **Stroke** palette, increase the stroke weight to **8 pt** (eight points). The highway now appears wider than the roads.

Both the Stroke and Appearance palette show that the item you have selected has a stroke of 8 pt, but the Appearance palette also tells you that the item you selected is a path and that it has a Fill of None. One of the best Illustrator habits you can develop is regularly using your Appearance palette. When Illustrator doesn't behave the way you expect, often the reason can be found—and corrected—using the Appearance palette.

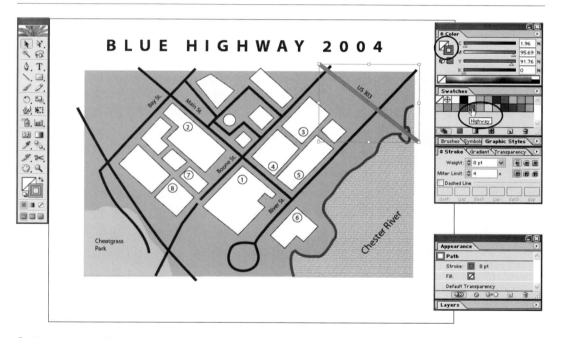

4. Make sure the **Stroke** square is on top, and click the **Highway** red swatch (circled above) to change the line's color to red. If you put your cursor over the red swatch and wait a moment, a tooltip appears saying "Highway."

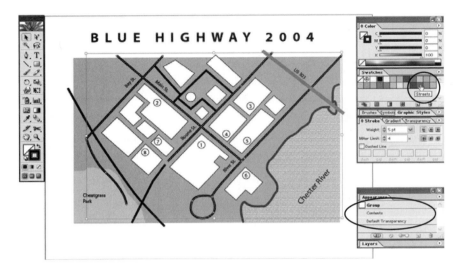

5. Click any of the roads with names on them. These roads are grouped, so selecting one selects the entire group. Make sure the **Stroke** square is on top and click the **Streets** medium-blue color swatch (circled above).

*Take a close look at the Appearance palette. Note that **Group** is the selected item rather than **Path**. This lets you know that you are applying this color to all the items in the group.*

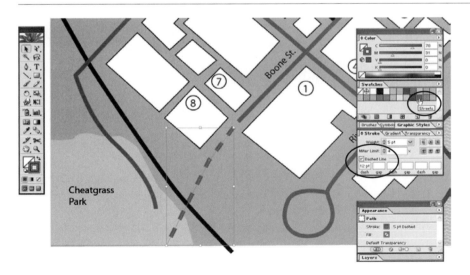

6. Select the section of street that is still black and runs south of town to the park (selected above). On the **Stroke** palette, check the **Dashed Line** box and then enter **12 pt** (twelve points) in the **dash** field. Stroke the dashed road with the same blue **Streets** swatch (circled above) you used in the previous step.

In this example, the road becomes dashed with both dashes and spaces 12 pts long. By entering different combinations of dash and gap lengths, however, you can create some pretty complex dashed lines. If you have more than one dash and one gap length, the pattern will repeat from the beginning to the end of the line.

TIP | Reversing a Dashed Stroke

A dashed stroke always starts with the dash, not the gap. If you dash a path and it starts with a gap, you are looking at the end of the path rather than the beginning. To swap the start and end points of a path, select the path and then choose the **Pen** tool. Click the point you want at the end of the line with the **Pen** tool and that will become the end of the path.

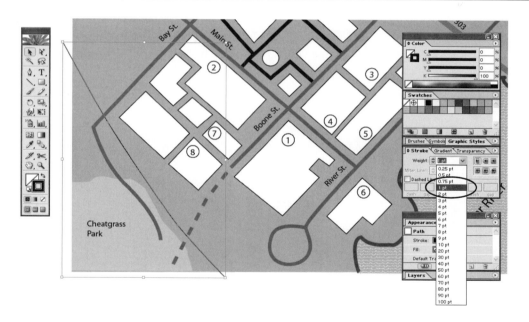

7. Click the path next to the park that crosses the dashed line and select it (see above). Using the **Stroke** palette, change the **Weight** of the stroke to **1 pt**.

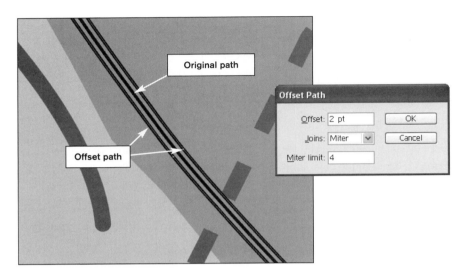

8. Choose **Object > Path > Offset Path**. The **Offset Path** dialog box will open. Change the **Offset** value to **2 pt**. Click **OK**.

Offset path creates a "box" around the path. The long sides of the box are parallel to the path you chose.

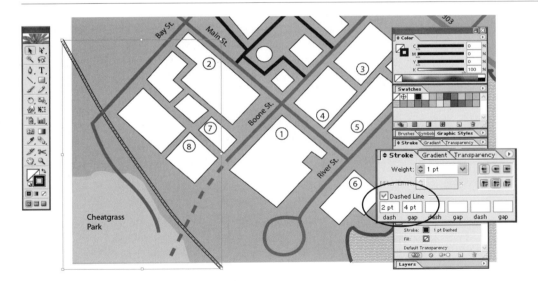

9. You now have three parallel paths. Select the original (center) path. Using the **Stroke** palette, change the **dash** value to **2 pt** and the **gap** value to **4 pt**.

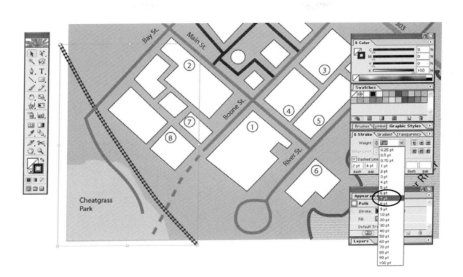

10. With the center line still selected, change the **Weight** to **7 pt**.

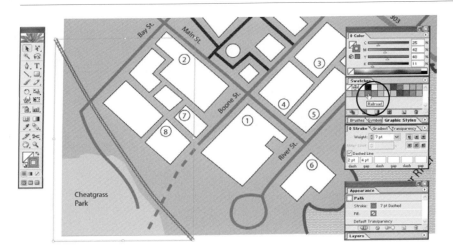

11. Set stroke color to the dark brown **Railroad** color (circled above) from the **Swatches** palette. Choose **Object > Arrange > Send Backward**. By changing the dash and gap values, you created artwork that gives the illusion of railroad tracks! Pretty slick, eh?

Be sure to choose Send Backward and not Send to Back. Send Backward puts the brown railroad ties behind the rails. Send to Back puts them behind everything on the map!

12. Save the file.

5. —————————Caps and Joins

In addition to weight and dashes, the Stroke palette controls the look of line corners and ends. Adjusting these joins and caps can make the difference between a good-looking illustration and a polished one.

1. Open **Map_05.ai** or continue from Exercise 4 if it is still open.

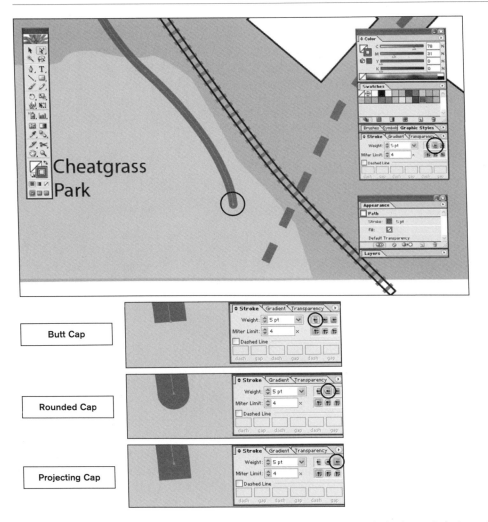

2. With the **Zoom** tool, click several times on the road that dead-ends in the park (selected above) to zoom in on it. With the **Group Selection** tool, select the dead-end road. On the **Stroke** palette, switch the end from a **Butt Cap** to **Rounded Cap**.

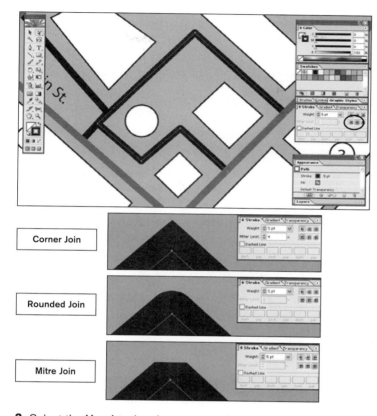

Corner Join	
Rounded Join	
Mitre Join	

3. Select the **Hand** tool and pan over to the back streets by the unnumbered buildings. Click twice with the **Group Selection** tool on the black streets with corners (selected above). Using the **Stroke** palette, change the join from a **Corner Join** to a **Round Join**.

Beneath the stroke Weight is a drop-down for the Miter Limit, which is only available with a corner join. The Miter Limit is the point at which a corner join will automatically become a bevel join. The default of 4 pt means that when the distance from the point on the path to the tip of the corner exceeds four times the stroke weight, Illustrator draws a bevel rather than a corner.

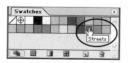

4. Stroke the streets with the **Streets** swatch (circled above) from the **Swatches** palette that you used for the streets in Exercise 3.

5. Double-click the **Hand** tool to see the entire map. Save the file and close it.

6. _____Linear Gradients

Gradients are fills containing multiple colors that blend from one to the next. Because they let you simulate light on objects, create the appearance of texture and depth, and smoothly blend colors, gradients are one of those core Illustrator tools you will use regularly. Illustrator's mesh tools allow for complex gradients over a shape, but even the basic gradients from the Gradient palette provide a lot of options.

1. Open **poster_05.ai** from the **chap_05** folder. Zoom out to see the entire poster by double-clicking the **Hand** tool in the Toolbox or pressing **Ctrl+0** (Windows) or **Cmd+0** (Mac) on your keyboard.

2. Select the sky by clicking anywhere on the sky with the **Selection** tool. The current solid fill color appears on the **Toolbox**, the **Color** palette, and the **Swatches** palette.

*The poster file contains the custom swatches used in the poster. The swatches are also available from the **chap_05** folder as **poster_swatches.ai**.*

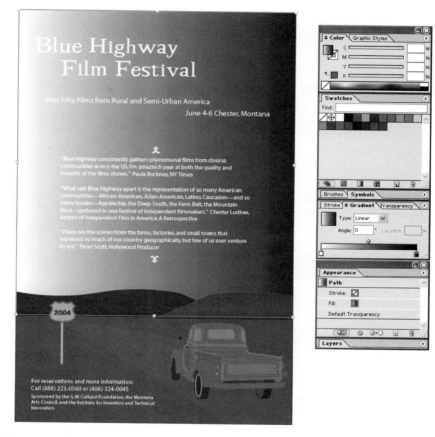

3. Click the **Gradient** button on the **Toolbox** (circled). The sky fills with the gradient and the **Gradient** palette comes to the front.

The Gradient button will fill the selected object(s) with the last gradient you used. Since you haven't created a gradient yet, it filled the sky with the default black-and-white gradient.

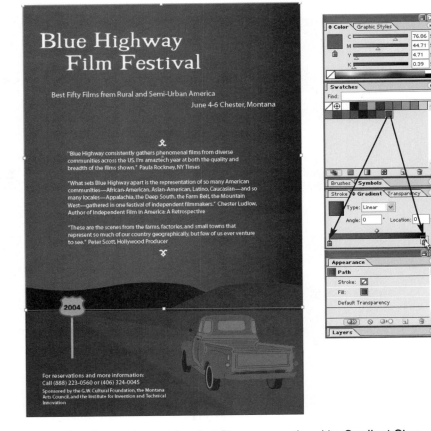

4. On the **Swatches** palette, drag the purple swatch called **Sky one** over the white **Gradient Stop** color on the **Gradient** palette. Purple replaces white in the sky gradient on the poster. Drag the dark blue swatch called **Sky two** over the black **Gradient Stop** to replace it.

The Gradient Stops determine the colors in the gradient fill. You can add as many colors to a gradient as you like by adding more stops to the bar on the Gradient palette. Click the signpost in the poster to see an example of a three-step gradient. To delete a color from the gradient, drag it off the Gradient palette and release the mouse. A gradient has a minimum of two colors, however.

5. With the sky still selected, select the **Gradient** tool on the **Toolbox**. Drag the **Gradient** tool from a point near the end of the road to the top center of the poster to set **gradient angle** and **gradient distance**.

The gradient angle is also adjustable from the Gradient palette and sets where the two ends of the gradient lie. An angle of zero degrees is a gradient from left to right. Ninety degrees is from bottom to top and so on. The gradient distance is more interesting. By default, the gradient starts at one end of the filled area and ends on the other side. But with the Gradient tool, you can drag a line that extends beyond the filled area, and part of the gradient will not be seen. You can also define a gradient that does not even reach the sides of the area.

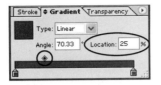

6. On the **Gradient** palette, slide the diamond-shaped gradient midpoint stop (circled above) from the middle of the gradient to a **Location** of **25%**. To enter the number manually, click the midpoint stop and then enter the number in the **Location** field.

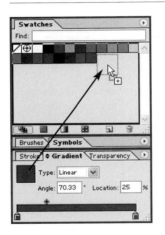

7. Drag the gradient from the **Gradient** palette to the **Swatches** palette.

By creating a gradient swatch, you can use the gradient anytime you want. These swatches are logically called gradient swatches. Cool!

8. Save the file and close it.

7. ——————————Radial Gradients

Radial gradients are different than linear gradients in that the gradient starts at some point in the filled area and extends equally in all directions, so there is no gradient angle. Other than that, the two gradient types are created and edited identically. Radial gradients are a great way to create the appearance of a sphere.

1. Open **map_05.ai**.

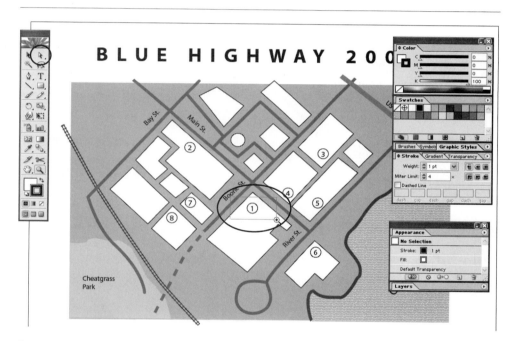

2. Draw a box (marquee) around **ball flag 1** (the circle with the number 1) with the **Zoom** tool to zoom in on it. Select the ball flag with the **Group Selection** tool.

The ball flags are not grouped, so you could use the Selection tool as well. The Group Selection tool does not show the bounding box however, so it's easier to see the gradient you are about to create.

3. Ensure that the **Fill** square is on top in the **Toolbox** or **Color** palette. Click the **Gradient** button on the **Toolbox**.

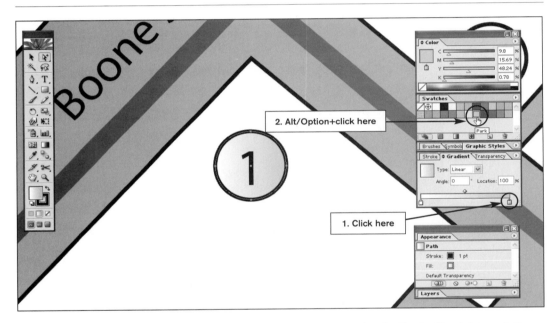

4. Click the black stop color (circled) on the **Gradient** palette to select it. On the **Swatches** palette, **Alt+click** (Windows) or **Option+click** (Mac) the light brown swatch (circled) to replace black with brown.

Simply clicking the swatch rather than Alt+clicking or Option+clicking will remove the gradient and fill the circle with solid brown.

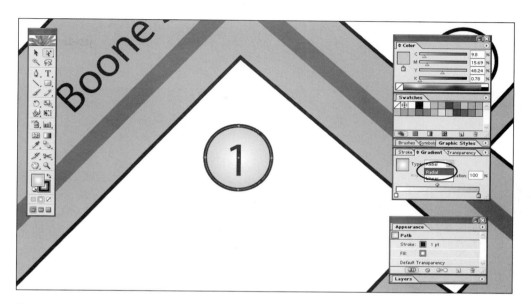

5. Using the **Gradient** palette, switch to a **Radial** gradient.

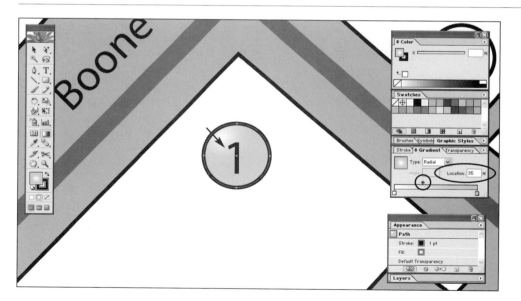

6. With the circle still selected, choose the **Gradient** tool from the **Toolbox** and drag from a point near the upper left of the circle to the center. In the **Gradient** palette, select the midpoint stop and move it to a **Location** of **35%**,

7. Using the **Color** palette or the **Toolbox**, set the stroke to **None**. Zoom out by pressing **Ctrl+−** (Windows) or **Cmd+−** (Mac) twice or choose the **Zoom** tool and hold down the **Alt** key (Windows) or the **Option** key (Mac) while clicking twice.

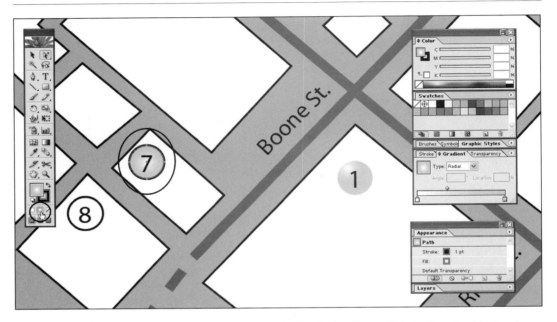

8. Select the **ball flag 7** (selected and circled above). On the **Toolbox**, click the **Gradient** button to apply your most recently created gradient.

The white-to-brown gradient filled the circle, but the gradient is symmetrical from the center, and the stroke is still visible. This information is not stored as part of the gradient fill itself. To see how to copy the gradient and the entire appearance of the ball flag, see Chapter 7, "Layers and Appearances."

9. Double-click the **Hand** tool to see the entire map and save the file.

8. ————————Multiple Strokes

One of the coolest additions to Illustrator in recent years was the capability to add multiple strokes and fills to the same path. Multiple fills are only useful when used in conjunction with effects and blending, which are discussed later in this book. Multiple strokes are simpler to use and can quickly create a highlighted or neon effect along a path.

1. Open **map_05.ai** or continue from Exercise 7 if the file is still open.

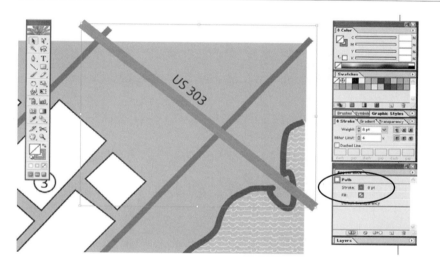

2. Zoom in on the road labeled "US 303" with the **Zoom** tool. With the **Selection** tool, select the red road under the words "US 303." Note the description on **Appearance** palette of a **Path** with an **8 pt** stroke.

3. From the **Appearance** palette flyout menu, choose **Add New Stroke**.

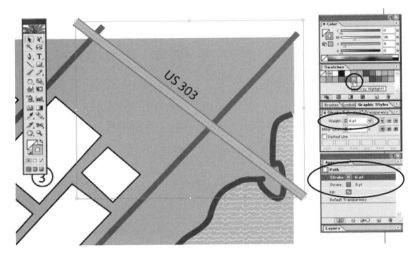

4. On the **Stroke** palette, change the **Weight** of the new stroke to **6 pt**. Click the pink **Highway Highlight 1** swatch (circled above) from **Swatches** palette to stroke it with a new color.

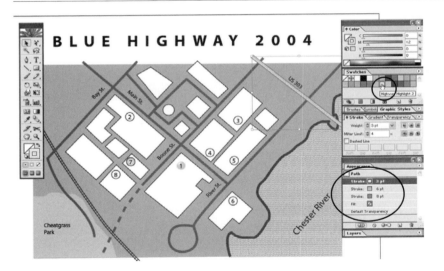

5. Repeat Step 4 to add a third stroke. Change **Weight** to **3 pt** and click the very light pink **Highway Highlight 2** swatch (circled above). Double click the **Hand** tool or press **Ctrl+0** (Windows) or **Cmd+0** (Mac) to zoom out and see the neon effect.

Note that the order of the strokes is visible in the Appearance palette. The thinner strokes are above the thicker ones in the list on the palette the same way they are stacked in the illustration. Rearranging the order in the Appearance palette will change the order in the illustration.

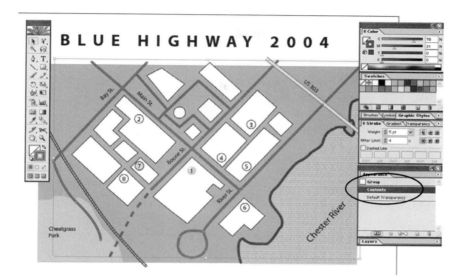

6. Using the **Selection** tool, select the main roads group (selected above). The **Appearance** palette shows a group is selected but shows no stroke or fill information.

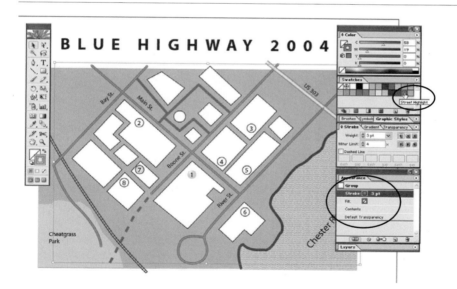

7. From the **Appearance** palette, choose **Add New Stroke** from the flyout menu. Set the weight to **3 pt** and change the color using the **Street Highlight** medium-blue swatch (circled above) on the **Swatches** palette. A lighter line appears over all the streets.

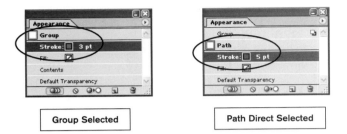

Look carefully at the information in the Appearance palette. It shows that you applied the blue 3 pt stroke to the group instead of the paths that make up the group. If you ever ungroup the streets, you will also delete the 3 pt stroke. If you select an individual street (path) with the Direct Selection tool, you can see why. As shown above, the path is only stroked with a 5 pt darker stroke. What makes this more confusing is that you applied the 5 pt blue stroke to the same group in Exercise 3, but the color applied to the paths and not the group! (It applied to the group this time because you added a stroke rather than simply changing the color.) The point here is that your Appearance palette is the best way to see exactly what is selected and the properties of that selection. When Illustrator seems to be acting oddly—such as strokes "randomly" disappearing—look at your Appearance palette first.

8. Save the file

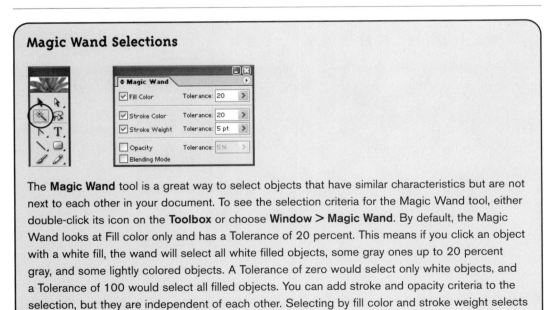

Magic Wand Selections

The **Magic Wand** tool is a great way to select objects that have similar characteristics but are not next to each other in your document. To see the selection criteria for the Magic Wand tool, either double-click its icon on the **Toolbox** or choose **Window > Magic Wand**. By default, the Magic Wand looks at Fill color only and has a Tolerance of 20 percent. This means if you click an object with a white fill, the wand will select all white filled objects, some gray ones up to 20 percent gray, and some lightly colored objects. A Tolerance of zero would select only white objects, and a Tolerance of 100 would select all filled objects. You can add stroke and opacity criteria to the selection, but they are independent of each other. Selecting by fill color and stroke weight selects all objects that match the fill *or* the stroke rather than the fill and the stroke.

MOVIE | **monkey.mov**

To see some example of what you can do with the Magic Wand tool, watch the movie **monkey.mov** online at **http://www.lynda.com/books/hot/illcs/movies/**. After watching the movie, try it yourself by opening the file **monkey.ai** located in the **chap_05** folder on the **H•O•T CD-ROM**.

Whew! This was a long, but critical chapter to build your skill set to create more interesting (and colorful!) art projects in the future. Take a break and stretch your mind and mouse hand.

6.

Transformations

| Precision Rotation and Scaling | Reflection |
| Scaling Strokes and the Transform Palette | Shearing |
| Free Transform Tool |

chap_06

Illustrator CS
H•O•T CD-ROM

The capability to transform objects is one area where the computer reduces your workload like no other tool. Because Illustrator is a vector-based drawing program, you can make transformations such as scaling, shearing (stretching the top and bottom of an object in opposite directions), reflecting, and more—without the artwork becoming fuzzy or grainy. You have already learned basic scaling and rotation transformations using the bounding box, but Illustrator has a set of tools and dialog boxes that allow for much more extensive, flexible, and precise transformations. One of the best parts about using these tools is they are really fun. You can completely modify the look of your work in one or two quick steps. By the end of this chapter you will know some of the possible uses for the transformation tools and some important options.

I. ————————Precision Rotation and Scaling

In Chapter 4, "*Basic Shapes*," you used the bounding box to scale and rotate objects. In this exercise, you will use the scale and rotate tools to perform similar tasks, but with much greater control, precision, and fun!

1. Copy the **chap_06** folder from the **H·O·T CD-ROM** to your hard drive. Open the file **north.ai**. The file includes the basic building blocks for a compass rose.

There is a completed, red compass rose on the lower part of the artboard so you can see what the final product looks like.

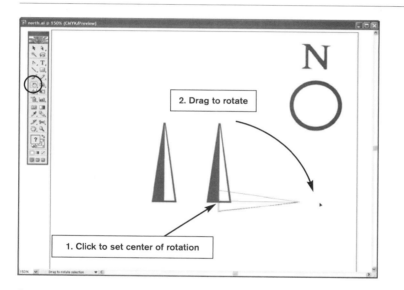

2. Select two-color triangle on the right. Select the **Rotate** tool from the **Toolbox**. Click once in the bottom center of the triangle to set the center of transformation. Note that after you click, the cursor changes. Next drag from a point above the triangle to rotate the triangle as close to 90 degrees clockwise as you can.

*This exercise step shows off two powerful features of the Rotate tool that differ from using the bounding box. The first click with the Rotate tool defines the **center of transformation**, which is in this case the point about which the selection will rotate. The rotation point you set does not even need to be on the selection. It can be anywhere on the artboard. Once the point is set, you can drag from anywhere on the artboard. This has the benefit of letting you zoom in, using Ctrl-+ or Cmd-+, or zoom out, using Ctrl+− or Cmd+−, before rotating and letting you rotate from a point far away from the center of rotation. The farther you are from the center of rotation, the easier it is to move something only a few degrees.*

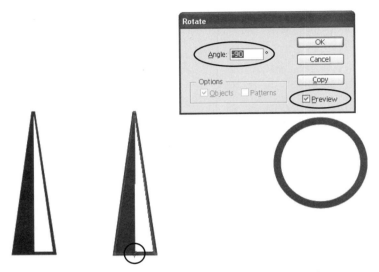

3. Your manual rotation was probably close to 90 degrees, but not exactly 90 degrees. Choose **Edit >** **Undo** to undo the rotation. With the **Rotate** tool still selected, **Alt+click** (Windows) or **Option+click** (Mac) at the bottom center of the right-hand triangle, (circled above) as you did in the previous step. When the **Rotate** dialog box opens, enter a value of **−90** degrees and check the **Preview** box so you can see the effect. Click **OK**.

This dialog box is a great tool to use when you want to create precise rotation transformations. You can open it by Alt+clicking (Windows) or Option+clicking (Mac) the object you want rotated or by double-clicking the Rotate tool on the Toolbox. If you double-click the Rotate tool on the Toolbox, however, the object rotates about its center.

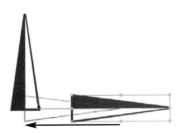

4. Select the **Selection** tool. Select the rotated triangle and drag it so the ends of the two triangles overlap (as you see here).

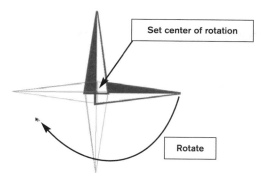

Set center of rotation

Rotate

5. Select both triangles by **Shift+clicking** using the **Selection** tool. Select the **Rotate** tool, and click where the two triangles overlap (as shown here) to set the center of transformation. Next, move the cursor near the point of the horizontal triangle. Finally, hold down **Alt+Shift** (Windows) or **Option+Shift** (Mac) and drag down and to the left to rotate both triangles, constrain to them 90 degrees, and copy them all at once!

Just as when you use the Selection tool, holding down Alt or Option while you drag with the Rotate tool will copy the object and holding down Shift will constrain the motion to 45- or 90-degree increments.

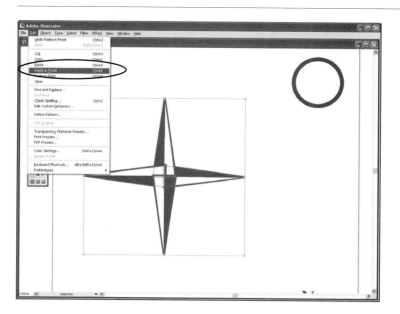

6. Select all four triangles by clicking each one with the **Selection** tool while holding down the **Shift** key. Choose **Edit > Copy**. Next choose **Edit > Paste in Front**.

Paste in front and paste in back commands are a great way to duplicate an item in exactly the same location on the artboard.

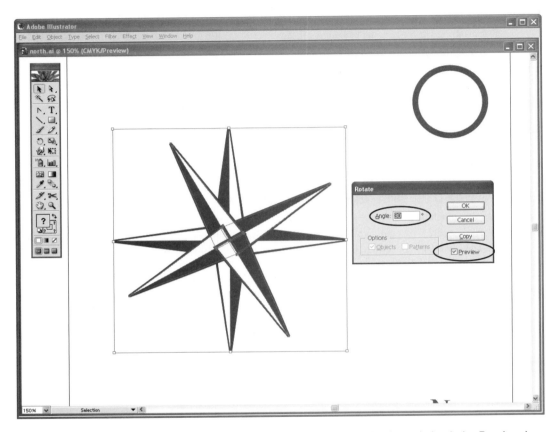

7. Choose **Object > Transform > Rotate**. Enter **30 degrees** as the **Angle** and check the **Preview** box so you can see the result. Click **OK**.

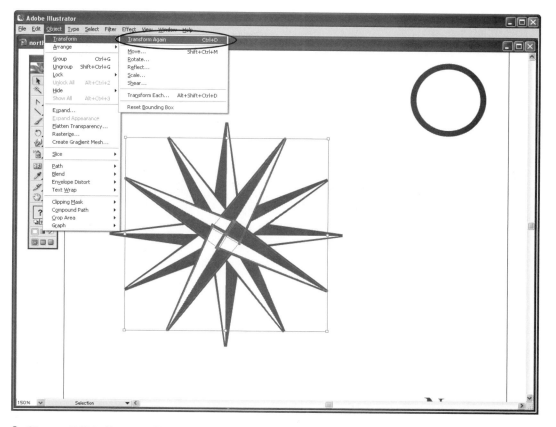

8. Choose **Edit > Paste in Front** again. If you look closely, you will see a new four-point star is sitting on top of the one you just rotated. Choose **Object > Transform> Transform Again** and then **Object > Transform> Transform Again** a second time. The new star has rotated 30 degrees twice for a total of 60 degrees.

*The shortcut for Transform again is **Ctrl+D** (Windows) or **Cmd+D** (Mac). This is a super-handy shortcut and works for whatever transformation—rotation, scaling, moving, reflection—you did last.*

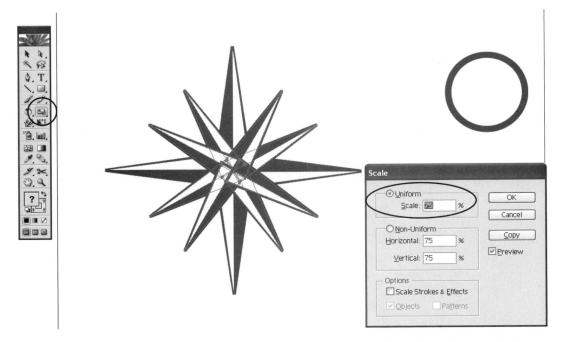

9. Hold down the **Shift** key while you select the eight rotated points with the **Selection** tool. Double-click the **Scale** tool on the **Toolbox**. In the **Uniform** section of the dialog box, enter a **Scale** of **75%**. Click **OK**.

When you double-click the Scale tool, the center of scaling defaults to the center of the selection. You can click once with the Scale tool to set a different point as the center of transformation, just as you did with the Rotate tool. You can then drag with the mouse to scale the object. If you hold down the Shift key as you drag, the scaling will be uniform. If you do not hold down the Shift key, you can create stretched or squashed looking objects, too.

TIP | Incremental Scaling

To slowly scale something up or down and see how it looks, Select the object you want scaled and double-click the **Scale** tool to open the **Scale** dialog box. Enter **105%** (to scale up) or **95%** (to scale down) in the **Scale** field and click **OK**. Next use **Ctrl+D** or **Cmd+D** to transform again and again until it scales up or down to the right size.

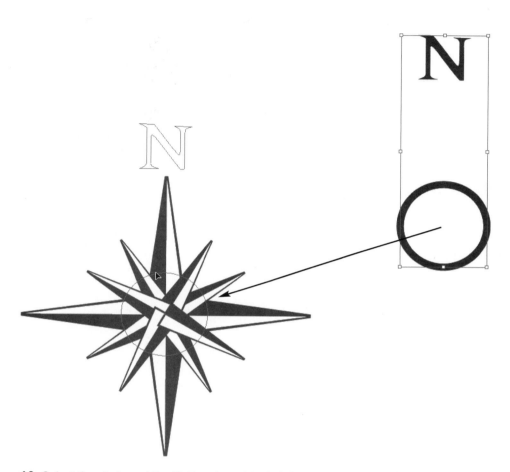

10. Select the **circle** and the **N**. Drag it so the circle is centered on the compass rose.

11. Save the file

2. —————————Reflection

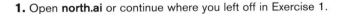

The **Reflect** tool lets you make a mirror image of your selection. This tool is not only handy for creating an image and its reflection, it is also a good way to simply change the look of an illustration, as you will see in this exercise.

> **1.** Open **north.ai** or continue where you left off in Exercise 1.

> **2.** Suppose your client loves your compass rose, but they want the dark part of the parts of the triangle under the **N** to be on the right rather than the left. (Clients are like that sometimes.) Choose **Edit > Select All**. Click and hold on the **Rotate** tool on the **Toolbox** until the flyout menu appears and then select the **Reflect** tool.
>
> *This selects the N as well, which we do not need to rotate, but it is easier to see the results when the N reflects, too.*

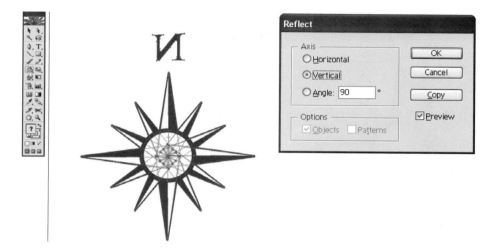

3. Double-click the **Reflect** tool or choose **Object > Transform > Reflect**. Choose **Vertical** from the dialog box and click **OK**. Now the compass rose is colored correctly, but the N is backward.

As with the other transform tools, the center of transformation is the center of the object unless you specify otherwise. The compass rose reflected precisely on its vertical axis.

4. Let's use the reflected N to better see how the **Reflect** tool works. Choose **Select > Deselect** to unselect everything, then click the **N** with the **Selection** tool. Select the **Reflect** tool from the **Toolbox** and click once to the right of the **N** (circled above) to set the center of transformation.

With the Reflect tool, the center of transformation becomes a point halfway between where the current image is and where the reflection will appear.

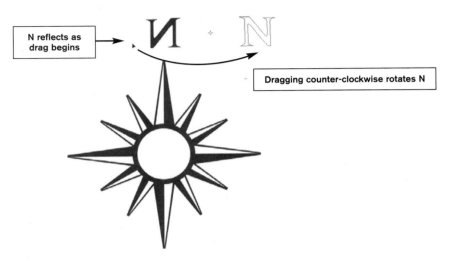

N reflects as drag begins

Dragging counter-clockwise rotates N

5. Drag the **N** down and counter-clockwise until it is opposite the original **N**. Release the mouse button.

The Reflection tool essentially did two things. As soon as you clicked, the N was replaced by its mirror image. As you dragged, the reflected N rotated around the point you set as the center of transformation. The reason is that when you first clicked, you reflected the N at an angle of 90 degrees. As you dragged, you changed the angle up to 270 degrees.

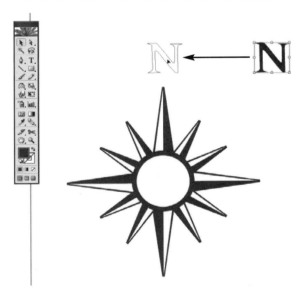

6. Select the **Selection** tool and drag the **N** back over the top of the compass rose. Choose **Select > All**.

7. The compass rose is now complete and ready to put on the map in Exercise 3. To make sure all the parts stay positioned correctly relative to each other from now on, choose **Object > Group**.

Grouping was covered in more detail in Chapter 4, "Basic Shapes."

8. Save the file.

NOTE | Transform Each

The transformations Scale, Move, Rotate, and Reflect are all accessible through **Object > Transform > Transform Each**. Using Transform Each with the preview function is a great way to try a number of manipulations all at once. Transform Each even supplies a random function for totally random amounts of transformation. The grid between the Reflect check boxes and the Random check box (circled above) sets the center of transformation about which all the transformations occur.

MOVIE | transform_each.mov

One key difference between Transform Each and the other Transform commands is that when you have several ungrouped objects selected, each object is transformed individually rather than as a group. To see what this means in practice, watch the **transform_each.mov** movie online at **http://www.lynda.com/books/hot/illcs/movies/**.

3. —————————————Scaling Strokes and the Transform Palette

Transformations have their own palette in Illustrator. Much like Transform Each, this palette lets you control several transformations at once. It also controls some very important options, as you will see in this exercise.

1. Open **map_06.ai** and **north.ai** from the **chap_06** folder. If you did not complete **north.ai** by finishing Exercises 1 and 2, open **north_complete.ai**.

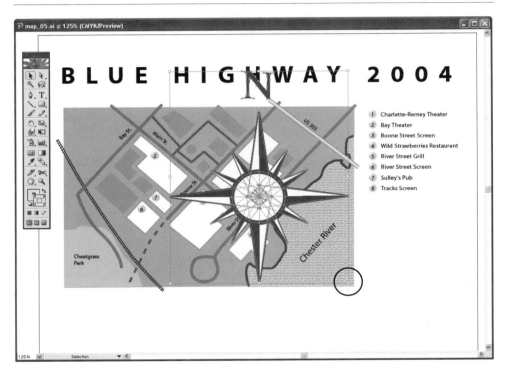

2. Copy the compass rose from **north.ai** and paste it onto **map_06.ai**. Choose **Object > Arrange > Bring to Front** if needed. Position the symbol so its lower-right corner matches up with the lower-right corner of the map.

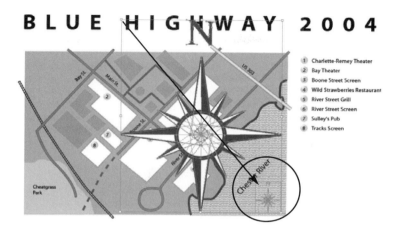

3. Scale down the compass rose to the size you see here by holding the **Shift** key and dragging the bounding box, as you learned to do in Chapter 4, "*Basic Shapes.*"

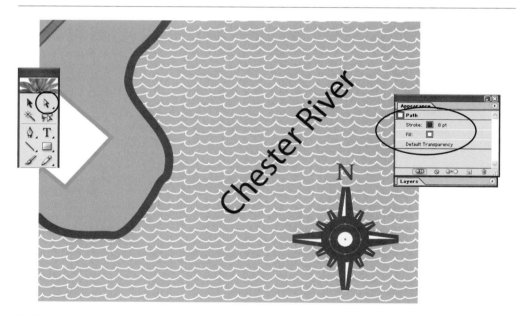

4. Choose **Select > Deselect** to deselect the compass rose. Select the **Group Selection** tool and click the center circle of the compass rose to select only that circle and not the entire group. On the **Appearance** palette, note that the **Stroke** of the center circle is **8 pts**.

The path of the center circle did scale, but the stroke did not. A stroke 8 pts wide looked fine when the compass was large, but looks terrible on the newly scaled down compass. The N looks fine because the path that defines the shape of the letter is filled but not stroked.

5. Choose **Edit > Undo** to undo the scaling. Choose **Window > Transform** to see the **Transform** palette. Choose **Scale Strokes & Effects** from the flyout menu.

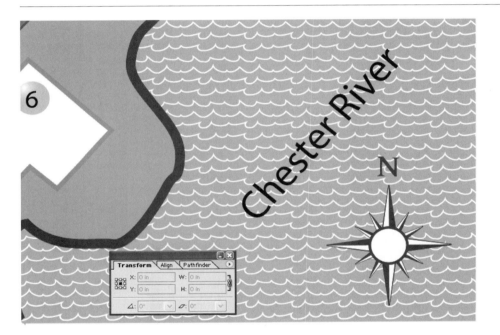

6. Using the **Selection** tool, scale down the compass rose again as you did in Step 3 of this exercise. Now that **Scale Strokes & Effects** is checked, the strokes scale down, and the smaller compass looks great.

You might wonder why scaling strokes is not the default. Scaling strokes is desirable with large changes of scale but undesirable with small ones. Imagine you create three identical squares with a 2 pt stroke. Now you make one only slightly smaller. The smaller one would now have a stroke that was, perhaps, 1.85 pt and would look odd next to its 2 pt neighbors.

7. Save the file and close it.

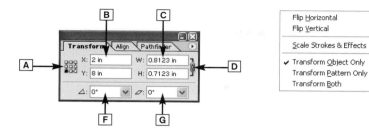

Transform Palette	
Item	**Purpose**
A	Position of the center of transformation relative to the selection. This example shows the lower-left corner of the selection chosen.
B	Position of the center of transformation relative to the artboard. This example shows 2 inches in from the left and 8 inches up from the bottom of the artboard. Changing either the X or Y value will move the selected object.
C	Width and Height of the selection. Changing either the W (Width) or H (Height) values will scale the object.
D	Uniform Scaling. When the chain appears, as shown in the previous screen shot, changing either the W or H value will automatically change the other one so the scaling remains uniform. Click the chain to make it disappear and allow non-uniform scaling.
E	Shear angle. Any value other than 0 will shear the selected object. (Shearing is explored in Exercise 4.)
F	Rotation angle. Any value other than 0 will rotate the selected object.
Flip Horizontal / Flip Vertical	Checking either one will reflect the selected object either horizontally or vertically.
Scale Strokes & Effects	If selected, strokes and effects will scale when the object is scaled.
Transform Object/Pattern/Both	When an object is filled with a pattern, the object will scale, but the pattern will not. You can alternately scale only the fill pattern within an object or both the object and its fill pattern.

4. ——————————Shearing

The **Shear** tool is one of those specialty tools that isn't used that often, but when you need it, nothing else will do. It comes in handy for adding an illusion of motion to a two-dimensional illustration and for creating very basic perspective, as you will do in this exercise.

1. Open **film reel.ai**. Choose **Window > Transform** to show the **Transform** palette.

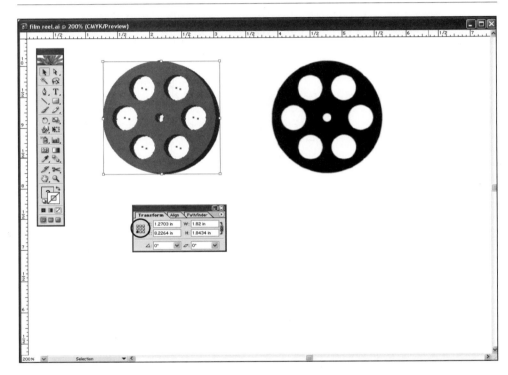

2. Select the **Selection** tool and select the bluish reel. On the **Transform** palette, set shear point to the bottom-left corner of the object.

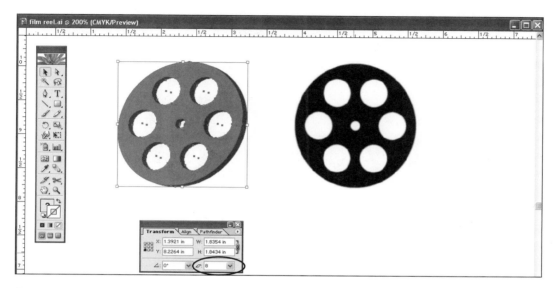

3. Click the **Shear** field on the **Transform** palette and type in a value of **8 degrees**. Press **Enter** (Windows) or **Return** (Mac).

There are shear several values available from the pop-up menu on the Transform palette, but you can enter any number you wish.

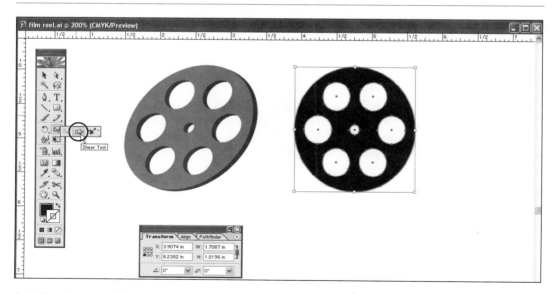

4. Select the fuzzy black reel with the **Selection** tool. Click and hold on the **Scale** tool until the flyout menu appears. Select the **Shear** tool from the flyout menu.

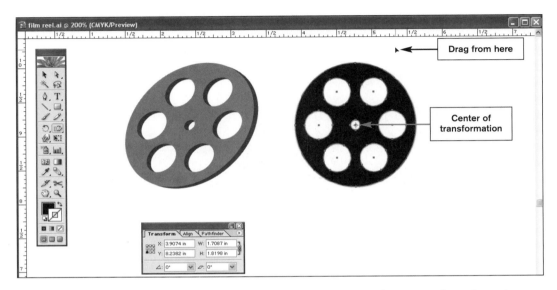

5. Click once with the **Shear** tool in the center of the black reel to set the center of transformation. Next, position the cursor above the reel to drag to the right.

As with the other transform tools, the farther you position the cursor from the center of transformation before you drag, the better control you have over the amount of transformation.

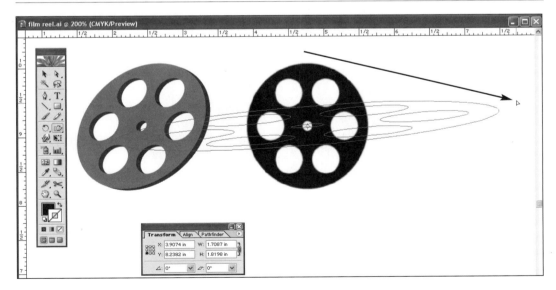

6. Drag down and to the right until the black shadow reel is very elongated and flattened.

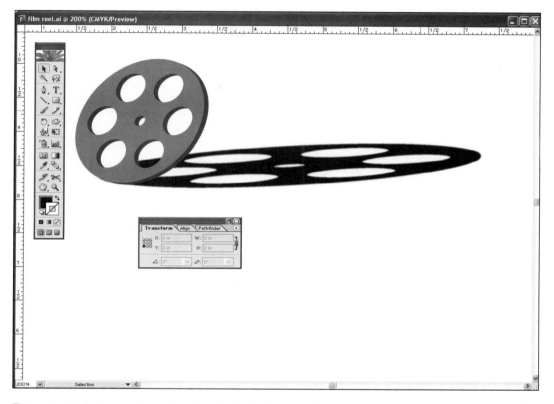

7. Use the **Selection** tool to select the black shadow reel drag it under the blue reel (as shown here).

8. Save the file and close it.

5.————————Free Transform Tool

As you saw in the previous exercise, the Shear tool lets you create some basic perspective quickly and easily. For anything more complex, a better choice is the **Free Transform** tool. This tool is very handy when you need to transform a group of objects that could not be easily drawn in perspective. The box in this exercise would be easy to draw in perspective rather than transform it, but the text on each surface would be a challenge. The Free Transform tool lets you manipulate each box side and its text as a single object.

1. Open the file **crate.ai** from the **chap_06** folder. The file shows two pieces of artwork. The left one consists of three panels you will transform into a crate. The right one is the final product for comparison.

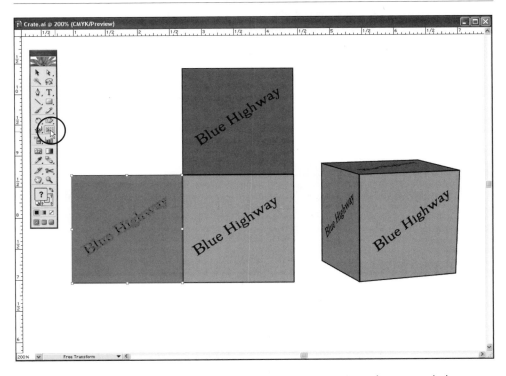

2. Select the left box. It is a grouped object that contains a square and some angled text. Select the **Free Transform** tool from the **Toolbox**.

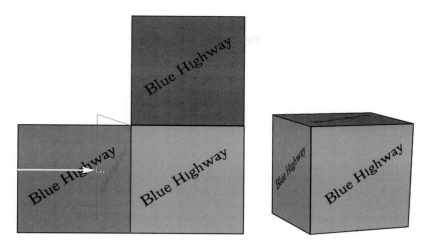

3. Click and hold the center-left handle. *While* you are holding down the mouse button, hold down the **Ctrl** key (Windows) or the **Cmd** key (Mac) and drag up and slightly left. Release the mouse button when the side of the box looks about right.

You must hold down the mouse button before *you hold down Ctrl or Cmd. If you do not, the tool will temporarily change from Free Transform into a Selection tool and move the shape rather than transform it. The system is awkward at first, but you get used to it.*

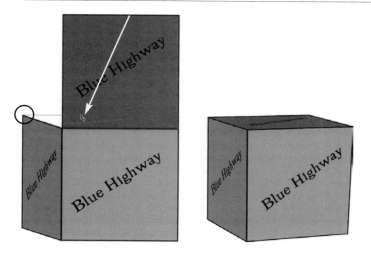

4. Hold down the **Ctrl** (Windows) or **Cmd** (Mac) key to temporarily change the **Free Transform** tool to the **Selection** tool. Click the upper panel of the crate to select it. Release the **Ctrl** or **Cmd** key to return to the **Free Transform** tool. Click and hold upper-right handle. Hold the **Ctrl** or **Cmd** key while dragging down and to the right until the corners of the top and left side of the box match up.

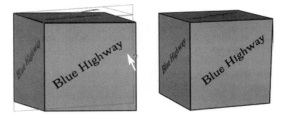

5. Hold down the the **Ctrl** (Windows) or **Cmd** (Mac) key to temporarily switch to the **Selection** tool and hold down the **Shift** key. Click all three sides of the crate to select them. Release the **Ctrl** or **Cmd** and **Shift** keys to return to the **Free Transform** tool. Click and hold the right-center handle. Hold the **Ctrl** or **Cmd** key while dragging up and slightly left for perspective.

You can see on this step that the order in which you perform transformations matters. The top and left sides of the box needed to be in place before the front was sheared so that the common sides would all move together. The same result could be achieved in a different order, but it might take several more steps to get it all right.

6. Hold down the the **Ctrl** (Windows) or **Cmd** (Mac) key to temporarily switch to the **Selection** tool and select the left panel only. Release the **Ctrl** or **Cmd** key and click and hold the lower-left handle. Hold the **Ctrl** key or **Cmd** key while dragging up for perspective.

7. Hold down the the **Ctrl** (Windows) or **Cmd** (Mac) key to temporarily switch to the **Selection** tool and select the front panel. Release the **Ctrl** or **Cmd** key and click and hold the lower-right handle. Hold the **Ctrl** key or **Cmd** key key while dragging slightly left and up for perspective.

The box is now very close to done, but a few more tweaks are needed to get the perspective just right.

8. Hold down the the **Ctrl** (Windows) or **Cmd** (Mac) key to temporarily switch to the **Selection** tool and select the top panel. Release the **Ctrl** or **Cmd** key and click and hold the upper-center handle. Hold **Ctrl+Shift** or **Cmd+Shift** to shear the top to the left. Stop when the right top side of the box looks correct to you.

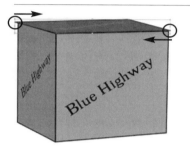

9. Alternately choosing the upper-left and lower-right corners of the top of the crate, make any final adjustments so all three top corners line up correctly. Hold **Ctrl+Shift** (Windows) or **Cmd+Shift** (Mac) after you click and hold on a corner to constrain the **Free Transform** tool to only horizontal movement.

There's a saying that 50 percent of the work gets 80 percent of the job done. That's definitely true in transformations, where you can get a good result from a few choice transformations, but many small adjustments are needed to get it just right. You can also make tiny final adjustments to corner points of the box using the Direct Selection tool on the corners of any of the three sides of the crate. These adjustments will not affect the text, but for tiny changes the difference is not noticeable.

10. Save the file and close it.

> **MOVIE | crate.mov**
>
> To view the complex steps of this exercise as they are performed, watch **crate.mov** located in the **movies** folder on the **H·O·T CD-ROM**.

Now you have learned how to perform one-step transformations and some very involved ones. When you're ready, move on to the next chapter and one of Illustrator's most important features: layers.

7.

Layers and Appearances

Layers and Sublayers	Selecting, Organizing, and Renaming
Targeting and Appearance	Duplicating Appearances
Duplicating Layers	Moving Layers Between Documents	Opacity

chap_07

Illustrator CS
H•O•T CD-ROM

To use Illustrator to its fullest, you must master the use of layers. Don't let this intimidate you! You have already used the idea behind layers without thinking about it. When you built a film reel shape by stacking simple circles and rectangle back in Chapter 4, you built it up one layer at a time. It was simple to build a single film reel, but now imagine managing all the objects in a document with 100 film reels. Then add dozens of lines of type, photographs, special effects, and more. With layers, managing the artwork in even very complex documents is made much easier.

Achieving full control of how your layers look in the final document sometimes requires using the Layers palette and the Appearance palette together. You have already used the Appearance palette to see detailed information about objects in your illustration. Now it's time to go further and use the Appearance palette in conjunction with the Layers palette to make changes to your artwork. As you work through the exercises in this chapter, you will see that there is a good reason these two palettes open together.

I. ————————Layers and Sublayers

In this exercise, you will work with the Layers palette and see how you can use it to organize your artwork and isolate exactly the items you want to edit.

1. Copy the **chap_07** folder from the **H•O•T CD-ROM** to your hard drive. Open **map_07.ai** from the **chap_07** folder.

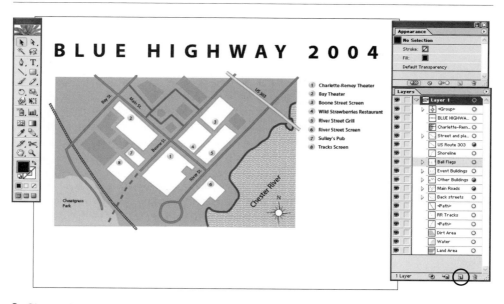

2. Choose **Window > Layers**. Drag the lower-right corner of the **Layers** palette down enough to see all the items on **Layer 1**. Since the **Layers** palette shares a window with the **Appearance** palette by default, you may already have the **Layers** palette visible from exercises in earlier chapters.

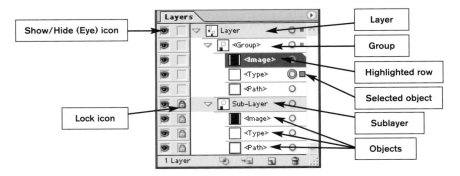

Layers Palette

Item	Description
Show/Hide (Eye) icon	Click the eye to show or hide this object in your artwork. Clicking a layer or group row in the Layers palette will hide all the objects on that layer or in that group.
Lock icon	An empty box allows editing of that object. A lock prevents editing. Click the lock or empty box to toggle editing on and off. Locking a layer or group row in the Layers palette will lock all the objects on that layer or in that group.
Layer	Layers are used to organize your artwork. All layer and sublayer rows in the Layers palette have a shaded background. The shading is very subtle on the Mac—especially on an LCD screen.
Group	Groups have the small triangle to show their contents, but their background color is white rather than shaded.
Objects	Every object in your document—paths, images, type, blends, and so on—has its own row in the Layers palette.
Sublayer	Used to organize your art. Sublayers are simply layers that are part of other layers.
Highlighted row	Clicking the middle of a row in the Layers palette highlights it but does not select the artwork artboard. The exact color of the highlight depends on your system settings. The default for Windows XP is dark blue. The default for Mac OS X is cyan.
Selected object(s)	Clicking the right side of a row in the Layers palette selects that art on the artboard.

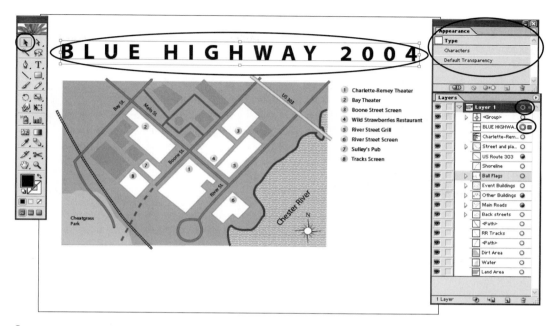

3. With the **Selection** tool, click the title "Blue Highway 2004" in your artwork to select it. The path containing that text highlights in the **Layers** palette with a large square next to the text path and a small square next to the layer. The **Appearance** palette also shows information about the selection.

The small square next to Layer 1 tells you that something, but not everything, on this layer is selected. When you select something on a layer that is not expanded, this handy feature shows you where to find it.

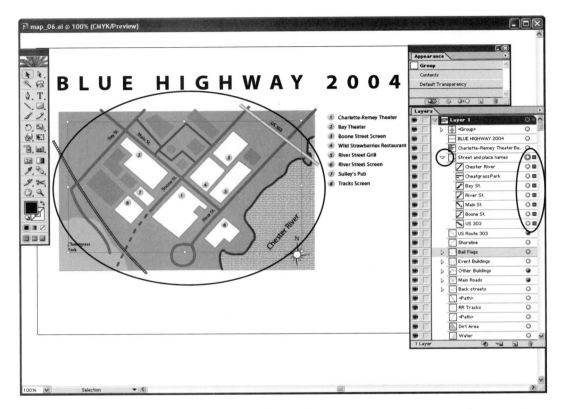

4. Click the words "Chester River" on the map. Since this text is part of a group, the entire group is selected, and a red square appears next to the group name. Click the small triangle to expand the group. Since all the objects in the group are selected, colored boxes appear next to each item in the group and the group name.

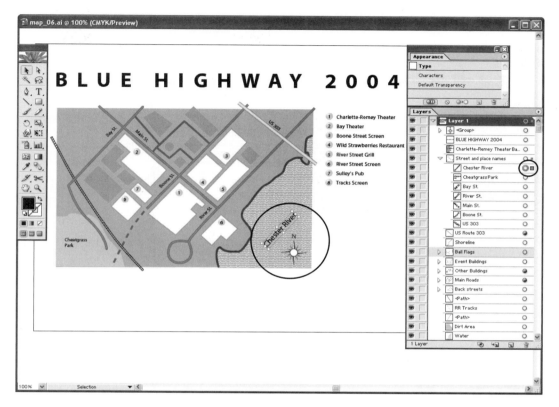

5. On the **Layers** palette, click to the right of the **Appearance** button (looks like a small circle) that appears to the right of "Chester River" (circled above). You have now selected only that text object.

Selecting objects in your illustration via the Layers palette is a great feature. You can easily select objects that may be hard to find or hidden behind other objects. If you select a group on the Layers palette, all the objects in the group are selected, but if you select a single object within a group, only that object is selected—much like using the Direct Selection tool. Holding down the **Shift** *key while you click items in the Layers palette will select multiple objects.*

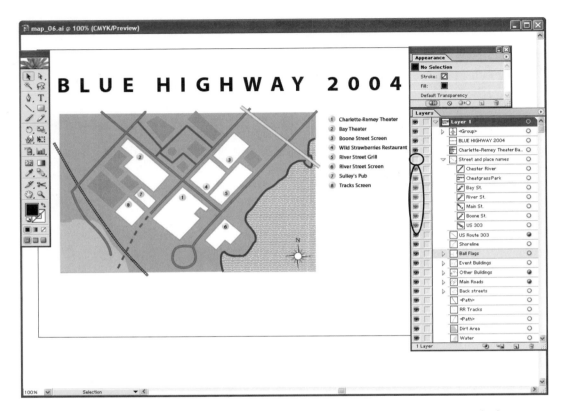

6. Click the **Eye** icon to the left of **Street and place names** to hide that group. All the text in the group disappears, and the **Eye** icons for the paths in the group are grayed-out, indicating that they have been hidden. Click the **Eye** icon again to show all the objects in the **Street and place names** group.

Hiding objects is a great way to declutter your art to work on a specific part of your artwork. You cannot select hidden objects in your illustration, but you can still select them via the Layers palette if you want.

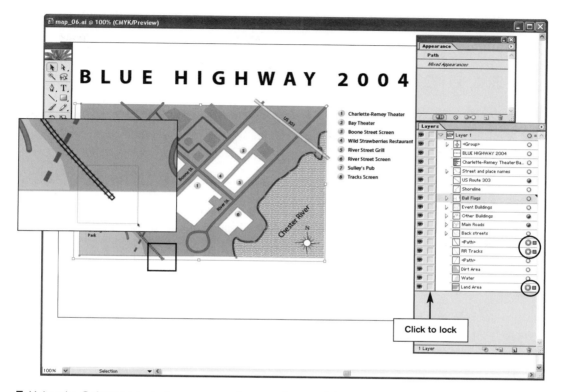

7. Using the **Selection** tool, drag a square (marquee) around the railroad tracks and green land area. Note on the **Layers** palette that the land and the two paths that make the railroad are selected. Click the **Item Locked** icon (the empty square to the right of the **Eye** icon) on the **Land Area** on the **Layers** palette. The locked icon appears. Because the layer is locked and cannot be edited, the land area is automatically deselected.

Locked objects, groups, or layers cannot be selected or edited. Locking objects underneath the art-work you are editing prevents you from accidentally messing up one part of your art while working on another.

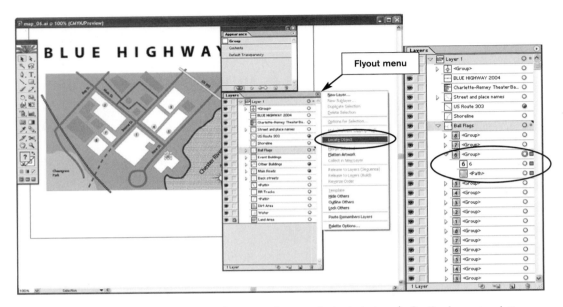

8. Using the **Selection** tool, select **ball flag 6** on the map (selected above). On the **Layers** palette flyout menu, choose **Locate Object**. The **Layers** palette expands whatever layers and groups are necessary to show you the selected object. Look for the red squares on the right side of the rows in the **Layers** palette. These are the rows for the object or objects you selected in the artwork.

*Note that the **Ball Flags** object on the Layers palette has a shaded background rather than a white one. The only other object on the Layers palette with a beige background is **Layer 1**. **Ball Flags** is not a group. It is a sublayer. Sublayers let you collect objects for organization without having to group them. When you selected ball flag 6, the other ball flags remained unselected. If they were a group, selecting one would have selected everything in the group.*

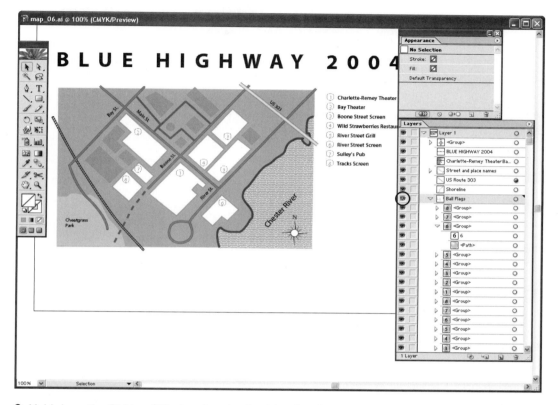

9. Hold down the **Ctrl** key (Windows) or the **Cmd** key (Mac) while clicking the **Eye** icon on the **Ball Flags** sublayer (circled above). The **Ball Flags** layer switches from **Preview** view to **Outline** view. Hold down the **Ctrl** key (Windows) or the **Cmd** key (Mac) while clicking the **Eye** icon again to switch the view back to **Preview** view.

You saw Outline view back in Chapter 2, "Interface," but only for all objects in the document. Applying preview to a sublayer is a slick trick that can be essential when aligning many overlapping objects. You can only use this feature on a layer or sublayer, which are indicated by the shaded background on the Layers palette.

10. Save the project and leave it open for Exercise 2.

TIP | Speeding Up Layer Thumbnail's Performance

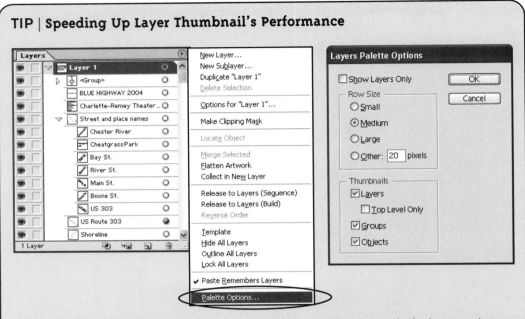

Rendering many thumbnails—the small images of each row item's contents in the Layers palette—slows performance dramatically on older or slower machines. Simply keeping the layers you are not using compressed (triangle turned to hide the layer contents) is usually enough layer management, but you can change the look of the Layers palette by choosing **Palette Options** from the **Layers** palette flyout menu. Unchecking **Thumbnails** for **Objects** and/or **Groups** will speed up the redrawing of the **Layers** palette as you work. Reducing the **Row Size** lets you see more rows at once, but the thumbnails are harder to see. Choosing a small **Row Size** turns off all thumbnails. Checking **Show Layers Only** hides everything except the layers and sublayers.

2. ———————Selecting, Organizing, and Renaming

Building on where you left off in Exercise 1, in this exercise you will use the Layers palette to edit and reorganize your artwork.

1. Open **map_07.ai** or continue from Exercise 1.

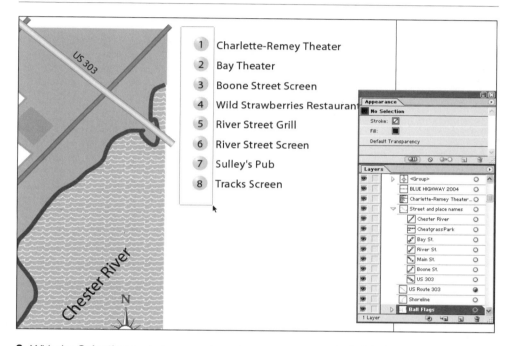

2. With the **Selection** tool, drag a rectangular marquee around all eight ball flags near the text (shown above) to select them.

*In previous chapters, many of the objects in the Layers palette were locked so you could not accidentally select them. In **map_07.ai**, all the layers are unlocked, so ensure that you select only the ball flags and not the text or part of the map.*

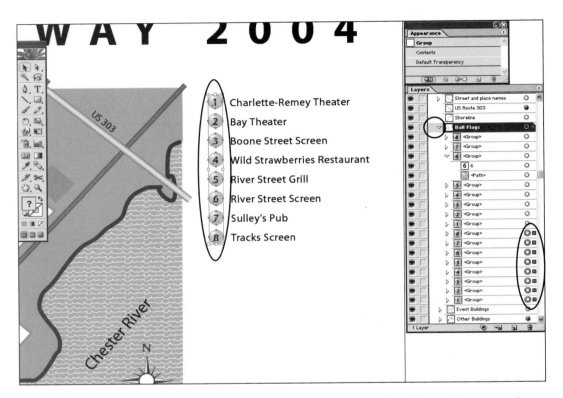

3. Expand the **Ball Flags** sublayer on the **Layers** palette and note that the eight ball flags are really eight groups each containing a ball and a number. Eight rows on the **Layers** palette takes up a lot of space. Create a new group out of these eight groups by choosing **Object > Group** or pressing **Ctrl+G** (Windows) or **Cmd+G** (Mac).

You can nest groups within groups, groups within layers, and layers within groups as many times as you wish.

4. On the **Layers** palette, find the new group. (It will have a red square on its row since the objects in that group are still selected). Double-click the word **<Group>**. In the **Options** dialog box that opens, name the group **Key Numbers** and click **OK**. It's good practice to name layers whenever possible; even when they contain groups.

5. Select everything on the **Ball Flags** layer by clicking the small red square on the right side of the row. Hold down the **Shift** key and click the red selection square for the **Key Numbers** group to deselect it. Now only the ball flags on the map are selected in the artwork and in the **Layers** palette.

Here's a good example of how selecting objects via the Layers palette is much simpler than hunting around your document to find them all.

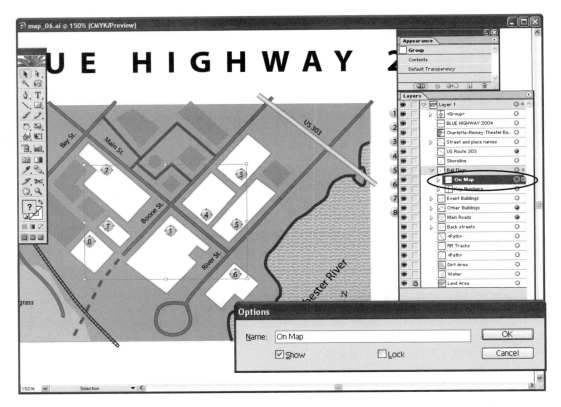

6. Choose **Object > Group**. Double-click the new group in the **Layers** palette and name it **On Map**.

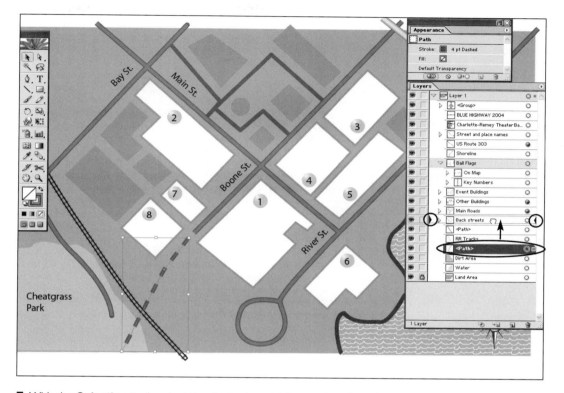

7. With the **Selection** tool, select the dashed road (shown above) on the map by clicking its artwork. On the **Layers** palette, locate and click the selected **<Path>**. It will highlight. Next drag the row upward in the **Layers** palette until two large triangles (circled above) appear on either side of the group **Back streets**. Release the mouse button to add the dotted road to the **Back streets** group.

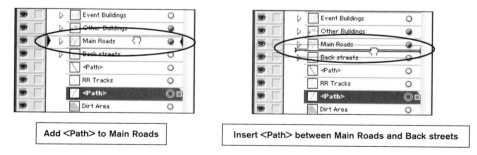

Add <Path> to Main Roads	Insert <Path> between Main Roads and Back streets

As you drag, you will see a two different indicators on the Layers palette. The big triangles indicate that you are adding a row to a group or sublayer, which is a quick way to add an object to a group. The dark line indicates that the row will insert between two rows, which might be needed to stack the objects in the right order to get the desired look in your artwork.

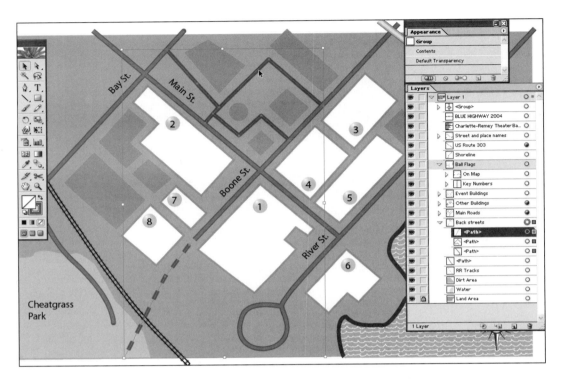

8. With the **Selection** tool, select the back roads on the map (shown above). The dotted line is selected too since it is now part of the group.

The Layers palette is a great way to manage groups since you can add or remove items without ungrouping them. You cannot create an empty group, however. If you remove all the items from a group on the Layers palette, the group row on the Layers palette disappears.

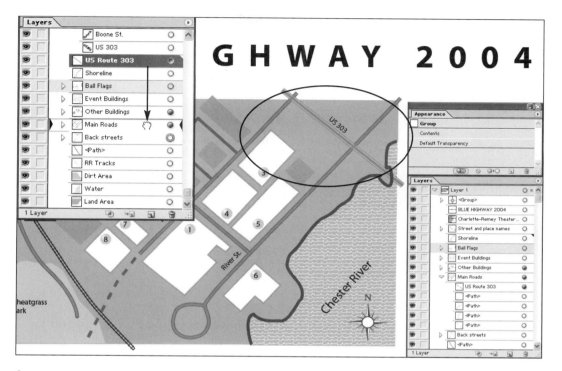

9. US Route 303 could be part of the main roads group as well. Choose **Select > Deselect** to deselect everything. Drag the row for **US Route 303** down into the **Main Roads** group. Unfortunately, this puts an extra purple stroke on the highway. You added this extra purple stroke to all objects in the **Main Roads** group in Chapter 5, "*Fills, Strokes, and Color*," to make the neon effect on the roads. The highway is now under the shoreline as well. Choose **Edit > Undo**. There is a better way to gather the streets together.

The order of objects in the Layers palette determines how the art looks on the artboard. The Land Area row is on the bottom of the Layers palette, and it is behind all the other objects in the artwork. US Route 303 must remain above the streets in the Layers palette to stay on top of them in the artwork.

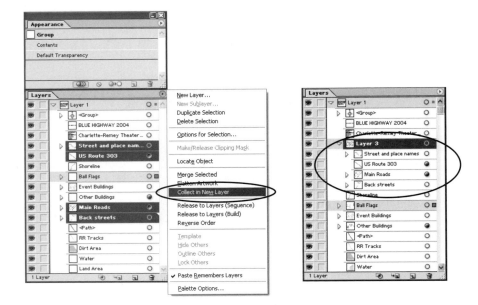

10. There is a better way to gather the streets together in the **Layers** palette. Click the middle of the **US Route 303** row in the **Layers** palette again to select it, and then hold down the **Ctrl** key (Windows) or the **Cmd** key (Mac) while you click the **Street and place names**, **Main Roads**, and **Back streets** rows. From the **Layers** palette flyout menu, choose **Collect in New Layer**. The objects all appear in a new sublayer, as shown above on the right.

11. Double-click the new layer row in the **Layers** palette to see the **Layer Options**, change the **Name** to **Streets**, and click **OK**.

*Layers have many more options than groups. **Show**, **Lock**, and **Preview** are the same as using the **Eye** icon and **Lock** icon you did in Exercise 1. Unchecking **Print** means you will see the layer in the document, but it will not print. **Dim Images** is a way to partially fade out images, such as JPEG or GIF files, to trace them or create a dimmed effect. **Template** is a function discussed in Chapter 20, "Templates and Actions." The **Color** is the color of items when they are selected. Having different layer colors is handy for ensuring you aren't selecting items on two different layers unintentionally.*

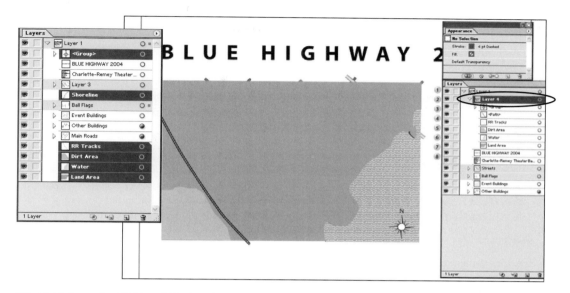

12. Hold down the **Ctrl** key (Windows) or the **Cmd** key (Mac) while you click the middle of the rows for **Land Area**, **Water**, **Dirt Area**, **RR Tracks**, **Shoreline**, and the compass rose (labeled **<Group>**). From the **Layers** palette flyout menu, choose **Collect in New Layer** again.

The new layer is created where the highest object was. In this case, that was the compass rose, on top of everything else. Now the land area is on top of all the roads and buildings.

13. Put the **Land Area**, and other members of the new layer, where they belong by dragging the new layer down to the bottom of the list. Double-click the new layer to see the layer options, rename the layer **Land Features**, and click **OK**.

14. Save the file and keep it open for the next exercise.

Sublayers Versus Groups

At first glance, sublayers and groups may seem redundant, but each offers some unique features. Every Illustrator document contains at least one layer, which appears at the top of the Layers palette. You may add more layers, sublayers, and groups as you wish. In general, you use a sublayer when you want to collect a bunch of objects for organization but want to edit them individually. You use a group when you want to take a bunch of separate objects and treat them as a single object. Here's a list of some of the differences between layers and groups

Layers Versus Groups	
Layers	**Groups**
Selection tool selects object individually.	Selection tool selects the entire group.
Selection tool moves objects individually.	Selection tool moves all objects at once.
Special effects are applied to all individual objects.	Effects are applied to group as if it were a single large object.
Images on a layer may be dimmed.	Images in a group appear at 100% opacity.
Can view in preview or outline.	No control over view.
Can be used as non-editable template.	No template function.
Can be made non-printing.	No non-printing option.
Can control color of selected objects.	No control over selected object color.

The Appearance Palette

The next two exercises involve appearances. Although you have worked with the Appearance palette when applying color to paths and to type. It's time to look at appearances a bit deeper and see how the Appearance palette and Layers palette work together.

Path has effects or extra fills and strokes applied

The Appearance palette was introduced in Illustrator 9 to manage the increasingly complex layering of effects on each Illustrator path, group, or layer. Any fills, strokes, effects, or changes in transparency applied to a path beyond a single fill and stroke is noted on the Layers palette by a shaded Appearance button. Groups and layers also have Appearance buttons because you can apply fills, strokes, and effects to the group. If any fills, strokes, or effects are applied to a group, the Appearance button is shaded.

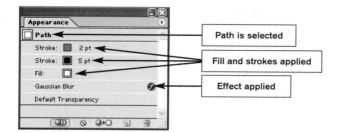

When an object is selected on the Layers palette, details of its appearance are visible on the Appearance palette. In the above example, the selected path has a 2 pt red stroke on top of a 5 pt black stroke on top of a white fill with a Gaussian Blur applied to everything and 100% opacity (the default).

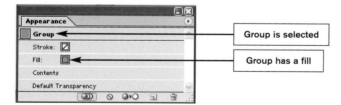

If the path is part of a group, that is also shown in the Appearance palette, along with an icon if there are fills, strokes, or effects applied to the group. If you want to see the appearance of the group, you can double-click **Group** on the Appearance palette.

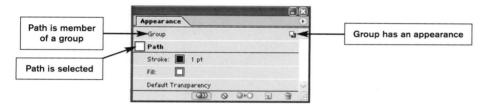

The entire group becomes selected on the Layers palette and its appearance is shown in the Appearance palette. If you double-click the **Contents** line on the palette, you will select all the contents of the group. If all the contents have the same fill and stroke, it will show the fill and stroke in the Appearance palette. If the group contents are varied, such as type, an image, and paths, it will say "Mixed Objects."

(3.) ————————Targeting and Appearance

The Layers and Appearance palette open together for a good reason. They complement each other well and are often used together—especially when objects aren't appearing quite the way you expect.

1. Open **map_07.ai** or continue from Exercise 2.

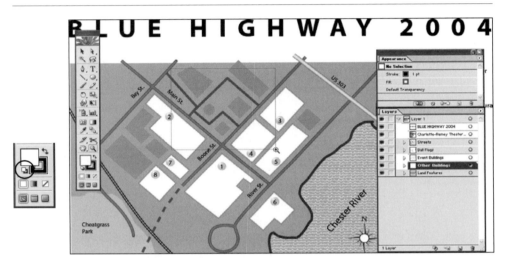

2. On the **Toolbox**, click the **Default fill and stroke** icon (circled above) or press **D** on your keyboard. This will ensure that the next object you draw has a 1pt black stroke and a white fill. Select the **Zoom** tool and drag a rectangular marquee around the back streets in the top center of the map.

3. On the **Layers** palette, click in the middle of the **Other Buildings** row. This highlights the row, but the objects in the group are not selected. Click the small triangle to see the group contents.

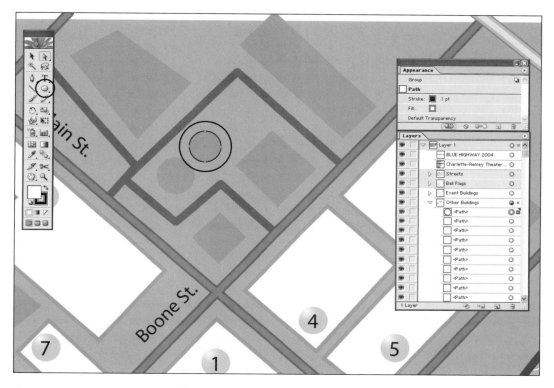

4. Select the **Ellipse** tool. Hold down the **Shift** key while you drag to draw a circle next to the green circle on the map. The circle will appear with a green fill on top of a black stroke.

The new object was added to the group Other Buildings, which you highlighted on the Layers palette in Step 3. If a layer or group row is highlighted on the Layers palette, the next object you draw is added to that layer. If an object row is highlighted, the new object is drawn directly above the highlighted object. Note that the Other Buildings group became unhighlighted after you drew the circle. Also notice that the circle is green with a black stroke, not the default black and white color setting that you selected in Step 2. You'll learn why next.

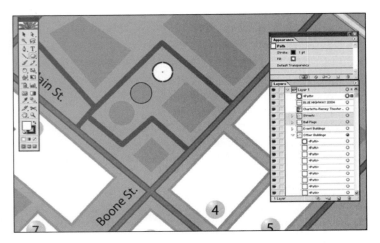

5. With the **Ellipse** tool still selected, draw a third circle near the second one. This circle appears with a white fill and a black stroke.

What's going on here? Two things are happening. The first is that after you started drawing, the Other Buildings group became unhighlighted. If nothing is highlighted on the Layers palette, Illustrator draws new objects at the top of the highest layer on the Layers palette. The second is that the Other Buildings group is creating the green fill, so when the new circle was drawn outside of the group, it appeared without a green fill. Still a bit confused? Steps 6 through 8 should make things a bit clearer.

6. Use the **Layers** palette to add the third circle to the **Other Buildings** group by dragging the new <Path> row into the **Other Buildings** row in the **Layers** palette.

Since the Other Buildings group has a green fill applied, all the objects in that group have a green fill. Since both circles are now part of the group, both circles have the green fill. Next you need to fix the unwanted stroke.

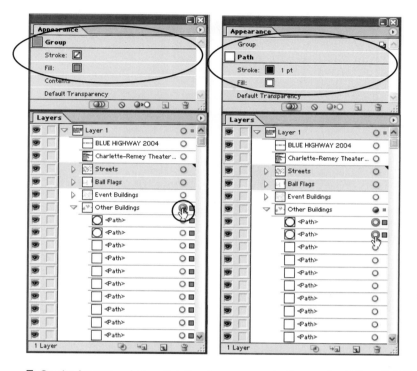

7. On the **Layers** palette, click the **Appearance** button on the **Other Buildings** row (circled above on the left). Note on the **Appearance** palette that the entire group has a green fill applied to it. Next select both of the new circles individually by clicking the **Appearance** button for one circle (circled above on the right) and then holding down the **Shift** key while clicking the other one. Note on the **Appearance** palette that both of these circles have a black stroke and a white fill.

The Appearance button for the group is shaded because the group has some stroke, fill, or effect applied to it. Normally, groups have no fills, strokes, or effects, so Illustrator shades the Appearance button to alert you of this unusual condition. The Appearance buttons for the two new circles were not shaded because both circles had only a single fill and stroke, which is the normal appearance (also called a basic appearance) for a path.

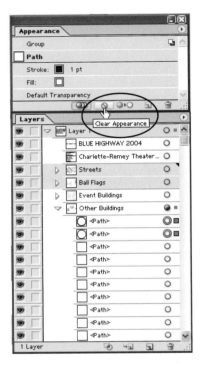

8. With the two new circles selected on the **Layers** palette, click the **Clear Appearance** button on the **Appearance** palette.

This removes the black stroke, which was visible around the edges of the green fill, from these two circles. It also removes the white fill, which was hidden underneath the group's green fill. Clear appearance works with both basic appearance (Appearance button not shaded) and complex appearances (Appearance button shaded).

9. Save the file and keep it open for the next exercise.

MOVIE | appearance.mov

To view the complex steps of this exercise, watch **appearance.mov** located in the **movies** folder on the **H•O•T CD-ROM**.

4. ————————Duplicating Appearances

After you get just the right color and look for part of your artwork, the ability to apply that appearance to other objects is a huge timesaver. As you will see in this exercise, the Layers palette, the Eyedropper tool, and the Paint Bucket tool are ready to help.

1. Open **map_07_unfilled.ai** or continue from Exercise 3.

2. Using the **Zoom** tool, drag a rectangular marquee around all the white buildings on the map to zoom in on them.

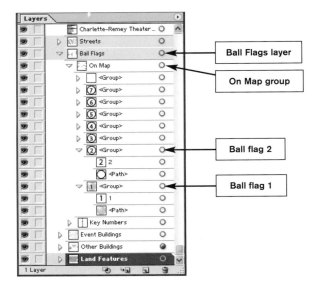

3. On the **Layers** palette, expand the **Ball Flags** sublayer, expand the **On Map** group, and find the groups for ball flag 1 and 2 by looking at the thumbnail images and expand them as well.

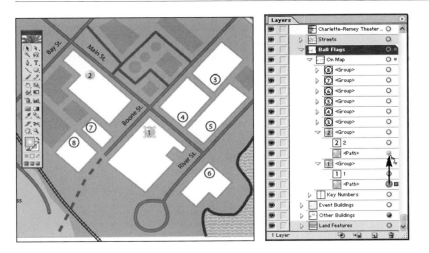

4. Drag the **Appearance** button from the gradient-filled circle of ball flag 1 over the **Appearance** of the **<Path>** ball flag 2. Ball flag 2 now appears with the correct gradient fill, including the gradient angle.

Back in Chapter 5, "Fills, Strokes, and Color," you tried to copy a gradient fill, but the gradient angle was lost, and the black stroke around the ball flag remained. This is what's so cool about copying an appearance, it copies everything that affects the look of the object and removes unwanted strokes and fills from the target.

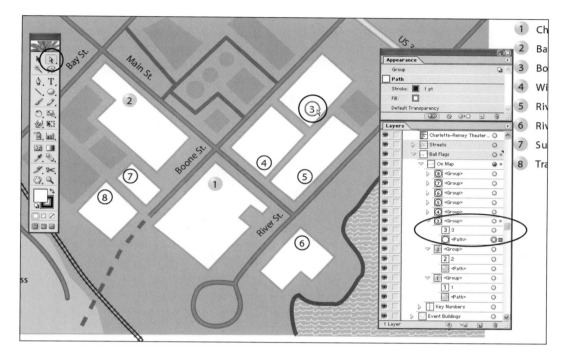

5. It would take a while to fix all the ball flags by dragging attributes. Expand ball flag 3 on the **Layers** palette. Choose the **Direct Selection** tool and click the circle around ball flag 3. On the **Layers** palette, you can see that only the circle is selected.

If you used the Selection tool rather than the Direct Selection tool, you would have selected the entire group.

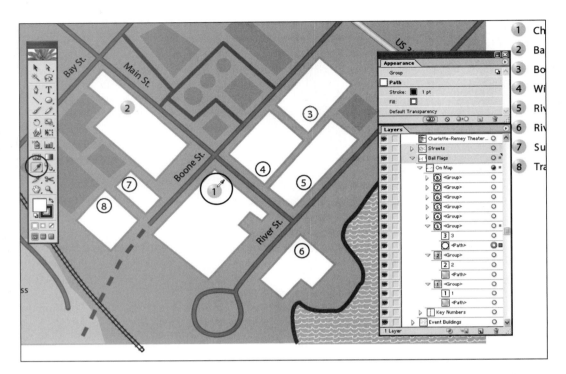

6. Choose the **Eyedropper** tool from the **Toolbox**. Click with the **Eyedropper** on the circle of **ball flag 1** on the map (circled above). The appearance is copied to the circle **ball flag 3**.

*Be careful where you click! If you click the number 1, you will copy the number's appearance—no stroke and black fill—onto ball flag 3. If this happens, choose **Edit > Undo** and try again.*

7. That was cool, but there is still a better way to copy one appearance to many objects. With ball flag 3 still selected, click and hold on the **Eyedropper** tool on the **Toolbox** to choose the **Paint Bucket** tool from the flyout menu.

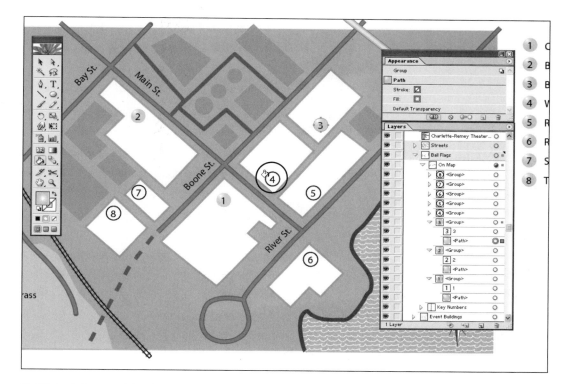

8. Click all the remaining ball flag circles with the **Paint Bucket** tool. The tip of the paint dripping out of the bucket is the tip of the tool. They will fill with the appearance of the selected ball flag 3.

The Eyedropper and Paint Bucket are similar tools with different results. The Eyedropper picks up attributes from whatever you click and applies them to whatever is selected. The Paint Bucket picks up attributes from the selected object and applies them to whatever you click. When you want to copy an appearance from one object and apply it to the object you have selected, use the Eyedropper. When you want to take a single appearance and apply it to several objects, as is the case in this step, use the Paint Bucket tool for the job.

9. Save and close the file.

NOTE | Eyedropper and Paint Bucket Options

Eyedropper/Paint Bucket Options

Eyedropper Picks Up:

- ☑ Appearance
  - ☑ Transparency
  - ☑ Focal Fill
    - ☑ Color
    - ☑ Transparency
    - ☑ Overprint
  - ☑ Focal Stroke
    - ☑ Color
    - ☑ Transparency
    - ☑ Overprint
    - ☑ Weight
    - ☑ Cap
    - ☑ Join
    - ☑ Miter limit
    - ☑ Dash pattern
- ☑ Character Style
- ☑ Paragraph Style

Paint Bucket Applies:

- ☑ Appearance
- ☑ Character Style
- ☑ Paragraph Style

OK
Cancel

Raster Sample Size: Point Sample

The **Eyedropper/Paint Bucket Options** dialog box gives you detailed control over what characteristics the tools copy from one object to the other. By default, both tools will copy the complete appearance, but if you want characteristics of the fill, stroke, or transparency copied, turn down the small triangle by **Appearance** (circled above). If all you want copied is the fill or stroke color, you can hold down the **Shift** key while you click with either the **Eyedropper** or the **Paint Bucket** and only the color will be copied.

5. ————————Duplicating Layers

In this exercise, you will see how a quick duplication of a layer can save you a lot of time and effort.

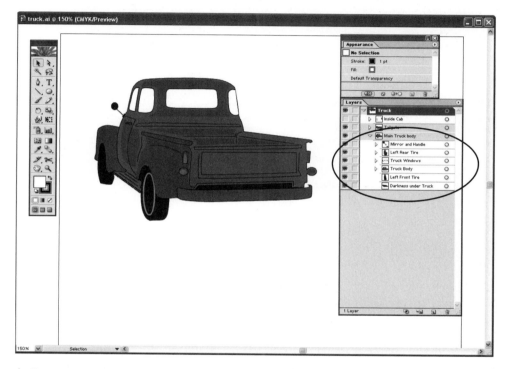

1. Open **truck.ai** from the **chap_07** folder. Expand the **Main Truck body** sublayer by clicking the small triangle.

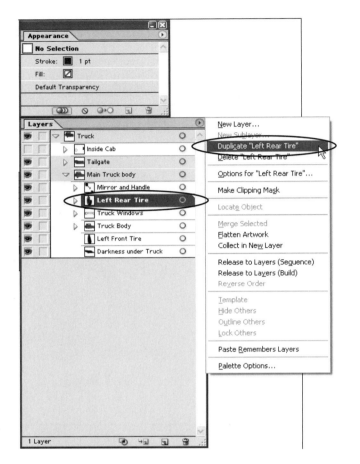

2. Click the middle of the **Left Rear Tire** row on the **Layers** palette to highlight it. From the **Layers** palette flyout menu, choose **Duplicate "Left Rear Tire."**

Be sure to highlight the row on the Layers palette so that it highlights rather than select the object and make the red selection square appear on the right side of the row.

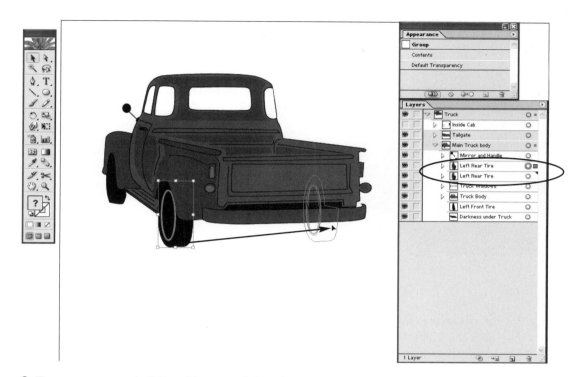

3. There are now two **Left Rear Tire** rows. Select the top one by clicking the right side of the row in the **Layers** palette so the selected square icon appears. Select the **Selection** tool. On the artwork, drag the duplicate tire to up and to the right to create the truck's right rear tire.

4. To avoid confusing the tires, double-click the row for the tire you moved and rename it **Right Rear Tire** and click **OK**.

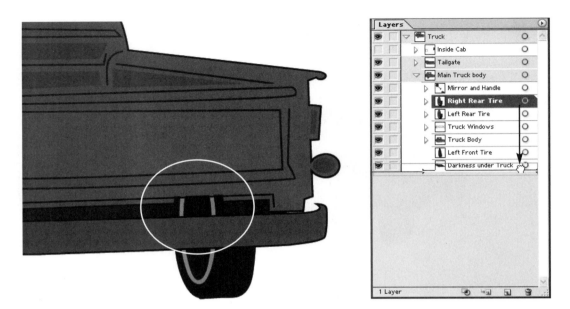

5. If you look closely between the bumper and the truck, you will see that the right tire is visible on top of some truck parts. While the row is selected on the **Layers** palette, drag **Right Rear Tire** down to the bottom of the stack so the tire appears behind the bumper and the entire truck body.

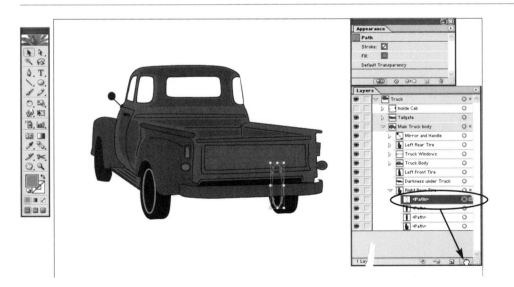

6. Click the small triangle for **Right Rear Tire** to show all the objects in the group. Drag the top **<Path>** in the list to the **Trash**. This removes the white circle from the tire.

7. Save the file and keep it open for the next exercise.

TIP | Layer Backups

Since duplicating a layer copies everything—each path, group, and sublayer—in exactly the same organization, its also a great way to try out an idea without messing up your original artwork. Duplicate the layer you want to experiment with. Next, hide and lock the original layer by clicking the **Eye** icon and the **Lock** icon. Now you can mess up the duplicate all you want. If you like the result, keep it. If you don't, drag the layer to the **Trash** and unhide and unlock the original.

6. Moving Layers Between Documents

Many Illustrator artists build pieces of their artwork in separate documents to later assemble them together in one document. There is nothing tricky about doing this, but there are a few techniques to understand in order to get exactly the result you want.

1. Open **truck.ai** or continue from Exercise 5.

2. Select the entire **Truck** layer by clicking the right side of the top row on the **Layers** palette (circled above). Choose **Edit > Copy**.

*Be sure to select the art using the Layers palette rather than **Select > All**. There is a hidden object used in a later exercise that will not be copied if you use the **Select > All** command.*

3. Open **poster_07.ai** from the **chap_07** folder. Highlight the **Landscape** layer by clicking the middle of the row. Click the **Create New Layer** icon on the bottom of the palette.

The new layer inserts immediately above the highlighted layer.

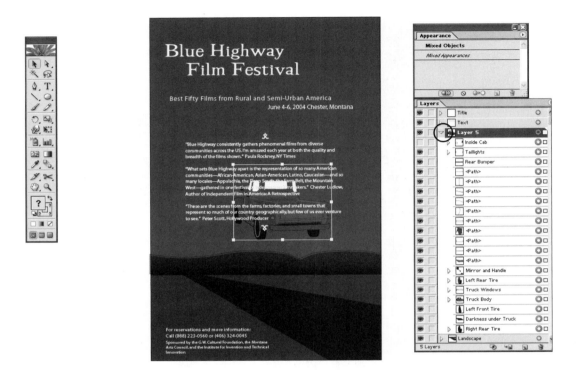

4. Choose **Edit > Paste**. A new layer appears in the **Layers** palette. Click the small triangle to the left of the new layer to reveal its contents.

The truck pasted onto the new layer, but all the sublayers from the original art were lost, and the paths from those layers are now unorganized. The groups, such as Right Rear Tire, were preserved. As long as you didn't care about the loss of sublayers for organization, this would work fine. But there is better way!

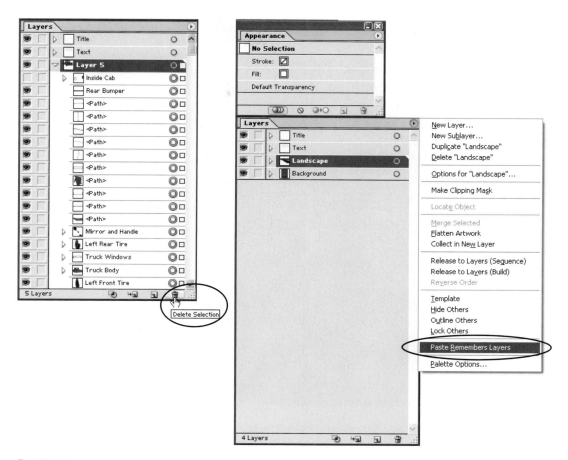

5. With the new layer still highlighted, click the **Delete Selection** (Trash) icon on the bottom of the **Layers** palette and click **OK** to confirm the deletion. Next, choose **Paste Remembers Layers** from the **Layers** palette flyout menu.

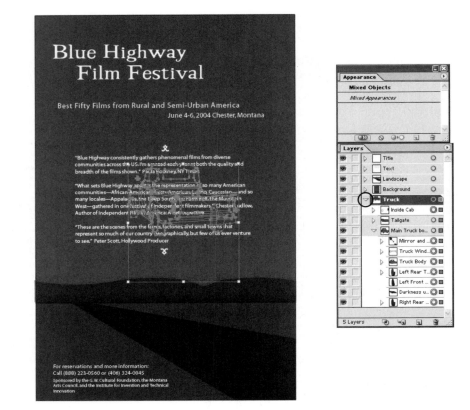

6. Choose **Edit > Paste** again. A new layer appears as the bottom row of the **Layers** palette. Click the small triangle to see all the sublayers intact.

Paste Remembers Layers also applies when you work within a document. With Paste Remembers Layers turned off, when you paste an object, it pastes onto whatever layer is highlighted in the Layers palette. With Paste Remembers Layers turned on, the object always pastes back onto the layer you copied from. This is annoying if you wanted to move an object to a different layer, so Paste Remembers Layers is turned off by default.

7. On the **Layers** palette, drag the **Truck** layer above the **Landscape** layer. Select the entire **Truck** layer by clicking the right of the **Truck Layer** row (circled above). With the **Selection** tool, drag the (now visible) truck down onto the road in the artwork.

8. Save the file and keep it open for the next exercise.

7. ——————Opacity

Photoshop users know and love the opacity setting on the Photoshop Layers palette. Illustrator has the same functionality, but it is found on the Transparency palette. True transparency was introduced in Illustrator version 10 and was a very welcome addition. It allows you to make some cool effects quite easily that would be very difficult to achieve any other way.

1. Open **poster.ai** or continue from Exercise 6.

2. Select the **Zoom** tool and drag a rectangular marquee around the truck to zoom in on it. On the **Layers** palette, click the triangle to expand the **Truck** layer and then click the triangle to expand the **Main Truck body** sublayer.

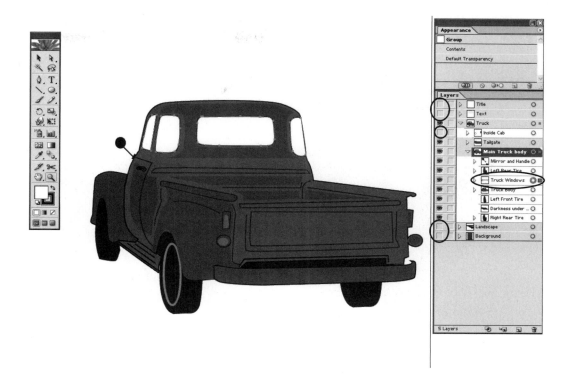

3. On the **Layers** palette, select **Truck Windows** by clicking the right side of the row (circled above). Hide all the other top-level layers (**Title**, **Text**, **Landscape**, and **Background**) by clicking their **Eye** icons (circled above).

WARNING | Deleting Hidden or Locked Layers

If you hide or lock objects that are part of a layer or group and then delete that layer or group, the hidden and locked objects are deleted as well. The danger is that you might hide something temporarily, forget it was part of a group, delete the group, and then a hour later go to unhide the object and discover it is gone! When working with hidden and locked layers, use your Layers palette to delete layers or groups so you can see what they contain.

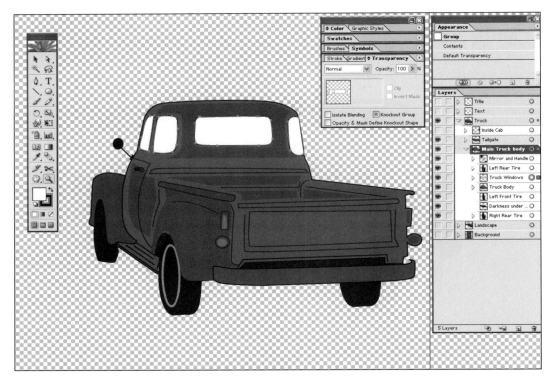

4. Choose **View > Show Transparency Grid** and **Window > Transparency**.

The transparency grid is a checkerboard background that lets you see transparency better than the white page.

5. On the **Transparency** palette, click the small triangle to the right of **Opacity**. Drag the slider to set an opacity of **75%**. Press **Enter** (Windows) or **Return** (Mac) on your keyboard. Now you can see the transparency grid through the truck windows.

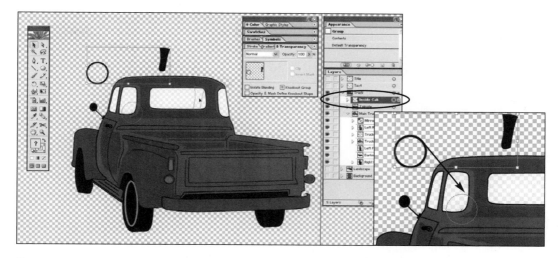

6. On the **Layers** palette, unhide the **Inside Cab** row. The truck steering wheel and front window post appear. Select the steering wheel with the **Selection** tool and drag it down so the center of the steering wheel is at the corner of the small window (see above).

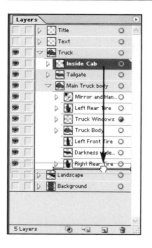

7. Put the steering wheel "inside" the truck by dragging the **Inside Cab** row on the **Layers** palette to the bottom of the **Main Truck body** sublayer.

Notice how the steering wheel and post become grayer when you put them behind the truck windows on the palette. You are now seeing the steering wheel through the 75% opaque windows. Very cool! You are also using the 100% opaque body of the truck to mask the unseen part of the steering wheel. That lets you adjust exactly how much of the steering wheel you see by simply moving the circle up or down. Very cool again!

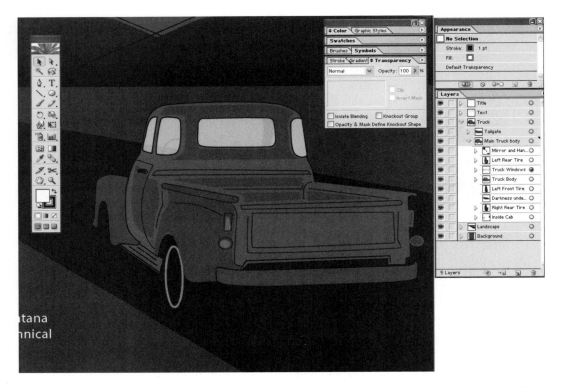

8. Choose **View > Hide Transparency Grid**. Click the center of the **Truck** row on the **Layers** palette to highlight it and then choose **Show All Layers** from the **Layers** palette flyout menu.

Now you can look through the truck windows, over the steering wheel and see the landscape. Extremely cool!

9. Save the file.

There are several more options on the Transparency palette. You will get to use these in Chapter 14, "Masks and Blending Modes."

NOTE | Merging and Flattening

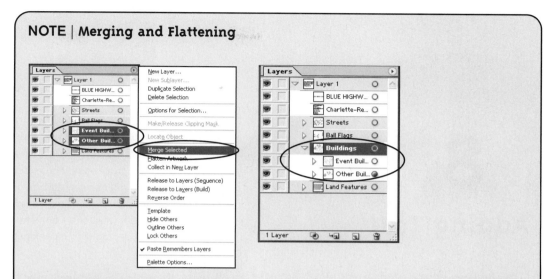

The **Merge Selected** option on the **Layers** palette flyout menu is an easy way to combine several layers, groups, or objects into a single layer for better organization or control. Highlight the layers you want by holding down the **Ctrl** key (Windows) or the **Cmd** key (Mac) and clicking in the center of each row. You must select at least one layer or group to get the Merge Selected option. All the merged items are collected in a single group or layer. Any sublayers are converted into groups.

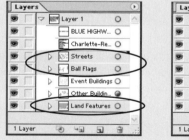 

The **Flatten Artwork** option appears immediately below **Merge Selected** and is a "super-merge" in that it converts all layers and sublayers into groups. Flatten Artwork also deletes any hidden layers (with a warning of course). Flattening artwork is helpful when the artwork is ultimately part of a larger illustration and you no longer want many sublayers for editing purposes.

Congratulations! Another long chapter under your belt. Now that you have learned about paths and shapes, fills and strokes, and layers and appearances, you understand the fundamentals of creating art in Illustrator. You can do much more with Illustrator than basic artwork, however, so it's time to insert some text.

8.

Adding Text

Type Containers	Type at a Point
Type in an Area	Type on a Path
Placing Text	Character Formatting
Paragraph Formatting	Threaded Text

chap_08

Illustrator CS
H·O·T CD-ROM

Even though Illustrator CS is widely known as an illustration program, good typography can make the difference between a professional and unprofessional publication. Fortunately, Illustrator CS offers masterful typography tools that support excellent typography automatically while offering the freedom to take typography to its highest art form.

Illustrator CS ships with over 100 fonts of its own and provides support for the various font formats you may already own. Once you select the right font for your art, Illustrator CS does an excellent job of making your type look terrific on the page automatically while offering precise, manual control over almost any aspect of the type. Illustrator does handle type a bit differently than other applications you may have used, even other Adobe products, so a little time spent reviewing how Illustrator does it is time well spent.

Type Containers

When you add text to your artwork, Illustrator records three things. First, it records the characters you typed in on the keyboard. If you type the word "Fun," it records the characters "F," "u," and "n." Second, it records the font, font size, and any other type features you assign to the text. Third—this is the part that is unusual—it attaches the type to a point, path, or shape on the artboard. This point, path, or shape is the **type container**. You must decide which kind of type container you want before you start typing. Different type containers behave in different ways.

NOTE | Text Versus Type

In this book, you will see references to both "text" and "type." The two terms can be used interchangeably, but in this book, "text" refers to content, and "type" refers to formatting of that content. The sentence "The dog fetched the stick." is text. The font 18 pt Myriad Bold with leading of 22 pt used to format that sentence is type. The tools used to select and format the text in Illustrator are called the **Type** tools.

Type at a Point

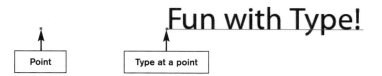

The simplest type container is a single point. Think of the point as a thumbtack stuck into the artwork that holds a string of text in place. If you select the point and move it somewhere else, the line of type will move with it.

Type on a Path

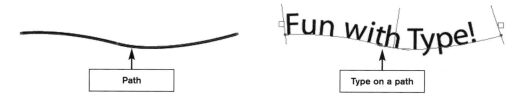

Type can also follow a path in your document. If the path curves, the type follows the curve. If you change the curve of the path, the type reformats and follows the new curve.

Type in an Area

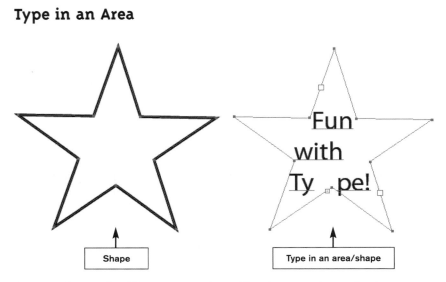

Area type is type that fills an area or shape. The shape can be as simple or as complex as you want, and Illustrator will fit the type inside it as best it can. If you change the shape, the type rearranges to fit the new shape.

Selecting Text

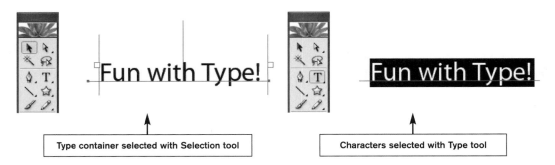

Because text is always associated with a type container, there are two ways to select text. You can select the type container using the selection tools, or you can select the characters themselves using the Type tool. You will select type both ways as you work the exercises in the next two chapters. Since doing is the best way to learn, it's time for Exercise 1!

I. ——————Type at a Point

Perhaps the most intuitive way to add text to an Illustrator document is to select the Type tool, click somewhere on the artboard, and start typing. Since all text objects need to be associated with a point, path, or shape, Illustrator chooses the simplest route and creates a single point where you click and lets you start typing from there.

1. Copy the **chap_08** folder from the **H•O•T CD-ROM** to your hard drive. Open the file **poster_08.ai** from the **chap_08** folder.

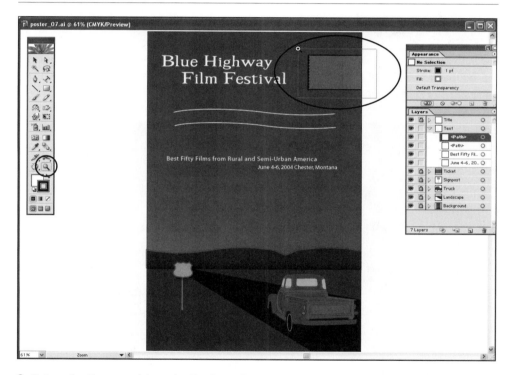

2. Select the **Zoom** tool from the **Toolbox**. Zoom in on the green ticket in the upper-right corner of the poster by dragging a rectangular marquee around it.

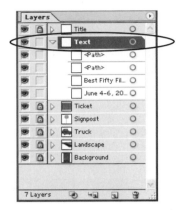

3. Choose **Window > Layers** to open the **Layers** palette if it is not already open. Click in the middle of the **Text** layer to highlight it. Any new type you add will appear on this selected layer. Click the small triangle to see the layer contents.

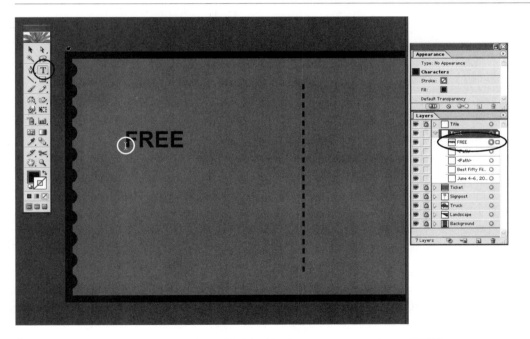

4. Select the **Type** tool on the **Toolbox**. Click inside the green area and type **FREE**.

When you click with the Type tool, the cursor will change to a flashing insert icon. A new object labeled "<Type>" also appears on the Layers palette. As you type, the word "FREE" replaces "<Type>" on the Layers palette.

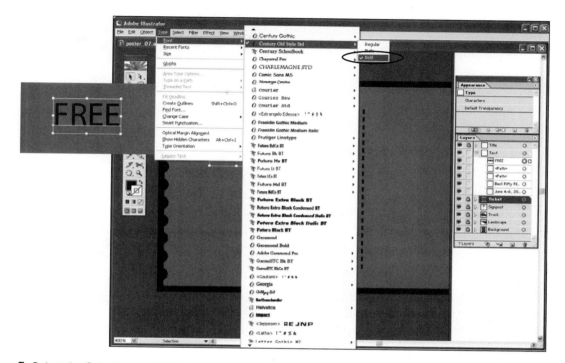

5. Select the **Selection** tool. A bounding box appears around the word "FREE" to indicate the type object is selected and you are not entering text anymore. Choose **Type > Font > Century Old Style Std > Bold**.

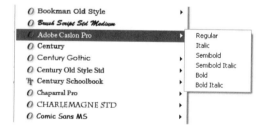

The appearance of the font name in the **Type > Font** menu is an example of the regular version of that font. Illustrator's system for handling fonts may be new to you. In addition to the list of fonts accessed by **Type > Font**, many fonts have additional submenus to choose bold or italic versions of the font. Some fonts also have special versions such as semibold. You wont find any bold or italics buttons in Illustrator; you must choose the version of the font you want to use. If a font does not have a submenu, you cannot make it bold or italic even though you may be able to bold or italicize the exact same font in other programs. This is because when you click a bold or italic button in a program like Microsoft Word, the program creates something that the font designer did not intend. This kind of type manipulation is called "faux" (for fake!) and is frowned upon by professional typographers.

6. Bring your cursor to the upper-right corner of the bounding box. Hold down the **Shift** key while you drag the corner of the box down and to the left to constrain the rotation to increments of 45 degrees. Rotate the type **90** degrees.

7. Drag the rotated type over to the dotted line on the green ticket.

8. Bring your cursor to the lower-right corner of the rotated bounding box. Drag down and to the right so the word "FREE" is the same length as the dotted line and is the tall enough to fill most of the space between the dotted line and the side of the poster.

One of the cool things about resizing type this way is you can stretch the height and width independently rather than simply selecting a larger font size. Of course, the font designer might not like the resulting type since it is no longer proportional to his or her original type design. Sometimes you just can't please everybody.

9. Recenter the word "FREE" over the dotted line if necessary and save the file. Keep the file open for the next exercise.

Fonts

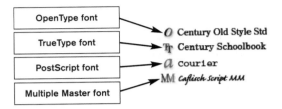

Illustrator supports the three major font formats in use today: **OpenType**, **TrueType**, and **PostScript**. In addition, Illustrator supports **Multiple Master** fonts, which are an enhanced version of PostScript fonts. The **Type > Font** menu indicates the type of each of your installed fonts with a small icon to the left of the font name. You can use any combination of font types you wish in your document, but each type has slightly different properties you should know.

OpenType

OpenType is touted as a relatively new type specification developed jointly by Adobe and Microsoft. OpenType actually uses the older TrueType and PostScript font formats but encloses them in a file that works on both Windows and Macintosh systems. This makes OpenType the first true cross-platform font standard. OpenType also uses Unicode so it can contain over 65,000 individual characters, including all Western characters and accents and many non-Western characters. OpenType fonts also provide easy access to its additional characters, known as glyphs, which are discussed in Chapter 9, "*Type Appearances and Styles.*" Finally, OpenType lays the groundwork for many typography improvements in the future.

TrueType

TrueType fonts were developed jointly by Microsoft and Apple using a simple system for defining the shape of each character in the font. Some printers balked at using TrueType fonts, and there were some early problems with TrueType technology, which gave them a bad reputation with some designers. The problems have since been corrected, and the technology works just fine on both platforms. TrueType fonts are more common on Windows systems due to Microsoft's aggressive support of the file format. TrueType fonts often look better onscreen than the equivalent PostScript font. If you have a choice between TrueType and PostScript for onscreen and Web artwork, use the TrueType font.

PostScript

PostScript fonts were developed with printing in mind, although some PostScript fonts don't print well on some low-end printers. There are many versions of PostScript font types with different characteristics and capabilities. In general, PostScript fonts define characters more precisely than TrueType, but often each version of the font (bold, italic, and so on) requires its own file to print correctly. PostScript fonts are still the standard for most professional printing. If you send a TrueType font with your artwork to a print service, they may substitute the equivalent PostScript font. This may result in a slight change in the look of the final artwork.

Multiple Master

Multiple Master fonts are a version of PostScript fonts that allowed typographers to create their own versions of the font by adjusting up to three font characteristics. For example, the typographer could select a font weight between regular and bold by adjusting a slider for character weight. The custom font could also be saved for later use. Illustrator CS lets you use Multiple Master fonts, but there is no Multiple Master font palette for creating the custom changes. To use custom Multiple Master fonts, you must make the custom font file in a font program such as Adobe Type Manager Deluxe, save it as a version of the Multiple Master font, and then select that font in Illustrator CS. If you use custom Multiple Master fonts, you must include the original Multiple Master font files and any custom files when you send out your artwork to print, or you must convert all the custom type to outlines. Converting to outlines is covered in Chapter 9, "*Type Appearances and Styles.*" Adobe supports using Multiple Master fonts, but it is focusing its efforts on OpenType.

NOTE | Windows and Mac Font Choices

Some font suppliers supply only the TrueType version of a font for Windows and the PostScript version of the font for the Mac. If you are just printing on your own printer or using the type in artwork for the screen, this shouldn't be a problem. If you are sending out a file to print, make sure the print service has the appropriate version of the font.

---

2. ——————Type in an Area

Area type in Illustrator is the best way to add multiple lines of type to your artwork and contain it within a given area.

1. Open **poster_08.ai** or continue from Exercise 1. Highlight the **Text** layer by clicking in the middle of that row on the **Layers** palette. If you aren't already zoomed in on the green ticket, select the **Zoom** tool and drag a rectangular marquee around the green ticket in the upper-right corner of the poster.

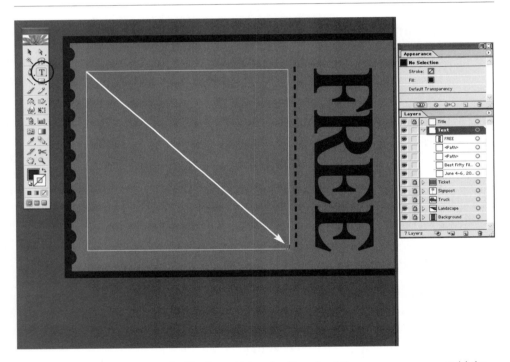

2. Select the **Type tool** from the **Toolbox**. Using the **Type tool** the same way you would the **Rectangle Shape** tool, drag a square so that its height is the same as the dotted line and it is as wide as the empty green area.

You now have a type area with a flashing cursor. In a sense, this is an invisible square that "fills" with text as you type on your keyboard.

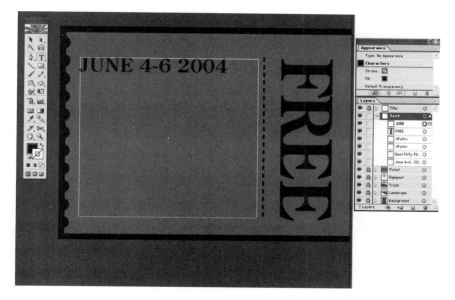

3. Type **JUNE 4-6 2004** in the type area.

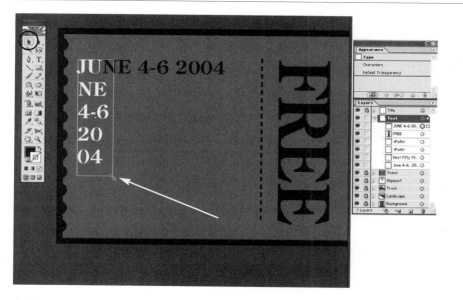

4. Select the **Selection** tool and drag the lower-right corner up and left.

Note how the text wraps to fit in the type area, but the type does not resize. This is a big difference between type at a point versus type in an area.

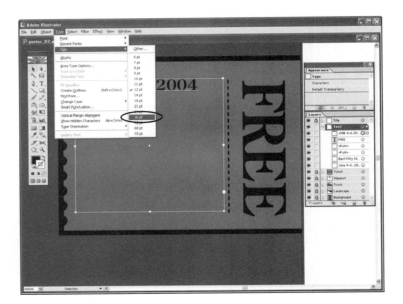

5. Choose **Edit > Undo Scale** to set the type area back to its full size. Choose **Type > Size > 36 pt**. The larger type now wraps in the type area and is three lines high. It no longer fits properly, but you'll fix that next!

6. On the lower right of the type area, there is now a red plus icon, indicating that there is hidden type because the area is too small. With the **Selection** tool, drag the bottom-center handle of the type area down until the missing type reappears.

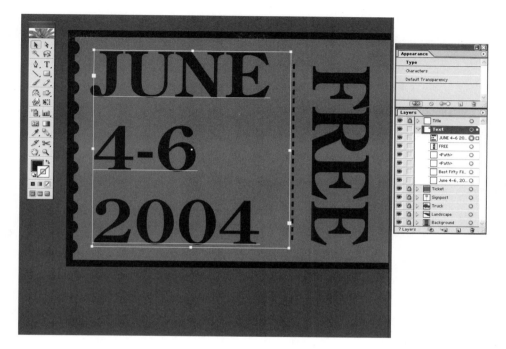

7. The larger type area may no longer be centered vertically on the ticket. With the **Selection** tool, recenter the type on the ticket and save the file. Keep the file open for the next exercise.

NOTE | Rotating a Type Area

> When you rotate a Type Area, the area rotates but the type remains upright and wraps to fill the new space.
>
> When you rotate a Type Area, the area rotates but the type remains upright and wraps to fill the new space.

Rotating a type area by dragging a corner handle of the bounding box rotates the area but not the type inside. The type rewraps to fit in the new shape instead. If you want to rotate the area and type inside it, use the **Rotate** tool.

Area Type Options

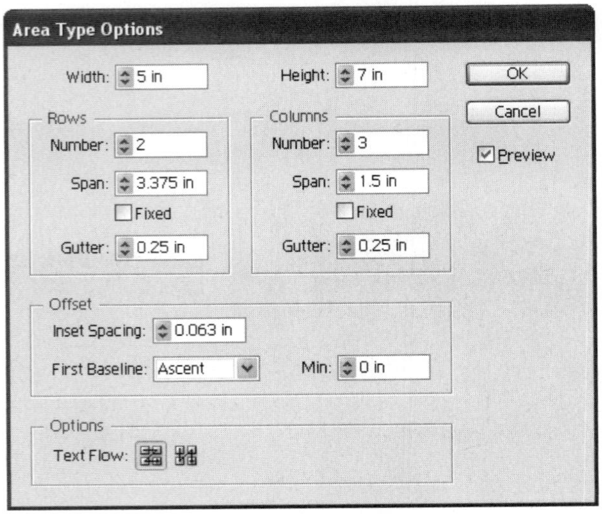

Double-clicking the **Type tool** when area type is selected or choosing **Type > Area Type Options** opens the **Area Type Options** dialog box. The following chart details some of its options.

Area Type Options	
Item	**Use**
Width and **Height**	Setting the width and height of a rectangular type area or the width and height of the bounding box around a type area.
Rows and **Columns**	Dividing a type area into rows and columns. Useful for fliers, brochures, and similar design projects.
Offset	Creating a space between the edge of the type area and the type within the type area.
Options	Setting the order of text flow from one row or column to the next within a type area. Has no effect when rows and columns are both set to 1.

3. ——————Type on a Path

Your third option for adding type to your artwork is to put the type on a path. This option is similar to type at a point, except that the type will follow any curves or corners along the path. With type on a path, typing along a circle, spiral, or any other path is no problem at all.

1. Open **poster_08.ai** or continue from Exercise 2.

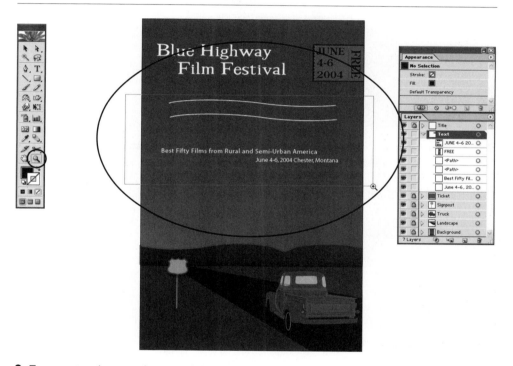

2. Zoom out and center the artwork by double-clicking the **Hand** tool or pressing **Ctrl+0** (Windows) or **Cmd+0** (Mac). Zoom in with the **Zoom** tool by dragging a rectangular marquee around the festival subtitle, dates, and two wavy lines.

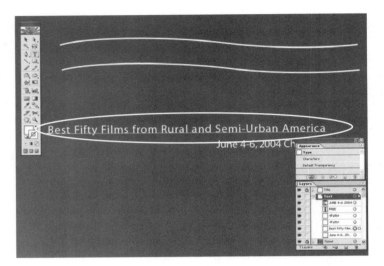

3. Select the **Selection** tool. Click once anywhere inside the line "Best Fifty...." Choose **Edit > Cut** or press **Ctrl+X** (Windows) or **Cmd+X** (Mac).

You do not need to select the type with the Type tool to cut it and put it on the clipboard.

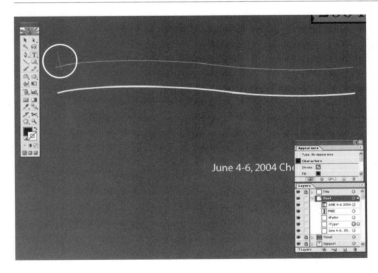

4. Select the **Type tool**. Click the left end of the top wavy line (circled above). The stroke on the line disappears and a flashing cursor appears.

You have converted the path into a type container, so it has no stroke and no fill. If you started typing on your keyboard, the type would appear on the path.

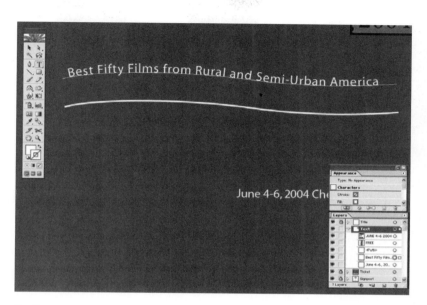

5. Choose **Edit > Paste** or press **Ctrl+V** (Windows) or **Cmd+V** (Mac). The poster subtitle appears following the wavy line.

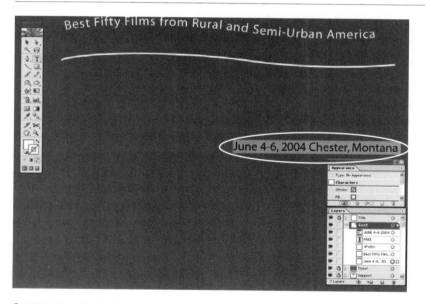

6. With **Type tool**, click anywhere inside "June 4-6…." Choose **Select > All** or press **Ctrl+A** (Windows) or **Cmd+A** (Mac).

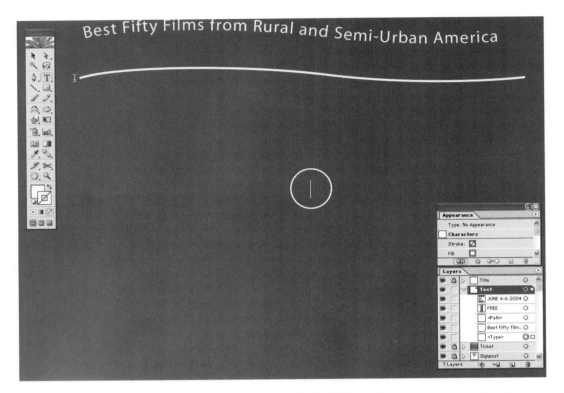

7. Choose **Edit > Cut** or press **Ctrl+X** (Windows) or **Cmd+X** (Mac). The dates disappear, but the flashing cursor remains.

Back in Step 3, you selected the text and cut it to the clipboard by selecting the entire type container with the Selection tool. This time you selected the text itself with the Type tool and cut it, but the type container—the point, path, or area associated with the text—did not get cut. Illustrator is showing you a flashing cursor and is ready for you to type something to replace the text you cut. You cannot click the second wavy line to paste the date until you get rid of this flashing cursor. This demonstrates the advantage of selecting the type and its container with the Selection tool if you want to cut and paste type.

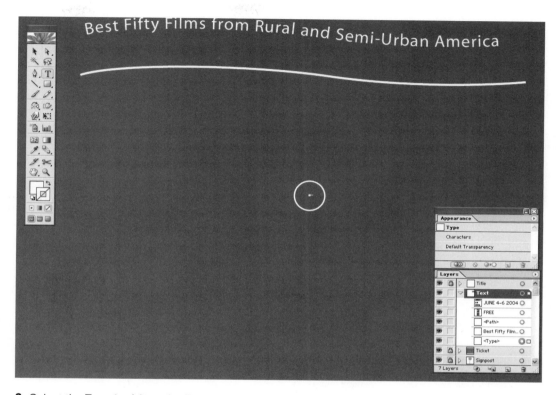

8. Select the **Type tool** from the **Toolbox** again. This will get rid of the flashing cursor, but there is now a single point selected where the date used to be. This is an empty type container, which appears on the **Layers** palette as **<Type>**. Press **Backspace** or **Delete** to delete the empty container or drag the **<Type>** layer to the **Trash**.

Empty type containers won't print and are generally harmless. It's still good practice to get rid of them just to ensure they don't cause problems later.

9. With the **Type tool** still selected, click the second wavy line under the word "Film" in the above line. Choose **Edit > Paste** or press **Ctrl+V** (Windows) or **Cmd+V** (Mac). The text appears where you clicked.

*Note: You could simply click the second wavy line and type "June 4-6, 2004 Chester, Montana" if you wanted. The **Edit > Paste** command is used here only to save you the bother of typing!*

10. Select the **Direct Selection** tool. Three handles appear on the path—one on the beginning of the text, one at the end of the line, and one in the middle of the other two.

You could use the Selection tool here, but the bounding box makes the three type handles harder to see.

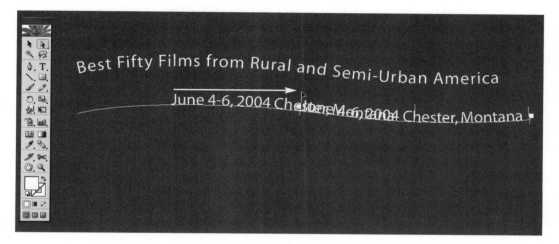

11. With **Direct Selection** tool, drag the handle at the beginning of the text to the right until the end of the word "Montana" reaches the end of the path, but does not disappear.

The handles on each end of the text determine how much of the path you want filled with text. When you put the type on a path, Illustrator assumes you want the text to start at the beginning of the path and continue to the end. By sliding the left-hand handle, you shorten the part of the path containing text and moved the starting point to halfway down the path. The middle handle lets you slide the text left and right on the path and even lets you flip the text so it hangs upside-down.

12. Save the file and keep it open for the next exercise.

NOTE | Type on a Path Options

By choosing **Type > Type on a Path > Type on a Path Options**, you can adjust the look of the letters as they follow the path and how the text aligns relative to the path. You can also flip the text so the letters hang upside-down from the path. Type on a Path Options are only available if you are editing path type or if path type is selected.

NOTE | **Type on Closed Paths Versus Area Type**

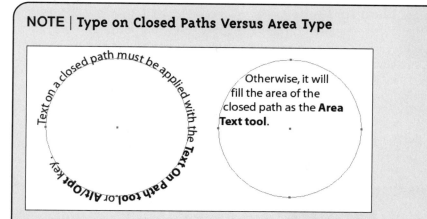

In the previous three exercises, you have created type at a point, type in an area, and type on a path all with the same tool—the Type tool. Illustrator makes the Type tool behave in different ways depending on where you click with it. There is a catch, though, if you want to put type on a shape rather than inside it. If you click a shape that is a closed path, such as a circle, Illustrator assumes you want that shape converted into a type area and fills the area with your text. If you want the text to follow the path instead, hold down the **Alt** key (Windows) or the **Option** key (Mac) as you click the path. Alternately, you could select the **Type on a Path** tool from the flyout menu under the **Type tool**. For more information on the other type tools, watch **type_tools.mov** at **http://www.lynda.com/books/hot/illcs/movies/**.

MOVIE | **type_tools.mov**

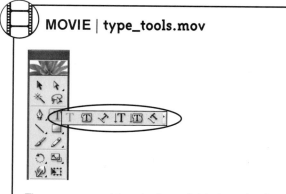

There are several type tools available from the flyout menu under the Type tool. Everything these tools offer can be achieved with the regular Type tool and keyboard shortcuts, but switching tools can be handy in certain situations. To explore how these tools work, watch the movie **type_tools.mov** online at **http://www.lynda.com/books/hot/illcs/movies/**.

4. _____Placing Text

Cutting and pasting is fine for small amounts of text but can be a pain when you want to place many paragraphs of text into your artwork. Illustrator comes with several built-in filters so you can insert text directly from a word processor and text documents.

1. Open **poster_08.ai** or continue from Exercise 3.

2. Zoom out and center the artwork by double-clicking the **Hand** tool or pressing **Ctrl+0** (Windows) or **Cmd+0** (Mac).

3. Choose **File > Place**. Locate the file **poster text.doc** in the **chap_08** folder. Click **Place**.

Poster text.doc is a Microsoft Word document, but you do not need Microsoft Word on your computer to import Word documents into Illustrator.

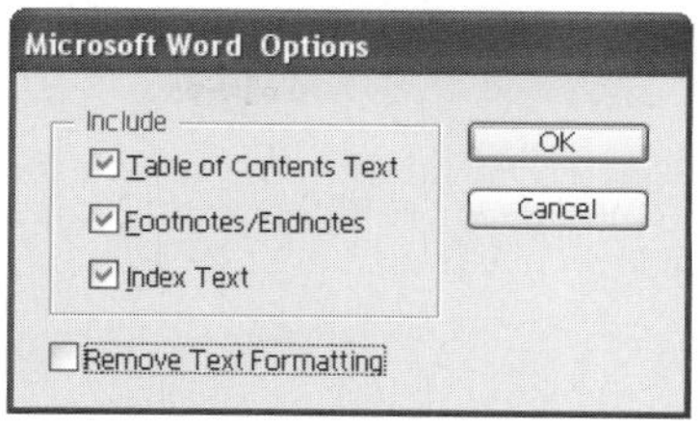

Microsoft Word Options

Include
- ☑ Table of Contents Text
- ☑ Footnotes/Endnotes
- ☑ Index Text

OK
Cancel

☐ Remove Text Formatting

4. When the **Microsoft Word Options** dialog opens, leave the **Include** options checked and leave **Remove Text Formatting** unchecked. Click **OK**.

With the Remove Text Formatting option unchecked, Illustrator will attempt to preserve the font selection, size, tabs, paragraph breaks and so on from the Word document.

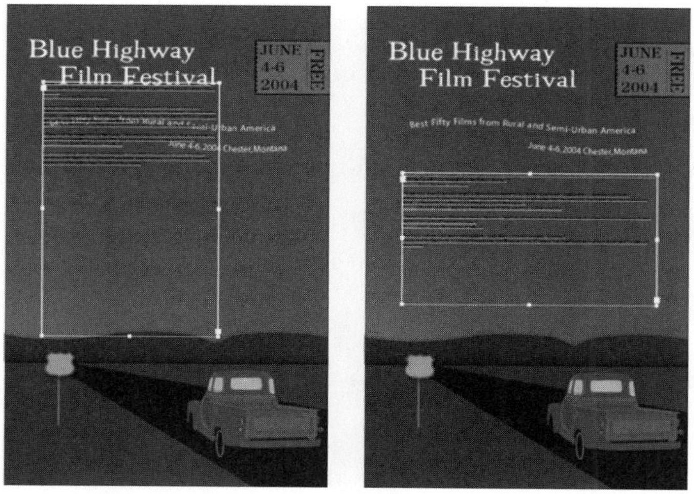

5. Placing the Word document creates a new type area the size of the area inside the margins of the Word document page, in this case 6 by 9 inches. Use the **Selection** tool to drag the type area down to the center of the poster and resize the type area to fit, as shown above.

6. Save the file and keep the file open for the next exercise.

NOTE | Styles and Placed Text

Although the text formatting is retained while placing text, any paragraph and character styles used in the original document are lost.

TIP | Problems with Placing Text

Sometimes placing text from a word processor document, such as Word, creates unwanted characters or other undesirable results. If you run into problems, try saving the Word file as a **R**ich **T**ext **F**ormat (RTF) document and placing it. If all else fails, save the document as text and place it. None of the formatting is preserved, but at least you won't have to type in the text yourself! To see what placing text is like, you can try placing the file **poster text.txt**, located in the **chap_08** folder, into the **poster_08.ai** file.

Spell Checker

Illustrator includes a basic spell checker to prevent you from embarrassing spelling mistakes when your art goes out to print or up on the Web. To start the spell checker, choose **Edit > Check Spelling** then click **Start**. The spell checker will scan all the text in your artwork, regardless of what was selected when you started it. The suspect words appear in the spell checker dialog box, and they are also highlighted in your document.

5. ——————— Character Formatting

One of the great features of Illustrator is that it offers precise manual control of type whenever you need it. In this exercise, you will edit the basic characteristics of type and see how to access advanced features through the Character palette.

1. Open **poster_08.ai** or continue from Exercise 4. With the **Zoom** tool, zoom in on the text placed in Exercise 4 by dragging a rectangular marquee around it.

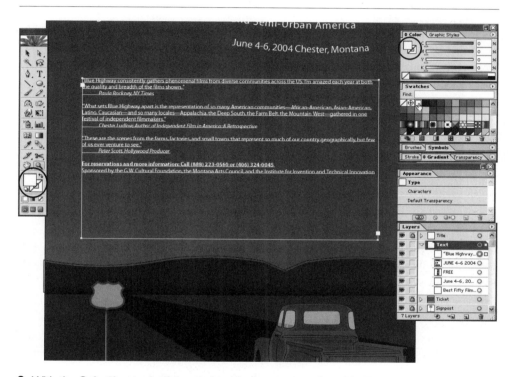

2. With the **Selection** tool, click anywhere in the text you placed in Exercise 4 to select it. Make sure the **Fill** square is on top in the **Toolbox** on the **Color** palette. On the **Swatches** palette, click the **White** swatch to make the black text a more readable white.

Type is designed to be filled with a color and have a stroke of None. You can add a colored stroke to type to achieve a particular effect, but if you are simply changing the color of the type, change the fill color only.

3. Color changes to type are done with the **Color** palette or the **Fill** and **Stroke** squares on the **Toolbox**. All other changes use the **Character** palette. Choose **Window > Type > Character** to open the **Character** palette.

4. The text you imported in Exercise 4 is in the Times New Roman font. On the **Character** palette, click the **Font** drop-down menu and change the font to **Myriad** (circled above). After you do, the font will show as **Myriad** and the font type will show as **Roman**.

Illustrator is a bit inconsistent on terminology here. Roman is the same as Regular on the font menu. Roman is the term for "normal" type used more often in typography.

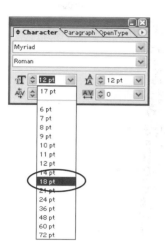

5. On the **Character** palette, click the drop-down menu for **Font Size** (circled above) and choose **18 pt**.

6. The type now appears very cramped. That's because the type is still using the line spacing, or leading, of 12 pt from the original Word document. Click the drop-down menu for **Leading** (circled above) and choose **Auto**.

As you change the leading, it appears that there is more space between each line of text. Leading is actually the height of the background on which type is drawn. Auto leading changes the leading to work with whatever font size you select. The leading amount chosen by Illustrator appears in parentheses so you know the value is being automatically adjusted.

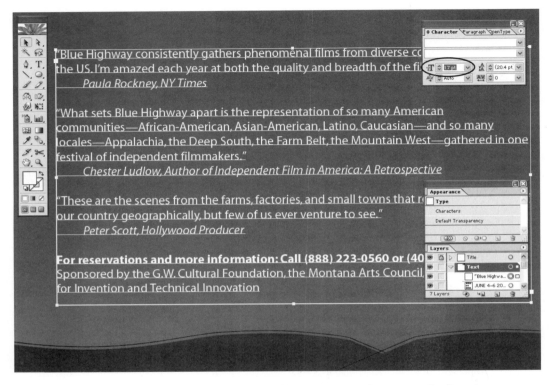

7. Click once in font size where it says **18 pt**. Press the **down arrow** key on your keyboard once to reduce the size to **17 pt**. The auto leading automatically changes from **21.6 pt** to **20.4 pt** to account for the smaller type.

The down and up arrow keys are a great shortcut to adjust a font size up and down until it looks just right on the screen. This shortcut works on all of the fields on the Character palette.

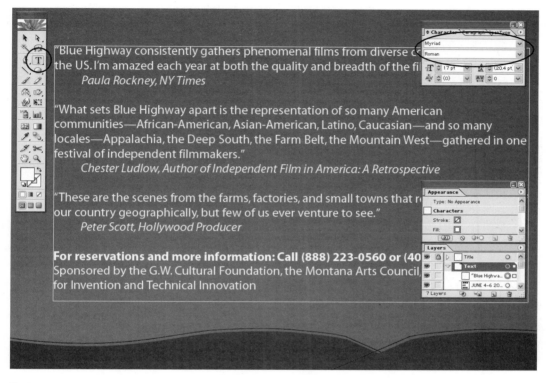

8. Select the **Type tool**. Double-click the first word of the first paragraph ("Blue") to select it. On the **Character** palette, the font name and style of the word "Blue" appears. The font is **Myriad** and style is **Roman**.

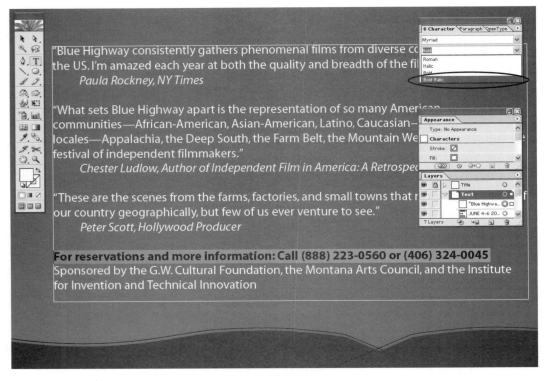

9. Check that you still have the **Type tool** chosen. Select the entire line that begins "For reservations and…" by clicking three times on any word in that sentence. On the **Character** palette, change the type style from **Bold** to **Bold Italic**.

As was mentioned before, there are no bold or italic buttons to format type in Illustrator. You must choose the roman, bold, italic, or bold italic version of that font.

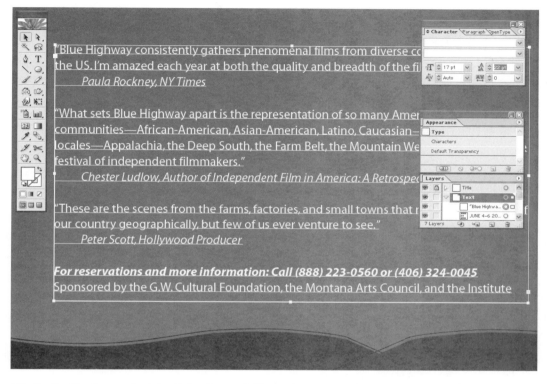

10. On the **Toolbox**, select the **Selection** tool. The entire text area becomes selected. On the **Character** palette, note the Auto Leading of **(20.4) pt**. Click once on number **20.4** to select it. Type **22** to change the leading to **22 pt**.

Increasing the leading adds visual space to your type, making it more legible at a distance. Since you have fixed the leading at something other than Auto, the leading will not change if you change the font size.

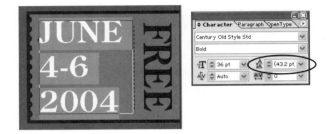

11. Hold the spacebar to temporarily select the **Hand** tool. Pan up the page to see the green ticket on the top right of the poster. Select the **Type tool**. Click the word "June" three times to select the date. The leading is automatically set to **43.2 pt**.

A triple-click with the Type tool selects an entire sentence. The date "June 4-6 2004" appears on three lines because it is wrapping in the type box, but it is still only one sentence.

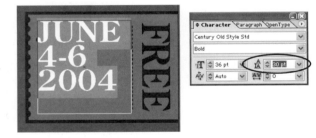

12. On the **Character** palette, change the **Leading** to **34 pt**.

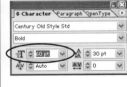

13. Using the **Type tool**, drag over the numbers "4-6" to select them. Change **Font Size** to **60 pt** in the **Character** palette.

The space is still okay below the numbers "4-6," but the type overlaps the line above that says "JUNE." This problem illustrates an important subtlety to leading. Leading and type are measured from the bottom up. If the type is too tall for your leading, it will stick out the top and overlap the line above. If you have a problem with the space between two lines, change the leading on the lower of the two lines to fix it.

14. With the numbers "4-6" still selected, change **Leading** to **50 pt**. The problem is now fixed.

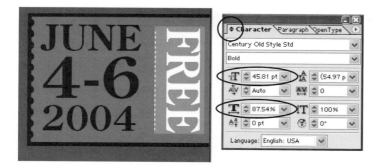

15. With the **Type tool**, double click the word "FREE" to select it. On the **Character** palette, double-click the **expansion** icon (circled above) to show the additional fields on the **Character** palette.

Note the type size and type width (both circled above). When you resized the word "FREE" in Exercise 1, Illustrator automatically changed the font size to the necessary height and adjusted the width of the font to compress the letters slightly. The result was approximately a font size of 45.81 pt that was compressed to 87.54 percent of its original width. Your results will be slightly different depending on exactly how much you resized the type.

16. Save the file.

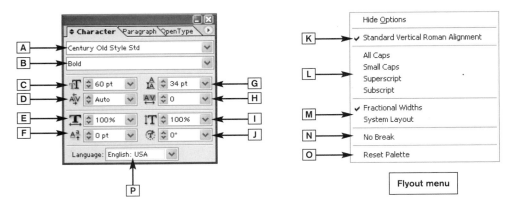

Flyout menu

Item	Name	Use
		Character Palette
Item	**Name**	**Use**
A	Font Name	Selecting a font
B	Font Style	Selecting a font style
C	Font Size	Selecting a font size
D	Kerning	Adjusting the space between two characters
E	Character Width	Stretching or squashing character width
F	Baseline Shift	Moving baseline of characters up or down relative to their normal position
G	Leading	Adjusting the space between a line of type and the line above it
H	Tracking	Adjusting the space between all the characters in a word or line of type
I	Character Height	Stretching or squash character height
J	Character Rotation	Rotating each character individually
K	Std. Vert. Roman Alignment	Correcting alignment when mixing Asian and Roman type

continues on next page

	Character Palette *continued*	
Item	**Name**	**Use**
L	Case and Position	Quickly substituting case or position of type
M	Fractional Widths	Making type more readable in artwork used on the Web or onscreen
N	No Break	Preventing line breaks in selected type
O	Reset	Returns palette to default settings
P	Language	Access features for various languages

MOVIE | char_palette.mov

To see what the different character palette adjustments look like in action, view **char_palette.mov** online at **http://www.lynda.com/books/hot/illcs/movies/**.

TIP | Mac OS X Font Locations

If you have fonts installed on your Mac that are not appearing as an option in Illustrator, be sure that a copy of the font (not an alias) is in the folder **Library > Fonts**. If the problem still persists, put a copy the font into the folder **Library > Application Support > Adobe > Fonts**.

6. ————————Paragraph Formatting

The horizontal alignment, left and right margins, and indentation of paragraphs' first lines are all controlled on the Paragraph palette. The Paragraph palette is a bit simpler than the Character palette since it has significantly fewer options.

1. Open **poster_08.ai** or continue from Exercise 5. Drag a box with the **Zoom** tool around the text placed in Exercise 4 to zoom in on it, if necessary.

2. The **Paragraph** palette shares a window with the **Character** palette. Bring the **Paragraph** palette to the front by choosing **Window > Type > Paragraph** or click the **Paragraph** tab on the window containing the **Character** palette.

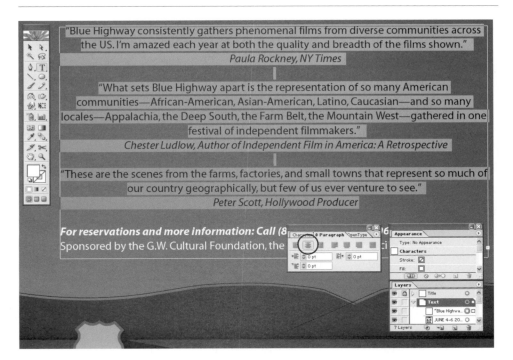

3. Select the **Type tool**. Drag the **Type tool** over the first three paragraphs of the text. Click the **Align Center** button (circled above) on the **Paragraph** palette. The sentences are all centered.

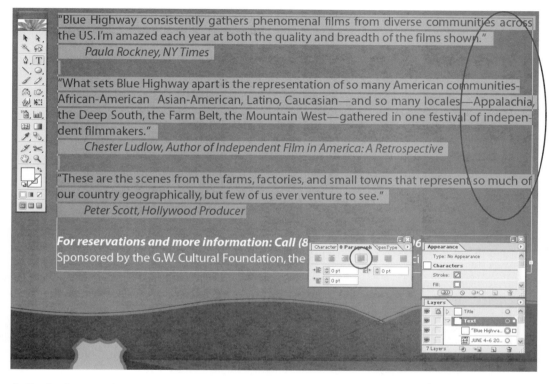

4. On the **Paragraph** palette, click the **Justify With Last Aligned Left** button (circled above).

There are three Justify With Align Last options; one for right, left, and center. There is also a traditional Justify button. Justify will adjust the space between the letters and words (tracking) so that both margins of the paragraph are flush with the sides of the type area, but allowing the last line to align left, right, or center results in much better character spacing.

"Blue Highway consistently gathers phenomenal films from diverse communities across the US. I'm amazed each year at both the quality and breadth of the films shown."

Paula Rockney, NY Times

"What sets Blue Highway apart is the representation of so many American communities—African-American, Asian-American, Latino, Caucasian—and so many locales—Appalachia, the Deep South, the Farm Belt, the Mountain West—gathered in one festival of independent filmmakers."

Chester Ludlow, Author of Independent Film in America: A Retrospective

"These are the scenes from the farms, factories, and small towns that represent so much of our country geographically, but few of us ever venture to see."

Peter Scott, Hollywood Producer

For reservations and more information: Call (8...6
Sponsored by the G.W. Cultural Foundation, the...ci

5. Click the **Align Left** button and set **First Line Left Indent** to **18 pt**. The text aligns left and indents.

6. Hmm. Perhaps the centered type is better for the poster. Set the first line indent back to **0 pt** and click the **Align Center** button. See how easy it is to change your mind with these new skills?

7. Save the file.

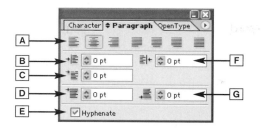

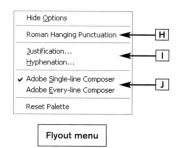

Flyout menu

Paragraph Palette

Item	Name	Use
A	Alignment	Controls horizontal alignment of each line
B	Left Indent	Sets distance between edge of type container and paragraph
C	First Line Indent	Creates indented or hanging first line
D	Space Above	Adds space before each paragraph
E	Hyphenate	Toggles automatic hyphenation on and off
F	Right Indent	Sets distance between edge of type container and paragraph
G	Space Below	Adds space after each paragraph
H	Roman Hanging Punctuation	Hangs quotes beyond left margin
I	Justification and Hyphenation	Access justification and hyphenation options
J	Composer	Toggles between standard (single-line) and advanced (every-line) line break and spacing rules

(7.)——————Threaded Text

If your text does not fit in a single type area or on a single path, you can **thread** the text through several type areas or paths. Any text that does not fit in the first area appears in the second one, and any text that still does not fit appears in a third, and so on. If you add or remove text, the remaining text is redistributed as needed. Threaded text is also a great way to experiment with breaking up a single type area into smaller ones, as you will see in this exercise.

1. Open **poster_08.ai** or continue from Exercise 6. Drag a box with the **Zoom** tool around the text placed in Exercise 6 to zoom in on it, if necessary.

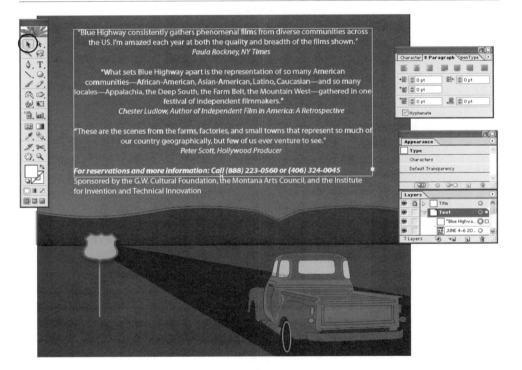

2. Select the **Selection** tool and select the entire type area by clicking any text in the type area. Drag the bottom-center handle of the bounding box upward so the last line you can see is "For reservations…" Release the mouse button, and the last two sentences will be hidden from view.

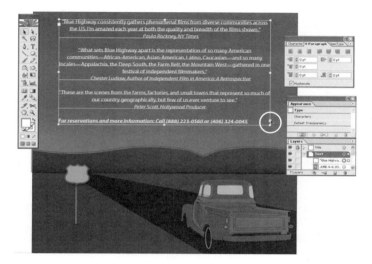

3. When you released the mouse in Step 2, a small, red plus sign appeared on the right side of the type area indicated there is text hidden from view. Click the **plus** icon. The cursor changes to an insert type area symbol.

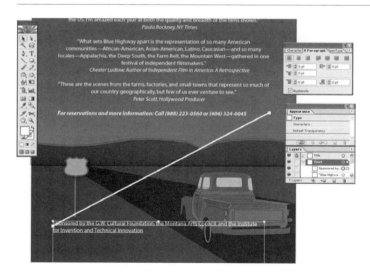

4. Click underneath the highway sign. A new type area appears with the remaining text, and a line connects the two type areas. The line indicates that the two type areas are threaded, meaning that any text that cannot fit in the first area will overflow into the second.

You can alternately drag a rectangular area rather than simply click. The text will flow into the area you define.

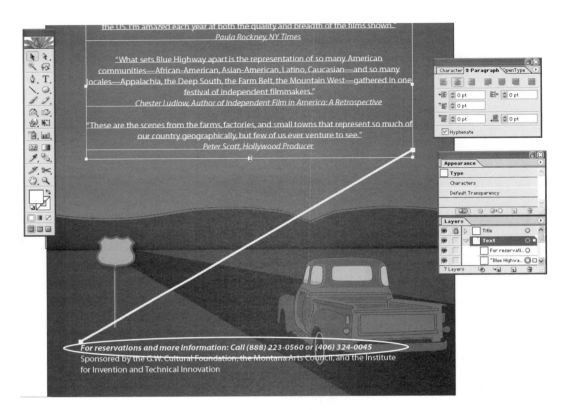

5. With the **Selection** tool, drag the center handle on the upper type area upward until the sentence "For reservations…" flows into second window.

Having text flow from one type area to another is also great with brochures and fliers that may contain many paragraphs of text. By threading the text, you can focus on getting the size of each type area exactly right for your design and let Illustrator redistribute the content between the type areas as needed. You can also thread text between type areas and type on a path.

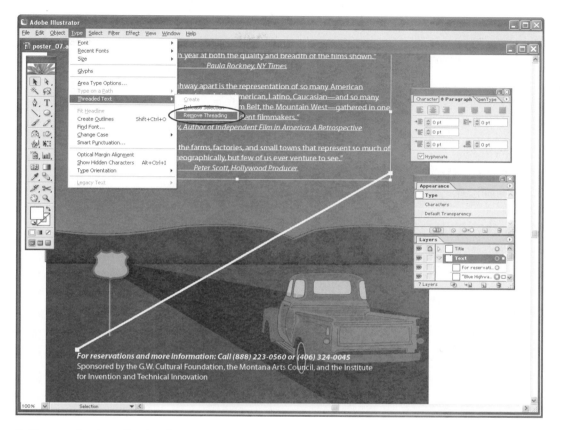

6. Remove the threading by choosing **Type > Threaded Text > Remove Threading**. The line connecting the two type areas disappears. Now, edits to one type area will have no effect on the other.

---

7. Save the file and close it.

Now you have the fundamentals for adding and format type in your documents. Read on to use some more advanced tools that make working with type easier and give you even more creative control.

9.

Type Appearances and Styles

The Eyedropper Tool and Type	Setting Custom Tabs
Paragraph Styles	Character Styles
OpenType and Glyphs	Creating Outlines

chap_09

Illustrator CS
H•O•T CD-ROM

Now that you know how to add type to your work, it's time to learn some of the techniques that save time, avoid frustration, and create professional-quality typography. Illustrator CS introduces two very cool new features with regard to type. The first is paragraph and character styles. Styles have been in use in word processing and page layout software for years, and they are a welcome (and perhaps overdue) addition to Illustrator.

The other addition is OpenType support. You have already worked with OpenType fonts in Chapter 8, "*Adding Text*," but in this chapter, you will see how OpenType really shines by using two new palettes: the OpenType palette and the Glyphs palette. The OpenType palette takes advantage of OpenType's capability to automatically substitute characters; the Glyphs palette provides direct access to all the characters and their variants. Before you get into the cool new features of OpenType, you will learn a few tricks for successfully formatting any kind of type.

I. ——————The Eyedropper Tool and Type

In Chapter 8, "*Adding Text*," you selected type and used the Color palette to change its color. You can also use the eyedropper to apply a color to type, but this process is not as straightforward as you might expect. Problems when using the eyedropper with type are some of the most common frustrations reported by people learning Illustrator. In this exercise, you will learn how selecting your artwork in the correct way is crucial to getting the desired eyedropper result every time.

1. Copy the **chap_09** folder from the **H•O•T CD-ROM** to your hard drive. Open the file **poster_09.ai** from the **chap_09** folder.

2. Double-click the **Hand** tool or press **Ctrl+0** (Windows) or **Cmd+0** (Mac) to see the entire poster.

3. Double-click the **Eyedropper** tool to open the **Eyedropper/Paint Bucket Options** dialog box. Make sure the **Appearance** check box is checked under **Eyedropper Picks Up**.

Having the Eyedropper tool pick up an entire appearance is the default when Illustrator installs and is important for working with effects and graphic styles.

4. Select the **Type** tool. Click inside the word "Best' on the upper wavy line of text to put the flashing text cursor on that line. Choose **Select > All** or press **Ctrl+A** (Windows) or **Cmd+A** (Mac) to select the entire line.

5. Note on the **Appearance** palette that you have **Characters** selected. Select the **Eyedropper** tool. Click inside the light blue colored square to the left of the poster. The type fills with the blue color. Choose **Select > Deselect** to see it better.

Remember, type is normally filled with a color and has a stroke of None.

6. Select the **Selection** tool. Click the lower wavy line of text to select it. Note on the **Appearance** palette that you have **Type** selected. Select the **Eyedropper** tool. Click inside the light blue colored square to the left of the poster. The type changes, but it's a now a brighter white with a hint of blue!

What happened? The difference is subtle, but very important. When you selected the upper wavy line in Step 4, you used the Type tool, and in Step 5, you used the Selection tool. When you use the Selection tool to select type, you might not realize that what you are doing is selecting the Type container, and not the actual type within. Type containers are discussed in Chapter 8, "Adding Text."

NOTE | Graphic Styles

Illustrator 10 and earlier had a palette called the Styles palette. This palette has been renamed the Graphic Styles palette to avoid confusion with the Paragraph and Character Styles palettes. For more information on graphic styles, see Chapter 18, "*Graphic Styles.*"

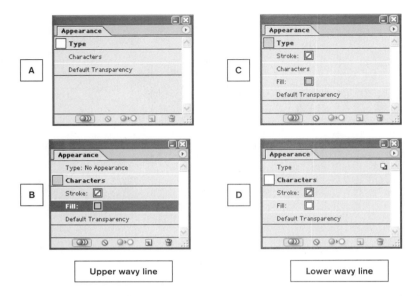

Upper wavy line   Lower wavy line

7. Select the **Selection** tool. Click the upper wavy line of text and look at the **Appearance** palette (shown in A above). The type *object* has no fill and no stroke. Select the **Type** tool and click three times on the word "Best" on the first wavy line to select all of the text. Look at the **Appearance** palette now (shown in B above). The *characters* are filled blue. Select the **Selection** tool and click the lower wavy line. On the **Appearance** palette (shown in C above) you see that the type *object* has a blue fill. Select the **Type** tool and click the word "June" three times on the lower line to select the text. Look at the **Appearance** palette (shown in D above) one more time. Here's the problem! The *characters* on this line still have a white fill! This white character fill is sitting on top of the blue object fill you added with the eyedropper and making the two lines of text appear as different colors. (Example C, above, shows that the characters are above the blue fill.)

Problems applying color to type are commonly discussed on the Adobe user-to-user forum for Illustrator. Confusion about selecting type objects versus characters is almost always the reason.

TIP | Hidden Type Fill and Stroke

If you ever select type and can't change the color, or the wrong color appears, change the way you selected it. If you used the Selection tool, try using the Type tool instead. If you used the Type tool, try using the Selection tool instead.

8. With the characters on the lower wavy line of type still selected with the **Type** tool, Select the **Eyedropper** tool and sample the light blue square again.

Now the two lines are similar, but still not identical. The lower one is still filled twice, once at the character level and once at the type object level.

9. Double-click the **Type** line in the **Appearance** palette, and the selection will change. The characters are no longer selected, and the type container is selected. Click the **Clear Appearances** button or drag the extra fill to the **Trash**. Now the two lines appear the same color.

Double-clicking a line on the Appearance palette is a great shortcut for switching between a type object and characters. Clear Appearances is a great tool for getting rid of problems and handling conflicting strokes and fills. Sometimes problems are readily apparent on screen. Other times they aren't noticeable until you print.

10. Double-click the **Hand** tool to zoom out. With the **Selection** tool, click on the type "For reservations…" at the bottom of the poster to select that entire text area.

11. Select the **Eyedropper** tool. Hold down the **Shift** key and click the upper colored square. The blue is copied to the characters correctly, instead of added to the type object.

Shift+clicking with the Eyedropper tool is the same as unchecking the Appearance check box on the eyedropper or paint bucket options. Holding down the Shift key also works for copying a single color out of a gradient, effect, or image such as a photograph.

12. Save the file and keep it open for the next exercise.

TIP | Gradients on Type

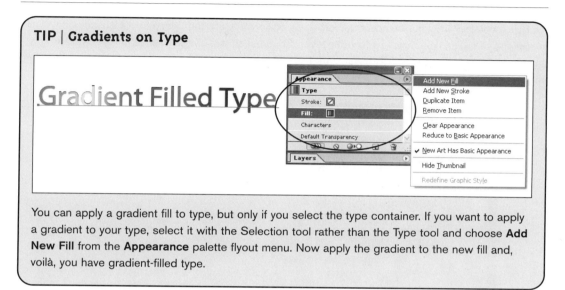

You can apply a gradient fill to type, but only if you select the type container. If you want to apply a gradient to your type, select it with the Selection tool rather than the Type tool and choose **Add New Fill** from the **Appearance** palette flyout menu. Now apply the gradient to the new fill and, voilà, you have gradient-filled type.

2. ⎯⎯⎯⎯⎯⎯⎯Setting Custom Tabs

No type formatting system is complete without a way to control tabs. The Tab palette in Illustrator functions similarly to tab rulers you may have used in a word processor, with the difference that you can drag it anywhere you need on the artboard. Tabs are typically used as mechanisms to align type for formatting charts and reports that require columns of information.

1. Open **poster_09.ai** or continue from Exercise 1.

2. With the **Zoom** tool, zoom in on the text quotes in the center of the poster. Select the **Selection** tool and click the text to select it.

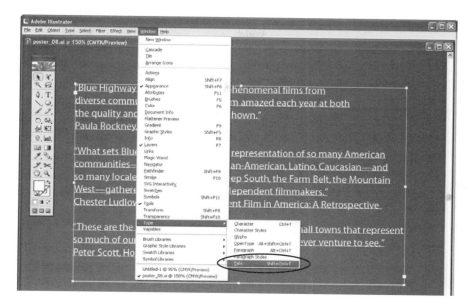

3. Choose **Window > Type > Tabs** to see the **Tab** palette. Choose **Window > Type > Paragraph** if the **Paragraph** palette is not already visible.

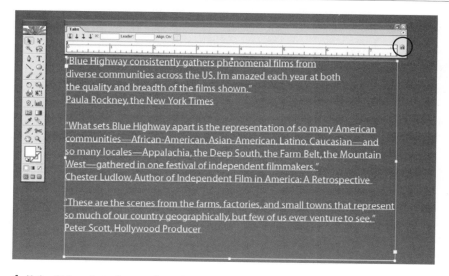

4. If the **Tab** palette is not aligned over the top of the text, click the **magnet** icon.

The magnet aligns the Tab palette over the selected text. If no text is selected, clicking the magnet has no effect.

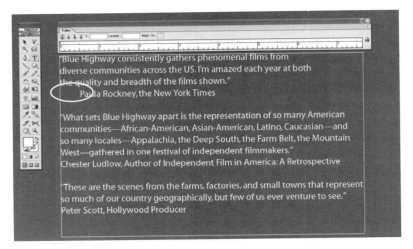

5. Click once with the **Type** tool in front of the name "Paula." Press **Tab** on your keyboard to enter a tab. The author's name indents.

Because no tabs are set on the Tab palette, the name indents to the default of every one-half inch.

6. Click the **Left Justified Tab Stop** button (circled above) on the **Tab** palette. Place a left justified tab at **3 inches** by either clicking on the tab ruler (circled above) or entering the number in the field on the tab bar. The author byline moves.

Once you add a custom tab stop to the Tab palette, the default tab stops before the new tab stops are no longer used. The tab in front of the author name now aligns the name with the tab stop you added to the tab ruler.

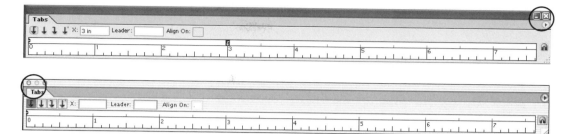

7. Close the **Tab** palette. Save the file and keep it open for the next exercise.

TIP | Better Looking Quotes

When you have a quote in front of several lines of left aligned or justified text, the quotation marks indent the first line relative to the rest of the paragraph. To fix this and maintain a straight left margin, choose **Roman Hanging Punctuation** on the **Paragraph** palette flyout menu. This hangs the quotes beyond the margin so all the type aligns correctly on the left margin.

3. ——————Paragraph Styles

Paragraph and character styles are a common feature on word processing and page layout programs but are included for the first time in Illustrator CS. Styles let you format a section of type using the Paragraph and Character palettes, and then apply that formatting to as many other sections of type as you wish. Changing the format of the style updates all the type using that style at once, rather than selecting and changing every instance of the style separately. The standard use of styles is to set the format of the whole paragraph with a paragraph style first and then make exceptions to single words, such as bold or different colors, using character styles.

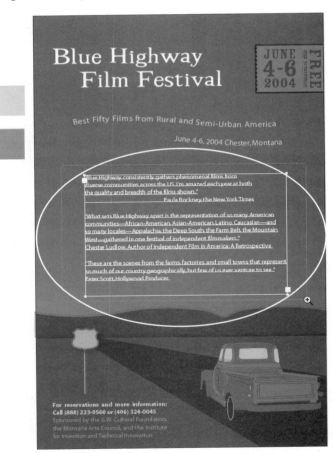

1. Open **poster_09.ai** or continue from Exercise 2. With the **Zoom** tool, zoom in on the quotes in the center of the poster by dragging a rectangular marquee around them if the file is not already zoomed in.

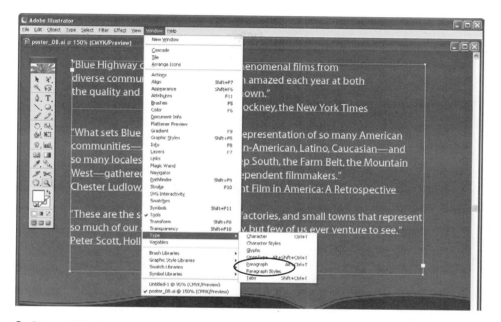

2. Choose **Window > Type > Paragraph** to see the **Paragraph** palette and choose **Window > Type > Paragraph Styles** to see the **Paragraph Styles** palette.

3. Select the **Type** tool. Click three times in the third paragraph of the quotes to select the entire paragraph.

Unlike many applications where there are several default styles to choose from, Illustrator documents open with only one default style—the Normal Paragraph style. The Normal Paragraph style includes left justified black type. Since you have edited the formatting of the selected paragraph so it no longer matches the default style, a plus symbol appears next to Normal Paragraph Style, alerting you to the difference. Differences between the selected text and the highlighted style in the Paragraph Style palette are called **overrides**.

4. Choose **New Paragraph Style** from the **Paragraph Styles** flyout menu. Name it the new style **Quotes** and click **OK**.

You can redefine the Normal Paragraph style (default style) if you want, and then all new paragraphs you create will use this style. In general, it's good practice to create your own styles for clarity, however.

5. With the last quote still selected, click **Quotes** on the **Paragraph Styles** palette. On the Paragraph palette, click the **Align Center** button to center the text. The paragraph style now appears as **Quotes+**. This indicates there is an override. From the **Paragraph Styles** flyout menu, choose **Redefine Paragraph Style**.

*Redefine Paragraph Style changes the definition of Quotes so that it matches the selected text. In some cases, the Quotes paragraph style may still show as Quotes+. If this happens, click the **Quotes** row on the **Paragraph Styles** palette to clear the override and make the plus sign go away.*

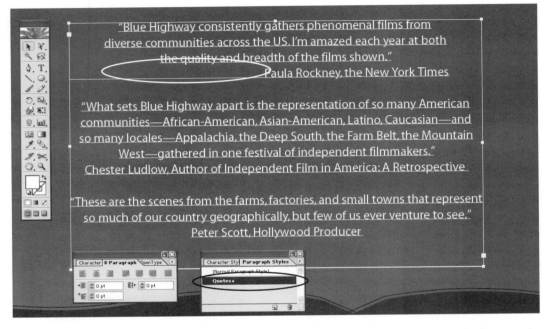

6. Select the **Selection** tool to select the entire text area. Now nothing is highlighted on the **Paragraph Styles** palette. Click **Quotes** once. The paragraphs are now center aligned. There is an override symbol (plus sign) next to **Quotes** because of the tab setting, which is not part of the Quotes paragraph style, in the paragraph containing the name "Paula Rockney." Click **Quotes** again. The override is cleared and the nonconforming tab setting is removed.

7. With the **Selection** tool, select the light blue color square to the left of the poster. If the **Color** and **Swatches** palettes are not visible, choose **Window > Color**. Drag the blue color from the **Color** palette to the open area at the bottom of the **Swatches** palette to add it to the swatches. You will need this color on the **Swatches** palette for the next few steps.

8. Double-click **Quotes** on the **Paragraph Styles** palette. The **Paragraph Style Options** dialog box opens.

The General section of the dialog box shows you all the items the style currently controls. For example, the Quotes style currently ensures the font size is 17 pt on 22 pt leading and the alignment is centered. Note that the paragraph style controls formatting found on both the Character palette (such as font size) and the Paragraph palette (such as alignment). This can be confusing when you first work with styles. Just remember that paragraph styles can control all the formatting for everything in a paragraph—fonts, alignment, tabs, color, and much more.

9. Click **Character Color** on the left side of the dialog box. Scroll down the list on the right. Click the **New Color Swatch** (probably at the very bottom of the list). Click **OK**.

This swatch is the blue color you added to the Swatches palette in Step 7 of this exercise. The Paragraph Style Options uses the Swatches palette for its list of colors, so you must put the color you want on the Swatches palette before you select the color in the Paragraph Style Options dialog box.

10. All the paragraphs with the **Quotes** paragraph style are now blue.

This is the beauty of styles. You can make a single change to the style, and all the instances of that style are automatically updated in your document.

11. Save the file and keep it open for the next exercise.

4. ————————Character Styles

Character styles work the same way paragraph styles do, but they are used to set the style for a individual words or letters within a paragraph. For example, if you wanted to emphasize certain words but weren't sure if you wanted to use bold type or semi-bold type, you could define a character style called Emphasis and then easily change the look of the emphasized words throughout your document.

1. Open **poster_09.ai** or continue from Exercise 3. With the **Zoom** tool, zoom in on the quotes in the center of the poster if you are not already zoomed in.

2. In the same window as the **Paragraph Styles** palette, click the tab for the **Character Styles** palette. Choose **New Character Style** from the flyout menu. Name the style **Quote Sources**. Click **OK**.

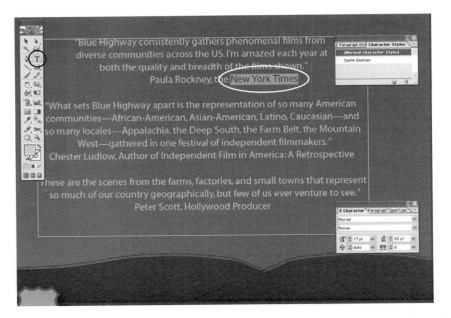

3. Select the **Type** tool. Select only the text "New York Times" by clicking with the **Type** tool once in front of the words and then dragging over them.

4. On the **Character Styles** palette, double-click **Quote Sources**. This sets the text "New York Times" to the **Quotes Sources** style and opens the **Character Style Options** dialog box.

The Character Style Options dialog looks just like the Paragraph Style Options dialog box except it has fewer choices on the left side. You cannot set paragraph-wide formats, such as the alignment of the entire paragraph, using character styles. Character styles are only for changing character formats for a string of type within a paragraph.

5. Click **Basic Character Formats** on the left side. Choose **Myriad** as the **Font Family** and **Italic** as the **Font Style**. If the **Preview** box on the lower left is checked, you will see the selected text change to italics in your artwork. Click **OK**.

Here you see how character styles are used for overriding the paragraph style for a section of type within a paragraph.

6. Save the file and keep it open for the next exercise.

MOVIE | type_styles.mov

To learn more about using paragraph and character styles, watch **type_styles.mov** online at **http://www.lynda.com/books/hot/illcs/movies/**.

TIP | Eyedropper and Styles

The Eyedropper and Paint Bucket tools copy paragraph and character styles, as well as type appearances. To prevent copying a style when you use the eyedropper or paint bucket, double-click the Eyedropper tool on the Toolbox and uncheck Character Styles or Paragraph Styles as needed.

5. —————————OpenType and Glyphs

One big advantage of OpenType fonts is that they allow quick and easy access to glyphs and other special characters. Glyphs are alternate versions of characters you can use for a more professional look or special effects. The glyphs are part of the font file, so not every OpenType font contains every glyph option.

1. Open **poster_09.ai** or continue from Exercise 4. With the **Zoom** tool, zoom in on the second wavy line of text.

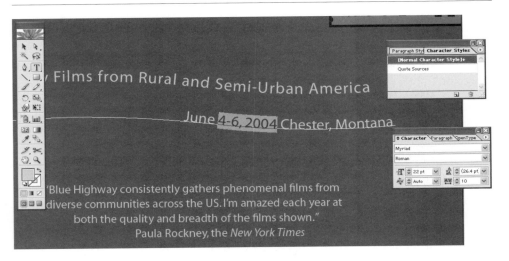

2. Select the **Type** tool. Select the numbers "4-6, 2004" in the date.

3. On the **Character** palette, change the font to **Myriad Pro**.

Glyphs are built into the font itself. Pro versions of a font usually contain more glyphs and special characters than the standard versions.

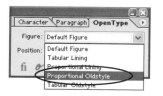

4. Choose **Window > Type > OpenType** or click the **OpenType** tab hidden behind the **Character** or **Paragraph** palettes. From the **Figure** drop-down menu, choose **Proportional Oldstyle**. The numbers are replaced with traditional, old-style figures.

The other Figures shown on the drop-down menu are for other special situations with numbers. Tabular figures are for use on tables so the numbers align precisely; Proportional Lining figures are for use when you combine numbers with type containing small caps.

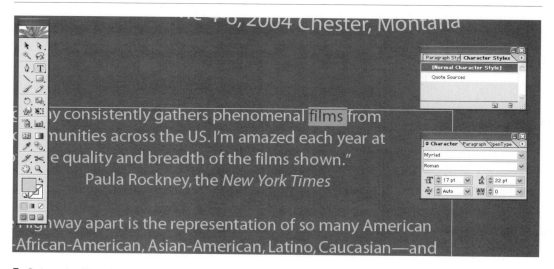

5. Select the **Hand** tool. Pan down with the **Hand** tool to see the first quote. Use the **Zoom** tool or **Ctrl+−** (Windows) or **Cmd+−** (Mac) to zoom out if necessary. Using the **Type** tool, click twice on the word "films" in the first sentence to select it.

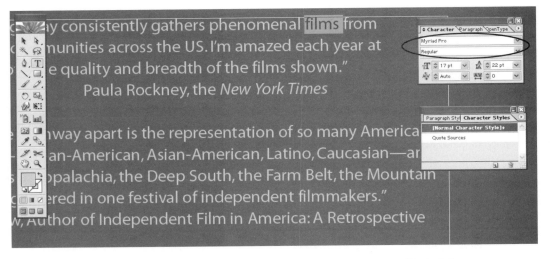

6. Click the **Character** palette tab to bring it to the front. Change the font to **Myriad Pro**.

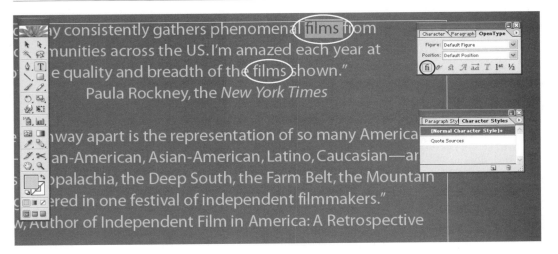

7. Click the tab for the **OpenType** palette to bring it to the front. Click the **Ligatures** button (circled above) on the **OpenType** palette. Note that the "f" and the "i" appear connected? That's a ligature. Compare the word "film" in the first line of the quote with the word "film" in the second line to see the difference. You'll learn about why ligatures are used in upcoming "Ligatures" sidebar.

The Ligatures button replaces any common ligature pair with the appropriate ligature. In this case, the "fi" in "film" is replaced.

NOTE | Ligatures

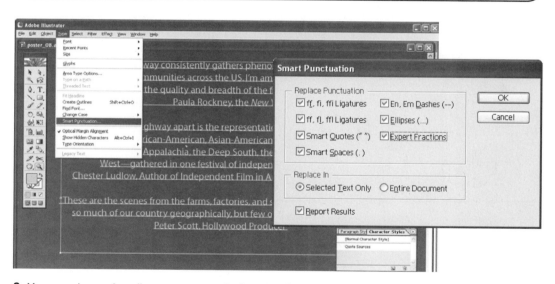

A ligature is when a single special character replaces a pair of characters that might overlap if printed together. The above example is the word "film" in the font Adobe Caslon (which is the poster child font for need for ligatures). In the nonligature version on the left, the dot on the "i" overlaps the top of the "f." In the ligature version on the right, the "i" and "f" are combined into a single character. Note how the top of the "f" visually replaces the missing dot for the "i." The common ligatures are "ff," "fi," "ffi," "fl," and "ffl."

8. You can also replace ligatures automatically using **Smart Punctuation**. With the entire text area still selected, choose **Type > Smart Punctuation**. Check all boxes and ensure **Selected Text Only** is selected. Click **OK**.

The OpenType palette affects only OpenType fonts. Ligatures are also available for many TrueType or PostScript fonts, depending on the font, but they cannot be accessed from the OpenType palette. Smart Punctuation is the best way to replace ligatures in these fonts. When using a PostScript font, old style figures and other special characters are accessed from a pro or expert version of the font. For example, the PostScript font for Poetica might use normal numbers, but if you select the numbers and change the font to Poetica Expert Set, they will switch to proportional old style. A big advantage of OpenType fonts is having only one font file where the same number of variants might require 4 or 5 (or more) PostScript font files.

9. Click **OK** on the report to close it. The ligatures and other corrections have been made in your text.

10. Save the file and keep it open for the next exercise.

TIP | Spell Check Before Ligatures

Spell check does not understand ligatures in PostSript and TrueType fonts, so it will return spelling errors for words that are spelled correctly but use a ligature. OpenType fonts do not have this problem. Spell check your artwork before you substitute ligatures when you are using non-OpenType fonts.

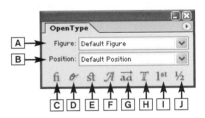

OpenType Palette		
Item	**Name**	**Use**
A	Figure	Selecting the appropriate kind of number for tables, small caps, or a classical look. This setting applies only to numbers.
B	Position	Setting the vertical position of superscripts, subscripts, and fractions.
C	Standard Ligatures	Replacing standard ligature pairs ("ff," "fi," "ffi," "fl," and "ffl").
D	Contextual Alternates	Replacing letter pairs in script fonts to appear closer to handwriting.
E	Discretionary Ligatures	Replacing additional pairs such as "st" or "ct." Options vary from font to font.
F	Swash	Replacing leading capital letters (first capital in a sentence) with a stylized (swash) alternative.

continues on next page

	OpenType Palette *continued*	
Item	**Name**	**Use**
G	Stylistic Alternates	Replacing letters with a more stylized alternative. Options vary from font to font.
H	Titling Alternates	Replacing capitals, numbers, and punctuation in titles with a lighter-weight alternative.
I	Ordinals	Automatically superscripting ordinals such as 1st and 3rd.
J	Fractions	Automatically superscripting numbers before a / to create fractions such as ½.

Access to Glyphs

The OpenType palette gives you access to many of the special characters in an OpenType font and is perfect for substituting characters throughout a range of text. You can access all the special characters in any kind of font by choosing **Type > Glyphs** to open the **Glyphs** palette.

If a character on your screen is selected with the Type tool, that character is replaced by choosing any glyph in this palette. Double-clicking any glyph inserts that character at the cursor where the Type tool has selected the text. Where a character has alternate forms available, a small black triangle appears. Clicking the triangle opens a grid where you can select alternate characters. The lowercase "b" in Adobe Caslon Pro (above) has its normal form, a superscript form, a small capital form, and an ornament you can use to accent your artwork. To the right of the circle, you can see the "fi" and "fl" ligatures for Adobe Caslon Pro as well. The glyphs on the Glyphs palette are the same glyphs inserted when you use the OpenType palette or Smart Punctuation. The difference is the Glyphs palette gives you access to all the glyphs in the font. If finding the right character is too difficult while looking at the entire font, you can choose to view only certain kinds of glyphs by using the **Show** menu in the upper-left corner of the palette. Additional glyphs options are available with Asian fonts as well. The Glyphs palette provides access to all the characters in any font, but it needs an OpenType font for full functionality.

6. ——————Creating Outlines

One of the problems with having type in your Illustrator documents is that anyone you share the Illustrator file with, including a print service, must have that font to see the artwork correctly. If you're not sure if someone has the font you are using, you can convert the type in your document to outlines. The outlines look exactly the same as your font, but they are shapes instead of text. Outlines cannot be edited with the Type tool, so you can't easily change what the text says. You can, however, edit the shape of the outlines to create cool effects.

1. Open **poster_09.ai** or continue from Exercise 5.

2. Double-click the **Hand** tool to see the entire poster. Select the **Zoom** tool, and zoom in on the green ticket in the upper-right corner by dragging a rectangular marquee around the ticket.

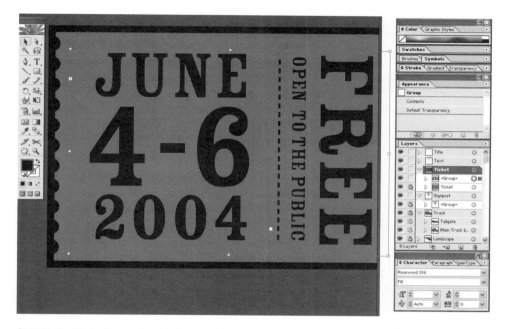

3. With the **Selection** tool, click the word "June." The type on the ticket is grouped so all the type is selected.

When you edited this ticket in Chapter 8, "Adding Text," you used the font Century Schoolbook. The type has now been replaced with Rosewood. This is a less common type (although it ships with Illustrator). If you sent this file out to a printer, you would have to include the font file for Rosewood or convert it to outlines.

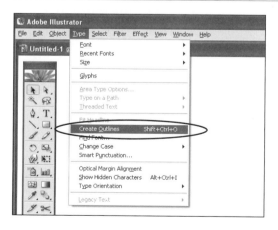

4. Choose **Type > Create Outlines**.

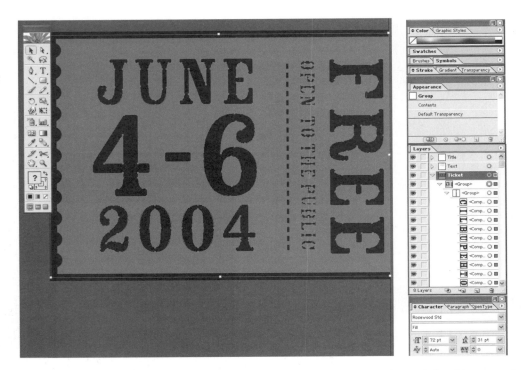

*Immediately, the selection looks different because each character is a shape defined by several points. These points are now highlighted in blue. The letters and numbers look the same, but they are no longer type and cannot be edited with the Type tool. They are now shapes (some are special paths called **compound paths**), which you could reshape with the Direct Selection and Pen tools if you wanted. Compound paths are a special kind of path discussed in Chapter 13, "Path Tools."*

5. Save the file.

TIP | Editing Outlines

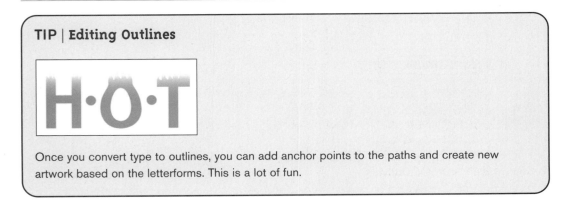

Once you convert type to outlines, you can add anchor points to the paths and create new artwork based on the letterforms. This is a lot of fun.

TIP | Find Font

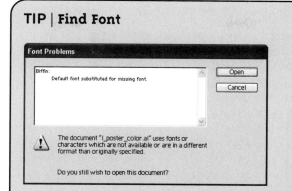

The title "Blue Highway Film Festival" on the poster is composed of a group of outlines rather than text. The original font was Biffin, which does not ship with Illustrator. If the title was not converted to outlines, you would see the message above when you opened the poster (unless you happened to have Biffin installed on your computer.

To find where a missing font is used in the artwork, click **Open** to open the file and then choose **Type > Find Font**. The missing fonts appear with asterisks. Click the name of the missing font in the upper window and then click **Find**. The problem text will highlight in your document. You can then replace the problem font with one from the lower window of the **Find Font** dialog box or tell the person who gave you the file that they need to send you the font or create outlines for that font and send you the file again.

Legacy Text

Illustrator CS uses a new system for controlling and displaying type. This isn't something you can see as a user, but it allows better file sharing between all the applications in the Adobe Creative Suite—Illustrator, Photoshop, InDesign, and Acrobat—and support for OpenType fonts. The change significantly affects opening your older Illustrator files or sharing files with people using Illustrator 10 and earlier.

When you open an older file, you have the option of updating the text to the Illustrator CS format or leaving it in the older, legacy format. If you do not update the text, you can still see and print the text, but you cannot edit it. If you do update it, you will have difficulty sharing that file with people using an older version of Illustrator. In addition, updated text may lose some or all of its formatting. If the text in your old documents updates poorly, the best solution is often opening the file in the older version of Illustrator and then copying and pasting it into a new Illustrator CS file.

You do not have to update all of the text if you do not want to. If you open the file without updating and then want to edit some of the text, click on it with the **Type** tool. A dialog box opens with the option of updating only that text object, copying the text object, or canceling. If you copy it, the original text remains visible for reference but at an opacity of 40%, so it's easy to tell the two apart.

Adobe Illustrator

⚠ Saving this document in an older format may convert all type to point type and may disable some editing features when the document is read back in. Do you want to continue?

☐ Don't Show Again

[Yes]   [No]

A more serious problem happens if you export an Illustrator CS file containing text to a legacy format so someone with an older version of Illustrator can read your files. To share your Illustrator CS files with older versions of Illustrator, you must choose **File > Export** and save the file as an **Illustrator Legacy.ai** file. When you do, you will receive a warning that your text may be converted to **point text**, a phenomenon also know as **split paths**. Split path text looks approximately correct on the screen, but what was a long sentence is now several individual paths containing one to three letters each. This is very annoying to edit. If you are sharing files with someone using Illustrator 10 or earlier, all the text editing should be done using the older copy of Illustrator.

Now that you know your way around the Type tools, it's time to move on. These chapters only brush the surface of the world of typography that you will discover as you experiment and explore on your own.

10.

Pen and Point Tools

| When to Pen | Drawing with the Pen |
| Converting Anchor Points |
| Tracing Images | Continuing and Joining Paths |

---
chap_10

Illustrator CS
H·O·T CD-ROM

The Pen tool is the only Illustrator tool that has remained relatively unchanged from the earliest days of Illustrator. It hasn't changed because its function is fundamental to the operation of Illustrator. The Pen tool gives you direct control over the points and handles that define each path on the artboard. Every shape you have drawn so far, even shapes that you have scaled, sheared, and otherwise transformed could have been drawn using nothing but the Pen tool.

That said, Illustrator's other tools exist because drawing complex shapes with the pen alone can be tedious and difficult. So the question is: "When to pen and when not to pen?" The exercises in this chapter will teach you what the Pen tool can do, but how often you use the pen will be a matter of personal preference. The majority of Illustrator artists report that the pen is one of their most used tools, but some artists hardly use it at all.

When to Pen

The pen has two primary uses. First, the pen is often the tool of choice when you want to draw a complex shape that is not easily built from simple shapes the way you did in Chapter 4, "*Basic Shapes.*" You can choose the Pen tool and start drawing, or trace a scanned-in paper sketch, digital photograph, or CAD drawing. Second, it is the ideal tool to tweak a path or shape that doesn't look quite right. In Chapter 4, you used the Direct Selection tool to move points and their handles, but with the Pen tool you can add and remove points or handles along a path.

Two other notable benefits of the pen are that you choose the direction of the overall path, and you choose the number of points. The direction of a path is important in how it responds to brushes, effects, and interaction with other paths. The number of points is important because, in general, the fewer points that define a path, the cleaner a path appears. Paths with excessive points also take longer to print and can cause print errors on lower-end printers.

Open and Closed Paths

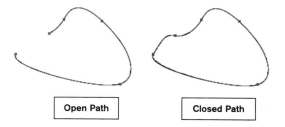

Open Path   Closed Path

There are two kinds of paths in Illustrator, open paths and closed paths. Open paths have different starting and ending anchor points. Closed paths have the same anchor point as the start and the end. You have already worked with both kinds, although you may not have realized it. The roads on the map were open paths–lines in that case. Rectangles, ellipses, polygons, and other shapes are closed paths. The distinction is important in the next few chapters because the Pen, Pencil, and Paintbrush tools let you create both open and closed paths depending on what effect you want in the final artwork.

I. ——————————Drawing with the Pen

The Pen tool icon is a nib (there's a handy Scrabble word for you), but this icon is misleading in that you cannot drag the Pen tool over the page and draw a path as you would with a real-world nib. Instead, think of the pen as a connect-the-dots tool where you place the dots and Illustrator does the connecting.

1. Transfer the **chap_10** folder to your hard drive from the **H•O•T CD-ROM**.

2. Open the **blank_pen.ai** file from the **chap_10** folder.

*This is simply a blank document with **View > Show Grid** and **View > Snap to Grid** turned on. Snap to Grid limits the placement of points and handles to gridlines, which will make following the rest of the exercise much easier.*

3. Select the **Pen** tool. Click the default stroke and fill button. This sets the stroke to **1 pt black** and the fill to **white**.

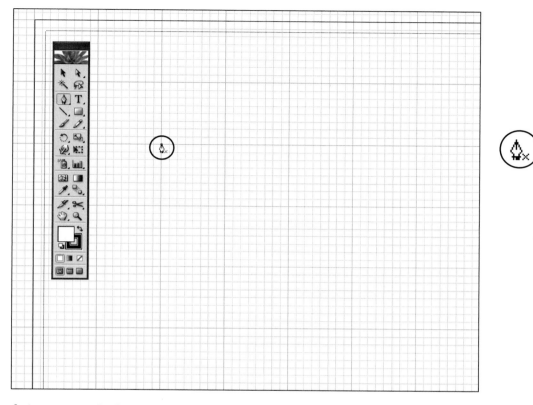

4. As you move the **Pen** tool over the artboard, a small x appears to the right of the **Pen** cursor. This indicates that your first click will begin a new path. Click once with the **Pen** tool at a point of the grid where two heavy gridlines intersect. This point is the origin and first anchor point for your new path.

Make sure you click and release without dragging the pen! Remember, you're creating a connect-the-dots shape rather than drawing a line.

NOTE | Pen Icons

The Pen icon sometimes doesn't behave as expected on slower, over-taxed machines. Don't worry if the Pen icon doesn't always appear the way described here. It's more important to know that the Pen tool can perform multiple functions whether or not the actual icon changes correctly.

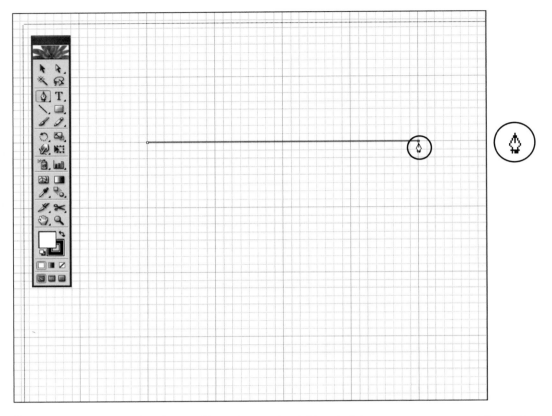

5. Move the **Pen** cursor four large grid sections to the right and click your mouse a second time. This defines the second anchor point, and Illustrator connects the two points with a straight line. Because you have Snap to Grid active, the line will be perfectly horizontal. You can also hold down the **Shift** key to constrain the pen to 45-degree and 90-degree lines.

After you click, the Pen tool cursor appears without the x, indicating that you are in the process of defining a path.

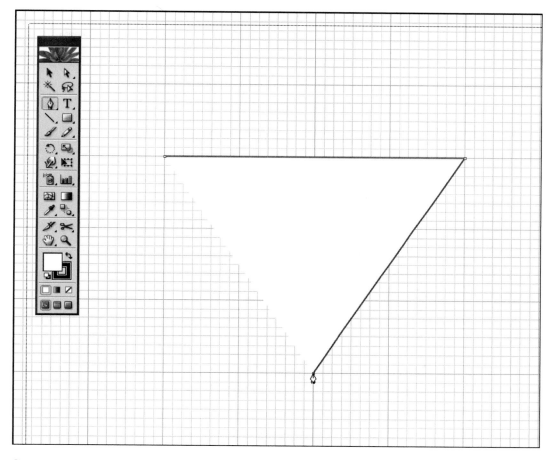

6. Move the **Pen** cursor three large grid sections down and two to the left. Click to define the third anchor point. Illustrator connects the second point to the third one and fills the space inside the shape with white.

The path was actually "filled" in Step 5, but when two points are connected by a straight line, you can't see any fill. As soon as the path bends, Illustrator will show the fill on the inside area of the line. Even though you can see a fill, this is still an open path with only two stroked segments. For more information on how Illustrator decides what is "inside," see Chapter 13, "Path Tools."

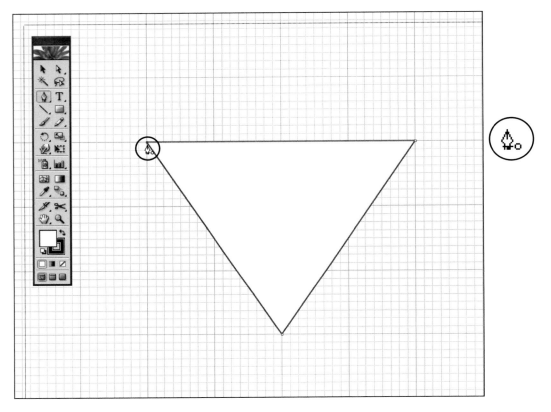

7. Bring your cursor over the first point you made. As you do, the **Pen** icon appears with a circle beside it to indicate that a click will close the path. Click the first point you made to close the triangle path. This does not create a new anchor point. Instead, it connects the point at the bottom of the triangle to the first one you made.

So why not use the Triangle (Polygon) tool? The Polygon tool would create an equilateral triangle that would not fit exactly on the grid. Of course, you could edit that triangle and make it fit, but the Pen tool let you create exactly what you wanted—a triangle three units high by four units wide.

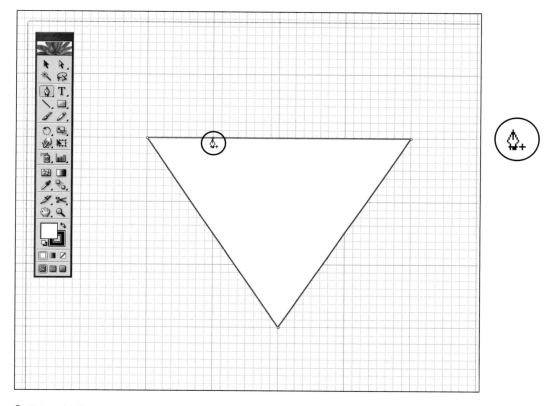

8. Bring the **Pen** cursor over the top, horizontal line where it intersects with the first heavy gridline. As you move over the line, the icon appears with a plus sign next to it. Click once on the line, and a new point is added to the path.

By now, you can see the Pen tool is context-sensitive. If you click a selected path, the tool assumes you want to add a point rather than create a new path. If you make a mistake and want to remove a point, simply click it with the Pen tool, and it is deleted from the path. When you bring the Pen cursor close to a point on a selected path, the Pen icon appears with a minus sign next to it, indicating that a click will delete the point.

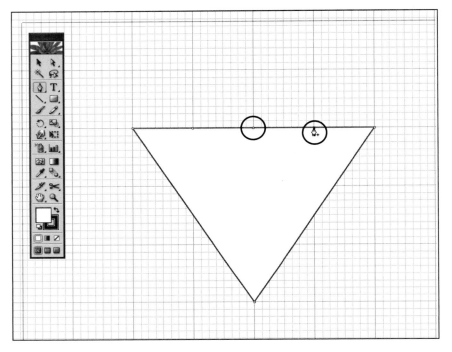

9. Add two more points to the top section of the path so that there is one at each large gridline.

10. Save the file and keep it open for the next exercise.

NOTE | Add and Remove Point Pen Tools

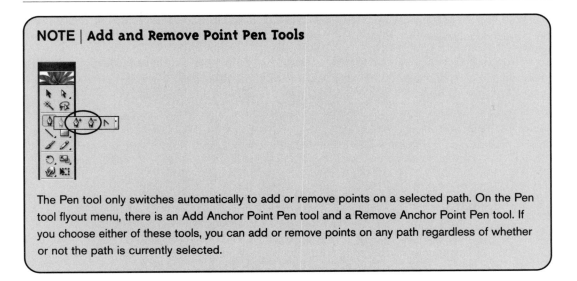

The Pen tool only switches automatically to add or remove points on a selected path. On the Pen tool flyout menu, there is an Add Anchor Point Pen tool and a Remove Anchor Point Pen tool. If you choose either of these tools, you can add or remove points on any path regardless of whether or not the path is currently selected.

2. ————————Converting Anchor Points

Creating paths by clicking with the Pen tool, as you did in Exercise 1, is only half the story with the Pen tool. In this exercise, you will take the points you created in Exercise 1 and add the direction handles needed to make curving lines and complex shapes.

1. Open the file **blank_pen.ai** or continue from Exercise 1.

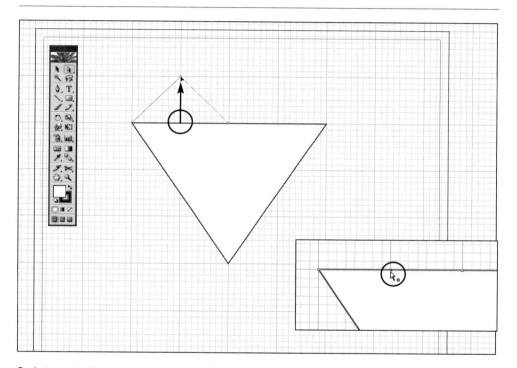

2. Select the **Direct Selection** tool. Click the triangle where the top line intersects the first heavy gridline (circled above). Drag the anchor point up to the next heavy gridline. The path is changed, and Illustrator adjusts the fill to cover the new area.

When you click to select the anchor point, it should appear as a filled blue dot with unfilled blue dots on either side. If does not, click anywhere outside the triangle to deselect the path and then try selecting the point again.

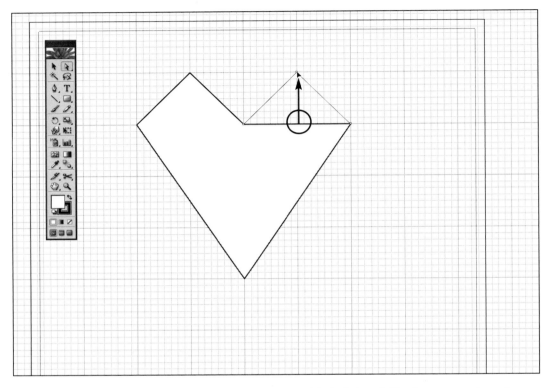

3. Repeat Step 2 for the fourth anchor point from the left (circled above). You have created a rather ungraceful heart.

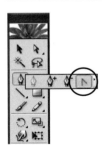

4. On the **Toolbox**, select the **Convert Anchor Point** tool. Instead of controlling points, as the **Pen** tools do, the **Convert Anchor Point** tool controls direction handles.

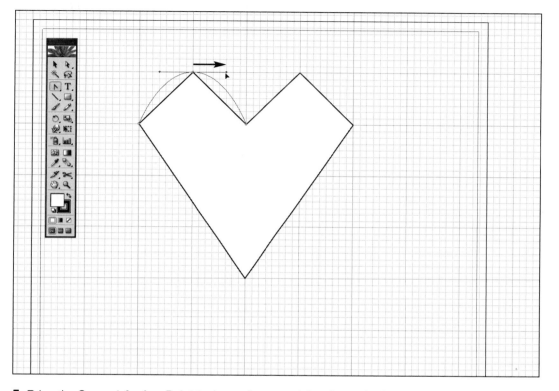

5. Bring the **Convert Anchor Point** tool over the upper-left point on the heart. Drag from the point horizontally to the right. As you drag, two handles extend from the anchor point, and a preview of the new curved path appears in blue. Drag right five small gridlines and release the mouse button.

*The Convert Anchor Point tool converted the anchor point into an smooth anchor point with equal-length handles. Because it is a smooth anchor point, the path follows a smooth curve as it passes through the point. Because the handles are equal, the degree of curve will be equal on both sides of the point. If you make a mistake and want to redo the handles, you can choose **Edit > Undo** or simply click once on the anchor point with the Convert Anchor Point tool, and it will convert back to a corner point with no handles.*

NOTE | Direction Matters

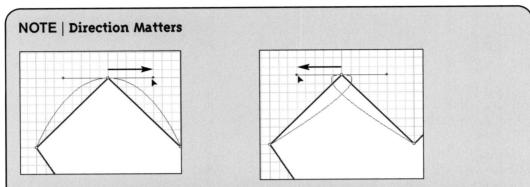

The direction you drag the handle is critical and frustrates many people until they understand it. When you pull a handle out from a corner point and convert it to a smooth point, the handle under your cursor curves the path segment between the point you are editing and the next point along the path. While you do this, a mirror image handle extends in the opposite direction and curves the path segment between the point you are editing and the previous point on the path. The two handles look identical, and you adjust both handles at the same time, but each one controls a specific part of the path. Since you created the path in a clockwise direction, you must drag the handles clockwise to curve the path outward (shown above on the left). Pulling the handle to the left (counter-clockwise) would create a curve that crossed its own path (shown above on the right). It would be handy if Illustrator could show you which way you made the path, in case you forget, but it cannot.

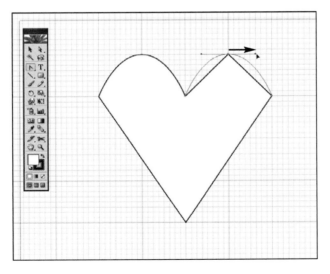

6. Repeat Step 5 to create a second curved top of the heart-shape.

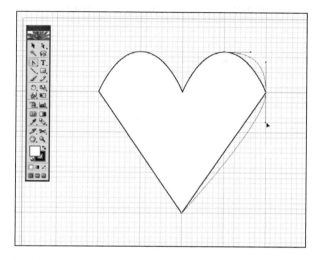

7. With the **Convert Anchor Point** tool, convert the right side anchor point to smooth points by dragging the right side anchor down five small gridlines.

Note that this adds more curvature to the top of the heart as well as curving the bottom. Since you created a handle on both sides of the right-side point, you affected the curve on both sides of the point.

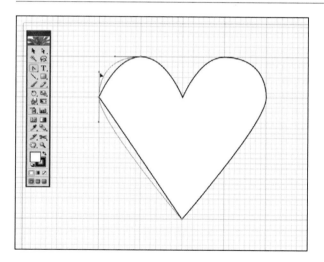

8. With the **Convert Anchor Point** tool, convert the left side anchor point to smooth points by dragging the right side anchor up five small gridlines.

You must pull the handle up on the left side of the heart because you built the path in a clockwise direction.

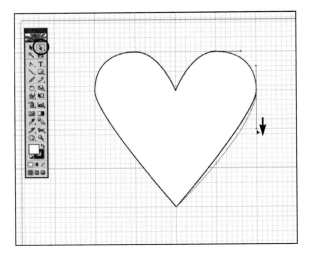

9. Select the **Direct Selection** tool. Drag the lower handle on right side down three more gridlines so it is on the heavy gridline. You now have a smooth point with unequal length handles. The curves on either side of the point are no longer symmetrical, but they still move smoothly through the point because the two handles still lie along a straight line, tangent to the curve. You are only adjusting the lower handle, so the curve of the top of the heart is unaffected.

The Direct Selection tool can only adjust a handle that already exists, so you must create the handle with one of the Pen tools before you edit it with the Direct Selection tool.

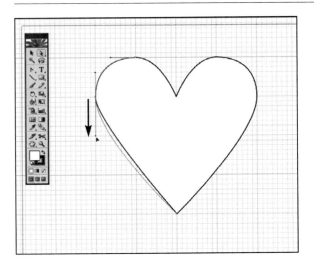

10. Repeat Step 9 for the left side of the heart by dragging the lower handle down to the heavy gridline.

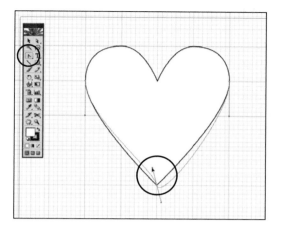

11. Select the **Convert Anchor Point** tool. Drag a handle out of the bottom point one gridline left and four gridlines up. You created another equal-length smooth point, but because one handle is inside the curving path and the other is outside, the result is an S-shape.

Clearly a smooth point is not what you want for the bottom of the heart, but the Convert Anchor Point tool will always create an equal-length smooth point when you first drag the handles. What you have done is set the handle for the part of the curve on one side and ignored the effect on the other side.

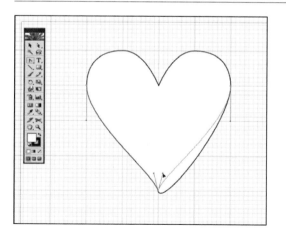

12. With the **Convert Anchor Point** tool still chosen, drag the right handle up to mirror the left one.

In Step 9, you adjusted a handle with the Direct Selection tool. In this step, you must use the Convert Anchor Point tool because you are converting the smooth point—where both handles always point in opposite directions—to a corner point. Corner point handles are totally independent of each other, so you can make curving paths that meet at sharp corners.

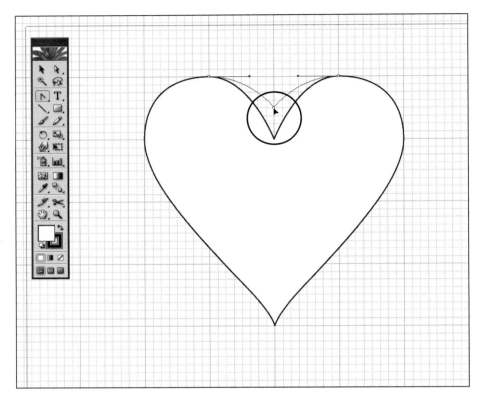

13. Hold down the **Ctrl** key (Windows) or the **Cmd** key (Mac) to temporarily switch your tool to the **Direct Selection** tool. Drag the upper-middle point on the heart up.

Holding down Ctrl or Cmd switches to the last selection tool you used. Since you used the Direct Selection tool in Steps 9 and 10, you get the Direct Selection tool now. If you had most recently used the Selection tool, then holding down Ctrl or Cmd would have switched to the Selection tool.

14. If you're in a romantic mood, fill the heart with red. Save and close the file.

If you had a really clear image of the heart in your mind before you began, you could have made almost the entire heart by creating all six anchor points and their handles when you initially created the path with the Pen tool. As you'll see in the next exercise, you can create both anchor points and handles without switching tools when you first define a point or path.

NOTE | Point Types

Now that you are precisely customizing anchor points on a path, it may be helpful to review the kinds of anchor points and how they are used. All of these shapes were created using the Pen tools.

Five Types of Anchor Points

Corner Points	Use
No handles	Sharp corners where two straight lines meet
One handle	Where a curve meets a straight line
Two handles	Where two curved lines meet at a sharp point

Smooth Points	Use
Equal-length handles	Symmetrical curves
Unequal-length handles	Asymmetrical curves

3. _____Tracing an Image

In the previous two exercises, you defined a path as a series of points and then added handles to those points to create the exact curves you wanted. Real mastery of the Pen tool comes when you can do both tasks at once. In this exercise, you will use the pen to trace a photograph and create both curved and straight segments as you draw the shape.

1. Open the file **highway.ai** from the **chap_10** folder.

2. Select the **Pen** tool. On the **Toolbox**, set the stroke to **black** and the fill to **none**.

3. At the top center of the sign, click to place the origin anchor point but hold the mouse button down. Now drag to the right and slightly down. As you do, the **Pen** tool will temporarily act as a **Convert Anchor Point** tool, and you will make this anchor point into a smooth point.

There will not be any blue preview of the line because there is only one point so far, and it takes at least two points to define a path. A mirror image handle also extends away from your cursor. Ignore this handle for now.

4. Click and hold on the next peak of the highway symbol. Now drag slightly up and away. The path between the two points will curve and follow the top of the highway symbol. Now for the tricky part. The handle under your cursor is for the next segment of the path—which you can't see yet because you haven't placed a third point—but it's mirror image is controlling the curve that follows the top of the highway sign. Move the handle under your cursor to adjust the mirror image handle and fit the curved path to the top of the sign.

5. The next segment of the highway symbol is straight, so simply click and release the mouse button at the next point on the symbol.

There is now an unwanted bulge at the previous point. To fix it, you need to get rid of the handle and change that point into a one-handle corner point.

6. Move the **Pen** tool away from the path you are creating. Hold down the **Alt** key (Windows) or the **Option** key (Mac) to temporarily change the **Pen** tool into the **Convert Anchor Point** tool. While holding down the **Alt** or **Option** key, drag the unwanted handle back to the point until it disappears. Release the mouse and the **Alt** or **Option** key.

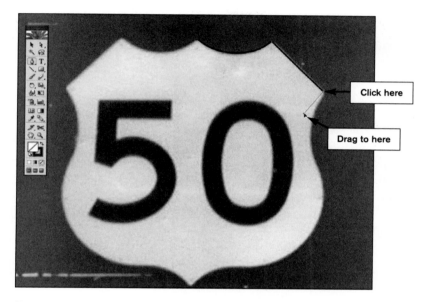

7. Bring the **Pen** tool over the last point on the path. Drag a handle out from this anchor point.

Clicking an endpoint of an open path with the Pen tool resumes building the path.

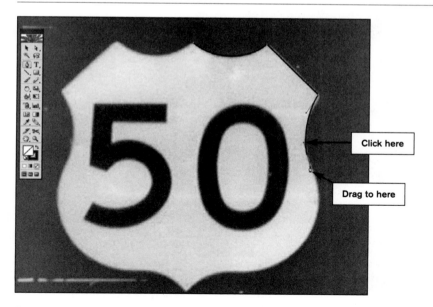

8. Continue the curve of the sign by placing anchor points with the Pen tool and dragging handles out of them before releasing the mouse button. Follow the curve of the sign as closely as you can.

Click here

Drag to here

9. Continue the path.

Drag to here

Click here

10. Near the bottom of the sign the symbol has a S-curve. Place the anchor point where the curve reverses direction (the middle of the S) and drag the handle out to match the curve.

11. Place an anchor point on the center bottom point of the sign and drag a a handle to down to match the right side of the curve. Without releasing the mouse button, hold down the **Alt** key (Windows) or the **Option** key (Mac) and drag the handle under your cursor upward. This will be a direction handle for the next section of the line.

Holding down the Alt or Option key changed the pen into a Convert Anchor Point tool, just like in Step 6, except you did it in one step rather than two.

12. Continue placing points and dragging handles up the left side of the symbol to mirror what you did on the right side up to the straight line.

TIP | How Many Points?

One of the challenges of the Pen tool is that you must select how many points to place and where to place them. For the smoothest looking artwork, the fewer points you place, the better. Too few, however, and you cannot match the line closely to complex curves. Try placing points every place the line changes direction abruptly (a corner), makes an S-curve, or curves more than 90 degrees. If you find that adjusting one part of a curve consistently messes up another part, you probably don't have enough points.

13. You don't want a handle for the next segment. On the other side, you fixed the unwanted handle after you drew the line, but there is a shortcut. Click once with the **Pen** tool on the point you just placed. The extra handle disappears. Now click to place a point and complete the straight line.

14. You now need a handle for the final curve. Bring the **Pen** tool over the last point you made and drag out a handle.

15. Try closing the path at the origin by clicking on the origin point and dragging a handle. Unfortunately, this alters the very first handle you set in this exercise because Illustrator will make the origin into a smooth point.

16. Choose **Edit > Undo** to remove the point. Hold down the **Alt** key (Windows) or the **Option** key (Mac), click the top-center point, and drag a handle. Because you held down the modifier key, you create a handle pointing back to the previous point, but the first handle you created remains untouched.

It looks a bit weird though. As you drag away from the point, no handle appears under your cursor. Only the mirror image handle appears onscreen.

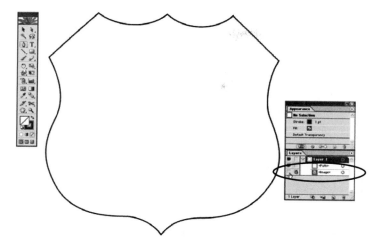

17. Choose **Window > Layers** to see the **Layers** palette. Hide the **<Image>** of the highway sign to see your work.

18. Save the file and close it.

Since your placement of points and handles is slightly different on the right and left sides of the highway sign, the resulting sign will have a slightly asymmetrical, hand-drawn look. In the next exercise, you'll see how to create perfect symmetry with the Pen tool and the Join command.

TIP | Try More Than Once

Don't hesitate to make several attempts at drawing a shape with the pen. Drag each one off to the side of the artboard or put it on a layer and hide it. Select and edit the best result or even mix and match pieces you like from different ones. There is no "correct way" to trace a shape and create a path. Rest assured that all new Illustrator users spend a lot of time practicing with the Pen tool. At first it seems counterintuitive and like a bizarre way to draw shapes. Once you have done it for a while, it actually becomes second nature, but it does require practice to get to the point where you don't have to think really hard about each move!

MOVIE | sign.mov

To view the complex steps of this exercise are performed, watch **sign.mov** located in the **movies** folder on the **H·O·T CD-ROM**.

4. ——————Continuing and Joining Paths

When creating paths with the Pen tool, there are times you need to combine two paths. You can do this with the Pen or the Join command. Join can either connect two points by creating a line between them or merge two points that overlap. The Join command is a great complement to the Pen tool. As you will see in this exercise, Join is ideal for creating complex symmetrical shapes.

1. Open the file **join.ai** from the **chap_10** folder.

2. Select the **Pen** tool. On the **Toolbox**, set the stroke to **black** and the fill to **white**.

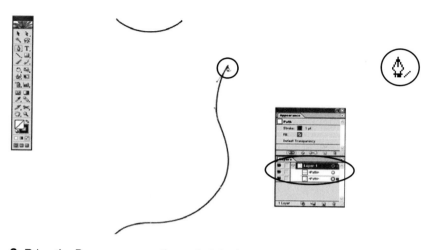

3. Bring the **Pen** cursor over the end of the longer path. The x next to the **Pen** icon changes to a /. Click the **Pen** tool on the end of the path. Instead of starting a new path, the long path highlights with the last point selected.

The next time you click with the Pen tool, it will continue the path. Before going on to Step 4, note that there are two paths on the Layers palette.

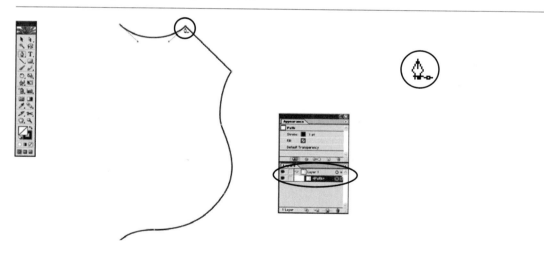

4. Bring the **Pen** cursor over the end of the short path. The icon changes again to show a small chain. Click the endpoint of the small path. The two open paths are now combined into one, and there is only one path on the **Layers** palette.

This technique works to join any two open paths, but when you simply want to connect to points with a straight segment, there is a faster way.

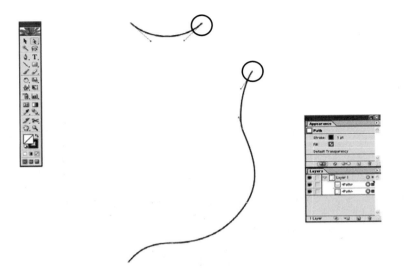

5. Choose **Edit > Undo** to remove the segment and get two paths again. The endpoints of each path are still selected.

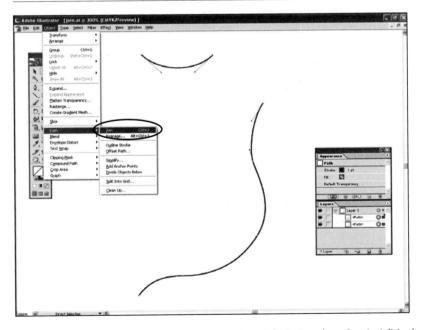

6. Choose **Object > Path > Join** or press **Ctrl+J** (Windows) or **Cmd+J** (Mac). The two points are joined by a straight segment.

NOTE | Joining Across Groups or Layers

Adobe Illustrator

To join, you must select two open endpoints. If they are not on the same path, they cannot be on text paths nor inside graphs, and if both of them are grouped, they must be in the same group.

☐ Don't Show Again

[OK]

You can join two open paths that are on different layers or are part of a group. You can't join paths that are in separate groups, however. When paths on separate layers are joined, they become a single path, which appears on only one of the two layers. A single path cannot exist on two layers at once. Likewise, when you join two paths, and one is in a group, the new combined path is made part of that group. This is why the joined paths cannot be in separate groups—Illustrator wouldn't know which original group to use for the new combined path. For a review of groups, see Chapter 4, "*Basic Shapes*." For a review of layers, see Chapter 7, "*Layers and Appearances*."

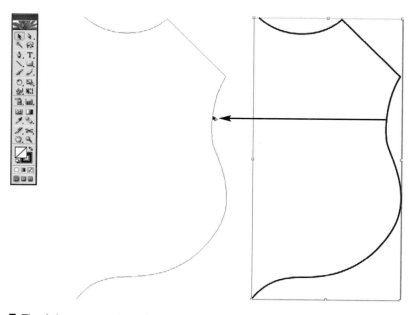

7. The **Join** command can be more complicated when points overlap. Select the **Selection** tool. Hold down the **Alt** key (Windows) or the **Option** key (Mac) to copy the path while you drag it to the left.

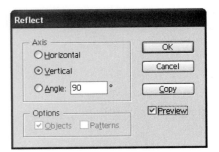

8. Choose **Object > Transform > Reflect** and select **Vertical** to reflect the copied path vertically. Click **OK**.

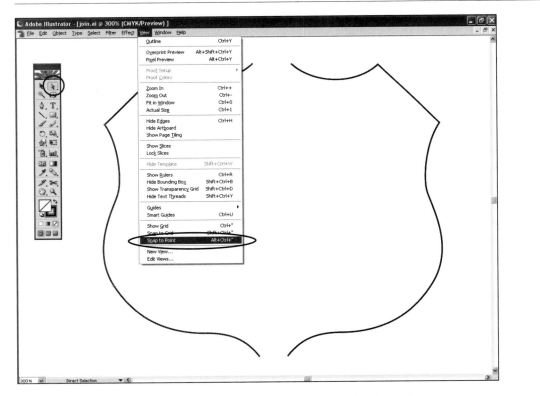

9. Choose **View > Snap to Point** and then choose the **Direct Selection** tool.

Snap to Point is a bit different from Snap to Grid in that the cursor, not the object, will snap to a point. If you are dragging a single point with the Direct Selection tool or dragging an entire path by the endpoint, the Direct Selection tool will "snap" directly on top of a point when it gets within two pixels.

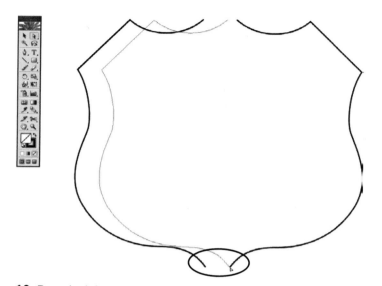

10. Drag the left section of the sign by dragging the bottom point to the right to overlap the endpoints. Because you have **Snap to Point** active, the two halves should snap exactly into place with the endpoints of each side overlapping.

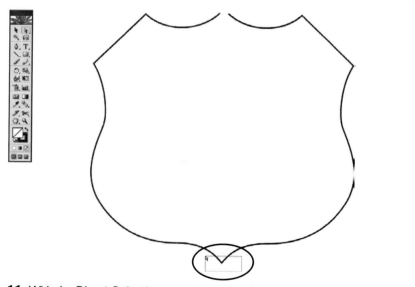

11. With the **Direct Selection** tool, drag a box around the overlapping points. This selects both endpoints and nothing else. Note that they look like a single point because one is exactly above the other. You might see all four handles, however.

12. Choose **Object > Path > Join**. If you overlapped the points, they merge into a single point, and you see a dialog box asking whether you want the single point to be a corner or smooth point. Select **Corner** to select a corner point. Click **OK**.

Make sure you see the dialog box if your intention is merging two points into one. If you do not see this dialog box, the two points weren't overlapping, and Illustrator joined the points by adding a small straight line that may be too small for you to see. This might look okay at first, but it can be annoying later when you try to edit the point and discover it is actually two points.

13. The top two points need merging, too, but they must both move to a center point. Select both points by dragging a box around both with the **Direction Selection** tool.

Average

Axis
○ Horizontal
○ Vertical
⊙ Both

[OK]
[Cancel]

14. Choose **Object > Path > Average**. Select **Both** for the **Axis** and click **OK**. Both points are moved to a position between the original points.

15. The shape looks complete, but there are still two overlapping points at the top rather than a single point. Choose **Object > Path > Join**. Choose **Corner** for the **Point Type** and click **OK**.

16. Save the file.

TIP | Average and Join at Once

Averaging and joining two points is so common that there is an undocumented command to do both steps at once with no dialog boxes. Select the two points and press **Alt+Ctrl+Shift+J** (Windows) or **Cmd+Option+Shift+J** (Mac) to average and join as a corner point in one slick step. The new point is always a corner point.

The pen is mighty. It gives you more direct control over your artwork than any other single tool. This is why so many Illustrator professionals name the pen as their most used tool. Next up, tools that place the points for you so you can let your creativity flow: the Pencil and Line tools.

II.

Pencil and Line Segment Tools

| Pencil Tool | Smooth and Eraser Tools |
| Line Segment Tool | Arc Tool |
| Spiral Tool |

chap_11

Illustrator CS
H•O•T CD-ROM

Illustrator's Pencil and Line Segment tools are fun and easy to use. You simply select the tool you want and start drawing. One of the best features of the Pencil tool is that as you drag the tool to draw the path, Illustrator decides where to put all the points and handles so you don't have to. This is in contrast to the Pen tool you used in Chapter 10, "*Pen and Point Tools*," where you have to decide the location of every anchor point and handle! The trade-off for this simplicity is that the resulting path may not be what you had in mind. Conveniently, the Pencil tools let you easily edit your work and get the right final look.

The Line Segment tools create shapes you could also draw with the pencil or pen, but they are big time-savers. Drawing arcs, spirals, and grids by hand can be tedious. With the Line Segment tools, they are a snap.

I. ──────────Pencil Tool

Unlike the Pen tool, which requires some practice and planning, the Pencil tool works just like icon indicates. Select the Pencil tool, drag across the artboard and a new path appears. This makes the Pencil tool a great choice for freehand illustration when you don't want anything to hinder the creative process. This pencil is also a great tool for tracing photos or scanned images.

1. Copy the **chap_11** folder from the **H•O•T CD-ROM** to your hard drive. Open the file **51_Chevy.ai**.

2. Select the **Zoom** tool and drag it around the windows of the truck to zoom in to that area.

TIP | Techniques for Tracing

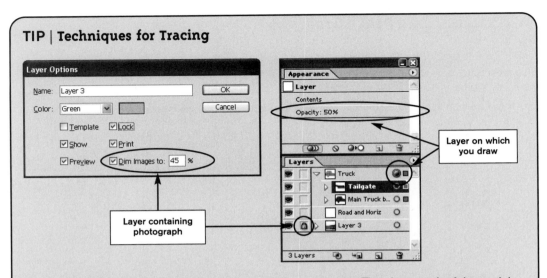

Layer on which you draw

Layer containing photograph

The file **51_Chevy.ai** uses two techniques to make tracing easier. The photograph of the truck is on a locked layer that has its opacity for its images set to 45%. Locking the layer containing the object you are tracing prevents you from accidentally selecting the image and moving it while you are working. Dimming the image is helpful with photos since it makes the borders between areas of rich color much easier to see.

The second technique isn't so intuitive. The entire layer you will draw *on* has a transparency setting of 50% opacity. This means you can see through your artwork as you create it. If you trace with the layer set to 100% opacity, the photo underneath becomes completely obscured as you work (unless you trace with **View > Outline** turned on). Opacity is discussed at the end of Chapter 7, "*Layers and Appearances*." **51_Chevy.ai** will open with these features already active, but you may want to try them for other tracing projects.

3. On the **Toolbox**, set the stroke to **black** and the fill to **none**.

The quickest way to do this is to click the small default fill and stroke icon to the lower left of the Stroke and Fill squares and then change the fill to none.

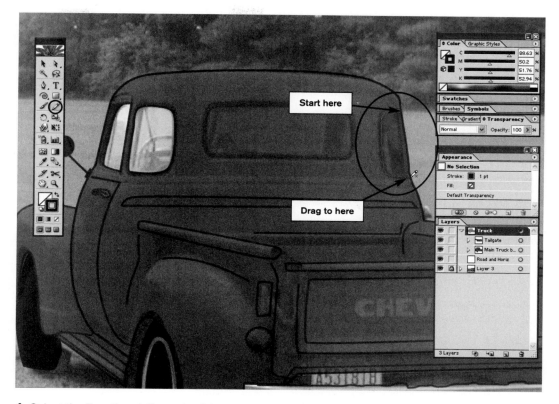

4. Select the **Pencil** tool. Trace the right corner window on the truck cab by starting at the top right of the window and dragging the **Pencil** tool around in a "C" shape using the photo as a guide. Release the mouse button when you get to the end of the window.

The "5-window cab" was a factory option on the 1951 Chevy pickups and is a favorite among vintage truck enthusiasts.

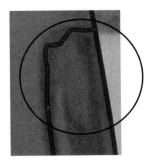

5. Unless you are a virtuoso with the **Pencil** tool, parts of the path won't match the photo as well as you would like. Edit part of the path by dragging the **Pencil** tool over that part of the path again. The original path is redrawn to match.

This easy redraw is possibly the Pencil tool's greatest feature. It lets you draw without worrying about making it perfect the first time. Once you have the basic shape, you zoom in on any problem areas and redraw them as much as you need. The Pencil tool can edit any Illustrator path—even if you created it with other tools such as the Rectangle, Ellipse, or Pen tools. The path must be selected before you start editing with the Pencil tool.

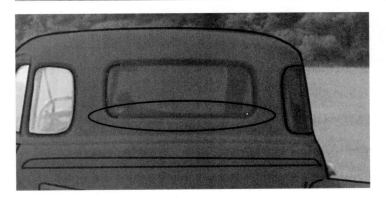

6. The **Pencil** tool can also continue an existing path. The trace for the truck's rear window is already started. Hold down the **Ctrl** key (Windows) or the **Cmd** key (Mac) to temporarily change the **Pencil** tool into a **Selection** tool. Click the path on the rear window once with the temporary **Selection** tool to select it and then release the **Ctrl** or **Cmd** key. Bring the **Pencil** tool over the last anchor point on the lower end of the path and start dragging. Release the mouse button when you get to the bottom-right corner of the window.

Continuing a path lets you take breaks as you draw so you don't have to draw the entire shape at once. The path must be selected before you extend it—the same way a path must be selected before you edit it, as you did in Step 4.

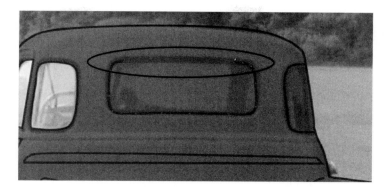

7. Continue your path with the **Pencil** tool around to the top right of the rear window. Hold down the **Alt** key (Windows) or the **Option** key (Mac) before you release the mouse button. Release the mouse button while holding the modifier key. The endpoints of the path are now connected with a straight line.

If you end a pencil path very close to the beginning of the path, it will close automatically. The modifier key guarantees that the path closes by connecting the two endpoints with a straight segment. The actual top of the window is slightly curved, so feel free to edit with the Pencil tool if you wish.

8. Select both new windows with the **Selection** tool and set the fill to **white**.

NOTE | Fill on an Open Path

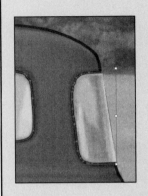

When you made the corner window on the truck, you did not close the path (meaning the starting point and the ending point are not the same anchor point). The inner area filled with white anyway. Filled open paths have an interesting visual effect. In this case it works well for the window which wraps around the corner of the cab out of view.

9. Select the **Hand** tool and pan over to the truck tailgate to see the taillights.

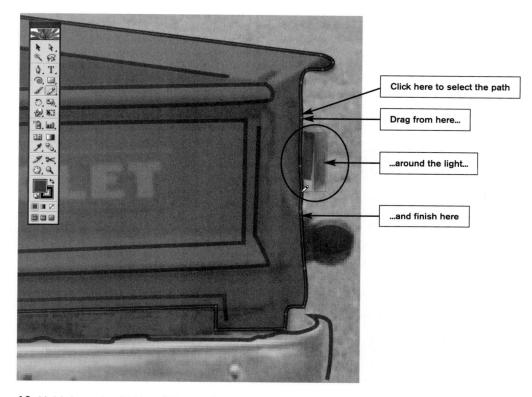

Click here to select the path

Drag from here...

...around the light...

...and finish here

10. Hold down the **Ctrl** key (Windows) or the **Cmd** key (Mac) to temporarily change the **Pencil** tool into a **Selection** tool. Click the edge of the truck bed to select the path and then release the **Ctrl** or **Cmd** key. Bring the **Pencil** tool over the path where the taillight should go and start dragging to the right, then down, then left, and finally down along the original path. The path is redrawn to bulge out and include the taillight.

This is no different than editing a line the way you did on the window, but it doesn't immediately occur to most people as a possibility. It helps to drag along the original path for a short distance before and after the part you want added to ensure the original path is edited instead of drawing a new path.

11. Save the file and keep it open for the next exercise.

MOVIE | trace.mov

To see the steps of this complicated exercise performed, watch the movie **trace.mov** located in the **movies** folder of the **H•O•T CD-ROM**.

2. ——————————Smooth and Eraser Tools

The Smooth and Eraser tools are alternate ways to edit a path. The Eraser tool function is simple—it erases paths. The Smooth tool is more interesting in that it smoothes and simplifies paths and gives your artwork a cleaner look.

1. Open the file **51_Chevy.ai** or continue from Exercise 1.

2. Select the **Zoom** tool and drag a box around the truck's rear bumper so it fills the screen. Select the bumper by clicking on it with the **Selection** tool.

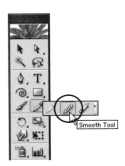

3. Click and hold on the **Pencil** tool until the flyout menu appears. Select the **Smooth** tool from the flyout menu.

4. Drag the **Smooth** tool over the long top section of the bumper following the line of the bumper. The rough path will smooth out. Repeat dragging the **Smooth** tool over any sections that don't smooth adequately on the first pass.

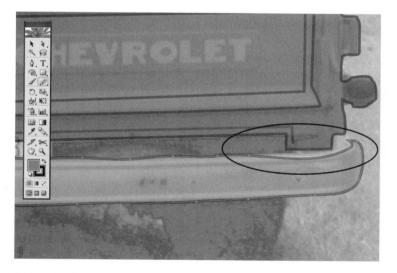

Using the Smooth tool may look the same as editing a path with the Pencil tool, but there are two key differences between smoothing and editing. The Smooth tool attempts to simplify the path by removing unnecessary points as it smoothes. When you edit with the Pencil tool, the number of points may decrease, increase, or stay the same. The Smooth tool can also move points, but it cannot make radical changes to a path. Some edits must be made with Pencil, Pen, or Direct Selection tools. The rear bumper of the truck contains a section (circled above) that is too far from the desired path to correct with the Smooth tool.

NOTE | Simplify Path

Another technique to smooth and simplify your paths is to select the path you want smoothed and choose **Object > Path > Simplify**. Check **Preview** and **Show Original** to see both the original path and the smoothed version on screen. Then adjust the sliders for **Curve Precision** and **Angle Threshold** until the smoothed version looks the way you want. Click **OK** and the smooth version replaces the original.

5. Select the **Hand** tool and pan over to the running board. Zoom in with the **Zoom** tool to see it better if needed.

6. Select the **Direct Selection** tool. Direct select the longer accent line on the running board.

The lines on the running board are grouped, so if you used the regular Selection tool, you would have selected the entire group.

7. Click and hold on the **Smooth** tool until the flyout menu appears. Select the **Eraser** tool from the flyout menu.

8. Drag with the **Eraser** tool over the unwanted part of the line extending past the running board.

The path must be selected for the eraser to function.

9. While the line is still selected, drag the **Eraser** tool over a short section of the line to cut it into two lines. Hold down the **Ctrl** key (Windows) or the **Cmd** key (Mac) to temporarily switch the tool to the last-used selection tool (the **Direct Selection** tool in this case). Click the other accent line on the running board and release the modifier key. Drag the **Eraser** tool over a short section of this line, too.

*Like the Pencil tool, the Eraser tool also works on any path regardless of what tool created the path. You can even switch between the Pencil and Eraser tools on the fly by choosing the Pencil tool and then holding down the **Ctrl** key (Windows) or the **Cmd** key (Mac) to temporarily change the Pencil tool into the Eraser tool.*

10. Save the file and keep it open for the next exercise.

NOTE | Pencil and Smooth Tool Preferences

Pencil Tool Preferences

Tolerances

Fidelity: 2.5 pixels

Smoothness: 0 %

[OK]
[Cancel]
[Reset]

Options

☑ Keep selected

☑ Edit selected paths

Within: 12 pixels

Smooth Tool Preferences

Tolerances

Fidelity: 2.5 pixels

Smoothness: 25 %

[OK]
[Cancel]
[Reset]

Double-clicking the Pencil or Smooth tools on the Toolbox opens their preferences. They have similar preferences, so it makes sense to look at them together. Both tools let you adjust their **Fidelity** and **Smoothness**. Fidelity is how closely the final path resembles the actual path you dragged with the tool. A fidelity of 0 (zero) pixels creates a path that matches your mouse motion exactly—and results in every tiny bump in your mouse motion appearing in your art! The greater the number of pixels in your Fidelity setting, the more Illustrator can ignore small bends in the path you drag. Smoothness determines how much Illustrator will attempt to smooth and simplify your path. In general, the further to the right both settings are, the smoother the resulting path. The default settings for both the Pencil and Smooth tool are 2.5 for Fidelity but 0% and 25% respectively for Smoothness. The defaults work well for most people. Experiment with these settings if the tools aren't giving you the result you need.

The Pencil tool options are for editing paths with the Pencil tool. By keeping the path selected, you can edit a path immediately after you draw it without pausing to select it. The **Edit selected paths** check box is what allows the pencil to edit paths, and the **Within** setting decides how close you must be to the selected path to edit it rather than start a new path.

3. ————————Line Segment Tool

The Line Segment tool is a straightforward tool to create straight lines. Although there is nothing fancy about the Line Segment tool, sometimes it is the perfect tool for the job.

1. Open the file **51_Chevy.ai** or continue from Exercise 2.

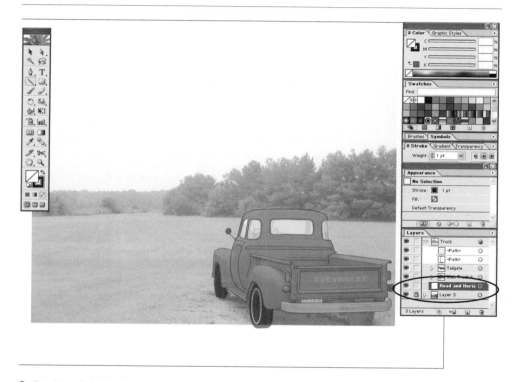

2. Double-click the **Hand** tool to see the entire page. Choose **Window > Layers** if the **Layers** palette is not visible. Click in the center of the **Road and Horiz** layer on the **Layers** palette to highlight it so the next object you create appears on that layer.

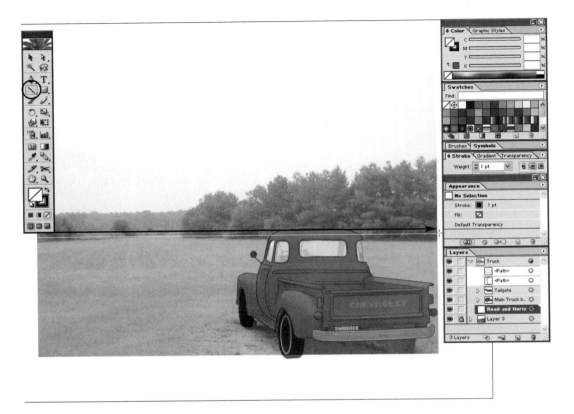

3. Select the **Line Segment** tool. Hold down the **Shift** key and drag with the **Line Segment** tool from the left to the right to add a horizon line to the layer.

The Line Segment tool uses the same modifiers you used in Chapter 4, "Basic Shapes." The Shift key constrains the Line Segment tool to 45- and 90-degree lines, and the Alt key (Windows) or the Option key (Mac) causes the Line Segment tool to draw out from the center in two directions at once.

4. Drag two more lines from the horizon to form a road for the truck and a vanishing point.

5. Save the file and keep it open for the next exercise.

TIP | Isometric Grids

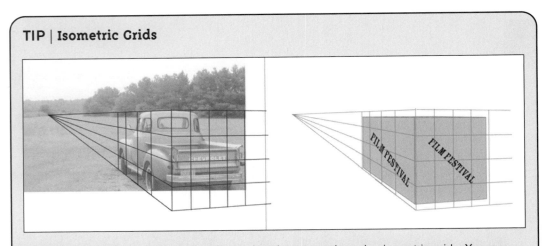

The Line Segment tool is ideal if you like to draw in perspective using isometric grids. You can create the standard 30-degrees isometric view or start with a photo or CAD diagram in the perspective you want. The above images were created by creating a new layer above the truck image and tracing a grid over it using the Line Segment tool. Once that grid was completed, the grid layer was locked and the truck was hidden. The crate was drawn on a third layer under the grid layer. While drawing the crate, the grid was used to determine the size of each part of the drawing so it was drawn in the same perspective as the truck. For example the crate is 3.5 gridlines high at the end closest to the viewer and the end farthest away.

4. ——————————Arc Tool

Sweeping arcs are easily made with the Pen tool, but the Arc tool is faster. The capability to modify the arc with keyboard keys makes it a better tool for experimenting with the exact look of the arc.

1. Open the file **51_Chevy.ai** or continue from Exercise 3. Double-click the **Hand** tool on the **Toolbox** to view the entire page. Choose **Select > Deselect** if you currently have any objects selected.

2. Click the **Eye** icon to hide the image on **Layer 3**. Drag the **Appearance** button on the **Truck** layer to the **Trash** to remove the 50% opacity on the truck. Now the truck is 100% opaque, and the truck, horizon, and road are the only art visible on the artboard. Finally, click in the middle of the **Road and Horiz** layer to highlight it so new art appears on that layer.

Opacity and appearances are discussed in Chapter 7, "Layers and Appearances."

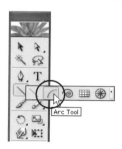

3. Click and hold on the **Line Segment** tool on the **Toolbox** until the flyout menu appears. Select the **Arc** tool from the flyout menu.

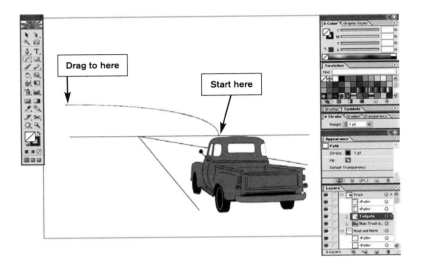

4. It's time to put some hills on the horizon. Put the cursor an the horizon and drag up and to the left, as shown above. The arc forms as you drag.

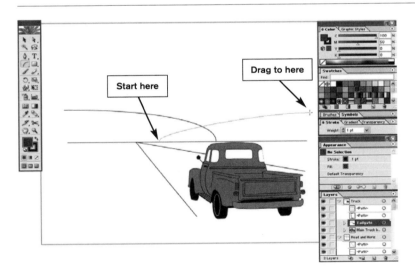

5. Put the cursor on the horizon and drag an arc to the right, as shown above, but before you release the mouse, press the **down arrow** key on your keyboard several times to flatten the arc. Release the mouse button to draw the arc. Choose **Select > Deselect** to deselect the arc.

The up arrow key will increase the bend in the arc. These keys are similar to the arrow keys changing the amount of roundness on the rounded rectangles you drew in Chapter 4, "Basic Shapes."

6. Make sure the **Fill** square is on top in the **Color** palette or **Toolbox** and then click the **Night Blue** swatch to set the fill color to **Night Blue**.

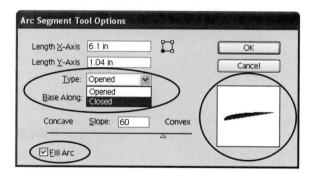

7. Double-click the **Arc** tool to see its options. Change the **Type** of arc to **Closed** and check the **Fill Arc** check box. Watch the preview window on the right side of the dialog box to see the effect of these two settings. Click **OK**.

Arcs can be drawn open, as the first two you made were, or closed where the ends of the arc are connected by two straight lines that meet at a right angle. The arc can have a fill of none, as is the default, or have a colored fill like any other shape.

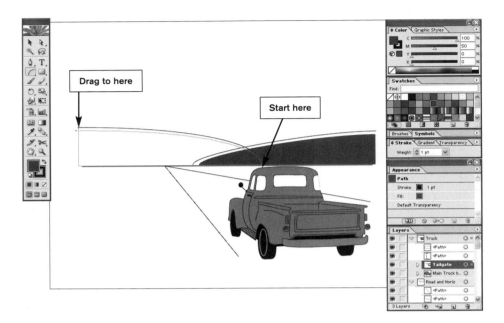

Drag to here

Start here

8. With the **Arc** tool, create two more arcs under the ones you created in Steps 4 and 5. These will be closed and filled since you changed the **Arc** tool options. The result is two solid hills in the distance with an accenting line above each one.

9. Save the file and keep it open for the next exercise.

NOTE | Arc Tool Modifier Keys

For a simple tool, the Arc tool has quite a few modifier keys you can use as you draw:

- Use the **up arrow** and **down arrow** keys to change the curve of the arc. (You used this in Step 5.)

- Press **C** to toggle between an open and closed arc.

- Press **F** to toggle between a convex and concave arc.

- Hold down **Alt** (Windows) or **Option** (Mac) to extend the arc from the center rather than an end.

- Hold down the **spacebar** to temporarily stop drawing and move the arc. Release the spacebar to continue drawing.

- Hold down **Shift** to freeze one axis of the arc while you adjust the other.

5. ——————————Spiral Tool

The Spiral tool is one of those very specific tools that don't get used very often but are huge timesavers under the right circumstances.

1. Open the file **51_Chevy.ai** or continue from Exercise 4. Double-click the **Hand** tool to view the whole page.

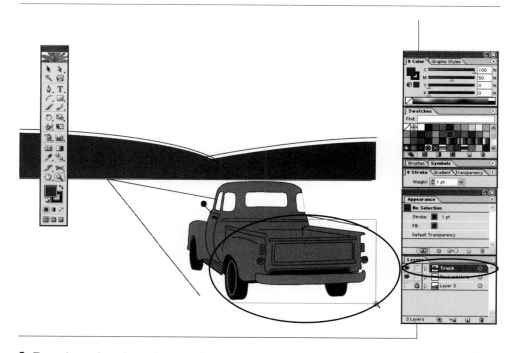

2. Zoom in on the tailgate by dragging a rectangular marquee around it. Click the **Truck** layer on the **Layers** palette to highlight it and make new art part of that layer.

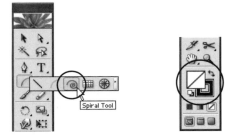

3. Click and hold on the **Line Segment tool** on the **Toolbox** and select the **Spiral** tool from the flyout. (The **Arc** tool might be visible in this spot from Exercise 4.) Set the stroke to **black** and the fill to **none** on the **Toolbox** or **Color** palette.

Spirals can be filled, too, which is great if you ever need to draw a Nautilus.

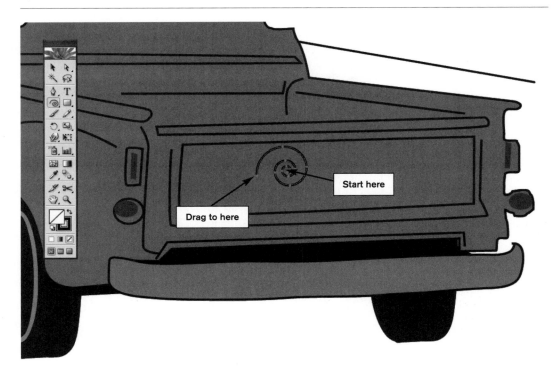

4. Put the cursor near the center of the tailgate and create a spiral by dragging to the left.

The center of the spiral is determined by where you first click. The open end of the spiral is set by the distance and direction you drag.

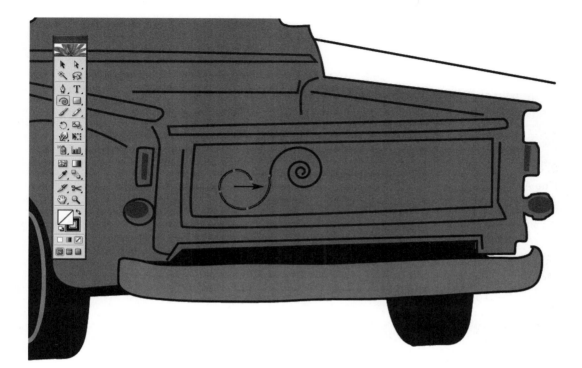

5. Move your cursor to the left and create other spiral by dragging to the right. Match the end of the new spiral with the end of the old one to form an "S" shape, as shown above, but do not release the mouse button. Press the **down arrow** key several times to decrease the number of turns of the spiral. Release the mouse when the spiral has only one complete turn.

The up and down arrow keys will increase or decrease the number of turns of the spiral from the inside out. The open end of the spiral always ends where you stop dragging and release the mouse button.

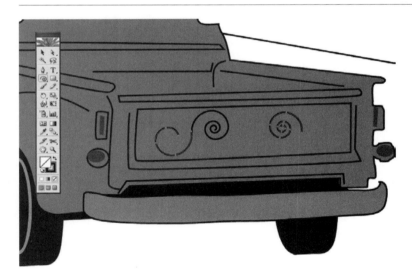

6. Click and release with the **Spiral** tool on the truck tailgate to see the settings for drawing a spiral. Change the **Style** to a clockwise spiral and click **OK**.

If you want to draw a spiral that winds in the other direction, you must change the spiral settings before you draw. But unlike the other Line Segment tools, there is no options dialog box for the Spiral tool. Notice that it says "Spiral" rather than "Spiral Options" on the dialog box. The only way to switch the direction of the spiral is to draw a spiral by clicking once and changing the settings. This is also the only way to switch the spiral direction back.

7. Press **Delete** or **Backspace** on your keyboard to remove the spiral you made by clicking with the **Spiral** tool. (This was just made to reverse the spiral direction). Drag the **Spiral** tool to the right and use the **up arrow** key to create a large spiral with many turns. Drag the **Spiral** tool to the left and use the **down arrow** key to create a small spiral with only one turn.

You could have copied and reflected the first spirals to achieve a similar effect, but drawing fresh spirals results in a more hand-drawn look.

8. Save the file.

MOVIE | grid_tools.mov

There are two tools on the Line Segment tool flyout menu designed for creating rectangular and circular (polar) grids. To see these tools in action, check out the movie **grid_tools.mov** online at **http://www.lynda.com/books/hot/illcs/movies/**.

That's it. Now that you have the Pen, Pencil, and Line Segment tools at your disposal, you can decide if you want precision anchor point control or free-form creativity.

12.

Paintbrush Tool

Calligraphic Brushes	Art Brushes
Custom Art Brushes	Pattern Brushes
Scatter Brushes	Brush Libraries

chap_12

Illustrator CS
H•O•T CD-ROM

In the earliest versions of Illustrator, the Paintbrush tool was little more than a way to draw a fat line. You could paint a pattern perhaps, but not much more. The Paintbrush tool has come a long way since then. Today it is a powerful calligraphic tool with support for pressure-sensitive pen tablets, a tool for reproducing and morphing artwork, a system for creating complex borders and woven patterns, and a tool for scattering objects throughout your artwork.

Part of the beauty of the Paintbrush tool is that you can use it with almost no training and get great results, but there are enough options and customization possibilities to keep you grinning for a long time. The brushes are organized into four categories: calligraphic, art, pattern, and scatter. They are a blast to use, so let's get going!

I.————————Calligraphic Brushes

Calligraphic brushes are the most intuitive of all the Illustrator brush types. They resemble a real paint-brush the way the Pencil tool resembles a real pencil. Select the brush you want and start painting. The calligraphic brushes offer many more options than the pencil. Adjusting these options lets you produce a dizzying array of artistic effects.

1. Copy the **chap_12** folder from the **H•O•T CD-ROM** to your hard drive.

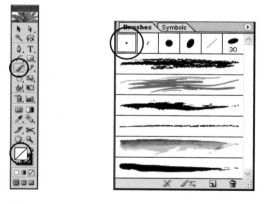

2. Choose **File > New**. Create a **Letter** size **CMYK Color** document called **Highway Sign**.

3. Select the **Paintbrush** tool and make sure the **Fill** square on the **Toolbox** is set to **None**. Choose **Window > Brushes** to bring the **Brushes** palette forward. The **Brushes** palette is grouped with the **Symbols** and **Graphic Styles** palettes below the **Color, Swatch**, and **Stroke** palettes you have already used. Click the **3 pt Round** brush on the **Brushes** palette.

The Brushes palette loads with a selection of brushes, including the 3 pt Round. These are only a few of the brushes that ship with Illustrator. To access all the brushes, see Exercise 5 in this chapter.

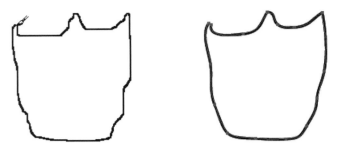

4. Using the **Paintbrush** tool, drag a complete highway shield (shown above) on the artboard.

The Paintbrush tool did two things. First, it created a path the same way the Pencil tool does (as you saw in Chapter 11, "Pencil and Line Segment Tools"). Second, it immediately stroked the path with the selected 3 pt Round brush.

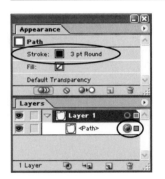

5. Choose **Window > Appearance** to open the **Appearance** and **Layer** palettes. Note that the stroke for the shape is **3 pt Round**—the selected brush. Look at the **Layers** palette. The **<Path>** you just created has a filled-in **Appearance** button. A brush stroke is more than a simple 3 pt line, so it is considered an appearance. This is indicated on the **Layers** palette.

6. Drag the **Paintbrush** tool over part of the path you drew to redraw it the same way you did with the Pencil tool in Chapter 11, "*Pencil and Line Segment Tools.*" Hold down the **Alt** key (Windows) or the **Option** key (Mac) to temporarily change the **Paintbrush** tool into the **Smooth** tool. Smooth the path.

Now you see that the Paintbrush and Pencil tools work almost identically. The biggest difference is that the Pencil tool strokes the path with whatever stroke is set on the Stroke palette, and the Paintbrush tool uses whatever brush is selected on the Brushes palette. The Paintbrush can continue a selected path the same way the Pencil tool does, as well.

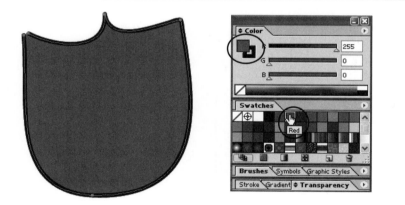

7. Choose **Window > Color** to see the **Color** and **Swatches** palettes. Make sure the **Fill** square is on top and then click the **Red** swatch to fill the path red. Painted paths can be filled just like a pen- or pencil-drawn path, but this isn't the way most of us think about a paintbrush and usually is not what you want when you select the **Paintbrush** tool. Click the **None** swatch to remove the fill.

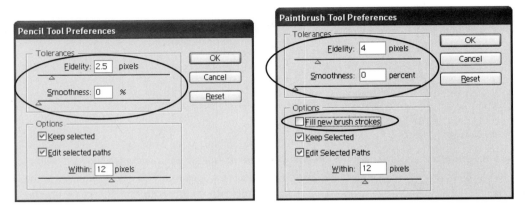

8. Double-click the **Paintbrush** tool on the **Toolbox** to see the **Paintbrush Tool Preferences** window. Uncheck **Fill new brush strokes**. Click **OK**.

It helps to keep this setting off as you learn the Paintbrush tool. The other Paintbrush tool options are identical to the Pencil tool options. The default setting for Fidelity is higher for the brush, so small zigzags in the strokes you draw are removed more than they are with the Pencil tool. Tiny zigzags usually look pretty ugly when stroked with a brush.

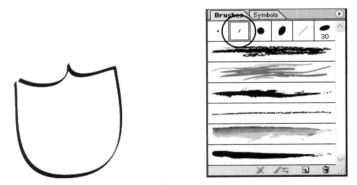

9. With the highway sign still selected, click the **6 pt Flat** brush on the **Brushes** palette. The path is restroked with the new brush.

Any path can be stroked with a brush by selecting it and then clicking the desired brush on the Brushes palette. It does not matter what tool created the path. Some of these default brushes don't look very vector-like, but they are vector art, which rescales well and prints clearly at many resolutions.

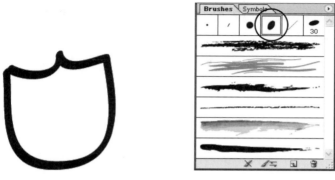

10. With the path still selected, click the **15 pt Oval** brush. Double-click the **15 pt Oval** brush to see its options.

11. Check the **Preview** check box. First, experiment with dragging on the oval brush in the white square to rotate and resize the brush and watch the changes to the stroke. Next, adjust the options for the paintbrush to match the settings shown above by entering the numbers using the keyboard. Set **Angle** to **60** degrees with a **Random Variation** of **90** degrees, a **Roundness** of **20%**, and a **Diameter** of **15 pt** with a **Random Variation** of **10 pt**. Note that as you adjust each parameter, the shape of the brush changes in the boxes above the parameters, and the look of the artwork changes. Click **OK**.

The Calligraphic Brush Options let you create virtually any brush stroke you can imagine. To help you visualize what the variation of random changes looks like, there are three examples of the brush above the brush settings that show the range of the brush. The smallest size and most counter-clockwise angle is on the left, the middle of the range settings is shown in the center, and the largest and most clockwise angle is on the right. If your brush uses only fixed settings, all three of these examples are identical.

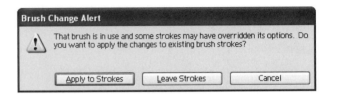

12. Since the brush you just changed is used on the highway sign, Illustrator needs to know if you want the sign restroked with the changed brush or left alone. When the **Brush Change Alert** dialog box appears, click **Apply to Strokes**. This applies the changes you made to the brush to all the instances of this brush in your artwork, and the highway sign will change in appearance. If you click **Leave Strokes**, the changes you made to the brush appear on all new strokes you make with the brush, but any existing artwork is left unchanged.

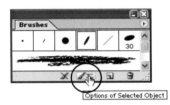

*If you want to change the look of a brush for only one piece of your artwork but leave the brush itself unchanged, select the artwork with the **Selection** tool and click the **Options of Selected Object** button on the **Brushes** palette. The same dialog box opens as when you double-click a brush in the Brushes palette, but any changes you make apply only to the brush strokes on the selected object or objects.*

13. With the path still selected, put the **Stroke** square on top in the **Color** palette and click the **Magenta** swatch on the **Swatches** palette. The brush stroke is now magenta.

14. Choose **File > Save** and click **OK** for the default save options. Close the file.

TIP | Multiple Brush Strokes on a Path

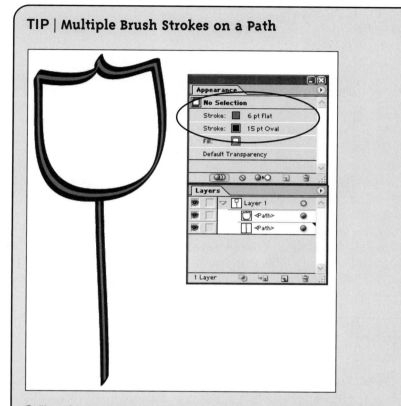

Calligraphic brush settings do not include a color, but you can make them any color you wish. A really cool effect can be achieved using the **Add New Stroke** command on the **Appearance** palette and putting two different brush strokes on the same path in different sizes and different colors.

NOTE | Unwanted Redraw

You drew the highway shield in this exercise as one long stroke. If you try drawing the top of the symbol by drawing one curve, releasing your mouse button, and then drawing the next curve, the first curve would have disappeared! This is due to the **Edit Selected Paths** option. With some shapes, Edit Selected Paths deletes the original path and replaces it with the next segment rather than extending the original path by adding a segment. There is no good workaround for this since turning off the Edit Selected Path option prevents you from extending the selected path at all. The Pencil tool has the same problem. If you run into this problem with certain shapes, your options are to use the Pen tool or draw the entire shape as one stroke with the Paintbrush or Pencil tool and then edit any problem areas.

NOTE | Pressure Sensitivity

If you have a pressure-sensitive pen and tablet, you can create brushes that change with the pressure you apply using the pen. The harder you press down, the wider the brush. The example above was created with a 15 pt brush that had a variation of 25 pt based on Pressure. If you find yourself drawing on the screen regularly, investigate getting a digital pen and tablet. Check out **http://www.wacom.com/index2.cfm** for more information on digital tablets.

2. ——————————**Art Brushes**

Art brushes are a very powerful and useful feature, but they function differently than most people imagine when they think of a "brush stroke." An art brush is made from a piece of art. This art often resembles something you might make with a real paintbrush, but any piece of art can become an art brush. When you use the brush, the art is stretched and bent as needed to follow the path you paint with the art brush. This is much easier to see than describe, as you will see in this exercise.

1. Open the file **1 pt Sign.ai** from the **chap_12** folder.

2. To see the art brushes only, open the **Brushes** palette flyout menu and uncheck any brushes except the art brushes so that **Show Art Brushes** is the only brush type checked.

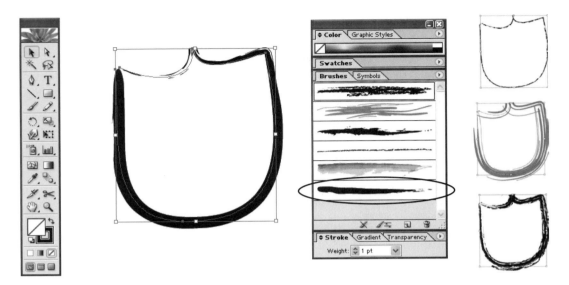

3. Select the highway sign with the **Selection** tool. Click the different art brushes to restroke the highway sign and see the effect. Do the **Fude** brush (circled above) last.

As you try the different brushes, look closely at the thumbnail image of the brush in the Brushes palette and the result on the highway sign. The image you see on the thumbnail is being stretched and twisted to fit on the path.

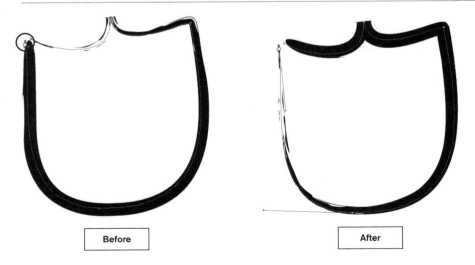

Before

After

4. Select the **Pen** tool. Click the endpoint of the path (circled above) to reverse the path direction. The **Fude** art brush also reverses the direction in which it follows the path.

Since an art brush places a piece of artwork on a path, it is affected by the direction of the path. The Fude art brush has an obvious difference between the beginning and the end of the art, so it's easy to see how it follows the highway sign in a counter-clockwise direction. This happens because the path was drawn counter-clockwise. By clicking with the Pen tool on the beginning of the path, you reversed the direction of the path. The art brush is now applied clockwise. If you extended the path by placing more anchor points with the Pen tool, the brush would stretch and continue following the path.

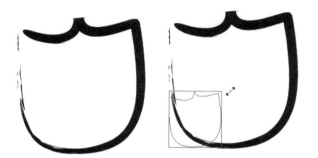

5. Switch to the **Selection** tool. Hold down the **Alt** key (Windows) or the **Option** key (Mac) while you drag the symbol to the right so you create a copy. Choose **Object > Transform > Scale** or use the bounding box to scale the copy down to **15%**. (It does not need to be exactly 15%.)

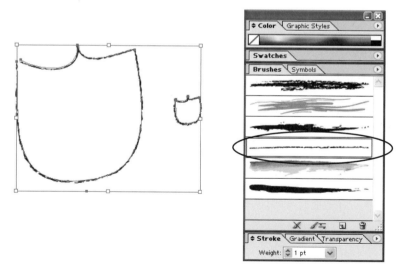

6. Select both objects with the **Selection** tool. Click the **Thick Pencil** art brush on the **Brushes** palette to restroke both paths with thick pencil. Click the **Options of Selected Object** button on the **Brushes** palette.

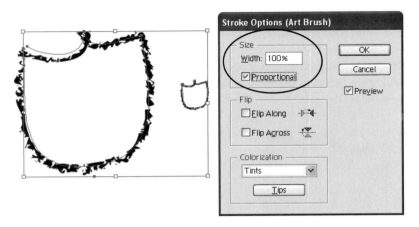

7. Check the **Preview** check box and then check the **Proportional** check box. Note the change on the artwork. Click **OK**.

*Since the artwork is stretched to fit on the path, Illustrator must decide if the height and width of the artwork remains proportional. By definition, the height of the artwork is the direction that follows the path, and the width is how far the art extends off the sides of the path. The **Flip Along** option has the same effect as reversing the path direction with the Pen tool (as shown in Step 4). The **Flip Across** option paints the artwork upside-down.*

8. Save the file and close it.

3. ——————Custom Art Brush

One of the cooler features of an art brush is how easily you can create your own. As you will see in this exercise, the brush can be a distinct piece of art instead of a paint effect.

1. Open the file **Fude Sign.ai**. Choose **Select > All** to select all of the artwork.

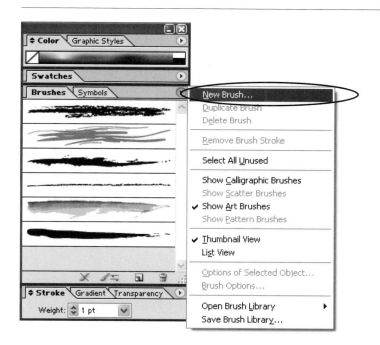

2. Choose **New Brush** from the **Brushes** palette flyout menu.

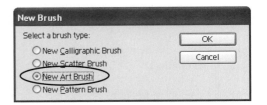

3. Choose **New Art Brush** and click **OK**.

4. Name the brush **Highway Sign**. Set the **Direction** by clicking the downward facing arrow (circled above) and check the **Proportional** check box. Click **OK**.

The selected art appears in the Art Brush Options dialog box automatically, but you must decide the direction the art is applied along the path. The large white window shows how the art will be drawn relative to the direction of the path with a blue arrow over your artwork.

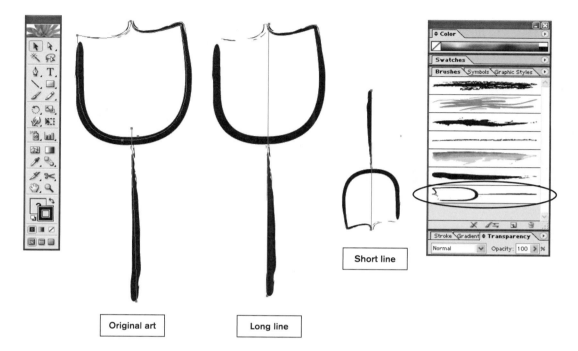

Short line

Original art

Long line

5. Select the **Line Segment** tool. Draw a vertical line the same length as the original art by holding the **Shift** key while dragging downward. Click the **Highway Sign** art brush, and the artwork appears along the line. Draw a shorter vertical line by holding the **Shift** key while dragging upward. Click the **Highway Sign** art brush, and the artwork appears along the line, but it appears upside-down because it is following the line from the bottom up.

Because you made the brush proportional, the width of the smaller sign is reduced to keep the relative dimensions of the artwork the same.

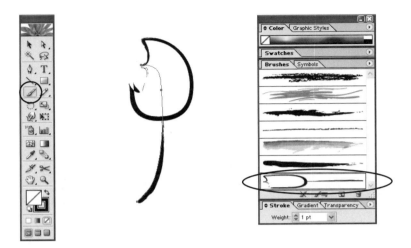

6. Select the **Paintbrush** tool. Select the **Highway Sign** art brush and draw a curved path with the **Paintbrush** tool. The image of the sign is warped to follow the path.

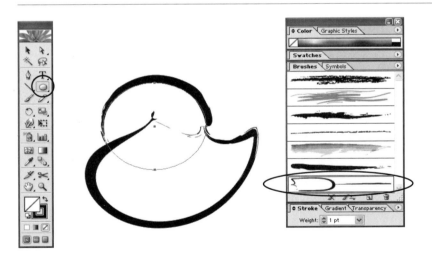

7. Select the **Ellipse** tool and draw an ellipse. While the ellipse is still selected, click the **Highway Sign** art brush to stroke the path with the artwork.

The Ellipse tool draws a closed path, so the starting anchor point and the ending anchor point are the same. There is still a direction to the path, however. The path is clockwise in this example with the start/end anchor point in the three-o'clock position.

8. Save and close the file.

4. —————— Pattern Brushes

Pattern brushes are like art brushes in that they take artwork and map it along a path. They do not stretch the art the way art brushes do. They repeat the art along the path similarly to how a pattern swatch repeats when you use it to fill an area. Pattern brushes have many options to ensure they look good as they turn corners on a path. Slightly curving paths can be stroked with a single piece of art and look great, as you will see in this exercise.

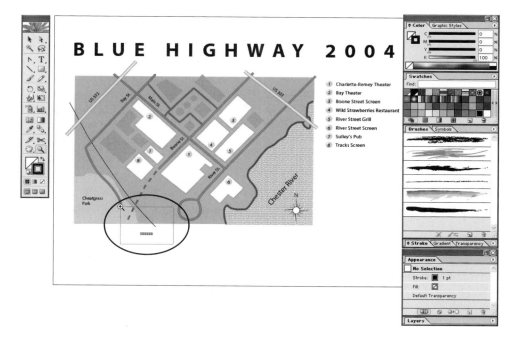

1. Open the file **map_12.ai** from the **chap_12** folder. Select the **Zoom** tool and zoom in on the bottom of the railroad track path and the small track segment.

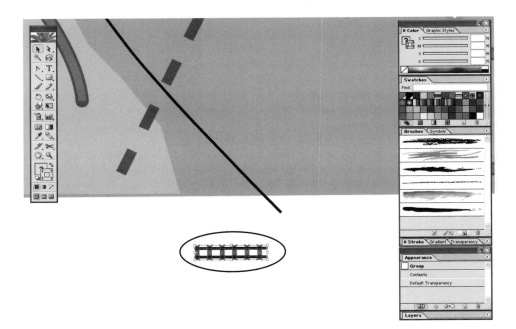

2. Select the **Selection** tool and click the small railroad segment to select it. It is grouped, so clicking any part selects the entire group.

3. Click the **New Brush** icon on the **Brushes** palette. Select **New Pattern Brush** and click **OK**.

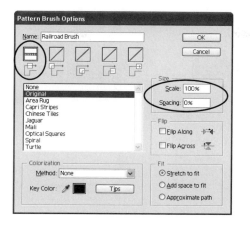

4. Name the new brush **Railroad Brush**. Note that the selected art appears in the first of five boxes under the brush name (circled above). This box represents the art that will be repeated along the path. The other four boxes are for variations of a brush that appear at corner points and optional brushes that appear at the ends of the path. Make sure that the **Scale** is **100%** and the **Spacing** is **0%** so the art won't change size and will appear without gaps as it is painted along the path. Click **OK**.

The other four swatches for the brush determine the behavior of the brush at corner points, the starting point, and the ending point. None of these apply to this exercise but are important if you continue using pattern brushes.

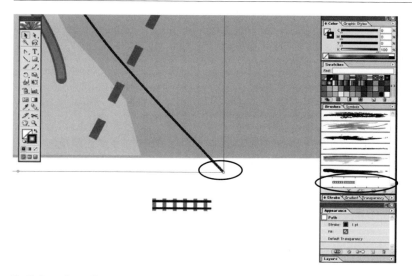

5. Select the railroad path by clicking on it with the **Selection** tool. Click the **Railroad Brush** pattern brush in the **Swatches** palette to stroke the path with the railroad pattern.

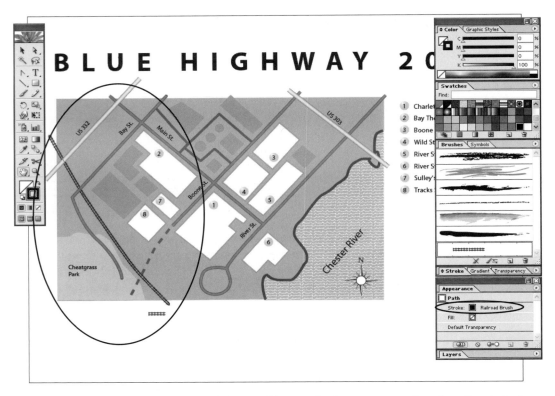

6. Double-click the **Hand** tool to see whole map. Note on the **Appearance** palette how the stroke for the selected path is **Railroad Brush**.

Creating the railroad with a pattern brush has several advantages over creating it with overlapping solid and dashed strokes as you did in Chapter 5, "Fills, Strokes, and Color." It takes fewer steps to make the railroad with the pattern brush, which saves you time. If you edit the path of the railroad, the pattern will automatically reapply to follow the new path. You can save Railroad Brush for use on future maps. See Exercise 6 for details on saving brushes.

7. Save and close the file.

MOVIE | pattern_brushes.mov

Pattern brushes can make dramatic effects including very cool borders. To see how this is done and better understand the pattern brush options, check out **pattern_brushes.mov** online at **http://www.lynda.com/books/hot/illcs/movies/**.

5. ——————— Scatter Brushes

A scatter brush is like a pattern brush with very bad aim. The scatter brush takes a piece of artwork and distributes it along a path. The distribution can be very regular, similar to the way a pattern brush repeats a pattern, or it can be quite wild with the artwork reproduced at random sizes, positions, and rotations.

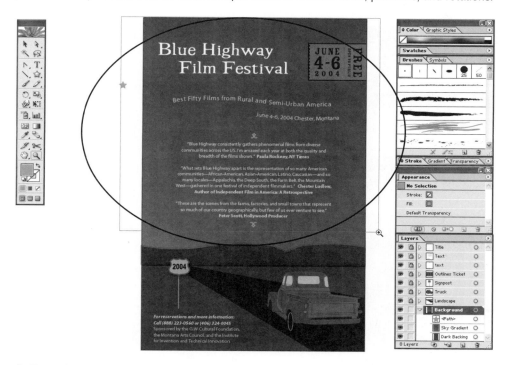

1. Open the file **poster_12.ai** from the **chap_12** folder. Select the **Zoom** tool. Zoom in on the upper two-thirds of the poster by dragging a box (marquee) around it.

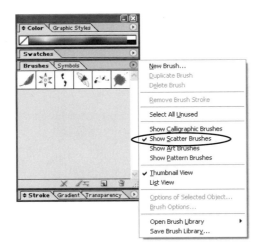

2. To see the scatter brushes only, open the **Brushes** palette flyout menu and uncheck any brushes except the scatter brushes so that **Show Scatter Brushes** is the only brush type checked.

3. Select the **Selection** tool and select the green star to the left of the poster (circled above). Drag it to the **Brushes** palette.

You could also select the star and click the New Brush icon as you did in Exercise 4. The result is the same.

4. Select **New Scatter Brush** and click **OK**. Name the brush **Starry Sky** and click **OK**.

Don't worry about skipping the options, you'll get back to them in a moment.

5. Click in the center of the **Background** layer on the **Layers** palette so new art appears on that layer. Select the **Line** tool. Drag a line across the poster under the title "Film Festival."

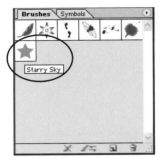

6. With the line still selected, click the **Starry Sky** scatter brush to stroke the line with the brush.

The result is the same as if you created a pattern brush—the art is repeated along the line. This is because no variation was set when you created the brush. It helps clarify how the brush works to see this look before you start creating the chaos of scattered art.

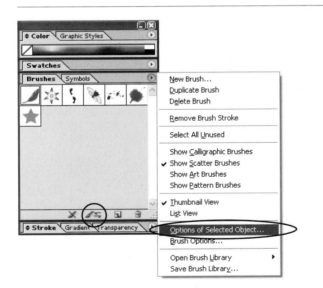

7. Choose **Options of Selected Object** from the **Brushes** palette flyout menu or click the **Options of Selected Object** button on the **Brushes** palette.

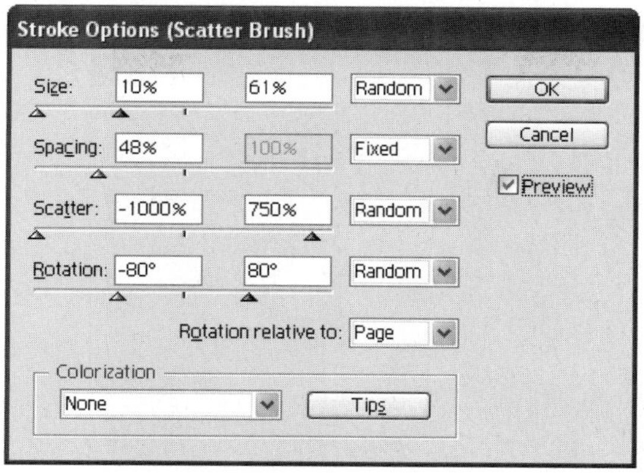

Stroke Options (Scatter Brush)

Size: `10%` `61%` Random OK

Spacing: `48%` `100%` Fixed Cancel

☑ Preview

Scatter: `-1000%` `750%` Random

Rotation: `-80°` `80°` Random

Rotation relative to: Page

Colorization

None | Tips

8. Check **Preview** to see changes as you apply them. Change **Size** to **Random** and values to **10%** and **61%**. Change **Spacing** to **48%**. Change **Scatter** to **Random** and values to **−1000%** and **750%**. Change **Rotation** to **Random** and values to **−80** degrees and **80** degrees. You must choose **Random** before you can enter a range of values. You can enter the range by typing the numbers in the field or using the sliders. Click **OK**.

That's a lot of variables, but that's what it takes to get the truly scattered final effect. Size is the size of the object relative to the original art, so a range of 10 to 61% means the smallest stars will be 10% the size of the original and the largest will be 61%. Spacing is how distributed they are on the line. Any spacing over 100% means some stars may overlap. Scatter is how far above or below the path the stars appear. −1000% means a star could appear below the line at a distance of 10 times the height of the original star. Rotation sets the limits for how much the star could appear rotated clockwise (positive number) or counter-clockwise (negative number).

TIP | Try More Than Once

If you use a scatter brush and like the settings but don't like the exact position of the scattered art, click a different brush (any brush will do) and then click the scatter brush again. Since much of the brush behavior is random, a new distribution of the art appears. Repeat this several times until you get the look you like.

9. Choose **Object > Expand Appearance**. The stars now become a group of individual objects and are unaffected by changes to that scatter brush. The original line is also part of the group as an unpainted object that you no longer need, but it will not appear in your artwork.

Once you have the look you like with a scatter brush, expanding it prevents you from unintentionally losing it by accidentally choosing a different brush. Since the distribution of the scattered art was random, you will never get exactly that distribution again.

NOTE | Expanding Brush Appearances

Selecting a path stroked with a brush and choosing **Object > Expand Appearance** will expand the appearance of any brush—calligraphic, art, pattern, or scatter. The result of expanding is a group of paths that look the same as the brush, but you can edit or delete them individually. Expanding the appearance of a brush is a good idea if you are sending a file out to print and want to ensure that the look of the brush strokes do not change. Expanding appearances is the paintbrush equivalent to creating outlines for type, which you did in Chapter 9, "*Type Appearances and Styles*."

10. Using the **Group Selection** tool, select and delete any stars that appear under type.

When you expanded the appearance of the scatter brush, the new paths were put into a single group.
The Group Selection tool is the best way to select individual stars and move, edit, or delete them.

11. Save the file and keep it open for the next exercise.

TIP | Scatter Brush on a Spiral

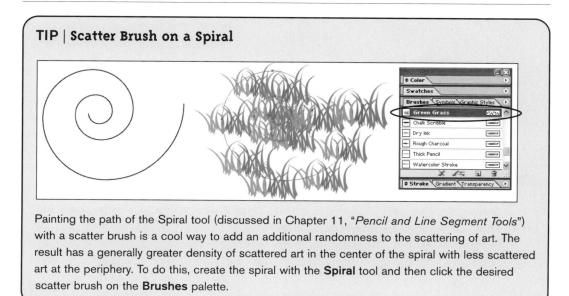

Painting the path of the Spiral tool (discussed in Chapter 11, "*Pencil and Line Segment Tools*")
with a scatter brush is a cool way to add an additional randomness to the scattering of art. The
result has a generally greater density of scattered art in the center of the spiral with less scattered
art at the periphery. To do this, create the spiral with the **Spiral** tool and then click the desired
scatter brush on the **Brushes** palette.

6. _____Brush Libraries

The brushes that appear on the Brushes palette by default are only a fraction of the dozens of brush libraries that ship with Illustrator. As you work with paintbrushes, you will undoubtedly want to create a few custom brush libraries of your own.

1. Open the file **poster_12.ai** or continue from Exercise 5.

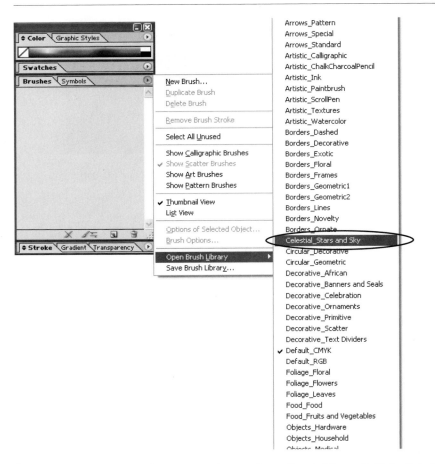

2. From **Brushes** palette flyout menu, choose **Open Brush Library > Celestial_Stars and Sky**. The library will open on its own palette.

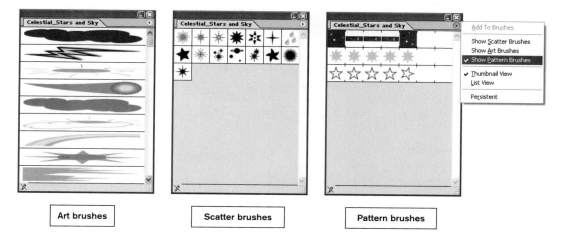

Art brushes **Scatter brushes** **Pattern brushes**

3. The **Celestial_Stars and Sky** library contains three different types of brushes. On the **Brushes** palette flyout menu, uncheck and recheck the different brush types to **Show Scatter Brushes**, **Show Art Brushes**, and **Show Pattern Brushes** individually. This is only one example of the many brushes that ship with Illustrator. Now it's time to add the **Starry Sky** brush to your saved brushes. Close the **Celestial_Stars and Sky** library palette.

Note that the different brushes have different thumbnail styles. Art brushes have a long thumbnail image. Pattern brushes use a thumbnail that shows the various swatches used by the brush. Scatter brushes use a square thumbnail. Calligraphic brushes use a square thumbnail too, but Celestial_Stars and Sky doesn't include any calligraphic brushes. Thumbnails help you identify the type of brush you are using in your art.

4. Since you expanded the **Starry Sky** scatter brush in Exercise 5, you need to use it once in your art before you save the brush. Select the **Paintbrush** tool and select the **Starry Sky** scatter brush. Drag a short line with the **Paintbrush** tool off to the side of your artwork.

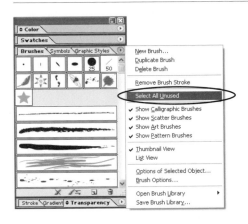

5. On the **Brushes** palette flyout menu, make sure all of the "Show…" options are checked for all brush types. Then choose **Select All Unused**.

You are selecting the unused brushes so you can delete them in the next step. The objective is to eliminate the unused brushes in this document, so you can isolate the brush you do want to save. This is why you needed to use the brush in Step 4. As with saving a swatch library, saving a brush library saves all the brushes on the palette even if you are not using them in your artwork.

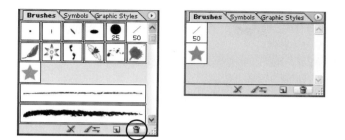

6. Click the **Trash** icon on the **Brushes** palette. Click **Yes** in the confirmation dialog box. Now only the brushes you are using remain on the palette, so only those brushes will be saved in the brush library.

You will discover that there is a 50 pt calligraphic brush used in the poster, too.

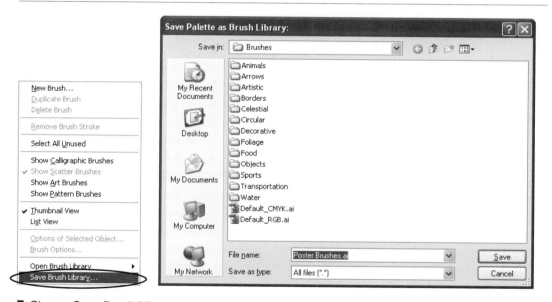

7. Choose **Save Brush Library** from the **Brushes** palette flyout menu. Name the file **Poster Brushes.ai** and click **Save** to save it in the **Illustrator CS > Presets > Brushes** folder. The next time you open Illustrator, **Poster Brushes** will be listed among your brush libraries.

TIP | Presets Folder

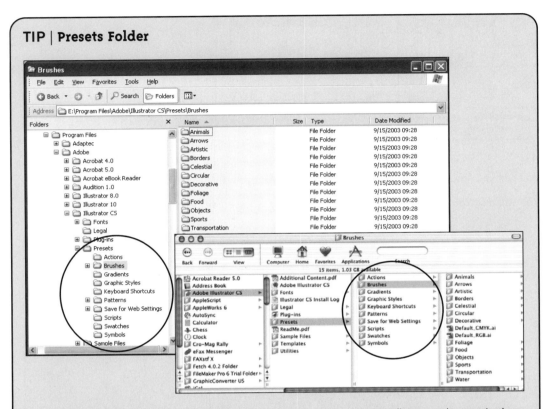

When Illustrator starts up, it loads a selection of swatches, brushes, gradients, and several other libraries. This loading takes time—a lot of time on older machines and operating systems. You can make Illustrator load faster by removing any unused libraries from the **Presets** folder, which is inside your **Adobe Illustrator CS** folder. The Adobe Illustrator CS folder is usually in **Program Files > Adobe** under Windows and in the **Applications** folder on Macs.

To move the preset libraries, quit Illustrator. Create a new folder called **Other Libraries** in your **Adobe Illustrator CS** folder and move all the libraries you rarely use to that folder. Start Illustrator. It should start up faster, and when you choose **Open Library** on a palette flyout menu, only the libraries you left in the **Presets** folder will be in the list. You can still load any of the others by choosing **Open Brush Library > Other Library** and navigating to the **Other Libraries** folder you created.

MOVIE | colorization.mov

Brushes have a special option for adjusting the colorization of the brush stroke as it appears in the document. To learn more about colorization methods, check out the movie **colorization.mov** online at **http://www.lynda.com/books/hot/illcs/movies/**.

Brushes are now a real power tool with lots of options for anyone who takes the time to explore and experiment. They are also just plain fun.

I3.
Path Tools

| Compound Paths | Knife Tool |
| Shape Modes | Pathfinders |
| Shape Modes Versus Pathfinders |

chap_13

Illustrator CS
H•O•T CD-ROM

All the paths you create with the Toolbox tools—lines, arcs, rectangles, circles, or free-form scribbles—have a single starting point, a single ending point, and usually several intermediate points all connected by path segments. Some of these paths are open, meaning the starting and ending points are different points and some are closed so the starting and ending points are the same point. These paths are all considered simple paths.

This chapter introduces a new concept: the compound path. A compound path is similar to a group in that it is a set of simple paths that are combined into a single object. They are different than groups in that a compound path has a single fill and stroke that applies to every area and path segment in the compound path. They also differ in that the path segments that make up a compound path interact to form "holes" in the filled area. Sound complicated? It's simpler in practice than it sounds and is easy to see when you start using Illustrator's tools for manipulating paths.

I. ————————Compound Paths

Compound paths are two or more paths that you intentionally overlap to create holes in their filled areas or to act as a single path. As you will see in this exercise, this feature lets you create some complex images simply and quickly. Illustrator uses a mathematical formula to decide whether or not to fill an area where two paths overlap.

1. Copy the **chap_13** folder from the **H•O•T CD-ROM** to your hard drive. Open the file **film_reel.ai** from the **chap_13** folder.

This file opens with the grid visible so you can see the effect of creating compound shapes as the exercise progresses.

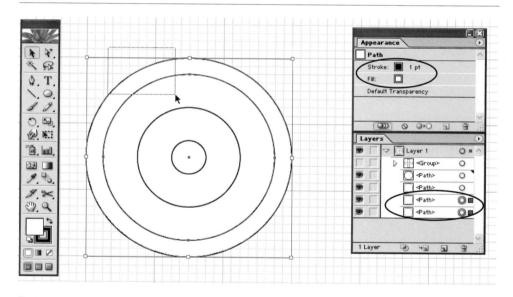

2. Select the **Selection** tool. Drag a rectangular marquee that crosses the largest two circles to select both of those circles. Choose **Window > Layers** if the **Layers** palette is not visible. Notice that the circles are two separate paths on the **Layers** palette and that each one has a 1 pt black **Stroke** and a white **Fill**, as shown on the **Appearance** palette.

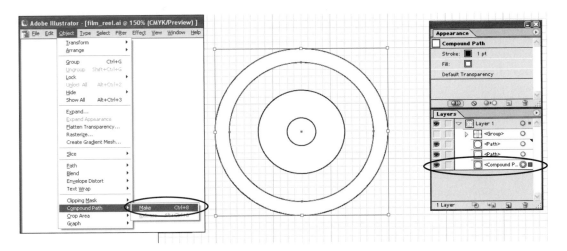

3. Choose **Object > Compound Path > Make**. Two things happen. First, the two paths on the **Layers** palette collapse into a single **<Compound Path>**. Second, the center of the compound path has no fill, allowing you to see the grid behind the shape. Essentially, the shape has become a ring.

When you made the two circles into a single compound path, Illustrator applied its formula to decide which areas were inside the shape defined by the compound path and filled only those areas. In this case, only the area between the two circles is considered the inside of the shape.

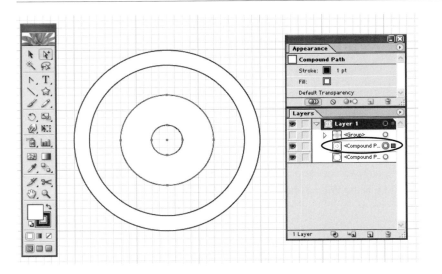

4. Select the inner two circles and choose **Object > Compound Path > Make**. Again the two paths on the **Layers** palette collapse into a single **<Compound Path>**, and the inner area becomes unfilled.

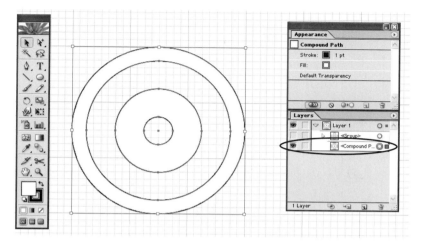

5. Choose **Select > All** to select both compound paths. Choose **Object > Compound Path > Make**. The two compound paths combine into a single compound path and every other ring is filled.

This is not a group. It is a single compound path. The center circle and the middle ring are now considered areas outside the path and are therefore not filled.

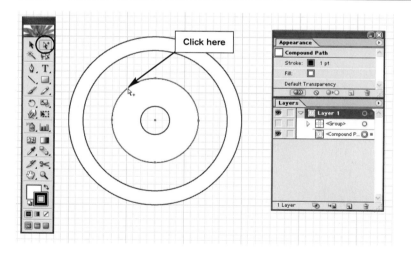

6. Click anywhere on the grid to deselect the compound path. With the **Group Selection** tool, select the inner-filled ring by clicking on the edge of the circle (as shown above).

The compound path is not a group, but the Group Selection tool can select one of the original paths if you click exactly on the path. Clicking in the filled area selects the entire compound path.

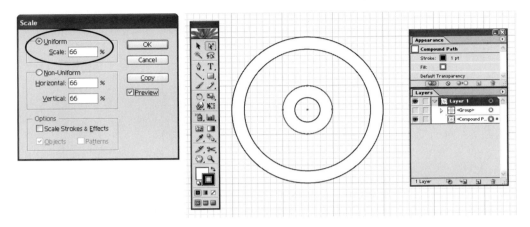

7. Choose **Object > Transform > Scale**. Make a **Uniform Scale** of **66%**. Click **OK**. The area between the innermost circle and the circle you just scaled is smaller, so the filled middle area is smaller, and more of the grid is visible through the hole in the compound path.

The real power of compound paths is that the original paths are still "live," meaning you can edit the component paths as you just did. An alternative to using the Group Selection tool is to choose Object > Compound Path > Release. This undoes the compound path, and you have the original simple paths again. The disadvantage with releasing the compound path is that you must remake the compound path to see the unfilled areas again.

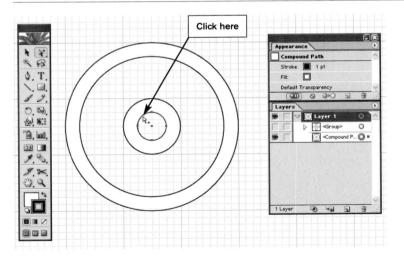

8. Click the inner edge of the inner-filled ring (circled above) with the **Group Selection** tool.

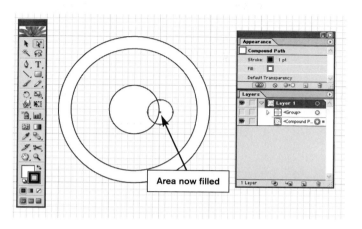

Area now filled

9. Drag the selected circle to the right so it overlaps the next circle. The areas of fill and no fill change.

Illustrator has recomputed which areas to fill and which ones not to fill. You probably wouldn't need to do something like this in your regular workflow, but it emphasizes the point that the compound path is a live object. Whenever you change a part of it, there can be an effect on the entire object.

10. Choose **Edit > Undo** to recenter the hole in the compound path. Save the file and close it.

NOTE | Outlined Type

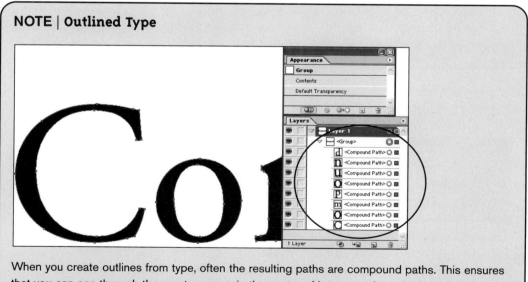

When you create outlines from type, often the resulting paths are compound paths. This ensures that you can see through the empty spaces in the center of letters, such as the letter "o." Creating outlines is discussed in Chapter 9, "*Type Appearances and Styles*."

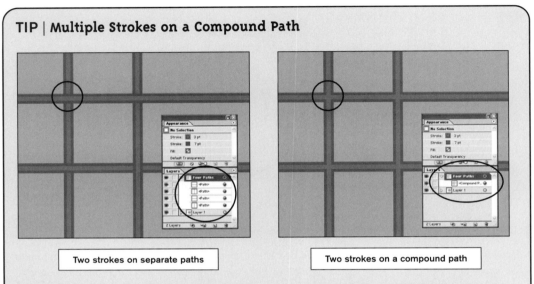

TIP | Multiple Strokes on a Compound Path

Two strokes on separate paths

Two strokes on a compound path

Shapes with holes aren't the only reason to use a compound path. Several straight lines can be made into compound paths too. If you put multiple strokes on two paths that cross, the intersection shows how one path is on top of the other. If you make these paths into compound paths by selecting them and choosing **Object > Compound Path > Make**, the paths merge into one and none appear to overlap. You can still edit the anchor points, using the Direct Selection tool. With the Direct Selection tool, you can select and move individual points even though they are part of a compound path (similar to using the Group Selection tool method you just learned about).

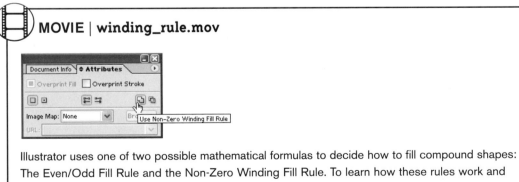

MOVIE | winding_rule.mov

Illustrator uses one of two possible mathematical formulas to decide how to fill compound shapes: The Even/Odd Fill Rule and the Non-Zero Winding Fill Rule. To learn how these rules work and how to control them, watch the movie **winding_rule.mov** at **http://www.lynda.com/books/ hot/illcs/movies/**.

2. ——————The Knife Tool

The Knife tool is a simple, freehand method for making compound paths.

> **1.** Open the file **big_circle.ai** from the **chap_13** folder.

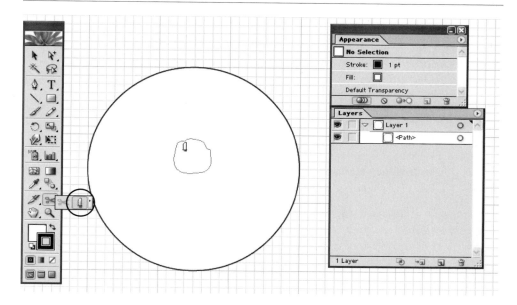

> **2.** Click and hold the **Scissor** tool and select the **Knife** tool from the flyout menu. Drag a circle in the center of the larger white circle. Be careful to finish the circle on the starting point so the Knife tool makes a closed path.

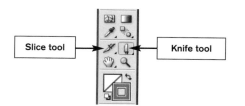

It's easy to confuse the Knife and the Slice tools. The Knife tool is the one that looks like a hand saw. The Slice tool is for cutting images into parts before using them in Web pages.

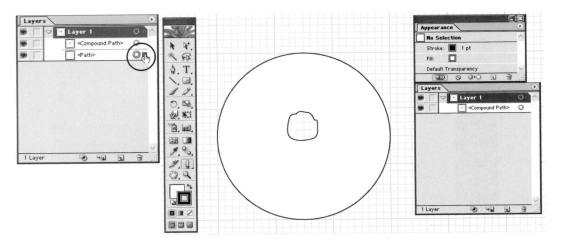

3. Click to the right of the appearance button on the **<Path>** row of the **Layers** palette to select only that path. Press **Delete** or **Backspace** on your keyboard. Only the compound path containing the hole remains. You have cut a hole out of the circle.

*If all you see on the Layers palette is a single row called <Compound Path>, the Knife tool cut an open path instead of a closed one. Choose **Edit > Undo** and redo Step 2.*

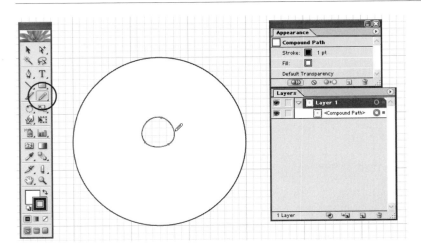

4. Select the **Smooth** tool. Smooth the inner circle.

You can edit paths within a compound path with tools such as the Pen, Pencil, or Smooth tools to fine-tune the work you did with the Knife tool.

5. Save the file and close it.

3. ——————Shape Modes

Similar to the compound paths you just made, shape modes create "live" compound shapes that you can edit to achieve exactly the effect you want. In this exercise, you will use the two most commonly used shape modes to edit a compound path.

1. Open the file **shape_modes.ai** from the **chap_13** folder.

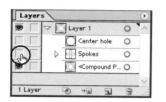

2. On the **Layers** palette, click the **Eye** icon to show the **Spokes** group. Choose **Window > Pathfinder** to see the **Pathfinder** palette.

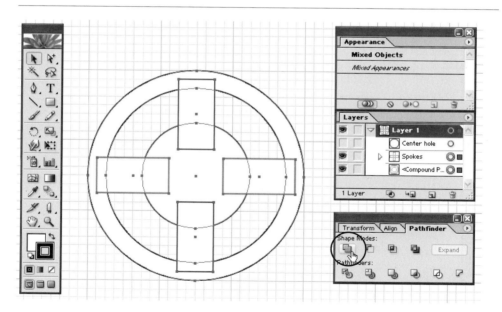

3. Choose **Select > All** to select the **<Compound Path>** and the **Spokes** group. Click the **Add to Shape Area** button on the **Pathfinder** palette (circled above).

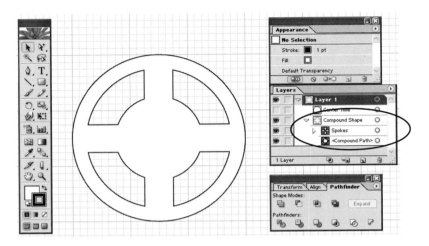

4. Click anywhere on the grid to deselect the objects and see the result. The compound path and four rectangles in the **Spokes** group have merged into a new object. On the **Layers** palette, click the expansion triangle for **Compound Shape**.

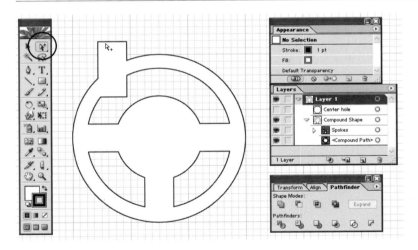

5. Choose the **Group Selection** tool and click inside one of the spokes to select that rectangle. Drag it up and to the left and release the mouse button. The shape changes accordingly. (Deselecting the object after you move the spoke allows you to better see the result.)

A compound shape is a kind of group, so if you select any part of it with the Selection tool, you select the entire group. If you use the Group Selection tool or the Layers palette, you can select individual parts and easily manipulate them.

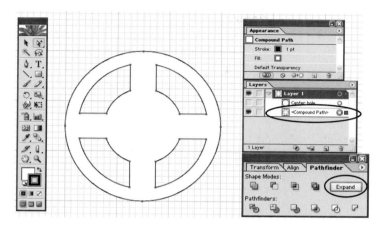

6. Choose **Edit > Undo** to move the spoke back. Choose **Select > All** to select the entire compound shape and then click the **Expand** button on the **Pathfinder** palette. The compound shape objects merge into a single compound path.

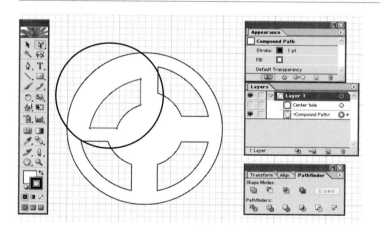

7. The new compound path looks identical to the compound shape, but there is a key difference. Click the edge of the top spoke with the **Group Selection** tool. Instead of the spoke becoming selected, the hole in the compound path is selected. Drag the selected hole down and to the right to see the effect.

Expanding a compound shape is essentially flattening it from two or more layers of shapes into a single layer containing only paths. Although it is still a compound shape, each component shape is editable. Once it is a compound path, only the paths are editable. What this means for your workflow is that you should keep the object as a compound shape as long as you want the ability to edit the basic shapes that created the compound shape. You should expand the compound shape into a compound path if you want to edit the points that create the holes in the object.

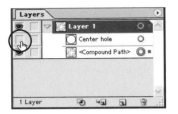

8. Choose **Edit > Undo** to restore the look of the film reel. Click the **Eye** icon to show the **Center hole**.

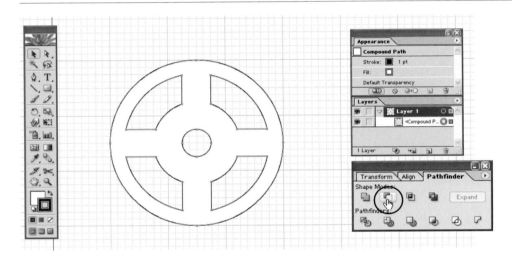

9. Choose **Select > All**. Hold down the **Alt** key (Windows) or the **Cmd** key (Mac) and click the **Subtract from Shape Area** button on the **Pathfinder** palette. The circle cut out of the resulting compound shape is immediately expanded into a compound path in one step.

Pathfinder shape modes all use the topmost shape to modify all lower selected shapes. With the Add function, it doesn't really matter which one is on top. With Subtract, be sure that the object you want to become a hole in the compound shape is the topmost object.

10. Save the file and close it.

NOTE | Shape Modes on Groups

You cannot select a single group and apply a shape mode. To use a shape mode on a single group, select the group, choose **Object > Ungroup**, and apply the shape mode.

4. ————————Pathfinders

Pathfinders are similar to shape modes in that they merge or cut paths where they overlap but instead of compound shapes, pathfinders always result in nonoverlapping simple or compound paths. Consequently, there is no Expand button for pathfinders. There are many, many uses for pathfinders—too many for one exercise! In this exercise, you will use the commonly used Divide pathfinder; which is fantastic for cutting up bigger shapes into smaller ones.

1. Open the file **pathfinder_poster.ai** from the **chap_13** folder.

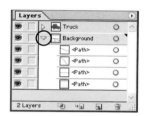

2. Turn down the expansion triangle on the **Background** layer on the **Layers** palette. Currently, the layer contains a large rectangle and three straight lines.

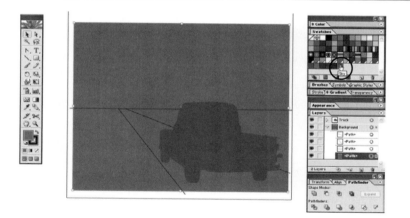

3. Select the **Selection** tool. Click anywhere inside the large rectangle to select it. Make sure the **Fill** square is on top. Click the **Sky** swatch (circled above) on the **Swatches** palette to fill the rectangle with blue.

This isn't the result you really want. The sky should be blue, the road gray, and the ground purple (for the poster). Right now, the ground and road are simply lines, so the areas between them can't be filled with a different color. The rectangle must be divided into four complete shapes so each one can be filled.

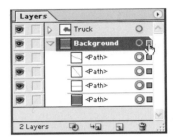

4. Click to the far right side of the **Background** row on the **Layers** palette to select all the objects on that layer.

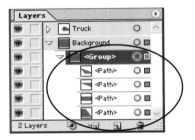

5. Click the **Divide** button on the **Pathfinder** palette. A new **<Group>** appears on the **Layers** palette. Turn down the expansion triangle to see that there are now four filled paths.

If you look closely on the artwork, you will also see that the parts of the lines that extended past the rectangle are gone. Only filled artwork remains after a divide. The lines were used to cut the rectangle into four sections and then deleted.

6. Select the **Group Selection** tool. Click anywhere outside the artwork to deselect everything. Click on the road to select only that area. Click on the **Grey Road** swatch on the **Swatches** palette to fill the road with gray.

NOTE | Divide Objects Below

If you are using only a simple path for a "cookie cutter," you can draw the path on top of the object you want divided, select both the path and the object, and use the command **Object > Path > Divide Objects Below**.

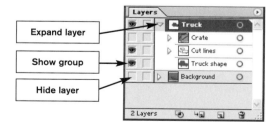

7. Divide results are easier to see on simple shapes, such as this landscape, but complex shapes are where it really shines. On the **Layers** palette, expand the **Truck** layer, click the **Eye** icon to show the **Cut lines** group, and hide the **Background** layer.

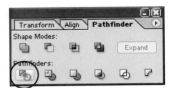

8. Choose **Select > All** to select all the visible objects. Click the **Divide** button on the **Pathfinder** palette.

9. Select the **Group Selection** tool. Click anywhere outside the artwork to deselect everything. Hold down the **Shift** key and click where each of the four truck windows should be. Click the **Default stroke and fill** icon on the **Toolbox** to quickly put a 1 pt black stroke and white fill on these paths.

You can continue selecting parts of the sectioned truck to color each one. The rest of this exercise shows the separate parts of the truck colored differently: the tires were selected and made black, the taillights red, the bumper gray, and the cab, tailgate, and running board stroked with a 1 pt black line.

10. Click the **Eye** icon on the **Crate** row on the **Layers** palette. A crate appears on top of the truck. Click the expansion triangle by the **<Group>** for the truck to see all the paths you created with the **Divide** pathfinder in Step 8. Drag the **Crate** row down on the **Layers** palette so it is directly beneath the first **<Compound Path>** you come to. Now the crate is behind the truck tailgate path but in front of the cab path, so it appears inside the truck bed.

Remember that at the beginning of this exercise the truck was a single solid object. You could not have put the crate behind only part of the truck without dividing it first. Inserting objects between parts of other objects is another common reason to use the Divide pathfinder.

11. Save the file and close it.

TIP | Clean Up

Pathfinder commands are notorious for creating unpainted paths (paths with a fill and stroke of none) that you can't see, don't want, and don't even realize exist until they interfere with some other part of your artwork. Illustrator can clean house for you at any time with the command **Object > Path> Clean Up**. Clean Up can also remove lone points that are not part of a path and can remove text objects containing no text. Clean Up has no effect on hidden or locked objects, and it doesn't matter what's selected.

Shape Modes Versus Pathfinders

Shape modes and pathfinders are related functions and can often achieve the same result, albeit by different routes. For example, using the Add shape mode and then expanding often produces the same result as the Merge pathfinder. To keep the two sets of functions straight, remember that all shape modes create a compound shape containing overlapping paths—which you can still edit individually—whereas pathfinders create a group of simple paths that do not overlap. Here are examples of all the shape modes and pathfinders used on the same original two paths.

Shape Modes

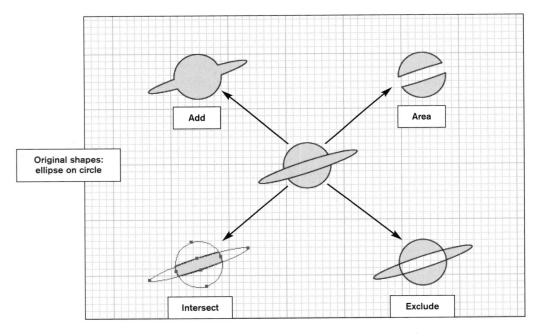

Note: The Intersect example is selected so you can better see the original paths.

Pathfinders

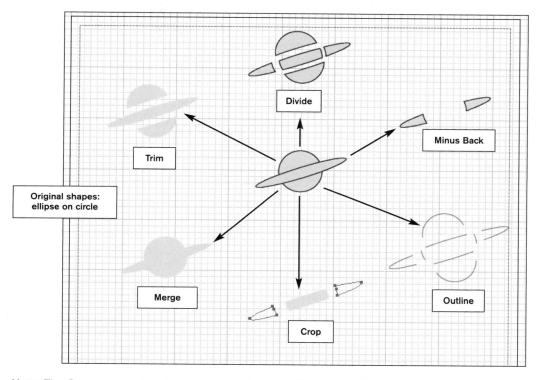

Note: The Crop example is selected to show the no stroke and no fill paths that pathfinders sometimes create.

MOVIE | autotrace.mov

Another path tool is the Autotrace tool. The Autotrace tool can replace the painstaking tracing of a complex path with the Pen or Pencil tool. To see the Autotrace tool in action, check out the movie **autotrace.mov** online at **http://www.lynda.com/books/hot/illcs/movies/**.

Compound paths, compound shapes, and the Pathfinder palette—the more you use them, the more you love them.

14.

Masks and Blending Modes

| Clipping Masks | Masking with Type |
| Opacity Masks | Blending Modes |

chap_14

Illustrator CS
H•O•T CD-ROM

This chapter describes how to use one or more objects in your work to modify another set of objects. The goal could be as simple as cropping out an unwanted part of a photograph or as complex as shifting colors and blending several objects of varying opacity. As with many Illustrator features, masks and blending modes are live effects. This means you can experiment with many possibilities and arrangements without degrading your original artwork. Masks are also a timesaver since they let you freely create without worrying about clean borders. Once you finish your art, you can mask it to get the right final look.

I. ————————Clipping Masks

Suppose you need to include only a piece of an image or drawing in your artwork. In many applications, you would simply crop the artwork, cutting off the parts you don't want. Illustrator does not have a conventional crop command (although there are commands to create the crop marks used when printing a document). Instead of cropping, Illustrator uses **clipping masks**. A clipping mask is a shape that hides part your artwork so only the desired portion is visible. The work is still there, but the clipped portion will not appear when printed or exported.

1. Copy the **chap_14** folder from the **H•O•T CD-ROM** to your hard drive. Open the file **map_14.ai** from the **chap_14** folder.

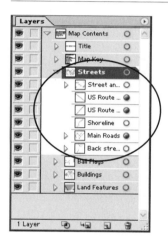

2. Click in the center of the **Streets** layer on the **Layers** palette to highlight it. Click the expansion triangle to expand the layer and see its contents.

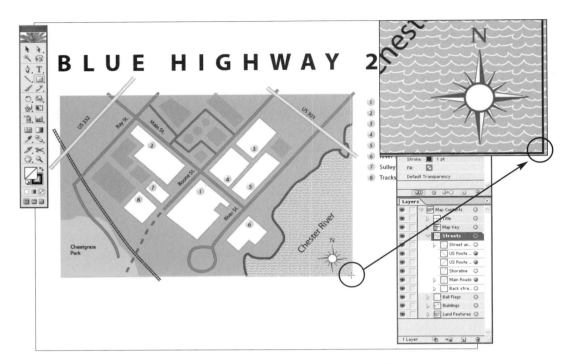

3. Select the **Rectangle** tool. Draw a rectangle around the map area with a border just inside the map itself. The rectangle will appear as a **<Path>** on the **Streets** layer because it was selected in the last step. Selecting a layer before you draw ensures that the new object appears within that layer.

4. Click to the right of the **Appearance** button on the **Streets** layer to select the new **<Path>** and all other layer contents. Selection squares appear for each row in the layer.

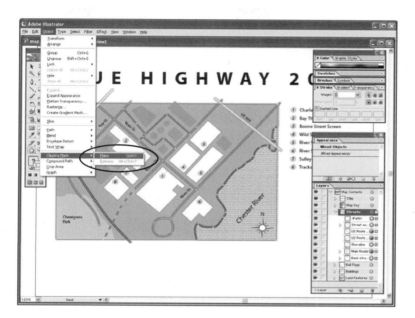

5. Choose **Object > Clipping Mask > Make**. Any section of street that extended past the rectangle that you just drew becomes invisible. The stroke on the rectangle also disappears.

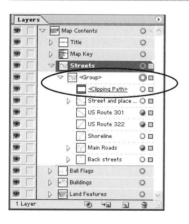

6. There is a new **<Group>** on the **Layers** palette. Expand the new **<Group>** to see the result of creating the mask.

*The **Clipping Mask > Make** command takes the top object in your selection and uses it to clip all lower selected objects. The rectangular <Path> was the top object, so it became a <Clipping Path>. The <Clipping Path> and all the clipped objects are grouped so you can see at a glance which objects are being clipped.*

WARNING | **Selecting Clipped Paths**

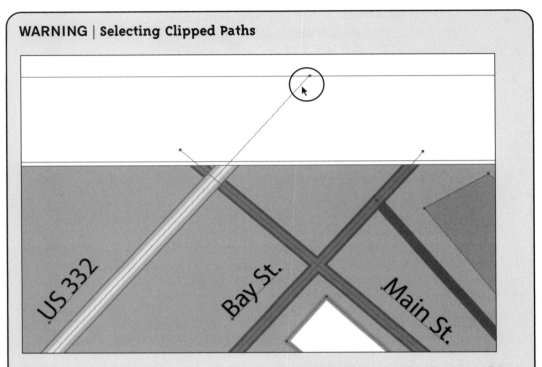

The paths and objects under a clipping path are still selectable, so it's possible for you to click what looks like empty space and accidentally select part of your artwork. The danger is that you could move or delete an object without realizing it. If you don't need to work on the clipped artwork, locking that group or layer avoids this potential problem. If you are editing the artwork, however, your only option is to be careful.

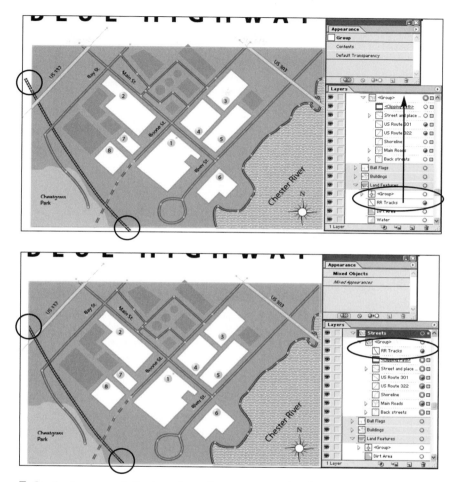

7. On the **Layers** palette, turn down the expansion triangle for the **Land Features** layer. Drag the **RR Tracks** row up into the **<Group>** containing the **<Clipping Path>**. The sections of the railroad track that extend past the clipping mask become invisible too. Clipping masks are "live," so any objects you add to the clipped group are also clipped.

The order of objects in the group doesn't matter. In this example, the RR Tracks row is above the <Clipping Path> on the Layers palette, but it is still clipped.

8. Make sure the **<Group>** containing the clipping mask is still selected. Choose **Object > Clipping Mask > Release**.

The art under a clipping mask is hidden but otherwise unchanged. Releasing the mask simply unhides the art.

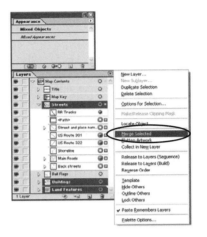

9. Hold down the **Ctrl** key (Windows) or the **Cmd** key (Mac) and click the **Streets, Buildings**, and **Land Features** rows on the Layers palette to highlight them. Be sure to click **Land Features** last. Choose **Merge Selected** on the **Layers** palette flyout menu, and all the layers merge onto the last layer you clicked: **Land Features**.

Clipped objects all end up in one group, so they must all be on one layer. If you select objects on multiple layers and create a clipping mask, Illustrator will group them on a single layer for you. By manually merging the layers, you choose where they go.

10. Drag the rectangular **<Path>** to the top of the layer. Click to right of the **Appearance** button on the **Land Features** row to select the entire layer.

You are about to make a clipping mask with the rectangle again, so you must make the rectangle the top-most object. When you make the mask, the object you use for clipping must be on top. After you make the mask, the clipping path can be anywhere in the group.

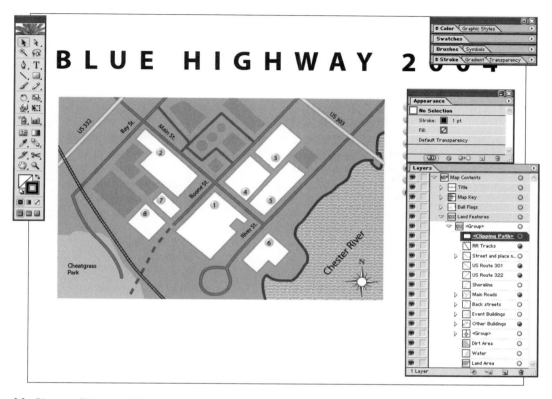

11. Choose **Object > Clipping Mask > Make.** Now all the map features are clipped.

12. Save the file and close it.

MOVIE | clipping.mov

To see the steps of this complex exercise performed, watch the movie **clipping.mov** located in the **movies** folder of the **H•O•T CD-ROM.**

2. ——————Masking with Type

Type can also be used to clip artwork. The result is type that is "filled" with the underlying image. Clipping with type creates some cool effects, and since the mask is live, the type is even editable!

1. Open the file **map_14_clipped.ai**.

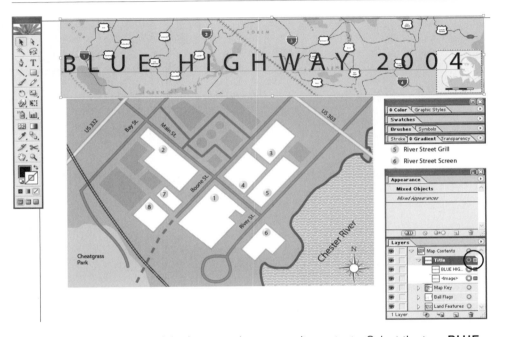

2. Turn down the **Title** row of the **Layers** palette to see its contents. Select the type **BLUE HIGHWAY 2004** and the **<image>** by clicking to the right of the **Appearance** button on the **Title** row of the **Layers** palette.

3. Choose **Object > Clipping Mask > Make**. The black type is "filled" with the image from the map graphic.

It's important to visualize what's going on here. You are seeing through the type to the high-ways image beneath it. It's as if you had a sheet of white paper with the letters "BLUE HIGHWAY 2004" cut out of the paper and you were looking through the cut-out letters and seeing the object below. The entire map image is still there, you just can't see most of it.

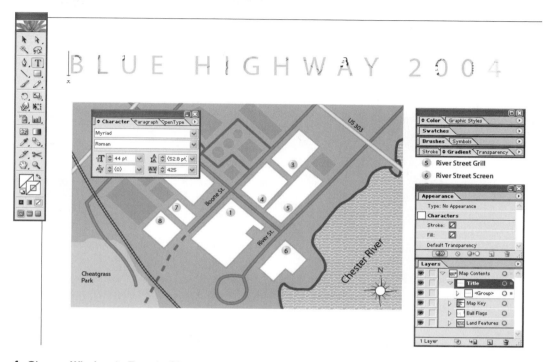

4. Choose **Window > Type > Character** to see the **Character** palette. Select the **Type** tool and click three times on the word "BLUE" in the title to select the entire paragraph.

As you learned in Chapter 8, "Adding Text," clicking on type once with the Type tool inserts the cursor. Clicking twice selects the word. Clicking three times selects the paragraph (in this case the entire title).

5. On the **Character** palette, change the font family from **Roman** to **Bold**. The type becomes wider and you can see more of the underlying image of the highways.

You could edit the type itself, too, and the map image would fill whatever text you typed in.

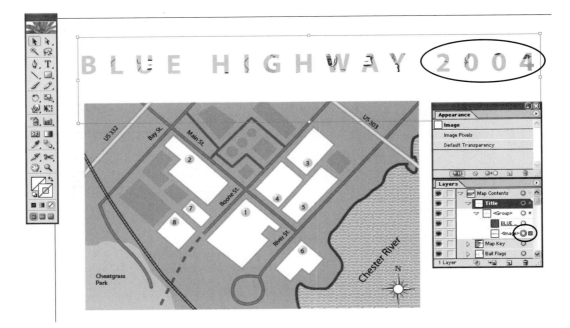

6. Turn down the expansion triangle for the new **<Group>** in the **Title** layer on the **Layers** palette. Click to the right of the **Appearance** button for the **<image>** row to select only the image. Select the **Selection** tool and drag the image behind the type down to hide the Lynda.com logo visible through "2004" and show more highway shields behind the type.

When you select the image, a bounding box appears, showing you the borders of the image. You can drag the image from anywhere inside this border even though you can only see the image through the type clipping mask. Since it is easy to accidentally select the type instead of the map graphic behind it, drag the image from a point away from the type.

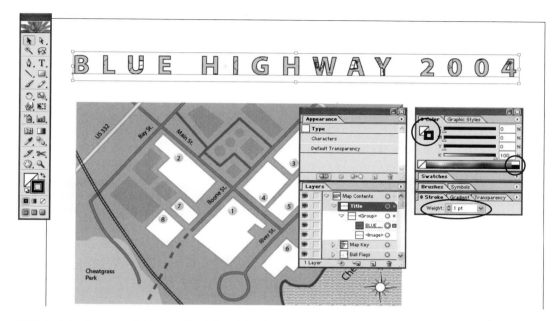

7. Select the type by clicking to the right of the **Appearance** button on the **BLUE HIGHWAY 2004** row of the **Title** layer in the **Layers** palette. Choose **Window > Color** if the **Color** palette is not visible. Click the **Stroke** square on the **Color** palette to make sure it is on top. Click the **black** area of the spectrum box to add a 1 pt black stroke to the type clipping mask.

When you create a clipping mask, any paint (stroke or fill) on the clipping object is removed. You can add one or more strokes back to the clipping mask to create a border. If you add fill to a clipping mask, it appears only where there is no object under the clipping mask. It is also possible to clip with a filled object of partial transparency. This is called an opacity mask, which is covered in Exercise 3.

8. Save the file and close it.

3. ——————Opacity Masks

Opacity masks are really two features in one. First, they allow you to adjust the opacity of any object so you can see through it. You can make the entire object opaque, or adjust the opacity of separate areas individually. You can also use the same opacity mask to clip objects so opacity masks can be clipping masks as well. They differ from standard clipping masks in that they use several objects to clip the art rather than a single path or compound path.

1. Open the file **map_14_masked.ai**.

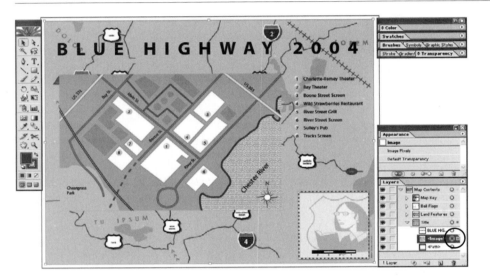

2. Turn down the expansion triangle on the **Title** row of the **Layers** palette. Select the green map graphic of the highways by clicking to the right of the **Appearance** button on the **<Image>** row of the **Layers** palette or by clicking the image of the highways on the artboard with the **Selection** tool.

3. Choose **Window > Transparency** to bring the **Transparency** palette forward. Double-click the expansion triangles on the **Transparency** tab until all the palette options appear, as shown above.

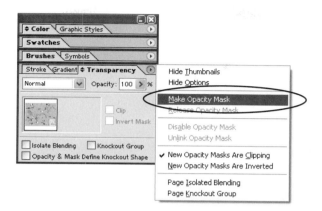

4. From the **Transparency** palette flyout menu, choose **Make Opacity Mask**. The green map graphic disappears.

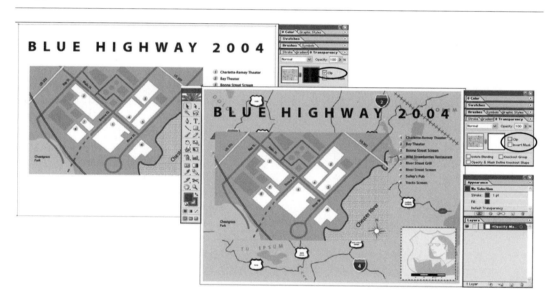

5. Uncheck **Clip** on the **Transparency** palette. The green map graphic reappears.

Opacity masks will clip by default. This behavior makes sense only after you have an object on the opacity mask, so be patient for a moment and you'll see how this works. You can change the default behavior from the Transparency palette options, but once you see how opacity masks work, you may want to keep the default setting.

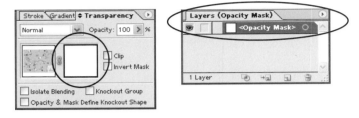

6. Select the opacity mask on the **Transparency** palette by clicking the right-hand square. The **Layers** palette changes to show a single row labeled **<Opacity Mask>**.

Using opacity masks involves different techniques than those with which you access most other Illustrator objects. You can edit either your artwork or the opacity mask, but not both at the same time.

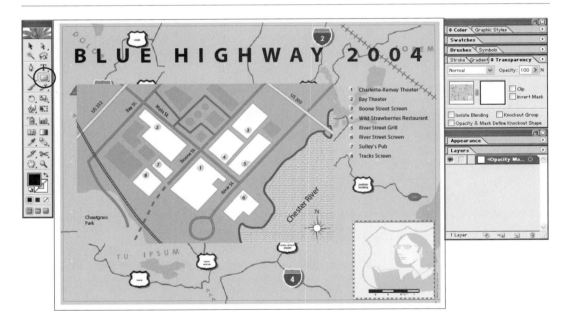

7. Select the **Rectangle** tool. Drag a rectangle over the map image, leaving a small border around the edges.

8. Choose **Window > Color** if the color palette is not visible. Using the color palette, change the fill of the new rectangle to **85%** black. The image of the highways under the rectangle becomes 15% opaque.

You drew this rectangle on the opacity mask and not on your artwork. When you changed the fill of the rectangle, you changed the opacity of the mask inside this rectangle from 100% opaque to 15% opaque. The amount of opacity for an object in the opacity mask is determined by the darkness of the fill. 100% black hides the underlying image completely and 0% black (also called white!) shows the image without any masking. It can get confusing since 100% black on the opacity mask makes an image 0% opaque, 25% black equals 75% opaque, 50% black is 50% opaque, and so on. It may help to remember that black sections of an opacity mask block out the masked artwork.

9. Check **Clip** on the **Transparency** palette again. Everything outside the 15% opaque rectangle is clipped. Uncheck **Clip** again.

Now you can see what Clip does. Clip creates a clipping mask out of the object or objects you put on the opacity mask. When you first created the opacity mask in Step 4, there were no objects on it, so Clip removed everything from view.

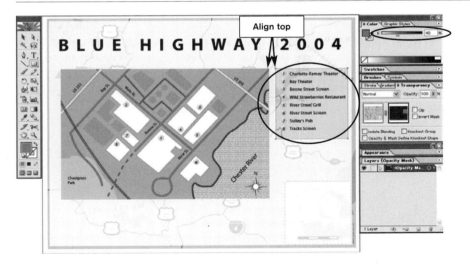

10. Create another rectangle over the ball flag map key with its top aligned with the top of the map of the festival streets. Using the **Color** palette, change the fill of this rectangle to **40%** black.

Since this rectangle is only 40% black, the map image underneath it is now 60% opaque.

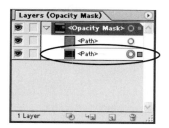

11. Click the expansion triangle on the **<Opacity Mask>** layer to see the paths. Select the larger rectangle.

Each object you draw on the opacity mask has its own row in the Layers palette, so you can control and edit each one individually. Remember, these objects are part of the opacity mask. They are not objects in your artwork.

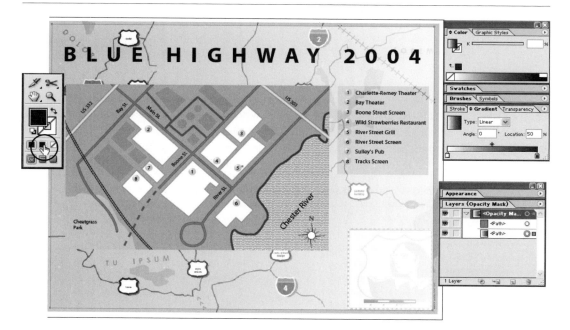

12. Click the gradient button in the **Toolbox** to fill the rectangle on the opacity mask with a gradient.

*If your mask doesn't fill with a gradient right away, choose **Linear** from the **Type** drop-down menu on the **Gradient** palette.*

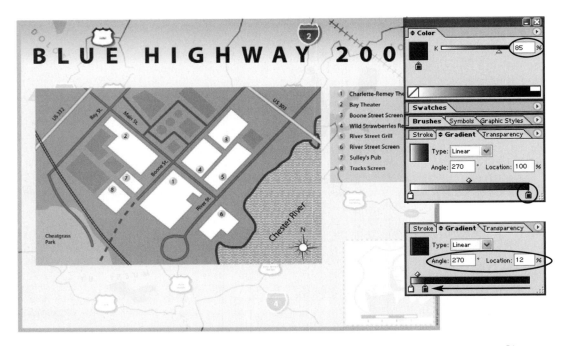

13. The **Gradient** palette will come forward in the same window as the **Transparency** palette. Change the **Angle** of the gradient to **270** to put the most masking at the bottom of the rectangle. Click the dark color stop on the **Gradient** palette and change its color to **85%** black. Slide the dark color stop to the left to a **Location** of **12%.** so the gradient is compressed into the top 12% of the rectangle.

You can fill an opacity mask object with solid fills, gradients, and even patterns!

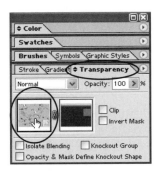

14. Click the tab for the **Transparency** palette to bring it forward. Click the left-hand square to stop editing the opacity mask and resume editing the artwork.

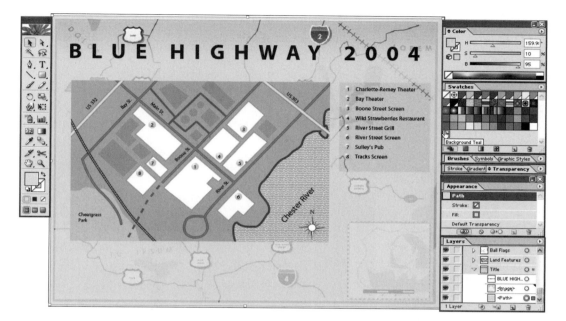

15. In the **Title** layer on the **Layers** palette, select the lowest **<Path>** by clicking to the right of the **Appearance** button. This is an unpainted rectangle behind all the artwork. Click the **Background Teal** swatch on the **Swatches** palette. The new fill color shows through all the semi-opaque areas of the opacity mask.

When you created the opacity mask, the area behind the image you were masking was white, so the mask made the image wash out but not change in color. Since opacity masks do affect opacity, any art behind the masked image will show through the areas that are not 100% opaque.

16. Save the file and close it.

MOVIE | more_masks.mov

There is a lot more to opacity masks than you saw in this exercise. To learn about such features as reversed masks, masking and clipping a color, knockout groups, and isolating blending, check out the movie **more_masks.mov** online at **http://www.lynda.com/books/hot/illcs/movies/**.

4. ——————Blending Modes

Blending modes are an option for transparency that allows the colors of two objects to interact. There are many uses for blending modes, and if you are a Photoshop user, you are probably familiar with some uses already. In fact, when you open a Photoshop file in Illustrator or an Illustrator file in Photoshop, the blending modes are preserved. The goal of this exercise is to use one of the blending modes to blend some stars into the background gradient on the poster so they stand out from the gradient at the top but fade in near the bottom.

1. Open the file **poster_14.ai** from the **chap_14** folder.

2. Select the **Zoom** tool and zoom in on the stars and gradient to the left of the poster.

This gradient is the same one used in the poster, and the stars are the same color. You will work here first to better see the effect of the blending and then apply the same effect in the poster.

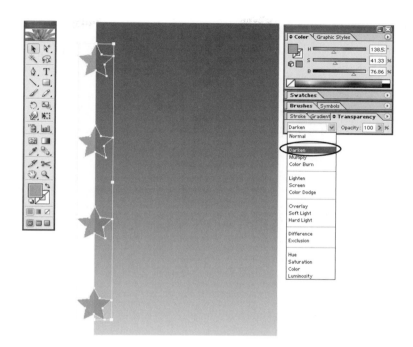

3. Select the group of four stars by clicking any one with the **Selection** tool. From the **Transparency** palette, choose a blending mode of **Darken**. Click outside the selected stars to deselect them and better see the results. All four of the stars darken, with the stars over the darkest part of the gradient affected the most.

The first group of blend modes could be called the "Color Same or Darker group." The three modes use different criteria and give different results, but in all three the resulting color for the blend is the same or darker than either original color.

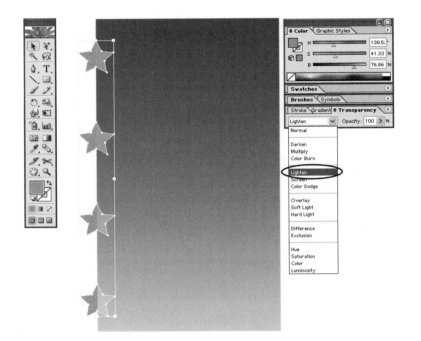

4. Select the group of four stars by clicking one with the **Selection** tool. From the **Transparency** palette, choose a blending mode of **Lighten**. Click outside the selected stars to deselect them and better see the results. All four of the stars darken, with the stars over the lightest part of the gradient affected the most.

The next group, which could be called the "Color Same or Lighter group," contains the complements of the first group. In each instance of this group, the resulting color for the blend is the same or lighter than either original color.

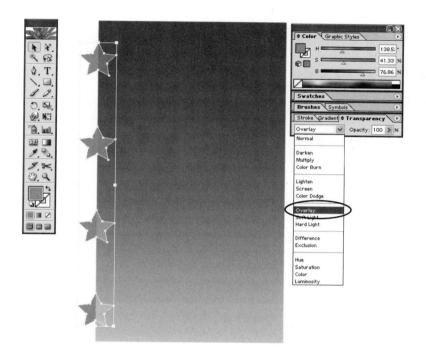

5. Select the group of four stars again and choose a blending mode of **Overlay**. Click outside the selected stars to deselect them and better see the results.

The effects of this group are a bit trickier. They all simulate the results of different light sources shining on the objects. You can think of them as the "Light Source group" and try them when you are simulating light shining on your artwork, such as a spotlight, or shining from one point within your art onto another, such as a sunset scene.

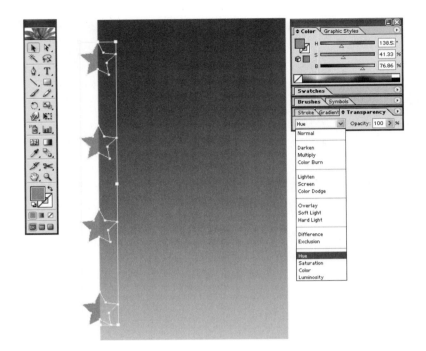

6. Select the group of four stars again and choose a blending mode of **Hue**. Click outside the selected stars to deselect them and better see the results.

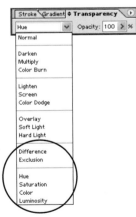

In this case, the green hue of the star is held constant, but its saturation and luminosity change to match areas on the underlying gradient. This is one example of what could be called the "Color Shifter groups." These last two groups all mix colors by taking a color property of one object and combining it with several properties of the other object.

NOTE | More About Blending Modes

Blending modes are best learned through experimentation, not written description. If you're still craving more information, the Illustrator Help files have good, concise descriptions of each blending mode. Look under **Using Transparency, Gradients, and Patterns > Working with transparency > Summary of blending modes**.

---

7. Select the stars one more time and choose **Lighten** for the blending mode. This mode showed the most promise for stars that faded in at the bottom but stood out at the top.

The Lighten blending mode compares the two colors and uses whichever color is lighter to determine resulting color. Since the gradient is lighter than the star at the bottom of the gradient, the lighter sky color predominates in the mix, and the star fades in. Since the star is lighter than the gradient at the top, the original star color predominates at the top.

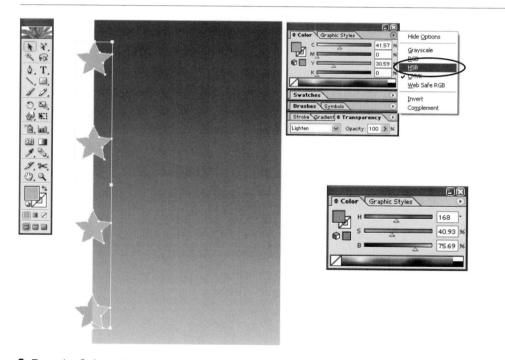

8. From the **Color** palette flyout menu, choose the **HSB** color model. Slide the color **Hue** to **168** degrees.

The green of the star is now closer to the blue of the sky, and the stars blend in more—especially on the bottom where the sky is lighter.

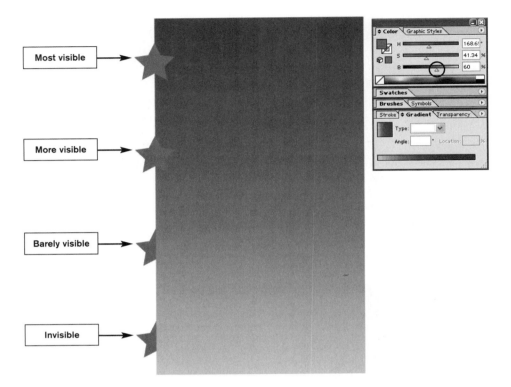

Most visible

More visible

Barely visible

Invisible

9. Slide the color **Brightness** to **60**% on the **Color** palette.

The Brightness also determines which color—sky or star—predominates. The brighter the stars are, the further down the sky stars will be visible. The dimmer the stars, the further up the gradient you must look to see the stars.

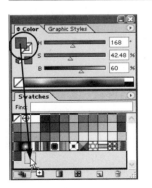

10. Drag the new star color to the **Swatches** palette.

11. Double-click the **Hand** tool to see the entire poster. Click any star on the poster with the **Selection** tool to select the entire group. Choose **Lighten** for the blending mode and click the new swatch to fill the stars with the correct color.

This applies the settings you experimented with on the small gradient and four stars to the entire poster. The stars on the poster now fade into the sky at the bottom and stand out at the top.

12. Save the file and close it.

MOVIE | better_blend.mov

An even better solution to the fading in of the stars than you saw here is to fill the group of stars with a gradient that uses the custom swatch color near the horizon and is the original green near the top of the poster. To see this technique demonstrated, view the movie **better_blend.mov** online at **http://www.lynda.com/books/hot/illcs/movies/**.

Congratulations! Another chapter under your belt. Now it's time to move on the very cool and mind-bending world of envelopes and blended paths.

15.
Envelopes, Meshes, and Blends

| Warp Distortion | Top Object Distortion |
| Mesh Distortion | Gradient Mesh and the Mesh Tool |
| Blending Paths |

chap_15

Illustrator CS
H•O•T CD-ROM

Envelopes, meshes, and blends are just plain cool. They open up a world of possibilities for changing the look of your art in ways that would be extremely difficult and time-consuming to draw by hand with the Pen or Pencil tools. Because envelopes are live objects, you can experiment with many different looks without ruining your original artwork. You can also easily edit a heavily warped piece of art—to change a color or word in response to a client request, for example—without re-creating the entire piece.

The live nature of envelopes and blends can be a challenge in that the appearance of warped or blended art you see on the screen is not the same as the actual paths of the original artwork inside the envelope. It's like looking at something in a fun-house mirror or through a fish-eye lens. This concept is a bit mind-bending at first and takes some getting used to. As you will see in the next several chapters, Illustrator relies heavily on this technique of changing the look of art without changing the art itself. Envelopes are a great place to start exploring this concept, so lets start warping some art!

I. ──────── Warp Distortion

Illustrator comes with many "ready-made" distortions. These distortions are easy to apply and edit with the Warp Options dialog box. The dialog box also gives you a good sense of how distortions work and ways they could be used, so warp distortions are a great place to start exploring.

1. Copy the **chap_15** folder from the **H·O·T CD-ROM** to your hard drive. Open the file **flag.ai** from the **chap_15** folder. Choose **Window > Layers** if the **Layers** palette is not open.

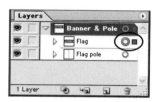

2. Expand the **Banner & Pole** layer on the **Layers** palette. Select the flag by clicking on the right side of the **Flag** row. **Flag** is a group containing all the paths that make up the flag.

3. Choose **Object > Envelope Distort > Make with Warp**.

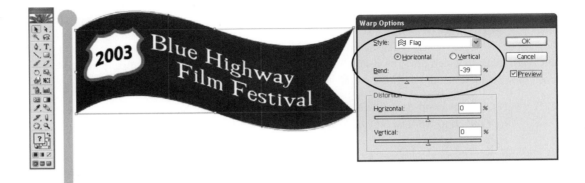

4. Check the **Preview** box. Choose **Flag** from the **Style** drop-down menu and make sure the **Horizontal** radio button is selected. Slide the **Bend** slider to the right and to the left to see the effect. Next slide it to **−39%** and click **OK**.

The Flag distortion is one of the simplest distortions, so it's easy to see what's going on. Feel free to try some other styles and bends to see the effect with the Preview box checked. When you are ready to go on, set things back to a Flag warp with the Bend set to −39% before you click OK.

5. Choose **Object > Envelope Distort > Reset with Warp**. The **Warp Options** dialog box opens again with the current warp settings. Check the **Preview** check box. Add a **Horizontal Distortion** of **−22%** and a **Vertical Distortion** of **−4%**. The horizontal distortion makes it more pennant-shaped, and the vertical distortion makes the top slightly wider than the bottom so the top appears to come out toward you a bit. Click **OK**.

6. Look on the **Layers** palette. The **Flag** group has been replaced by a row labeled **Envelope**. The envelope is a container for your art that warps the appearance.

As you will see, you can edit an envelope that contains art, or you can edit the art contained in the envelope, but you cannot edit both the envelope and its contents at the same time. This is similar to an opacity mask you used in Chapter 14, "Masks and Blending Modes," where you can edit the mask or the art behind it, but not both at once.

7. Choose **Object > Envelope Distort > Edit Contents**. An expansion triangle appears on the **Layers** palette, and the paths for the original artwork appear over the warped flag.

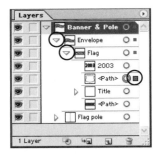

8. Turn down the expansion triangle for the **Envelope** and for the **Flag** group. Currently, all the objects in the group are selected. Click to the right of the **Appearance** button for the highway sign **<Path>** row to select that path only.

Selecting art inside an envelope is possible on the artboard too, but you must click where the unwarped art would appear, rather than where the warped art does appear. It's much easier to select art inside an envelope using the Layers palette.

9. If the **Swatches** palette is not visible, choose **Window > Swatches**. Make sure the **Fill** square is on top on the **Color** palette. Click the **Green Shield** swatch to fill the highway sign with green.

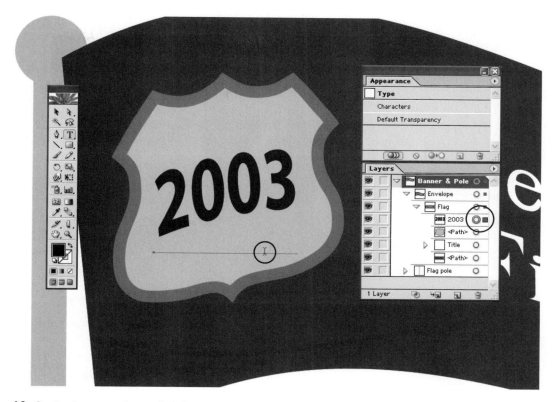

10. On the **Layers** palette, click the row labeled **2003**. This is a row of type, and the path containing the type appears as a straight blue line in your artwork. Select the **Type** tool and click it on the blue line under the **3**. Drag to the right to select the number 3.

This is an excellent example of the oddity of selecting art inside an envelope. You are selecting the 3, but you are dragging the Type tool over where the 3 would be without the envelope. Weird, huh?

11. Type **4** on your keyboard to replace the 3. Choose **Select > Deselect** to deselect the type.

The capability to edit the underlying art is part of what makes envelopes so great. Envelopes warp the way your art appears, but they do not change the original art in any way.

12. Select the **Selection** tool and click the flag to select the entire group. Choose **Object > Envelope Distort > Edit Envelope** to return to editing the envelope. Select the **Selection** tool and use it to drag a corner of the bounding box and resize the envelope slightly smaller.

The envelope is an object, so any transformation—scaling, rotating, reflecting, and so on—is possible. As you transform the envelope, the appearance of the underlying art changes accordingly.

> ### NOTE | Deleting an Envelope
>
> If you delete an envelope by dragging the Envelope row to the Trash on the Layers palette, you will delete the envelope and all the artwork inside it. To delete an envelope but keep your artwork intact, you must select the envelope and choose **Object > Envelope Distort > Release**. Releasing envelopes is demonstrated in the next exercise.

13. Choose **Object > Envelope Distort > Expand**. The envelope is removed, and the original artwork is changed to match the new look. This changed artwork appears as a new **<Group>** on the **Layers** palette.

Type in an expanded envelope is converted to outlines and is no longer editable with the Type tool. Converting type to outlines is covered in Chapter 9, "Type Appearances and Styles."

14. Save the file and close it.

2. ————Top Object Distortion

The envelope shapes available through the Warp Options dialog box are a sample of possible envelope shapes, but any shape can be used for an envelope. The results of creating an envelope from a complex shape can be difficult to predict, although through trial and error you can get some great effects. As you will see in this exercise, envelopes made from basic shapes are a bit easier to visualize and can be a great design technique.

1. Open the file **crate.ai** from the **chap_15** folder.

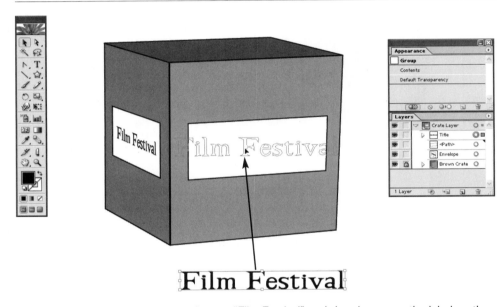

2. With the **Selection** tool, select the text "Film Festival" and drag it up over the label on the crate. It does not need to be centered under the white label.

The text in this exercise is type that was converted to outlines, so you won't see the text container or path when you select it, and you cannot use the Type tool to change what it says.

3. Choose **Object > Arrange > Send Backward**. This puts the text directly beneath the white label.

Be sure to choose Send Backward rather than Send to Back. Send to Back will put the text behind the entire crate.

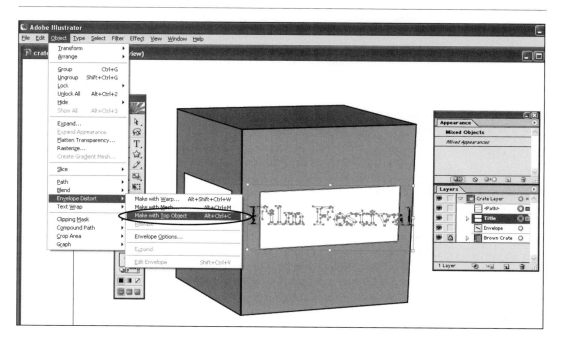

4. Hold down the **Shift** key and click the white label so both the text and the label are selected. Choose **Object > Envelope Distort > Make with Top Object**. This should use the label to warp the text.

Make with Top Object changes the top-most selected object into an envelope and puts all lower selected objects into that envelope. In this case, there was only one lower object selected, but it can be as many as you want.

5. The result is text warped to fit in the area of the white label. When the white label became an envelope, however, its fill and stroke became invisible. If you look closely, you can see that the text has been stretched out to touch the four corners of the envelope. This isn't what you need for the crate, so press **Delete** or **Backspace** on your keyboard to delete it.

Yes, delete it rather than choose **Edit > Undo.** *You are going to copy the label on the side of the box and look inside its envelope to see why it worked. Trust me.*

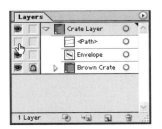

6. For your convenience, there is a second label for the box hidden in the **Layers** palette. Click the **Eye** icon for the hidden **<Path>** to have it appear in your artwork.

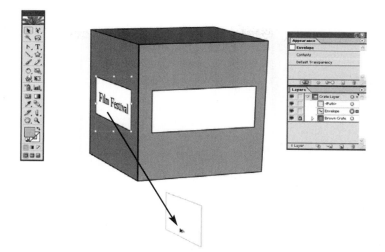

7. The label on the side of the crate was created using an envelope, too. To see how it was done, hold down the **Alt** key (Windows) or the **Option** key (Mac) and drag a copy of the left-side label down below the crate.

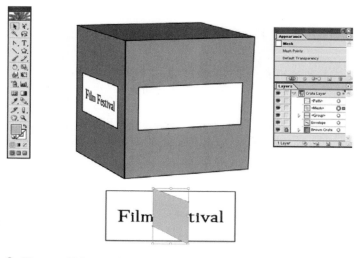

8. Choose **Object > Envelope Distort > Release** to release the envelope. The undistorted label and a gray shape appear. The gray shape is called a **mesh object**, and it defines the envelope. Click anywhere off the artwork to deselect the mesh object and its contents. Click the gray mesh object to select it and press **Delete** or **Backspace** to delete it.

Releasing the envelope reveals that the label on the side of the box was created by warping both the text and a white rectangle with a black border.

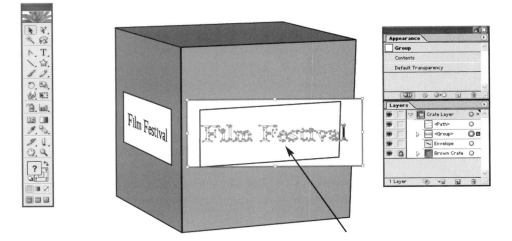

9. Select the undistorted label and drag it up under the label on the front of the box in your artwork. It does not matter if it is centered.

10. Hold down the **Shift** key and click the label on the front of the crate so it is selected as well. Choose **Object > Envelope Distort > Make with Top Object**. The crate now has a label in perspective.

This time the top object is warping both the text and the white rectangle. The cool part is that the relative sizes of the white rectangle and the text are maintained. The largest object, the white rectangle, is warped to fill the envelope while the text is warped in the same shape but is not stretched to fill the envelope as it was in Step 4.

11. Save the file and close it.

MOVIE | envelope_trick.mov

Sometimes you want an object warped slightly by an envelope, but you're not sure how much. You can group the object you want warped with four small unpainted (no fill and no stroke) objects—one for each corner of the envelope—and use them to control how much the visible object is warped. To see this technique performed, watch the movie **envelope_trick.mov** online at **http://lynda.com/books/hot/illcs/movies/**.

3. ——————————Mesh Distortion

Now that you have a sense of how envelopes work, it's time to dig deeper and explore the concept of the mesh object. An envelope is actually an object or objects that are warped by a mesh object. When you used the Make with Warp command in Exercise 1, the warps you were selecting from were a list of mesh objects. When you created an envelope from a top object in Exercise 2, the top object became a mesh object. Now it's time to edit mesh objects directly to understand how they work and how to achieve precise control over the way they look.

1. Open the file **barrel.ai** from the **chap_15** folder.

2. Select the flat label and drag it under curved label.

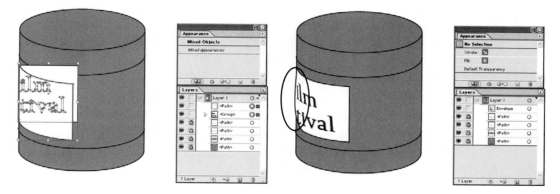

3. Just as you did in the previous exercise, hold down the **Shift** key and click the curved label so both the flat and the curved label are selected. Choose **Object > Envelope Distort > Make with Top Object**.

This time it doesn't work so well. Getting an asymmetrical curve to look correct in an envelope requires a more complex mesh object than can be achieved using the Make with Top Object command. It's still a good idea to try this simple technique first before messing with creating the custom mesh, just in case it does work out the way you wanted.

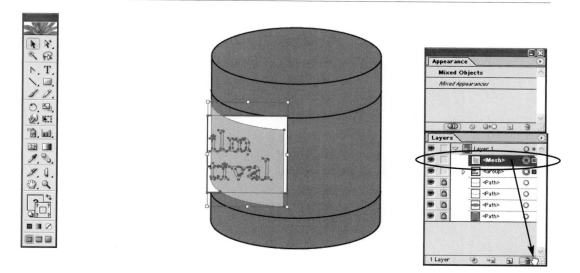

4. Choose **Object > Envelope Distort > Release**. On the **Layers** palette, drag the **<Mesh>** row to the **Trash** to delete it.

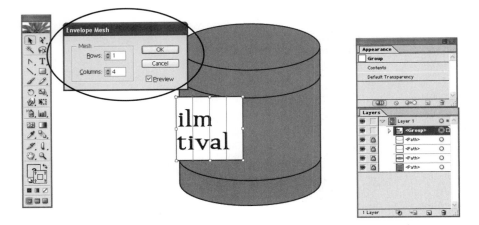

5. The flat (unwarped) label should still be selected. Choose **Object > Envelope Distort > Make with Mesh**. Choose **1 Row** and **4 Columns**. Click **OK**.

Why one row and four columns? The truth is that I experimented with several variations to arrive at this number. It was the simplest mesh that got the job done. As a general rule, try meshes with the fewest columns and rows possible at first. Four rows by four columns is often a good place to start. If you can't get the effect you want with that mesh, try more rows or columns as needed. Similar to drawing with a pen where fewer points make a smoother shape, fewer rows and columns in the mesh make a smoother envelope.

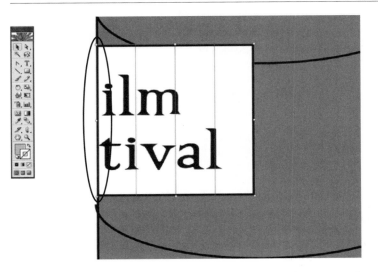

6. Select the **Zoom** tool and click three times on the label to zoom in on it. Select the **Selection** tool. Drag the entire label so the left edge is aligned with the edge of the barrel.

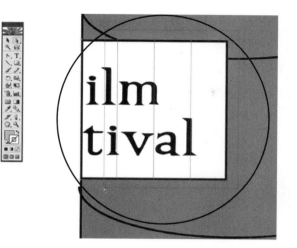

7. The mesh looks like three blue lines on the label, but there are really five lines. Two of them are hard to see because they are on the right and left sides of the label. These 5 lines are defined by 10 **mesh points**: 5 across the top of the label and 5 across the bottom of the label. Select the **Direct Selection** tool. Drag a rectangular marquee around the right eight mesh points—four on the top and four on the bottom—to select them.

You must use the Direct Selection tool because you want to select only some of the points in the mesh object.

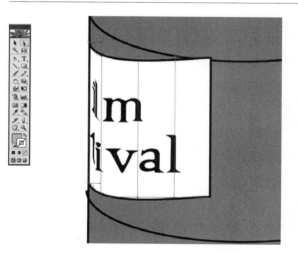

8. Drag the selected part of the mesh down and to the left. As you drag and change the shape of the mesh, the flat label warps accordingly. Moving the selected part of the mesh down causes the label to curve. Moving the selected part to the left compresses the part of the label visible in the first column.

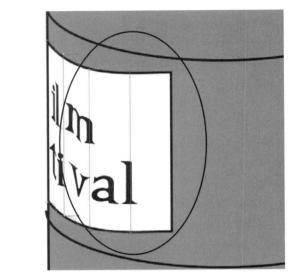

9. Drag a rectangular marquee around the right six mesh points with the **Direct Selection** tool and drag them down and slightly to the left so the curve of the label starts to match the curve of the barrel above and below. Since you want the text visible through the second column compressed less than the first, move these mesh points to the left (less than you did in Step 8).

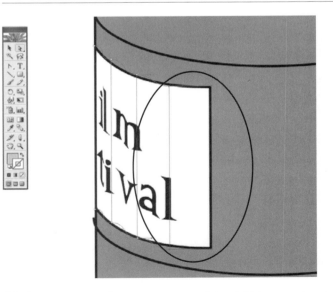

10. Drag a rectangular marquee around the right four mesh columns and drag them down and barely to the left.

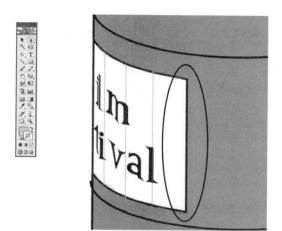

11. Drag a rectangular marquee around the right-most two mesh points with the **Direct Selection** tool and drag them straight down.

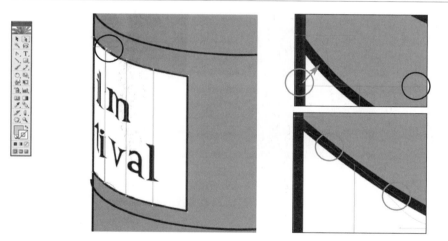

12. Now the label is curved to follow the bend of the barrel, but the text looks wavy rather than following a smooth curve. The next step is to tweak the direction handles on the mesh points. With the **Direct Selection** tool, click the second upper anchor point of the mesh in from the left (circled above). The direction handles appear. Drag the left handle up over the black line of the label so both handles are tangent to the curve of the label on the barrel. You are correcting the curve of the mesh the same way you use direction handles with the Pen tools to draw curved paths.

These mesh points are smooth points, so when you move one handle up, its reciprocal handle will automatically move down. For more information on direction handles and the Pen tool, see Chapter 10, "Pen and Point Tools."

13. Repeat Step 12 for the five other anchor points in the middle of the mesh (circled above) so all the direction handles lie tangent to the curve of the label. As you do this, the text on the label will change to appear more smoothly curved.

14. Select the upper-left anchor point (circled above) with the **Direct Selection** tool and move its single handle down so it lies tangent to the label as well. Repeat for the lower-left anchor point. Now the label looks correct.

That's a lot of work, but the result is a label that curves away in the correct perspective. The coolest part is that since the envelope is a live shape, you can edit the envelope contents and change what it says on the label without having to redo the mesh. This type is converted to outlines so you can't edit it with the Type tool. But if you put regular type inside the envelope, you can edit it, and the new type will appear to wrap around the barrel just like the original type.

15. Save the file and close it.

MOVIE | mesh_envelope.mov

To see the steps of this complex exercise performed, watch the movie **mesh_envelope.mov** located in the **movies** folder of the **H•O•T CD-ROM**.

NOTE | Envelope Options

While an envelope is selected, you can choose **Object > Envelope > Envelope Options** to adjust the options for that envelope. The **Rasters** settings control how the envelope will smooth and clip the raster image. (Yes, envelopes work on raster graphics, too!) The **Fidelity** setting determines how closely the edge of the warped art will match the border of the envelope. 100% is an exact fit but may result in a complicated path with many points that takes a long time to render onscreen. The check boxes determine what is warped by the envelope. **Distort Linear Gradients** and **Distort Pattern Fills** are unchecked by default. If you want an envelope to warp a gradient or pattern fill, and it isn't warping, fix the problem here.

4. ——————Gradient Mesh and the Mesh Tool

There is another kind of mesh called a gradient mesh. Gradient meshes can warp the underlying artwork like a mesh used in an envelope, but that is not their real purpose. Gradient meshes let you create a custom gradient that follows a warped grid. The gradient is created by defining different colors for each mesh point. Illustrator then creates gradients between all the mesh points that follow the curves of the mesh lines. The process can be painstaking, but the results are stunning. In this exercise, you will perform the first steps of creating a gradient mesh that simulates light on the truck fender.

1. Open the file **mesh_truck.ai** from the **chap_15** folder.

2. Select the **Zoom** tool. Drag a rectangular marquee around the fender to zoom in on it.

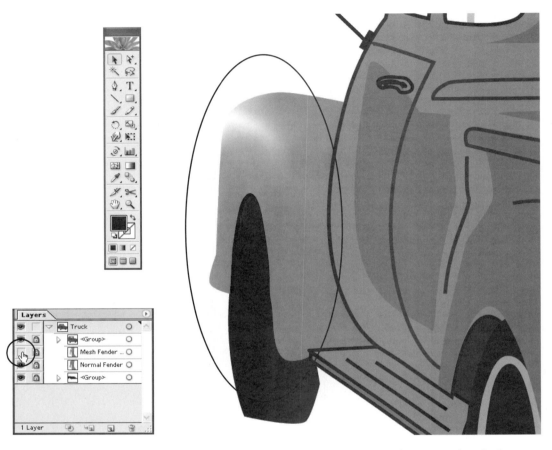

3. So that you can see what a gradient mesh looks like, choose **Window > Layers** to view the **Layers** palette. Click the **Eye** icon to show the hidden layer **Mesh Fender**. This fender has a complex gradient that simulates areas of light and dark and gives the illusion of depth. Click the **Eye** icon again to hide the **Mesh Fender** and reveal the normal fender you will convert into a gradient mesh.

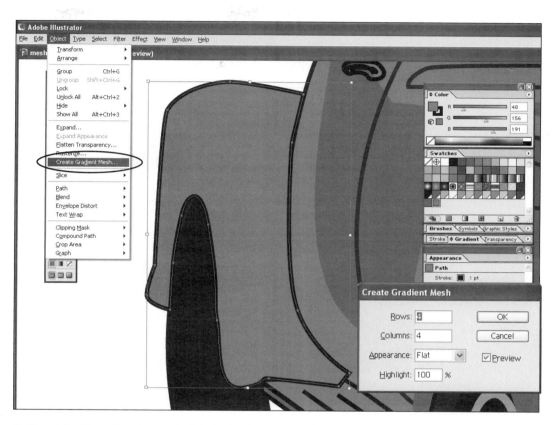

4. Select the **Selection** tool and click the fender to select it. Choose **Object > Create Gradient Mesh**. Choose **4 Rows** and **4 Columns** with a **Flat Appearance**.

*The Appearance determines how Illustrator creates a highlight for the mesh. **Flat** means there is no highlight, so the **Highlight** percentage is doesn't matter. The other two options for **Appearance** are **Center**, which lightens the center of the object as with a radial gradient, and **Edge**, which lightens all the edges of the object. The higher the percentage highlight, the more white the highlight becomes.*

WARNING | No Release for Gradient Mesh

Unlike envelopes, creating a gradient mesh alters the artwork itself. You cannot release a gradient mesh to reveal the original artwork later on. Make sure you have a copy of the artwork on a hidden layer, off to the side of the artboard, or in another file. It's a real bummer to want to restore the original shape you used for the gradient mesh after 20 minutes of work and realize you need to use **Edit > Undo** 150 times to get it.

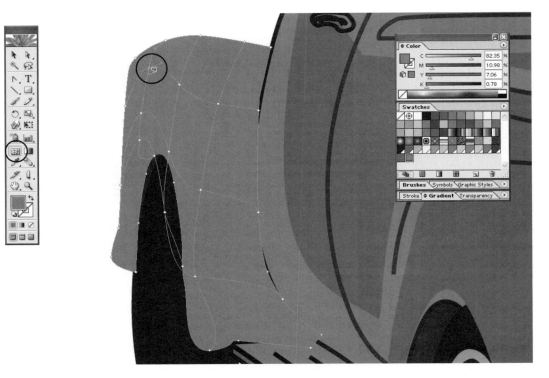

5. A mesh now appears on the fender that warps in a similar pattern to the bends of the fender. Right now, there is no gradient because all the mesh points are the same medium blue as the original object fill color. Select the **Mesh** tool. Click the **Mesh** tool on the mesh point circled above to select it. You'll know it is selected if four direction handles appear for that mesh point.

The Mesh tool has three uses. If you click a mesh point with the tool, it will select that point so you can edit it. If you click anywhere else on the mesh, it will add a new row and/or column to the mesh. If you click a normal object on the artboard with the Mesh tool, the tool will convert it into a mesh object with two rows and two columns. Be careful where you click with the Mesh tool!

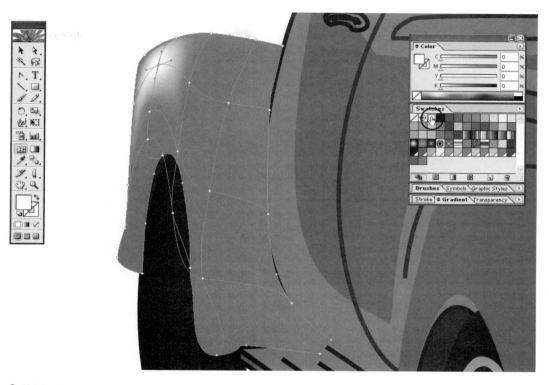

6. While the mesh point is selected, click the **White** swatch on the **Swatches** palette. The color at that mesh point is white, and a gradient appears going from white to the medium blue in all directions from that mesh point.

The gradient follows the mesh lines, so where the lines bend, the gradient bends. Where the distance between the mesh points is longer, such as the line going to the front of the fender, the gradient is stretched out.

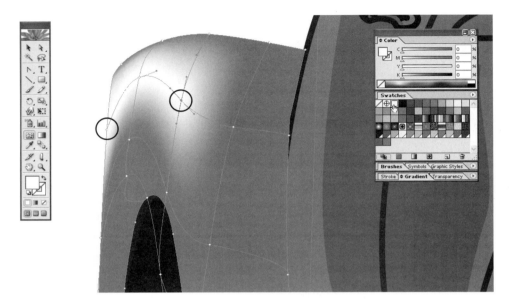

7. Select the mesh point to the left along the grid of the white mesh point (circled above) with the **Mesh** tool. Click the **White** swatch again. Select the mesh point to the right along the grid of the first white mesh point (circled above) with the **Mesh** tool and make it white as well.

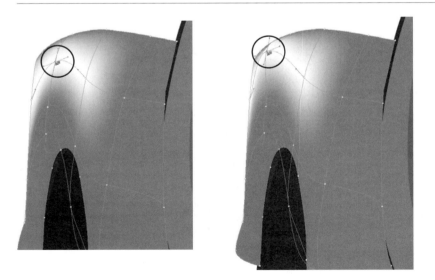

8. Select the first mesh point again (circled above) with the **Mesh** tool. Drag that point up and to the left with the **Mesh** tool. This will change the shape of the mesh, and the gradient will change accordingly.

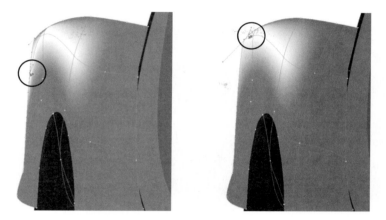

9. Select the next mesh point along the mesh to the left (circled above left), which you earlier changed to white. Hold down the **Shift** key and slide the mesh point up the line without moving the line. Slide it up so the white gradient seems to wrap around the front of the fender (circled above right).

This Shift key shortcut is great for working with gradient meshes. You can use it to slide any mesh point in the mesh along a mesh line, like a bead on a string, without disturbing the line.

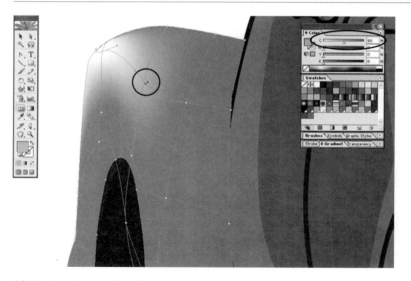

10. Select the right-hand mesh point that you made white (circled above) with the **Mesh** tool. On the **Color** palette, change the color to **50% Cyan**, **0% Magenta**, **0% Yellow**, and **0% Black**. This softens the gradient a bit.

Each mesh point is analogous to a color stop on the Gradient palette. By selecting custom colors across the mesh, you can make the gradient as subtle and complex as you wish.

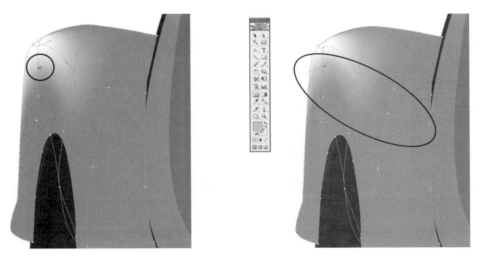

11. Click with the **Mesh** tool on the mesh line between the first white mesh point on the fender and the mesh point below it (circled above). A new row appears.

The new row will not change the appearance of your gradient immediately. Illustrator sets the color of the points along the new row to match the color of the gradient before the row was added.

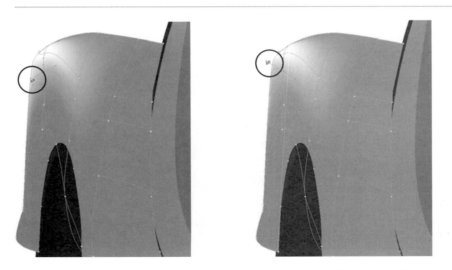

12. The point you added on the row is still selected. Using the **Mesh** tool, drag the left-hand direction handles up and left. This changes the shape of the mesh so the gradient is more compressed toward the front of the fender and more spread out toward the back.

The Mesh tool or the Direct Selection tool can be used to move mesh point direction handles.

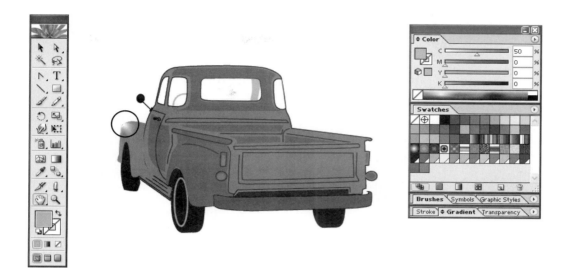

13. Choose **Select > Deselect** and double-click the **Hand** tool to see the full page and the result of your work. Not bad, but there is probably an odd dark spot at the front of the fender. Zoom way in on the odd dark spot by dragging a small square marquee around it with the **Zoom** tool.

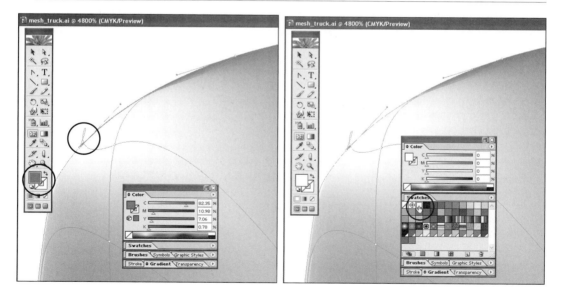

14. There are two mesh points close together at one side of the problem area. One is white the other medium blue. Select the medium blue one with the **Mesh** tool. You'll know you selected the correct one when the **Fill** square on the **Toolbox** shows medium blue. While it is selected, click the **White** swatch.

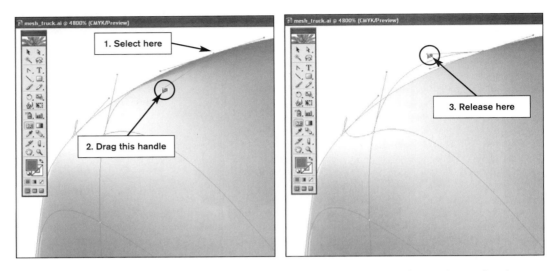

15. The other side of the problem is due to a direction handle on the mesh. Select the mesh point (shown with the arrow above) with the **Mesh** tool. Move its direction handle up and left. This will cover the dark area with the white gradient.

If you look closely at the right-hand picture above, the mesh line extends past the border of the mesh object. This is fine. The object shape did not change because this mesh line was not one that defined the border of the object. If you move either of the other two direction handles on that mesh point, you will change the shape of the object.

16. Save the file and close it.

MOVIE | gradient_mesh.mov

To see the steps of this complex exercise performed, watch the movie **gradient_mesh.mov** located in the **movies** folder of the **H•O•T CD-ROM**.

NOTE | Other Mesh Uses

These exercises focused on using envelopes and gradient meshes to warp vector art in perspective, but they are equally great for effects in flat artwork. The above example above uses a combination of envelopes for the text and gradient meshes for the background color effects.

5. ———————**Blending Paths**

Blending paths is a technique to take two or more objects and create a series of in-between shapes. You might think of it as a morph tool that lets you morph one shape into another. It would be easy to spend a whole chapter on looking at ways to blend paths, with many examples of using the Blend tool in artwork and animation. Blends are not complicated, however, and one exercise will give you the basics to start using blends in your work. Like envelopes, blends are live objects that change the appearance of your art but leave the original art intact. Be sure to check out the movie **power_blends.mov** for some additional techniques to get the most out of blends.

1. Open the file **blend.ai** from the **chap_15** folder. This file contains only a square and a star.

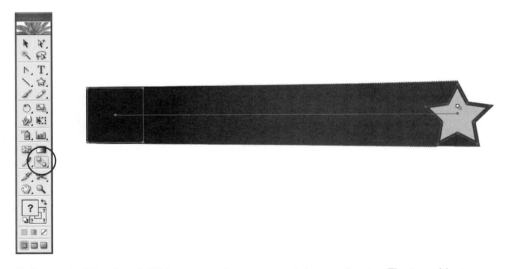

2. Select the **Blend** tool. Click once on the square and then on the star. The two objects are blended into a continuous shooting star. Cool, but it's difficult to see what is actually happening.

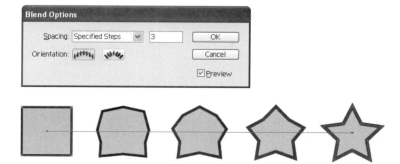

3. With the new blend still selected, choose **Object > Blend > Blend Options** or double-click the **Blend** tool. Change the **Spacing** to **Specified Steps** and set the number of steps to **3**. Click **OK**. Now there are two original shapes and three blend shapes, and it is much easier to see what is going on. Only the two end shapes are "real." The middle three are in-between objects that morph from the shape and colors of the square to the shape and colors of the star.

4. The square to star morph is cool, but not all that practical. Save and close the file **blend.ai** and open the file **poster_15.ai**.

5. With the **Zoom** tool, drag a rectangular marquee around the bottom of the poster to zoom in on it.

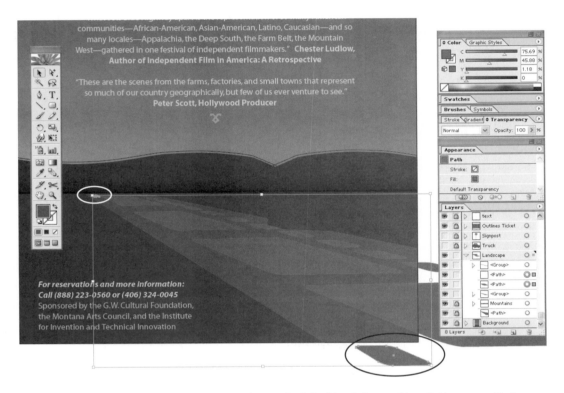

6. Select the two dark blue rounded rectangles on the left side of the road by clicking one with the **Selection** tool and the holding down the **Shift** key while you click the other. One is off the poster slightly and the other is near the horizon.

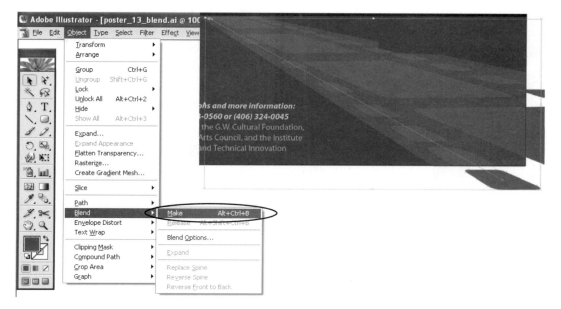

7. Choose **Object > Blend > Make**.

As with the square to star blend, only the first and last rounded rectangle in the series you see are "real." The others are steps in a series of shapes that starts out large like the largest shape and becomes progressively smaller to look more and more like the smallest shape. That is the blend. The progressively smaller rounded rectangles are actually evenly spaced from their centers, but the larger ones overlap, so it looks like there are more of them close to you than far away.

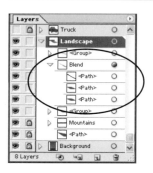

8. Choose **Window > Layers** if the **Layers** palette is not visible. Click the expansion triangle to expand the **Landscape** layer and the expansion triangle to expand the **Blend** row and see the blend contents. The blend consists of the two paths that make the rounded rectangles on each end and a third path. This path is a line connecting the two endpoints of the blend. This path is the blend spine. The in-between objects appear along the spine.

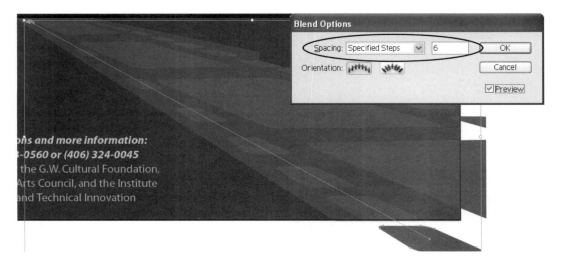

9. With the new blend still selected, choose **Object > Blend > Blend Options** or double-click the **Blend** tool. Make sure the **Spacing** is **Specified Steps** and set the number of steps to **6**. Click **OK**.

*The default of Smooth Color in the Blend Options dialog box is useful for a continuous blend between objects of different colors. Blends will blend object colors, patterns, and effects as well as shapes. The **Orientation** of the blend applies only when the spine is curved. Each step in the blend remains square to the bottom of the page by default but can rotate to match the curve of the spine if you choose.*

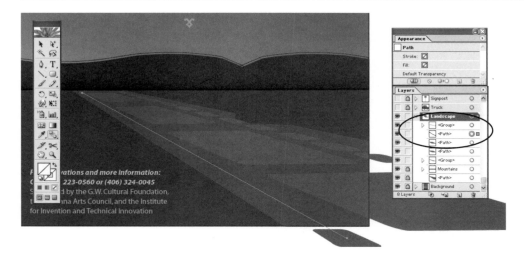

10. The result wasn't quite the desired effect, so choose **Object > Blend > Release**. After releasing a blend, the spine remains in your art as an unpainted path. Select the **<Path>** that was the spine on the **Layers** palette. Press **Delete** or **Backspace** on your keyboard.

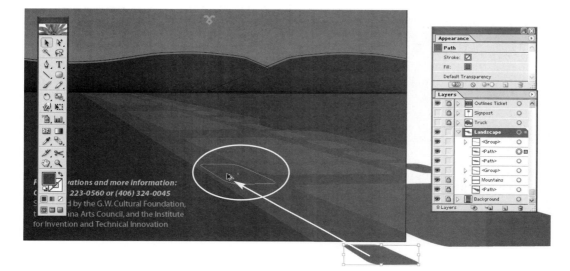

11. Select the **Selection** tool and hold down the **Alt** key (Windows) or the **Option** key (Mac) while you drag a copy of the larger rounded rectangle up and to the left.

12. Choose **Object > Transform > Scale**. Select **Uniform** and set the **Scale** to **70%**. Click **OK**.

13. Select the **Blend** tool. Click the largest rounded rectangle first, then the smaller, rescaled one, and then the smallest one. This creates a blend with three steps.

It does not matter what objects are selected when you create the blend using the Blend tool.

14. Double-click the **Blend** tool to see the **Blend Options**. Check the **Preview** check box. Make sure the **Spacing** is **Specified Steps** and change the number of steps to **2**. Now there are two blend objects between the first and second "real" rounded rectangle and two more blend objects between the second and third one.

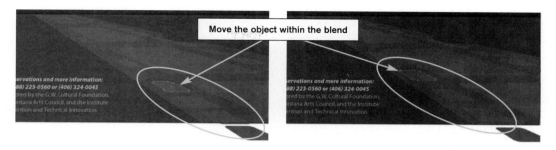

Move the object within the blend

15. Select the **Group Selection** tool. Click the middle rounded rectangle to select it. Move it toward the horizon a bit and release the mouse. The blend changes accordingly.

This is one area where blends really shine. Since they are live, you can move or edit the artwork used to define one step of the blend and change the look and/or position of the entire blend.

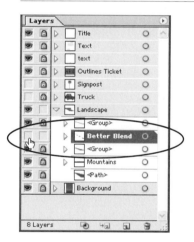

16. Click twice with the **Group Selection** tool on the middle rounded rectangle to select the entire blend. Press **Delete** or **Backspace** on your keyboard to delete it. On the **Layers** palette, unhide the group **Better Blend**.

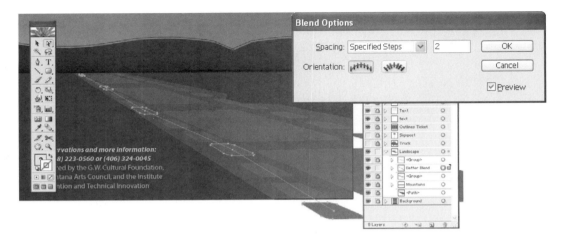

17. The **Better Blend** group is five rounded rectangles spaced to give a better final effect when blended. Select the **Blend** tool and click the five rounded rectangles from largest to smallest. Double-click the **Blend** tool and change the **Spacing** to **Specified Steps** with **2** steps. Click **OK**.

The more real objects you use to define a blend, the more control you have over the resulting look. In this case, having the Blend tool fill in the gaps between five real objects is more precise than having it fill in the difference between two or three. There is a point when it is easier to just draw all the objects, of course, but even small time savings add up on a big project.

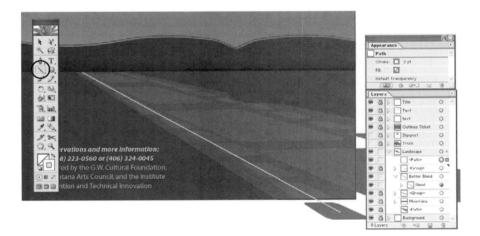

18. The rounded rectangles are now better spaced but poorly aligned because the five original shapes were not well aligned. This is easily fixed. Choose **Select > Deselect** to deselect the blend. Select the **Line** tool and drag a line directly from the center of the smallest rounded rectangle to the center of the largest one.

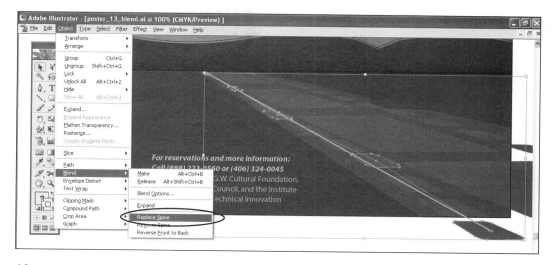

19. With the line still selected, select the **Selection** tool and hold down the **Shift** key while selecting the blend. With both the line and the blend selected, choose **Object > Blend > Replace Spine**. Now the shapes are aligned along the new spine.

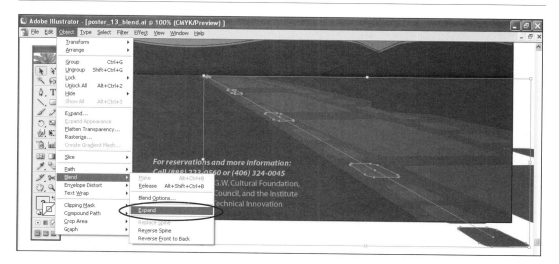

20. The blend is looking much better, but some custom tweaking might be needed to get each rectangle in exactly the correct position. With the blend selected, choose **Object > Blend > Expand**. Each step in the blend is now a "real" object of the correct size and shape. You can now use the **Group Selection** tool to adjust any positions you wish.

21. Save the file and close it.

NOTE | Blending Live Type

blending text
blending text
blending text
blending text
blending text
blending type
BLENDING TYPE
BLENDING TYPE
BLENDING TYPE
BLENDING TYPE

Something new to blends in Illustrator CS is the capability to blend live point-type objects. Point-type objects are discussed in Chapter 8, "*Adding Text.*" Create two or more point-type objects and choose **Object > Blend > Make** or click each object in sequence with the **Blend** tool. The blends appear between the type objects. The results of editing any type object immediately appear in the blend! This feature works only with point type. Type on a path or in an area cannot be blended unless it is converted to outlines first.

TIP | Duplication Through Blending

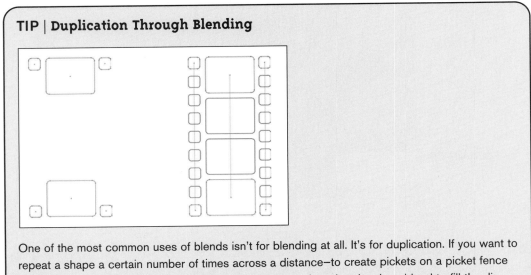

One of the most common uses of blends isn't for blending at all. It's for duplication. If you want to repeat a shape a certain number of times across a distance—to create pickets on a picket fence for example—you can create two identical objects for each end and make a blend to fill the distance between them. The filmstrip on the right was created from the objects on the left by creating three blends; two for the small rounded rectangles (one on each side) and one for the large rounded rectangles in the center.

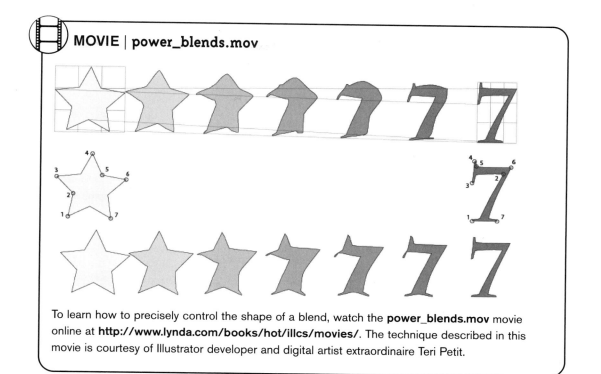

MOVIE | power_blends.mov

To learn how to precisely control the shape of a blend, watch the **power_blends.mov** movie online at **http://www.lynda.com/books/hot/illcs/movies/**. The technique described in this movie is courtesy of Illustrator developer and digital artist extraordinaire Teri Petit.

TIP | Illustrator CS Help

As you are getting to know meshes and blends, check out the Illustrator Help page **Using Transparency, Gradients, and Patterns > Working with gradients, meshes, and blends**. It provides a good overview and is a jumping-off point for several well-written and useful help pages.

Wow. That was a long and mind-bending chapter. Take a breather and think about all the possibilities for these cool tools. When you're ready, turn the page to learn about a great feature for creating and managing repeating images: symbols.

16.

Symbols

Placing Symbols	Modifying Symbols
Creating Symbols	Symbol Sets and the Symbol Sprayer
Symbol Stainer and Styler	Symbol Libraries

chap_16

Illustrator CS
H•O•T CD-ROM

Suppose you are making a company brochure, and the company logo appears in a dozen different places in an illustration. You draw the logo once and then duplicate it several times, resizing some copies larger or smaller. You spend an hour getting it just right. Just as you finish, someone from the marketing department walks in to tell you the company has changed its logo and hands you the new design. Sound like a nightmare? It would be if you created all 12 logo variations using copy and paste. If you used symbols instead, the entire change could be done in minutes.

Symbols are linked images. You create a single piece of art and keep it on a Symbols palette. You then place as many instances of this symbol in your artwork as you wish. Each instance can be warped, transformed, and even tinted individually. If you make a change to the original symbol, all the instances are immediately updated to reflect the change.

Symbols also act as a ready source of premade art—sort of like clip art on steroids. Illustrator provides a set of special symbolism tools to help adjust the look and placement of symbols in your work.

I. ────────Placing Symbols

The simplest use of symbols is taking some of the stock symbols that ship with Illustrator CS and placing them in your artwork. In this exercise, you will use some of these ready-made symbols and see how easily they are manipulated and managed.

1. Copy the **chap_16** folder from the **H•O•T CD-ROM** to your hard drive. Open the file **map_16.ai** from the **chap_16** folder.

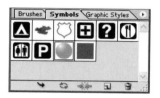

2. Choose **Window > Symbols** to open the **Symbols** palette.

*If you have looked at the Symbols palette before this exercise, you have probably seen several other symbols on it. The Symbols palette for **map_16.ai** contains only the symbols used in this chapter. As with most palettes, you can choose **Select Unused** from the flyout menu and delete the unused items.*

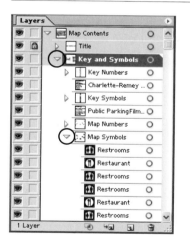

3. Choose **Window > Layers** if the **Layers** palette is not visible. Expand the **Key and Symbols** layer and then expand the **Map Symbols** group.

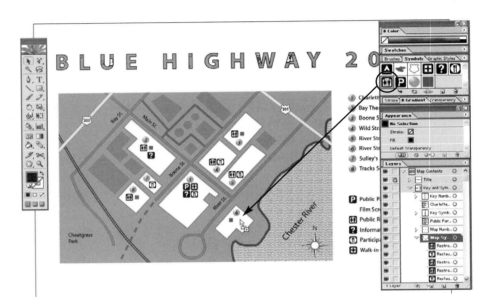

4. Drag the **Restroom** symbol from the **Symbols** palette to the map under ball flag **6** (shown above).

That's all there is to putting a symbol in your art—drag and drop!

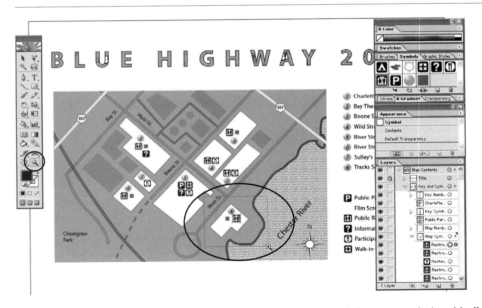

5. Select the **Zoom** tool and drag a rectangular marquee around the new symbol and **ball flag 6** to zoom in on that area.

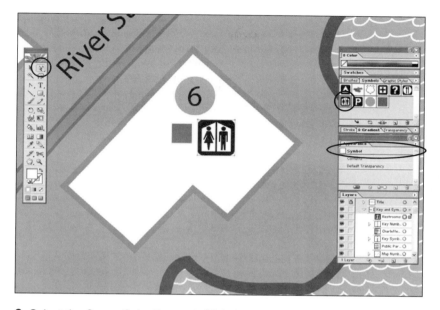

6. Select the **Group Selection** tool. Click the **Restroom** symbol to select it. Notice that even though it is selected, only a selection box with four corners appears. No paths or points are visible for the artwork; you don't see the points that define the circles for the people's heads, for example. This is because it is a symbol, and the art is kept on the **Symbols** palette. The **Restroom** symbol is highlighted on the **Symbols** palette, indicating that the **Restroom** symbol is selected in the artwork. The **Appearance** palette also provides feedback that you have a symbol selected rather than a normal path or group.

7. Choose **Object > Transform > Scale**. Enter **90%** for a **Uniform Scale** and click **OK**. The symbol instance resizes.

You have resized this instance of the symbol, but the original symbol on the Symbols palette is unchanged. You can change the look of individual instances of a symbol independently. Stroke weights and patterns on the symbol are always scaled when you scale a symbol.

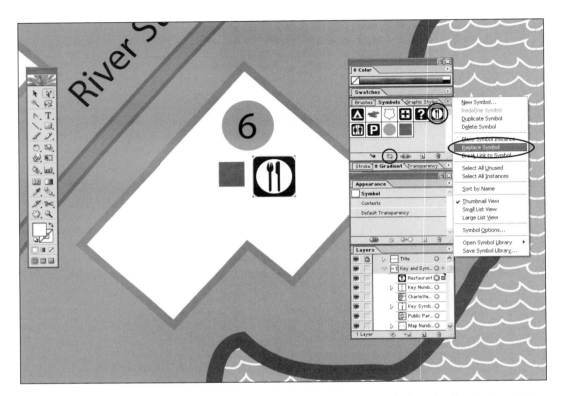

8. While the **Restroom** symbol is still selected, click the **Restaurant** symbol on the **Symbols** palette. Click the **Replace Symbol** button on the **Symbols** palette or choose **Replace Symbol** from the **Symbols** palette flyout menu. The **Restaurant** symbol replaces the selected instance of the **Restroom** symbol on the map.

Not only is it replaced, but it is automatically scaled down to 90%, just like the Restroom symbol was. This is part of what makes symbols so powerful. All the transformations and effects you apply to a symbol are remembered and applied to any replacement symbol.

9. Save the file and keep it open for the next exercise.

2.——————Modifying Symbols

Now that you know how to place symbols, the next step is modifying a symbol and making updates throughout the document. The process is two fold. First you must retrieve the symbol from the Symbols palette so you can edit it. Then you must replace the symbol on the Symbols palette with the new version. Once you replace the symbol on the palette, Illustrator automatically makes the changes throughout your document.

1. Open the file **map_16.ai** or continue from Exercise 1. Double-click the **Hand** tool to zoom out and see the entire map.

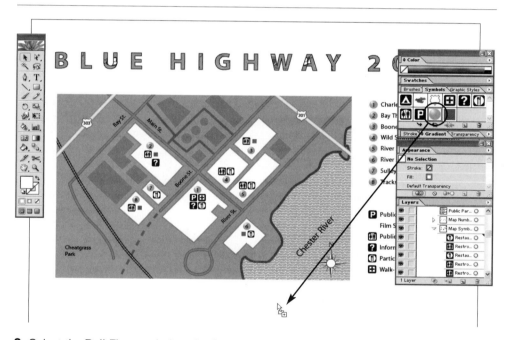

2. Select the **Ball Flag** symbol on the **Symbols** palette (circled above). Drag the **Ball Flag** symbol down to an empty area of the map, as shown above.

So far, you have simply placed an instance of this symbol on the map.

3. Click the **Break Link to Symbol** button on the **Symbols** palette or choose **Break Link to Symbol** from the **Symbols** palette flyout menu. The symbol changes (expands) into editable artwork; in this case a circle filled with a gradient.

*Breaking a link to a single symbol instance has an identical effect to choosing **Object > Expand**.*

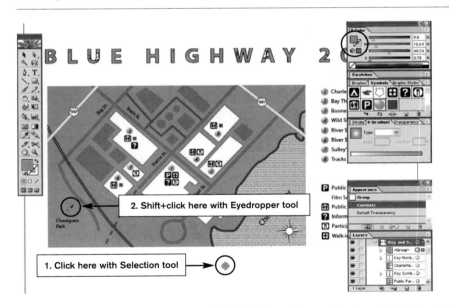

4. Make sure the **Fill** square is on top in the **Color** palette or **Toolbox**. With the circle still selected, select the **Eyedropper** tool. Hold down the **Shift** key to sample only the color rather than the appearance and click the beige area of the map labeled "Cheatgrass Park." This process will replace the circle's original gradient fill with the solid beige you just sampled.

There is no change to the symbols on the map yet. You'll learn how to make this happen next.

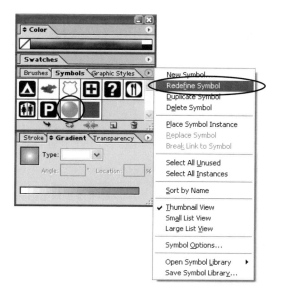

5. Make sure the **Ball Flag** symbol is still selected on the **Symbols** palette, and the solid beige circle is still selected in your artwork. Choose **Redefine Symbol** from the **Symbols** palette flyout menu. The symbol on the **Symbols** palette changes to a solid beige fill, and all the symbol instances update throughout the artwork.

---

6. While the beige-filled circle is still selected in your artwork, press the **Delete** or **Backspace** key on your keyboard to delete it.

The artwork for the symbol is saved in the Symbols palette and is part of your document even after you delete the original art in your artwork, so there is no need to keep this circle in the artwork.

---

7. Save the file and keep it open for the next exercise.

NOTE | Symbols and Older Versions of Illustrator

Symbols were introduced in Illustrator 10, so exporting a file containing symbols to version 9 or earlier causes all symbols to expand into groups containing editable paths. The links to the original symbols are broken, so they will not become symbols if you open the file from Illustrator CS again.

3. ———————Creating Symbols

The libraries of symbols that ship with Illustrator are a great starting point, but you will undoubtedly want to create custom symbols as you work on your own projects in the future. In this exercise, you will learn how to do so by taking a piece of original art, adding it to the Symbols palette, and integrating it into your artwork.

1. Open the file **map_16.ai** or continue from Exercise 2. Also open the file **small_reel.ai**.

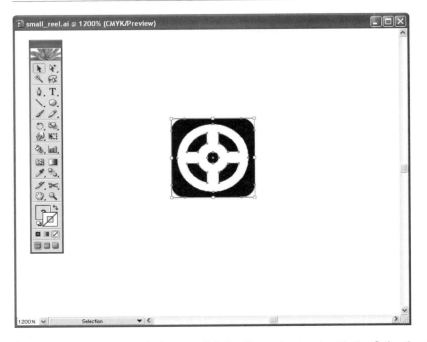

2. With the file **small_reel.ai** open, click the film reel artwork with the **Selection** tool or choose **Select > All** to select all the artwork. Choose **Edit > Copy**.

3. Choose **Window > map_16.ai** to switch back to the map artwork. Choose **Edit > Paste** to add the film reel art to the map.

4. Drag the pasted film reel next to the words "Film Screening Location," as shown above.

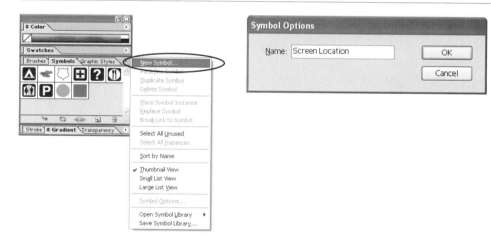

5. The next step is to create a symbol from this artwork. You could simply drag the art to the **Symbols** palette, and a new symbol would be created, but then you would still need to delete the original art and replace it with a symbol. Here's a great shortcut. With the film reel art still selected, hold down the **Shift** key and choose **New Symbol** from the **Symbols** palette flyout menu. Name the new symbol **Screen Location** and click **OK**. The new symbol is created, *and* your art is automatically replaced with the new symbol.

Replacing the original artwork that defined the symbol is a great idea if you don't need the artwork anymore. If you were making a whole series of symbols based on slight changes to one piece of art, you wouldn't want the art replaced by a symbol every time you created one, so Illustrator gives you the option of replacing the art by using the Shift key.

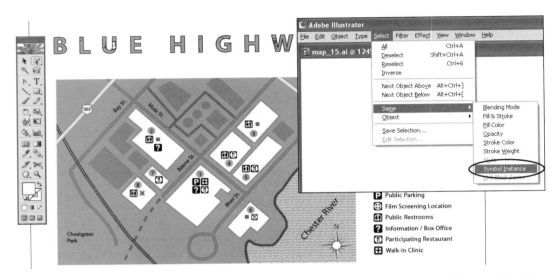

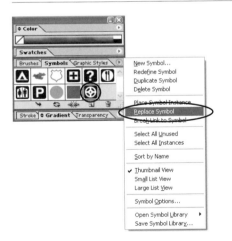

6. Select the **Group Selection** tool. Click any of the small red squares on the map. Choose **Select > Same > Symbol Instance** to select all the red squares.

These red squares are symbols. They were put on the map as placeholders to be replaced by the correct symbol at a later time.

7. Click the **Screen Location** symbol on the **Symbols** palette. Choose **Replace Symbol** from the **Symbols** palette flyout menu. The map is updated with the correct new symbols.

The placeholder symbols were already scaled down to 90%, so when the Screen Location symbol replaced them, it was scaled down to match.

8. Save the file. Choose **Window > small_reel.ai** and close that file.

NOTE | Almost Anything Can Become a Symbol

The only items that can't become a symbol are linked images and certain groups, such as groups of graphs. This leaves quite a few possibilities, including blends, envelopes, text, effects, gradient meshes, and so on. Symbols can even contain other symbols so you can build a complex symbol from simpler ones! Consider saving yourself some time and building symbol libraries of the artwork you find yourself using over and over, such as logos or icons.

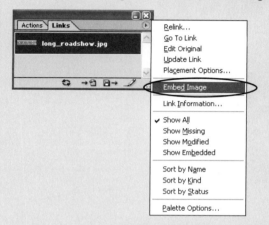

If you want to use a linked raster graphic as part of a symbol, go to the **Links** palette, click the linked image on the palette to highlight it, and choose **Embed Image** from the **Links** palette fly-out menu. This will embed the image in your Illustrator file, and changes to the original image will not be automatically updated in your Illustrator artwork. Images you inserted into your art using **File > Place** are linked to the original file by default.

4. ————————— Symbol Sets and the Symbol Sprayer

Illustrator provides a palette of Symbolism tools to help you work with symbols. The default tool is the Symbol Sprayer, which lets you create symbol sets, which are a group of symbols that behave as a single object.

1. Open the file **map_16.ai** or continue from Exercise 3.

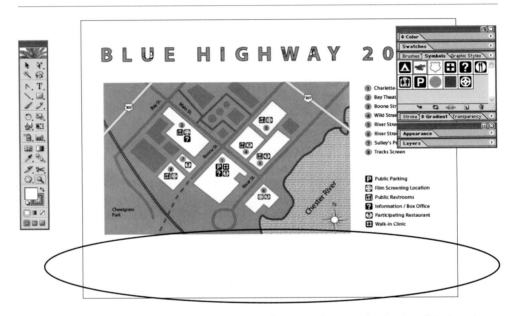

2. Select the **Zoom** tool. Hold down the **Alt** key (Windows) or the **Option** key (Mac) and click with the **Zoom** tool to zoom out. Stop when you can see the bottom area of the map.

The exact amount of zooming will vary with the size and settings for your computer monitor.

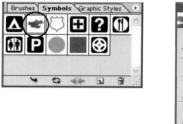

3. Click the **Ground Covering** symbol on the **Symbols** palette. On the **Toolbox**, select the **Symbol Sprayer** tool.

4. Move the tool to the lower-left corner of the map. A huge circle appears showing the area affected by the **Symbol Sprayer** tool. Click and drag with the **Symbol Sprayer** tool slowly from left to right. It applies dozens of instances of the **Ground Covering** symbol to your artwork. The symbols appear at the center of the circle and spread out as you spray. If you try to spray on top of symbols or fill in the gaps between symbols, symbols you have already placed actually move out of the way.

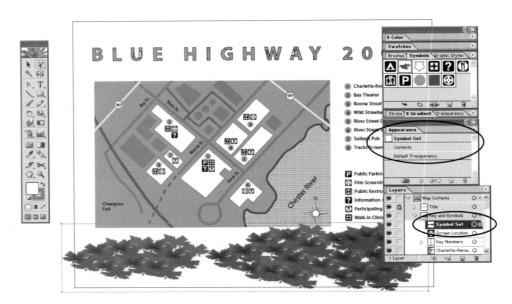

5. The pile of leaves contains many symbol instances, but it is a single object. On the **Appearance** palette and the **Layers** palette, note that it is referred to as a **Symbol Set**. This set is interesting, but a subtler arrangement of leaves might look better. Press **Delete** or **Backspace** on your keyboard.

6. Double-click the **Symbol Sprayer** tool to see the **Symbolism Tools Options**. Change the **Intensity** to **3**. This will slow down the stream of symbols. Click **OK**.

*The number of Symbolism Tool Options appears dizzying at first, but the key three are **Diameter**, which sets the size of the area affected by the tool; **Intensity**, which sets the rate at which the tool makes changes to the symbol set; and **Symbol Set Density**, which determines how much symbols are allowed to overlap. To learn more about the Symbolism Tool Options, watch the movie **symbol_sets.mov** online at **http://www.lynda.com/books/hot/illcs/movies/**.*

7. Spray the ground cover symbols again across the bottom of the map by dragging left to right and moving the mouse up and down slightly as you drag. Moving the mouse up and down will create a scattering of symbols rather than a straight line of them.

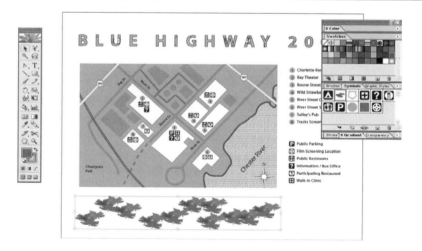

8. Select the **Selection** tool, and a bounding box appears around the symbol set. Hold down the **Shift** key to keep the symbols proportional and resize them slightly smaller.

Symbol sets behave as single objects but can have transformations and effects applied to them just like any other object. After the symbols are sprayed, you can resize, rotate, stain, and screen (adjust the transparency) of the symbols within the set using the other Symbolism tools.

9. Save the file and close it.

5. ——————————Symbol Stainer and Styler

Most of the Symbolism tools are only helpful when working with symbol sets, but two of the tools—the **Symbol Stainer** and the **Symbol Styler**—have applications for any symbol instance. These tools even provide features difficult to achieve on nonsymbol artwork.

1. Open the file **map_16_tools.ai** from the **chap_16** folder.

2. Select the **Selection** tool and click the symbol set of leaves to select them.

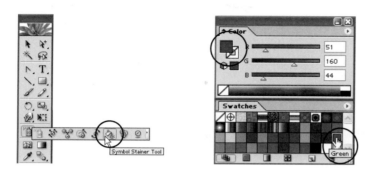

3. Click and hold on the **Symbol Sprayer** tool on the **Toolbox** until the flyout menu appears. Select the **Symbol Stainer** tool. Since the film festival is in the summer, green leaves would be a better look. Make sure the **Fill** square is on top in the **Color** palette and then click the **Green** swatch on the **Swatches** palette.

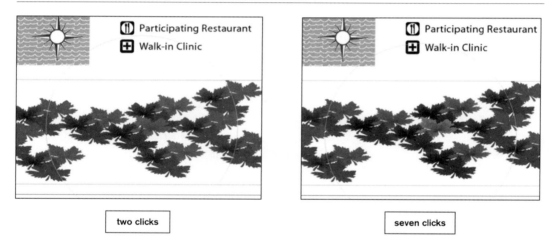

| two clicks | seven clicks |

4. Click with the **Symbol Stainer** tool twice on one of the symbols in the set. It will tint somewhat green, and any symbols nearby will tint slightly green. Click four more times. The symbol under the **Symbol Stainer** tool will be very green, and the surrounding symbols will have a various shades of green.

This is standard behavior for the Symbolism tools. They have the greatest effect under the tool and a progressively decreasing effect toward the edges of the circle showing the tool diameter.

5. Hold down the **Alt** key (Windows) or the **Option** key (Mac) and click four times with the **Symbol Stainer** tool. The stain is progressively removed with each click.

As with resizing symbols, staining doesn't change the original symbol, so you can always remove the stain.

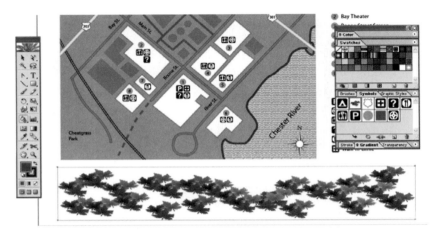

6. Double-click the **Hand** tool to see the entire page. Drag the **Symbol Stainer** tool back and forth across the entire symbol set for a count of 10 and release the mouse. The leaves are almost entirely green.

All the Symbolism tools can be applied one click at a time or continuously by holding down the mouse button. The longer you hold down the button, the more the tool is applied.

7. Drag a rectangular marquee with the **Zoom** tool around the **Highway** symbol over the highway in the upper-right corner of the map.

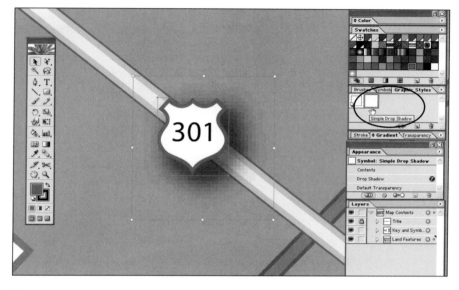

8. Select the **Selection** tool. Click the **Highway** symbol to select it. Click the **Graphic Styles** tab to see the graphic styles. Click the right-hand style **Simple Drop Shadow** to see it applied to the symbol.

Graphic styles are covered in Chapter 18, "Graphic Styles." For the time being, think of graphic styles as a ready-made special effect you can apply to a piece of art. In this case, it makes a drop shadow.

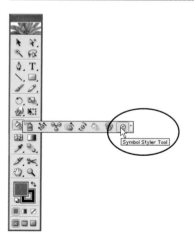

9. Now that you know what the style looks like when applied to the **Highway** symbol, choose **Edit >** **Undo** to remove the style. Click and hold on the **Symbol Stainer** tool to see the tear-off menu. Select the **Symbol Styler** tool.

Symbolism Tools Options

Diameter: 50 pt > Method: User Defined ▼   OK

Intensity: 3 > ☐ Use Pressure Pen   Cancel

Symbol Set Density: 5 >

Hold down the Alt key to decrease the amount of style.
Hold down the Shift key to keep the amount of style constant.

☑ Show Brush Size and Intensity

10. Double-click the **Symbol Styler** tool to see the tool options. Change the **Diameter** to **50 pt**. Since you are zoomed in on a single symbol, a smaller tool is easier to work with. Change the **Intensity** to **3**.

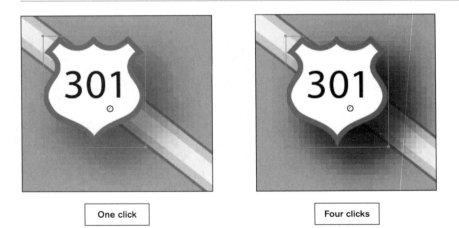

One click   Four clicks

11. Click the **Simple Drop Shadow** graphic style on the **Graphic Styles** palette again. Even though the **Highway** symbol is still selected, the drop shadow won't immediately apply to the symbol because the **Symbol Styler** tool is chosen. Click once over the **Highway** symbol with the **Symbol Styler** tool. The drop shadow is applied very lightly. Click three more times to apply the **Simple Drop Shadow** graphic style more intensely.

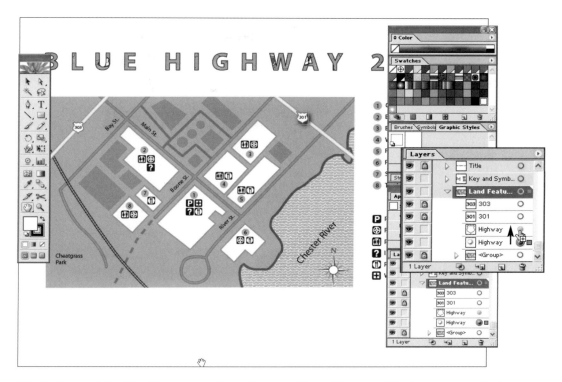

12. Double-click the **Hand** tool to see the entire page. Expand the **Land Features** row on the **Layers** palette. Hold down the **Alt** key (Windows) or the **Option** key (Mac) and drag the shaded **Appearance** button from the lower **Highway** row to the upper one. The effect is copied to the other **Highway** symbol on the map.

An effect is an appearance, so the Appearance button is shaded to show you that the appearance is present on this object. Once you've gotten the look you want with the Symbol Styler tool, you can copy the appearance to any object you want—even nonsymbols.

13. Save the file and keep it open for the next exercise.

MOVIE | symbol_sets.mov

There are a several other Symbolism tools that are important for working with symbol sets. To learn more, watch the movie **symbol_sets.mov** online at **http://www.lynda.com/books/hot/illcs/movies/**.

6. ——————Symbol Libraries

Saving a symbol library is probably even more useful than saving a swatch or paintbrush library, as you have done in earlier exercises, since symbol libraries can hold copies of all the art you regularly use in your work. The process for saving and opening the libraries is the same as with any other library.

1. Open the file **map_16.ai** or continue from Exercise 5.

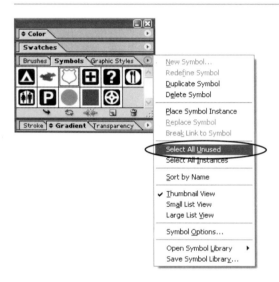

2. Choose **Select All Unused** from the **Symbols** palette flyout menu.

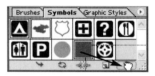

3. Drag selected symbols to the **Trash**.

This will remove any symbols you aren't using and probably don't want to save.

NOTE | Deleting Symbols

In Use Deletion Alert

⚠ One or more of the symbols are in use and cannot be deleted until their instances are expanded or deleted.

[Expand Instances] [Delete Instances] [Cancel]

If you delete a symbol from the Symbols palette that is in use in your artwork, Illustrator will notify you. You must either expand those instances of the symbol or delete them.

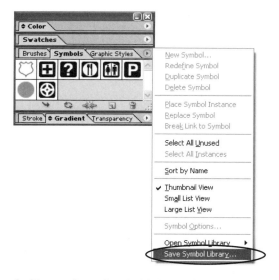

4. Choose **Save Symbol Library** from the **Symbols** palette flyout menu.

Save Palette as Symbol Library:

Save in: Symbols

My Recent Documents
Desktop
My Documents
My Computer
My Network

3D Symbols.ai
Arrows.ai
Artistic Textures.ai
Buildings.ai
Charts.ai
Communication.ai
Decorative Elements.ai
Default_CMYK.ai
Default_RGB.ai
Document Icons.ai
Food.ai
Hair and Fur.ai
International Currency.ai
Logos.ai
Maps.ai

Nature.ai
Networking.ai
Occasions.ai
Office.ai
People.ai
Science.ai
Weather.ai
Web Buttons and Bars.ai
Web Icons.ai

File name: map symbols.ai

Save as type: All files (*.*)

Save   Cancel

5. Name the file **map symbols.ai**. Click **Save**.

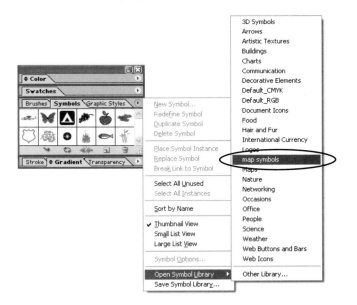

*The default location for saving a symbol library is in Illustrator's **Presets > Symbols** folder. If you save a symbol set in this folder, the next time you start up Illustrator, it will be listed in the Open Symbol Library submenu on the Symbols palette flyout menu.*

6. Close the file.

> ### TIP | **Remove Unused Symbols**
>
> Symbols can take up quite a bit of space in a document. The default Illustrator new document contains 12 symbols as examples. These symbols are saved as part of your document and take up 150 KB of file size. If you have 10 Illustrator files, that's 1.5 MB of symbols you aren't using! You can make slimmer files by selecting and removing unused symbols from the Symbols palette.
>
> Two other space hogs are the default brushes and the pattern swatches, which take up about 100 KB and 80 KB, respectively. To see how to change your startup files so these items do not load by default, see Chapter 20, "*Templates and Actions*."

That's it for Symbols. Since you got a taste of how easy it is to apply a drop shadow in Illustrator, it's time to find out what other cool items are waiting in the chapter on filters and effects.

17.
Filters and Effects

Filters Versus Effects	Enhancing Objects with Effects
Creating Dynamic Objects	Transforming Objects
Raster Art Filters and Effects	Target Practice with New Scribble

chap_17

Illustrator CS
H•O•T CD-ROM

The potential uses and techniques of Illustrator's filters and effects could fill a book all by themselves. Rather than try to show you all the possible uses of these tools, this chapter focuses on the difference between filters and effects, how they work, how the order you apply effects influences the final look, and how to adjust your document settings and workflow to get the most out of these powerful tools. Once you get the logic of how filters and effects work and see a few examples, you can experiment on your own with confidence. If you want to see more examples of how artists use filters and effects in their work, look for books with words like "WOW" and "Secrets Revealed" in the titles. Many of the Illustrator effects are equivalent to Photoshop filters of the same name, and many Photoshop design techniques can be used on your Illustrator artwork with similar results.

I. ─────────Filters Versus Effects

Many commands are available as both a filter and an effect. For example, the ever-popular drop shadow appears on both menus. As you will see in this exercise, an effect can do everything the equivalent filter can do and offer a great deal more. At the end of the chapter is a chart comparing the pros and cons of filters and effects.

1. Copy the **chap_17** folder from the **H•O•T CD-ROM** to your hard drive. Open the file **filters_and_effects.ai** from the **chap_17** folder.

2. Choose **Edit > Preferences > Units and Display Performance** (Windows) or **Illustrator > Preferences > Units and Display Performance** (Mac). Make sure your **General** units are set to **Inches**.

Artists working on Web graphics tend to use pixels for measurement. Artists working in print tend to use linear measures such as inches, centimeters, or points. The exercises for the next few chapters will all use inches.

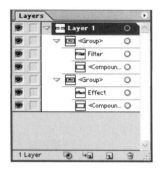

3. Choose **Window** > **Layers** if the **Layers** palette is not visible. Turn down the expansion triangles for the layer and both groups. Both groups contain a type object and a frame made using a compound path. The only difference between the groups is one contains a type object containing the word **Filter** and another contains a type object containing the word **Effect**.

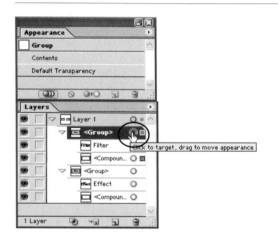

4. Click the **Appearance** button for the group containing the **Filter** type object to target that group. The **Appearance** button will show a double ring to indicate that the group is targeted.

Targeting an object is an important concept when working with filters and effects. Note that the group and both objects it contains are selected—as evidenced by the blue squares on the right of each row—but only the group is targeted. The filter or effect you choose will be applied at the group level.

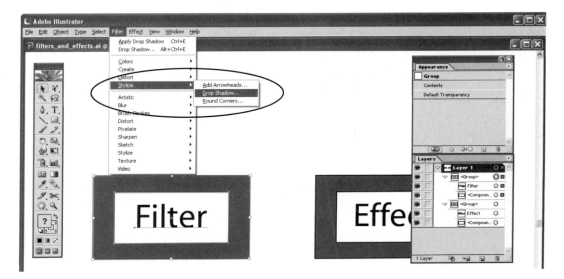

5. Choose **Filter > Stylize > Drop Shadow**. There are two **Stylize** items in the **Filter** menu. You want to use the upper one. The lower one works only with raster graphics, so its submenu items will be grayed out anyway.

6. The default settings are whatever you used when this filter was last applied, so it may or may not match what is shown here. Enter a (blending) **Mode** of **Multiply** with an **Opacity** of **75%** to create the shadowy darkness. Enter an **X Offset** and **Y Offset** of **0.15 in** to put the shadow below and to the right of the group, and a **Blur** of **0.04 in** to soften the shadow edge. Use **Darkness** of **50%** to make the shadow color match the background color and check **Create Separate Shadows** so that the shadows cast by the shape and the type are separate images. Click **OK**.

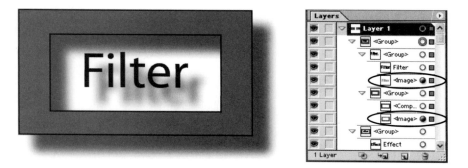

7. Turn down the expansion triangles on two new groups on the **Layers** palette to observe what changed. The drop shadow filter generated the drop shadow by creating two new raster images. One image is a shadowy rectangle that is grouped with the compound shape and the other is a shadowy word "Filter" that is grouped with the type.

8. Click the **Appearance** button for the group containing the **Effect** type object to target that group. Choose **Effect > Stylize > Drop Shadow**.

Be sure to get the correct menu here. It's easy to accidentally apply a filter when you meant to use the effect of the same name, and vice versa.

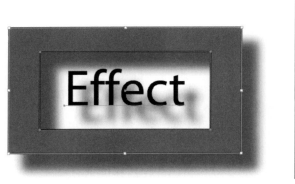

9. Enter the same settings you used in Step 6. Other than having a **Preview** and lacking a **Create Separate Shadow** option, this dialog box is identical to the one used by the filter.

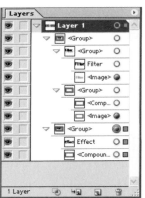

10. The drop shadow looks the same as it did with the filter (except that the shadow is of the word "Effect" this time), but the **Layers** palette looks very different. The only change is that the **Appearance** button for the group is shaded to indicate there is an appearance, in this case a drop shadow, on the group.

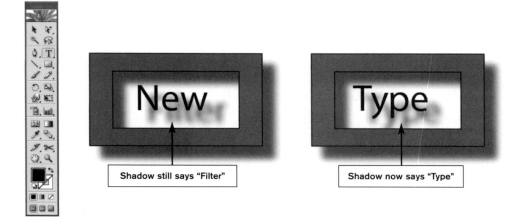

Shadow still says "Filter"

Shadow now says "Type"

11. Now it's time to see how the two drop shadows differ. Select the **Type** tool. Double-click the word "Filter" to select the type and type **New**. The type changes, but the shadow still says "Filter." Double-click the word "Effect" and change it to **Type**. The shadow that was generated using the effect changes to match the new word.

Because the effect is generated "live" from whatever is in the group, any changes to the group—changing an object, editing the type, adding or removing objects from the group—are immediately reflected in the effect. How cool is that?

12. Select the **Selection** tool and click the left-hand red rectangle on the screen. Since this rectangle is grouped, the rectangle, type object, and shadow images are all selected, and the group is targeted. Choose **Filter > Distort > Roughen**. Again, there are two **Distort** commands—you want the upper one. The lower one will have its options grayed out. Enter a **Relative Size** of **5%**, a **Detail** of **10/in**, and use **Smooth Points**. Check the **Preview** check box. Two things happen. One is that the compound path is now distorted, and you can see where dozens of new anchor points have been added to define the more complex shape. The second thing is that the type and images (shadows) have deselected. You cannot apply this filter to type unless you first convert it to outlines, and you cannot apply this filter to raster images at all. Click **OK**.

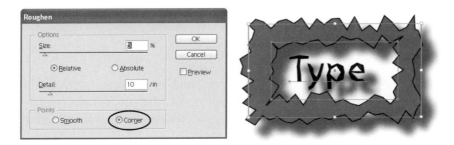

13. Click the right red rectangle on the screen with the **Selection** tool. Since the rectangle is grouped, the type is also selected, and the group is targeted. The shadows are effects, so they cannot be selected as separate objects. Choose **Effect > Distort & Transform > Roughen**. Both the type and the compound path remain selected, and both are roughened. If you look closely, however, you will see that there are no new anchor points showing. This roughen is an effect, the original art is unchanged. Enter the same settings as in Step 12 and click **OK**.

The shadows changed, too, but not because they are being roughened by the Roughen effect. The shadows are live objects, so when the compound path and type roughened, new shadows were created to match.

14. Since the **Drop Shadow** effect and the **Roughen** effect are appearances, they are listed on the **Appearance** palette. Double-click the **Roughen** effect row on the **Appearance** palette.

15. Change the effect from **Smooth Points** to **Corner Points** and click **OK**.

Effects are editable, which is a huge advantage over filters.

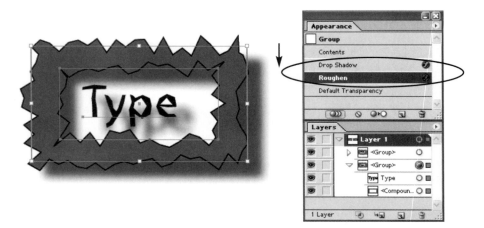

16. On **Appearance** palette, drag the **Roughen** row down underneath **Drop Shadow**. Now the compound shape is roughened but the shadow is not.

Effects are applied in the order listed in the Appearance palette from the top down. Because the Roughen effect is listed after Drop Shadow, the shadows are created from unroughened shape and type and then the shape and type are roughened. Customizing the order of effects in the Appearance palette can have some cool and mind-bending results. This is another big advantage to effects compared to filters.

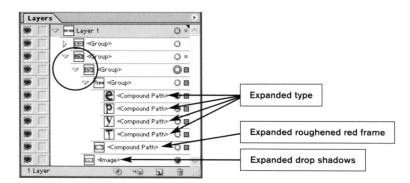

17. Choose **Object > Expand Appearance**. Turn down the three **<Group>** expansion triangles. The effects are made permanent by converting the type to outlines with extra anchor points, adding anchor points to the compound path, and converting the drop shadows into a single <Image>. Now the effect is similar to the filter in that the original artwork is changed.

18. Save and close the file.

Choosing Between Filters and Effects

Filters make immediate changes your artwork, and the only way to remove a filter is with the Undo command. Effects appear to change the artwork, but the anchor points or pixels in the artwork do not actually change. This is similar to the way envelopes warped your art without actually changing it in Chapter 15, "*Envelopes, Meshes, and Blends*." When the same command is available as either an effect or a filter, the effect is usually a better choice because you can edit the original art or remove the effect at any time. Since effects are appearances, objects with an effect applied have a shaded Appearance button on the Appearance palette. Effects can always be expanded with the **Object >** **Expand Appearance** command. Once you fully expand the effect, the underlying anchor points and/or pixels are changed, and the result is the same as applying a filter.

Sometimes you do not have a choice since a command is only available as a filter, such as **Filter >** **Create > Object Mosaic**, or as an effect, such as all the 3-D effects (**Effect > 3D**). Filters do have a few advantages over effects, as listed below, but expanding an effect negates these advantages. Since effects have much more versatility than filters, the rest of this chapter will focus on effects and only explore filters when no appropriate effect exists.

Effects Versus Filters

Effects Advantages over Filters

Effects are "live," so you can change the underlying art and get a new look to the effect. Filters add items to your artwork, such as the raster image drop shadow, or change the art permanently.

Effects can be edited or removed at any time. Filters cannot be edited or removed (except for using the **Edit > Undo** command).

You can change the order in which effects are applied at any time. Filters cannot be reordered.

Filters Advantages over Effects

Every time you edit an object with effects, all the effects are recalculated. This can take a long time when several effects are applied (especially processor-intensive effects like 3-D). Filters change the art, so the only delay is when you first apply the filter.

Filters give you immediate access to the anchor points for editing. Effects must be expanded to access the anchors points of the warped or changed shape.

Filters can be executed automatically by Actions while effects require a dialog box. For more information on Actions, see Chapter 20, "*Templates and Actions*."

Why Two Menus?

One of the more confusing things about filters and effects is that the many of the same commands appear on both menus and appear to do the same thing. To make matters a bit more confusing, some commands work only in the RGB color mode, some work only on raster graphics, and some work only vector graphics. The commands on the menus are grouped to help you know which commands are for what uses and in which color mode.

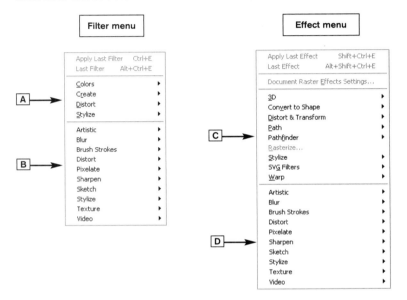

Color Modes and Applicability of Filters and Effects		
Group of Commands	**Color Mode**	**Vector or Raster**
A	RGB or CMYK, but with different commands in each mode	Both for many filters, but not all.
B	RGB only	Raster only.
C	RGB or CMYK	Both, but many affect only additional strokes and fills added to raster art.
D	RGB only	Both, but vector art is temporarily rasterized before the effect is applied.

After you use effects and filters on a few projects, you will get a better feel for which commands are most useful to your artistic style and workflow.

NOTE | The Future of Filters

Effects and the Effect menu did not exist until Illustrator 9. When effects were introduced, the Filter menu remained even though effects were more versatile and could be expanded to produce the same result as the filter of the same name. The rumor from inside Adobe is that the Filter menu will disappear in the next version of Illustrator, and the unique filters will be moved to another menu.

2. ———————— Enhancing Objects with Effects

The most common use of effects in Illustrator is probably to enhance vector art with attributes that would be difficult or impossible to draw with the standard Illustrator tools. Drop shadows, neon glows, and feathered edges are examples of raster-like effects that aren't easily drawn. Other effects, such as the Pathfinders or Distort effects, result in art you could draw from scratch with Illustrator tools, but using the effect saves you time and allows for easier editing later on. In this exercise, you will use the Outer Glow effect and the Add Pathfinder effect to create a glowing border for the truck.

1. Open the file **poster_17.ai** from the **chap_17** folder.

2. Select the **Zoom** tool in the **Toolbox** and drag a rectangular marquee around the truck to zoom in on it.

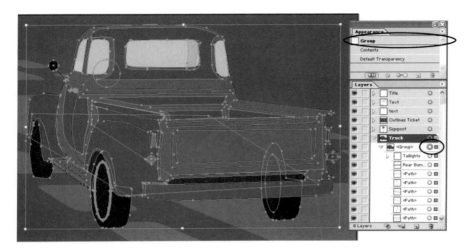

3. Select the **Selection** tool and click the truck on the screen. The truck is a group, so all the objects in the group are selected, but on the **Layers** and **Appearance** palettes, you will see that only the group has been targeted for an appearance.

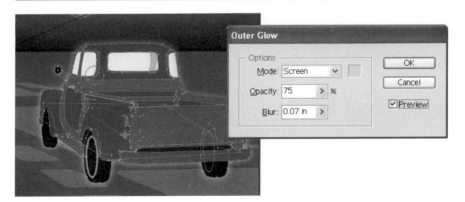

4. From the upper section of the **Effect** menu, choose **Effect > Stylize > Outer Glow**. Verify that the **Outer Glow** options are a (blending) **Mode** of **Screen**, an **Opacity** of **75%**, and a **Blur** of **0.07 in**. Change them to match these options if they are not and click **OK**. The border of the truck is now trimmed with an eerie yellowish glow.

That was easy. To create the same result without using an effect would require creating a path around the truck, using complicated mesh to make a gradient, and then applying that gradient to an opacity mask over a yellow fill. No thanks! The effect is also great in that it is easily edited. Changing the (blending) Mode changes how the color in the square beside the Mode interacts with the background colors. You can change the blend color by clicking on that colored square. Setting a greater Opacity makes the glow brighter. Setting a larger value for Blur spreads the glow out over a greater distance and softens the effect.

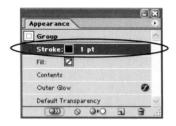

5. The next step is to add a thin stroke around the border of the truck to accent it a little more. While the group is targeted, go to the **Appearance** palette flyout menu and choose **Add New Stroke** to add a new stroke to the group. A new stroke appears on the truck and the **Appearance** palette, but it is difficult to see because it is a black stroke.

6. With **Stroke** on the **Appearance** palette still highlighted, choose the **white** color on the **Color** palette spectrum bar or click the **White** swatch on the **Swatches** palette to change **Stroke** to white. Now you can see the stroke, but it isn't just around the border the way the **Outer Glow** was. All the strokes on all the paths that make the truck are visible.

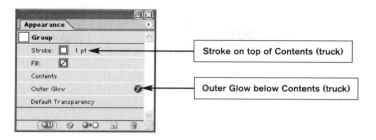

Stroke on top of Contents (truck)

Outer Glow below Contents (truck)

So why did the Outer Glow make an outline but the added Stroke did not? The reason is found in the Appearance palette. The Outer Glow effect was applied below (after) the Contents row. The Contents of this group is the truck, so the opaque fill of the truck masks any glowing edges that might appear inside the truck. The Outer Glow effect is designed to work this way and always appears below the Contents. You could drag the new Stroke row on the Appearance palette down underneath the Contents, too, and mask all the unwanted white lines, but the solution shown here is much better (and more elegant).

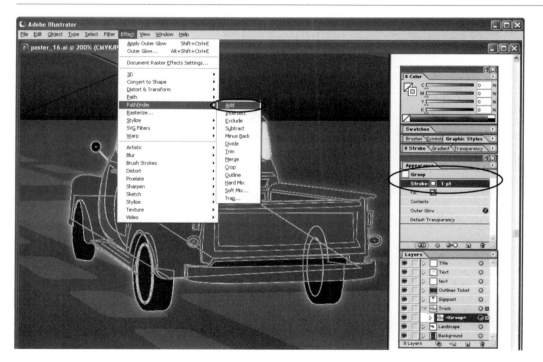

7. With the new **Stroke** row still highlighted on the **Appearance** palette, choose **Effect > Pathfinder > Add**.

The Add effect does the same thing as the Add Pathfinder explored in Chapter 13, "Path Tools." It merges several overlapping shapes into one large shape with one continuous border.

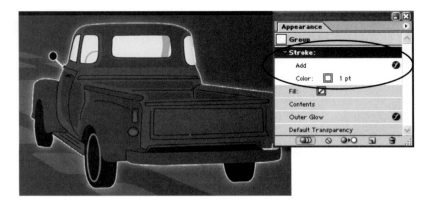

8. Look on the **Appearance** palette. The **Add** effect was applied only to the extra stroke. The shapes of the truck—the **Contents**—were unaffected, but the stroke is now only around the truck border. Cool! Since this border is an effect, any changes made to the trucks outer shape will immediately appear in the stroke as well.

You may need to deselect the truck to see the border well.

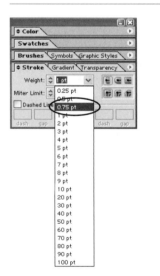

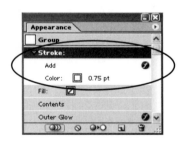

9. The **1 pt** border is a bit brash. Select the truck with the **Selection** tool (if you deselected it) and click the **Stroke** row on the **Appearance** palette to highlight it. On the **Stroke** palette, change the stroke to **0.75 pt.**

10. Double-click **Hand** tool to see the entire page and choose **Select > Deselect** to better see the results.

11. Save the file and keep it open for the next exercise.

3. ————————Creating Dynamic Objects

Since effects are "live," the look of artwork using effects changes whenever you edit the original paths or type. You saw this in Exercise 1, where the drop shadow changed to match a change in the type casting the shadow. This feature can be used to create objects that adjust themselves as you edit. Self-adjusting artwork can come in very handy, as you will see in this exercise.

1. Open the file **poster_17.ai** from the **chap_17** folder or continue from Exercise 2.

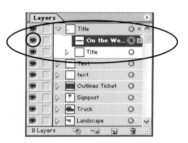

2. Turn down the expansion triangle for the **Title** layer and click the **Eye** icon to show the hidden type "On the Web...."

3. Select the **Zoom** tool and drag a rectangular marquee around the type to zoom in on it.

4. Select the type with the **Selection** tool and choose **Add New Fill** from the **Appearance** palette flyout menu.

5. On the **Color** palette, change the new fill color to **50% Cyan** and **0% Black**.

Since the new Cyan Fill is above the Black Characters in the Appearance palette, the type appears to change color.

6. Choose **Effect > Convert to Shape > Rectangle**. Make sure **Rectangle** is chosen for the shape and **Relative** is selected with **0.25 in Extra Width** and **Extra Height**. Click **OK**. The extra fill that was in the shape of the type is now a rectangle exactly .25 inches taller and wider than the type area.

Convert to Shape is an effect that makes no sense unless you apply it on an extra stroke or fill layer added in the Appearance palette. In this context, it is very cool, as you are about to see.

7. On the **Appearance** palette, drag the **Characters** row above the **Fill** row to put the black type in front of the cyan rectangle.

This rectangle is not a shape in the conventional sense. There are no visible anchor points you can edit, and you cannot select only the rectangle. It is an effect and is part of the Type object. What's great is that this rectangle will expand and contract as you edit the text, which you'll get to try in the upcoming steps.

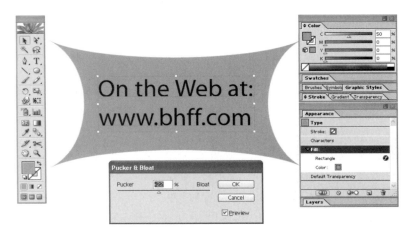

8. The rectangle needs a little pizzazz. Because it is an effect, you can only edit it using another effect. Click the **Fill** row on the **Appearance** palette to highlight it. Choose **Effect > Distort & Transform > Pucker and Bloat**. Enter a value of **−22%** and click **OK**.

Pucker leaves the anchor points of a shape unchanged, but bends the lines between the points inward toward the center of the shape. Bloat leaves the anchor points of a shape unchanged, but bends the lines between the points outward.

9. Double-click the **Hand** tool to see the entire page. Drag the type onto poster, as shown above. Once it's in place, zoom in on the type and background with the **Zoom** tool.

10. Now you that you have your cool type and background object in place, you find out that the Web address has changed to something very different. (I hate it when that happens.) Select the **Type** tool. Double-click the type "bhff" to select it. Type **bluehighwayfilmfest** to replace it. As you type, the background adjusts to match.

Some tweaking of the Pucker effect may be necessary to get the final look the way you want it, but that's still better than creating a new background object on short notice.

11. Save and close the file.

4. ——————**Transforming Objects**

Another great use for effects is taking a simple object and using it to create more complex ones on the fly. The powerful (and often overlooked) **Transform** effect is king in this area. This exercise is a quick and simple example of what can be done.

1. Open the file **map_17.ai** from the **chap_17** folder.

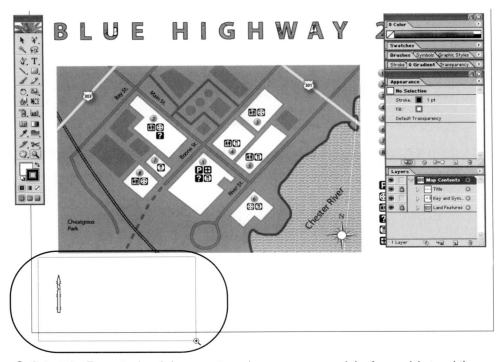

2. Select the **Zoom** tool and drag a rectangular marquee around the fence picket and the area to its right on the bottom of the map.

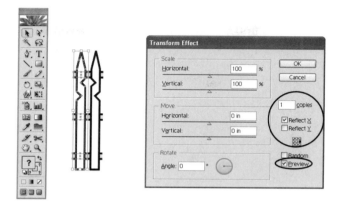

3. Select the **Selection** tool and select the fence picket. Choose **Effect > Distort & Transform > Transform**. Set the transform for **1 copies**, check the **Reflect X** check box, and put the center of transformation to the right-center position. Check **Preview** to see the results. Click **OK**.

Throughout this exercise, keep in mind that there is only one "real" fence picket. In this step, you copied the fence picket and reflected it along its right edge so it appears as if there are two pickets with a diamond cutout between them.

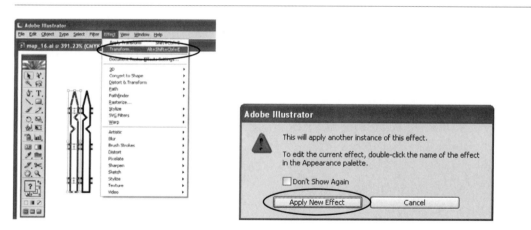

4. Choose **Effect > Transform**. Since this was the last applied effect it is second from the top of the list. (The **Apply Transform** option skips the **Transform Effect** dialog box and creates a second instance of the effect with exactly the same settings as the previous one). Click **Apply New Effect** when warned about a double instance of the effect.

*Resist the temptation to check the **Don't Show Again** check box for this particular warning. It's easy to accidentally apply an effect twice when you really meant to edit the original effect. To edit an effect, you must double-click the effect on the **Appearance** palette.*

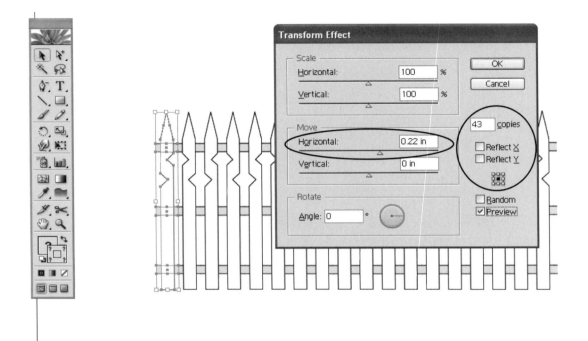

5. In the **Transform Effect** dialog box, set the effect for **Move Horizontal .22 in** and **43 copies**. Be sure that **Reflect X** is unchecked. Check **Preview** to preview the results. Click **OK**.

Since this is a second instance of the effect, it applies to the shape as it appears after the first instance of the effect. The result is that the two-picket fence you created in Step 3 is copied and moved .22 inches to the right, then that two-picket fence copy is copied and moved, and so on 43 times.

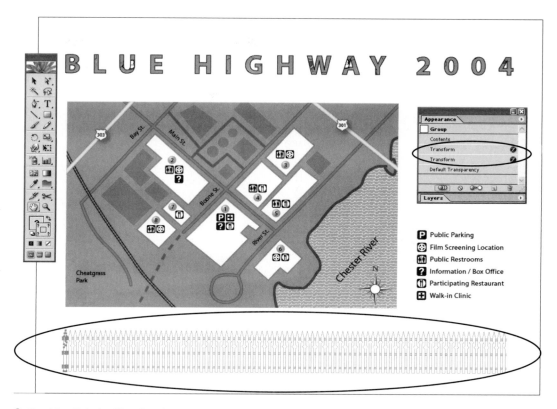

6. Double-click the **Hand** tool to see entire page. The fence extends across the page with the cutout section in perfect symmetry. Note that on the **Appearance** palette there are two separate **Transform** effects listed.

There is still only one selected group on the left of the fence. This is the only "real" picket. The entire rest of the fence is an effect. Any change you make to this one object is immediately applied to the entire fence, as you will see in the next step.

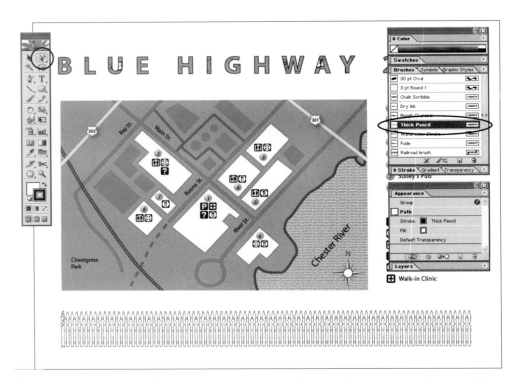

7. Select the **Group Selection** tool. Choose **Select > None** or click the outside border of the artwork to deselect the fence. Click the "real" (left-most) picket on the fence to select only the picket and not the small horizontal bars that appear behind the fence pickets. Choose **Window > Brushes** to show the **Brushes** palette. Stroke the picket with the **Thick Pencil** brush. The entire fence now has a more hand-drawn look. It is very important that you use the **Group Selection** tool and select only the one picket. Selecting everything will probably result in a memory error unless you have a very powerful computer with lots of available RAM.

*Combining brushes and effects is a great technique for a hand-drawn or painted look. If the names of the brushes are not visible, choose **List View** from the **Brushes** palette flyout menu.*

8. Save the file and keep it open for the next exercise.

MOVIE | transform_effect.mov

The Transform effect is very versatile and is underutilized by many artists. To see some other cool uses for the Transform effect, watch the **transform_effect.mov** movie online at **http://www.lynda.com/books/hot/illcs/movies/**.

5. ─────────Raster Art Filters and Effects

The bottom section of both the Filter menu and the Effect menu contains identical items and sub-menus. The list of commands is very similar to what you see under the Filter menu in Photoshop. In fact, many of these filters and effects are built from the Photoshop filters of the same name. The filters work only with raster art, so they will appear grayed out if you try to apply them to a path. The effects work on raster or vector art and have the advantage of leaving the original art unchanged. In this exercise, you will use a few filters and effects to integrate a photo (raster image) into your vector art.

1. Open the file **map_17.ai** from the **chap_17** folder or continue from Exercise 4.

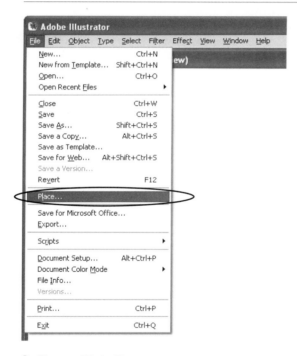

2. Choose **File > Place**.

3. Select the file **51_Chevy_side.psd**. Be sure the **Link** check box is unchecked. This will embed the images from the Photoshop file and make them part of the Illustrator file.

*Placed art is usually linked to the original file. This makes for smaller Illustrator files and allows you to update the original artwork in the original files and have the changes automatically appear in Illustrator. Most effects do not work on linked files. If you need to unlink a file after you have already placed it, you can do so by choosing **Window > Links** to see the **Links** palette, choosing the image you want embedded from the list, and choosing **Embed Image** from the **Links** palette flyout menu.*

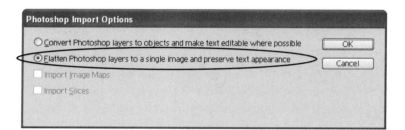

4. Choose the **Flatten Photoshop layers...** option and click **OK**.

In this case, there is no practical difference between the two options. For more information on working on files in both Photoshop and Illustrator, see the bonus Chapter 22, "Integration," on the **HOT CD-ROM**.

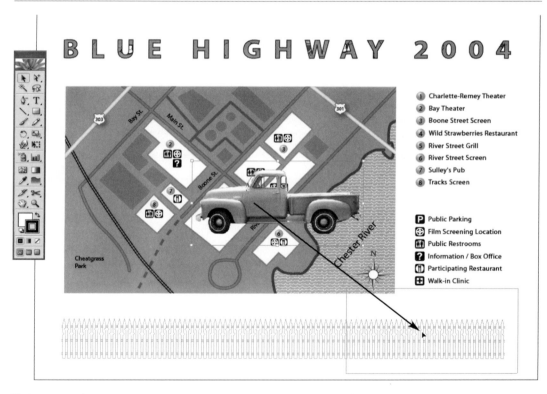

5. Select the **Selection** tool and drag the truck down to the lower-right corner, in front of the picket fence.

NOTE | Transparency and Alpha Channels

All raster art is rectangular, but sometimes the background color of the art is made transparent so you only see part of the raster image. In this case, the area around the truck is transparent, and you can see through its windows. The Photoshop file **51_Chevy_side.psd** includes a layer mask, which is equivalent to Illustrator's opacity mask. Both layer masks and opacity masks use something called an **alpha channel**, which is a layer of paths or pixels in varying shades of gray. The darker the shade on the alpha channel, the more transparent the object being masked. For more information on opacity masks in Illustrator, see Chapter 14, "*Masks and Blending Modes.*"

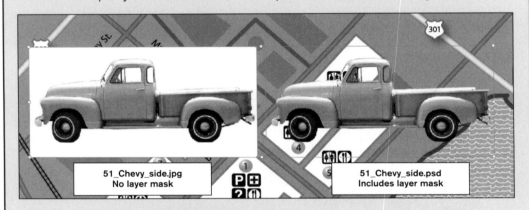

51_Chevy_side.jpg
No layer mask

51_Chevy_side.psd
Includes layer mask

I added this layer mask to **51_Chevy_side.psd**. If I had not, you would have seen the truck on a white rectangular background. Many common raster graphics formats, such as JPEG, do not support alpha channels. If you place a raster image into an Illustrator file and want part of the image to be transparent, you can add a layer mask in Photoshop, or use an Illustrator clipping path or opacity mask to get the same result.

One cool feature of using a Photoshop file with an alpha channel (layer mask) is that you can apply a drop shadow effect directly to the placed image, and Illustrator will make the shadow in the shape of the mask. This is a new feature in Illustrator CS.

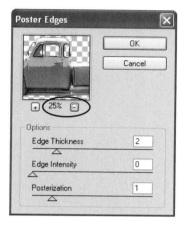

6. Choose **Effect > Artistic > Poster Edges**. The **Poster Edges** effect creates more uniform areas of color on the truck and darkens the borders between areas of color so it looks less like a photo and more like a painting. Click the **minus sign** to zoom out to **25%** to better see the truck. Enter settings of **Edge Thickness 2**, **Edge Intensity 0**, and **Posterization 1**. The **Edge Thickness** and **Edge Intensity** control the thickness and the darkness of the borders between colored areas. Both range from **0** to **10**, with **0** being a thin and not dark border and **10** being thick and very dark. **Posterization** sets the contrast between the colors and has a range of **0** (strong contrast) to **6** (subtle contrast). Click **OK**.

The dialog boxes for the raster effects are different from other Illustrator dialog boxes, but should look very familiar to Photoshop users. There is no Preview check box. Instead, a preview of the art with the effect applied appears in a small window. There are buttons to zoom the view in and out, and whenever your cursor is inside the box, it becomes a Hand tool so you can drag the image and see a different part. Here's a handy trick: When you click and hold with the preview window Hand tool, the image appears without the effect applied so you can compare the before and after looks of the image.

NOTE | Photoshop Filters in Illustrator

If the filters and effects in Illustrator seem identical to the ones you find in Photoshop, that's because they are the same. This means that most third-party filters or effects you have for Photoshop might work in your Illustrator files, too. To find out, quit Illustrator and copy the filter or effect from the Photoshop **Plug-ins** folder into the folder **Illustrator CS > Plug-ins > Photoshop Effects** or **Illustrator CS > Plug-ins > Photoshop Filters** as appropriate. When you restart Illustrator, the additional filters or effects should appear in the correct menus. There is no guarantee the filter or effect will work, however, and effects added this way might only work on raster art.

7. The truck looks more hand-drawn, but not enough. Choose **Effect > Artistic > Cutout**. The **Cutout** effect also simplifies the areas of color to make the image resemble a collage of colored paper. Click the **minus sign** to zoom out to **25%**. Enter settings of **No. of Levels: 4, Edge Simplicity: 2**, and **Edge Fidelity: 2**. **No. of Levels** determines how many colors there are in the final output and ranges from **2** to **8**. The fewer the colors, the simpler the final look. **Edge Simplicity** and **Edge Fidelity** control how much the borders between the new colored areas resemble the originals. The ranges for these two options are **0** to **10** and **0** to **3**, respectively. In both cases, the lower the number, the simpler the final output appears. Click **OK**.

Both Poster Edges and Cutout perform similar tasks—simplifying areas of color—but they use different algorithms and have different final looks. Cutout has a more radical look than Poster Edges. The reason you applied Poster Edges first is that the Cutout filter works best when there are clear borders between colors. The original photo did not have very clear borders, so Poster Edges was used to sharpen them and then Cutout was used on the Posterized photo. The order of applying the effects and the choice of settings for both effects was achieved through a combination of guesswork based on experience and simple trial and error.

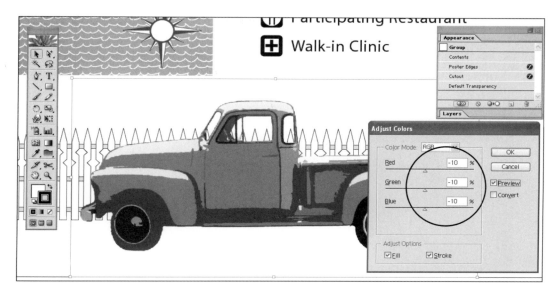

8. The truck is looking better, but the top is too washed out. Choose **Filter > Colors > Adjust Colors**. This filter lets you adjust the brightness of the red, green, and blue components of the image. Darken all three color channels by **−10%**. Check **Preview** to verify the result. Click **OK**.

This application is a filter, not an effect. It will not appear on the Appearance palette, and it will permanently change the photo of the truck. If you remove the Poster Edges and Cutout effects, you would see a photo of the truck that is 10 percent darker.

NOTE | The Stop Button

Since effects are live, Illustrator must recompute the look of an object every time you edit an object with effects. With multiple effects and an older computer, this can mean a lot of waiting and watching the Progress window shown above. If you do not need to see the final look of the object right away—perhaps you are making several changes and only want to see the final look after you make all the changes—you can click the **Stop** button on the **Progress** window. This stops Illustrator from recomputing the effect and makes the art appear on the artboard with no effects applied. The next time you add or edit an effect for the object, all the effects are recomputed and applied.

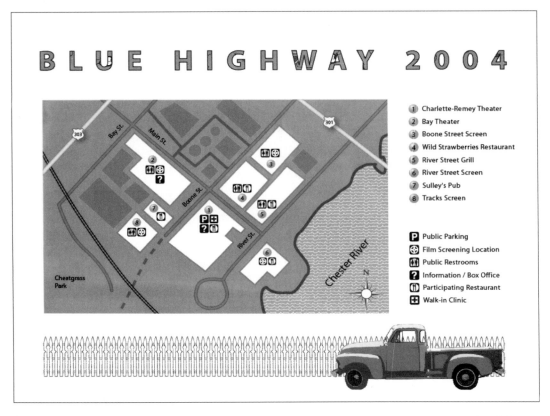

9. Double-click **Hand** tool to see the entire page. You now have a truck that looks much more hand-drawn.

*This is just one example of some effects to get a hand-drawn or painted effect. There are many other possibilities that would yield various final products. The **Artistic > Watercolor** and **Artistic > Underpaint** effects are other good ones to experiment with. The best way to learn how to use the dozens of available raster effects is to try them out and see what happens.*

10. Save and close the file.

Document Raster Settings

Document Raster Effects Settings

Color Model: RGB ▾   [OK]

                                          [Cancel]

Resolution
- ⦿ Screen (72 ppi)
- ○ Medium (150 ppi)
- ○ High (300 ppi)
- ○ Other: 300 ppi

Background
- ○ White
- ⦿ Transparent

Options
- ☐ Anti-alias
- ☐ Create Clipping Mask
- Add: 0.5 in Around Object

⚠ Changing these options may affect the appearance of currently applied raster effects.

This exercise looked at applying raster effects to raster art. You can apply raster effects to vector art, too. When you apply raster effects to vector art, Illustrator creates a temporary raster image and then applies the effect to that raster image. In order to do this, Illustrator must decide what resolution to use for the raster art. The higher the resolution, the better the art looks, but the longer it takes to compute and apply each filter. You control the resolution through the **Document Raster Effects Settings**. The default is **Screen (72 ppi)**. The unit **ppi** (**p**ixels **p**er **i**nch) is the equivalent of **dpi** (**d**ots **p**er **i**nch), which you may be familiar with from other applications. A Resolution of Screen (72ppi) may not be enough to see the fine details of effects applied to pattern- or gradient-filled vector art.

To change the resolution, choose **Effect > Document Raster Effects Settings**. Click a different ppi setting or click **Other** and enter a setting of your own. You can change these settings as much as you want. You can set the **Resolution** to **High** to get an effect just right and then set it back to **Screen** or lower when you work on other parts of the artwork. A **Background** of **Transparent** creates a mask using an alpha channel at the border of the vector art. The alpha channel is retained and appears as a layer mask if you open the document in Photoshop. You can also create a white border around the object if you wish. In this case, you can set options for whether the border color is blended into the colors of objects behind it (**Anti-alias**), and you can set the size of an optional clipping mask. If you choose a transparent background, the options have no effect.

These settings apply to all the vector art in the document. You can't set one piece of art for high resolution and another for low resolution using this dialog box. When you expand a piece of vector art with raster effects applied, it will permanently rasterize at the **Document Raster Effects Settings** resolution. When you print the document, the vector art with effects applied will print using the **Document Raster Effects Settings** resolution. For more information on printing, see Appendix C, "*Print Issues.*"

NOTE | Changing the Color Mode

Raster effects work only in the RGB color mode. If you have a CMYK document and you want to apply these effects, change the color mode for the document to RGB by choosing **File > Document Color Mode > RGB Color**. Most CMYK colors are reproducible in the RGB palette, so the colors in your CMYK document will probably not change. Many RGB colors are not reproducible in CMYK color, however, so be careful that you don't choose out-of-gamut colors if you plan to print your RGB document using CMYK process color. For more information on color mode, see Chapter 5, "*Fills, Strokes, and Color*."

MOVIE | outline_object.mov

You can use the outline object effect to apply fills and strokes to the borders of raster images placed in Illustrator. To learn more about this handy technique, watch the **outline_object.mov** movie online at **http://www.lynda.com/books/hot/illcs/movies/**.

6. ———————Target Practice with New Scribble

Illustrator CS has a new effect called **Scribble** that replaces the old Scribble and Tweak effect. The new Scribble is a very cool and flexible effect with loads of potential uses. Scribble is also a good effect to use for exploring how precise targeting for effects is crucial to getting just the look you want.

1. Open the file **scribble_truck.ai** from the **chap_17** folder.

2. Select the **Selection** tool and select the shield part of the highway sign. Note on the **Layers** palette that the **Sign** object is selected, indicated by the green square, and targeted for appearances, indicated by the double ring on the **Appearance** button.

When you select a single object, you automatically target that single object as well.

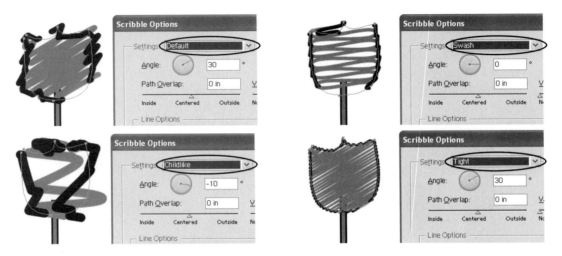

3. Using the upper **Stylize** submenu, choose **Effect > Stylize > Scribble**. Make sure **Preview** is checked and try several of the predefined scribbles available from the pull-down menu. When you are ready to go on, choose **Tight** and click **OK**.

As you try different scribbles, you will see the other settings in the window changing. Each named setting is simply a predefined group of settings for the Scribble effect.

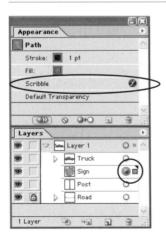

4. Note that the **Appearance** button for **Sign** on the **Layers** palette is shaded, indicating that there is an appearance (the **Scribble** effect) on this object. Also note that the effect also appears in the **Appearance** palette. The **Tight** scribble is a good place to see what all the **Scribble** settings do. To edit the **Scribble** effect you just applied, double-click the **Scribble** row on the **Appearance** palette. The **Scribble Options** dialog box opens again.

5. Change the **Angle** to **135** degrees to change the direction of the scribbled lines. Change the **Path Overlap** to **−0.08 in**. This brings the fill scribble inside the border of the path and makes the stroke scribble disappear. Change the **Variation** to **0.08 in**. This make the amount of overlap variable. It also makes the stroke scribble reappear because the **+0.08** in **Variation** is canceling out the **−0.08** in **Path Overlap**.

*The **Settings** also have changed to **Custom**. This happens whenever you stray from one of the predefined scribbles.*

6. In the **Stroke Width** field, select **0.01 in** with your mouse. Type in **.005**. (You can omit the leading zero and the "in" when entering values using the keyboard.) The scribble line will get narrower.

You can enter values lower than 0.01 inches, but they will still appear as 0.01 in the dialog box.

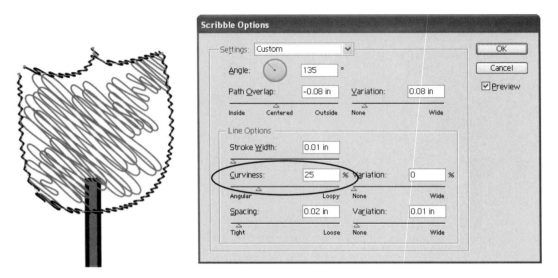

7. Set the **Curviness** to **25%**. The scribble becomes more **Loopy**. Changing the **Variation** would make the scribble randomly change between **Angular** and **Loopy** along its length.

8. Set the **Spacing** to **0.06 in**. The scribble becomes more spread out. Changing the **Variation** would make the scribble randomly change between **Tight** and **Loose Spacing**. Click **OK**.

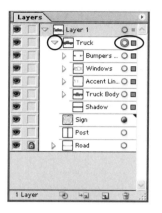

9. With the **Selection** tool, click the truck to select the entire group. On the **Layers** palette, turn down the expansion triangle for the **Truck** group. (Make sure all the objects in the truck group are selected, as shown above.) Note that the **Appearance** button for the **Truck** group is doubled. This means that any effect you apply now will be applied to the group, and all the objects will appear to have the effect. But suppose you want one kind of scribble for the wheels and a different one for the windows?

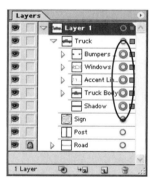

10. On the **Appearance** palette, double-click the **Contents** row. This selects the contents of the **Truck** group as individual subgroups or objects. Note the **Appearance** buttons on the **Layers** palette change to show that each subgroup or object is targeted separately. Choose **Effect > Scribble** and select the **Tight** scribble from the pull-down menu. Click **OK**. The tight scribble is applied to all the first level of subgroups and objects individually.

In both Step 9 and this step, all the objects in the truck are selected. The difference is that when you clicked the truck with the Selection tool in Step 9, the group was targeted. Now the group is not targeted, but the first level of subgroups and objects are targeted.

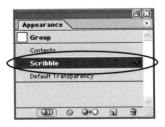

11. With the effect applied to each of the subgroups separately, there is now room to make changes to individual subgroups. On the **Layers** palette, target the **Truck Body** subgroup by clicking on the **Appearance** button on the **Truck Body** row. Be sure to click the **Appearance** button to target only that row. It should be the only **Appearance** button with a double ring, as shown above. Next, double-click the **Scribble** row on the **Appearance** palette to edit the effect for that subgroup only.

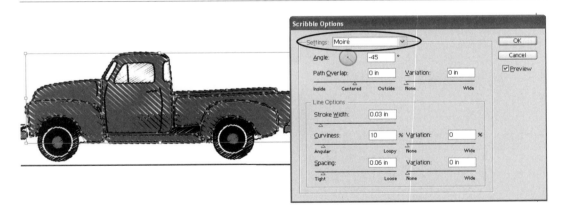

12. Change the **Setting** to **Moiré** and click **OK**. Now the body of the truck has the **Moiré Scribble** effect, and the wheels, windows, and bumpers have the **Tight Scribble** effect. You can take this combining of effects even further if, instead of groups, you target the individual paths or even individual fills and strokes.

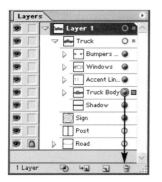

13. Drag the **Appearance** button of the **Truck Body** group to the **Trash** icon on the **Layers** palette. This removes the **Scribble** effect from the group.

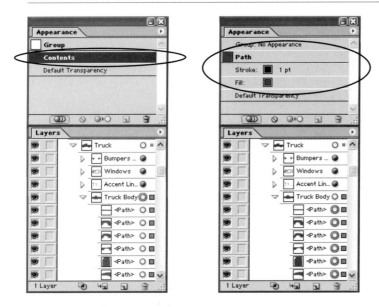

14. Turn down the expansion triangle for the **Truck Body** group. Double-click the **Contents** row on the **Appearance** palette to target the individual objects in the group. The **Appearance** palette now shows the stroke and fill for the individual objects in the group.

This works only because all the objects in the group have the same stroke and fill. If they had a variety of strokes and fills, the Appearance palette would show "Mixed Appearances."

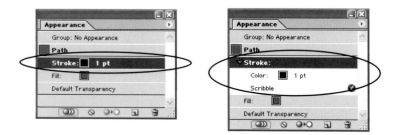

15. Click the **Stroke** row on the **Appearance** palette to target only the stroke. Choose **Effect >
Scribble** and choose **Moiré** from the drop-down menu. Click **OK**. Now the scribble is only on the
stroke of each object in the group. The **Scribble** effect now appears on a sublist under **Stroke** on
the **Appearance** palette.

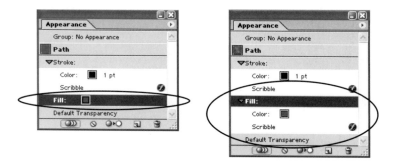

16. Click the **Fill** row on the **Appearance** palette to target only the **Fill**. Choose **Effect > Scribble** and
choose **Tight** from the drop-down menu. Click **OK**. Now the strokes of the truck body have a **Moiré
Scribble**, and the fills have a **Tight Scribble**. Wicked cool!

17. Note that the **Appearance** button for the groups is not shaded because the group itself has no appearance at all.

This example is two versions of the same effect, but you can use any combination of effects you want on strokes and fills individually. This works only with effects. You cannot apply a filter to a stroke or fill alone.

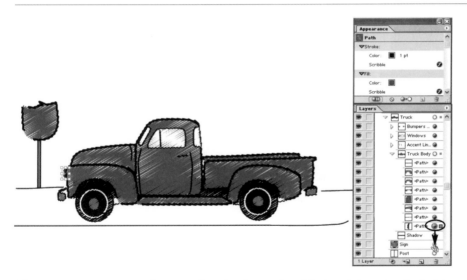

18. Hold down the **Alt** key (Windows) or the **Option** key (Mac) and drag the shaded **Appearance** button from the row of the last **<Path>** in the **Truck Body** group down to the **Sign** row in the **Layers** palette. This copies the custom appearance to the sign. Now the sign has a **Moiré** scribble on its stroke and a **Tight** scribble on its fill.

Once you get a combination of effects just right, this is one way to use them in other places. Another way is to define a graphic style. For more information see Chapter 18, "Graphic Styles."

19. Save and close the file.

TIP | Double Scribble

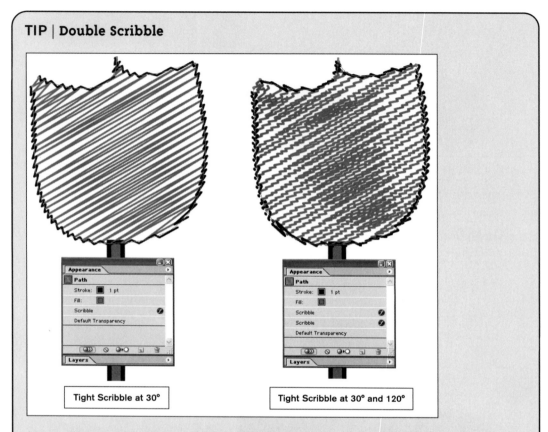

Tight Scribble at 30°

Tight Scribble at 30° and 120°

A cool effect one of the Illustrator CS beta testers came across was combining two scribble effects with a 90-degree difference in the angles. The result is a cross-hatch effect. Very cool.

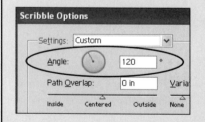

To do this, apply a **Scribble** effect to the artwork and note the angle for that effect before you click **OK**. Choose **Effect > Scribble** to apply a second instance of the **Scribble** and click the **Apply New Instance** button when prompted. Change the **Angle** for the second scribble effect to be 90 degrees different from what was set on the first effect and click **OK**.

NOTE | Appearance of New Art

When you create art with effects and then deselect the art, the Appearance palette retains the stroke, fill, and effect settings until you select another object or create a new object. The Appearance palette has an option to maintain these settings and apply them to any new objects. For example, if you just created a red filled heart with a bloat effect and a drop shadow, you could draw a rectangle and have it appear with a red fill, a bloat effect, and a drop shadow immediately applied. To do this, click the **New Art** button on the **Appearance** palette so that **New Art Maintains Appearance**. To deselect this feature, click the button again so that **New Art Has Basic Appearance**.

That was a long chapter, and it was only the beginning of what you can do with filters and effects. Now that you know how to target, arrange, and edit effects, you can explore on your own and discover all sorts of great effect combinations. Combinations of effects are the heart of the next chapter: "Graphic Styles." When you're ready to put your new effects skills into practice, read on!

18.

Graphic Styles

| Using Graphic Styles | Merging Graphic Styles |
| Editing Graphic Styles | Creating and Saving Graphic Styles |

chap_18

Illustrator CS
H•O•T CD-ROM

Graphic styles are power painting tools built from layers of strokes, fills, and effects. As you gain experience using Illustrator effects, you will find yourself using certain combinations of effects again and again. Rather than adding all the effects to an object one at a time, you can define a graphic style containing all the steps and apply it to objects in your art with a single click.

This chapter is where all your hard work understanding the Appearance palette and the concept of targeting objects or groups really pays off. Graphic styles commonly use multiple fills and strokes on the same path—something that can only be controlled using the Appearance palette. Often, the different fills and strokes will have different effects applied simultaneously just the way you applied one scribble to the truck stroke and a different one to the truck fill in the previous chapter. Unlike a simple effect, graphic styles can actually add or replace the fill and stroke on objects in your art, so it is important to know whether you are adding paint to an object, group, or layer. As always, the best way to understand how it all works is to try it yourself.

1. _____Using Graphic Styles

Illustrator CS ships with 11 libraries of graphic styles. These graphic styles are a great resource for adding pizzazz to your art and for sampling what can be done with Illustrator effects. As you apply some of these graphic styles, you will see how important your understanding of targeting groups or objects is in getting the desired result. You will also see how to clear out any unwanted fills and strokes that interfere with the graphic style you choose.

1. Copy the **chap_18** folder from the **H•O•T CD-ROM** to your hard drive. Open the file **styles_truck.ai** from the **chap_18** folder.

Document Raster Effects Settings

Color Model: RGB

OK

Cancel

Resolution
- ○ Screen (72 ppi)
- ○ Medium (150 ppi)
- ⊙ High (300 ppi)
- ○ Other: 300 ppi

Background
- ○ White
- ⊙ Transparent

Options
- ☐ Anti-alias
- ☐ Create Clipping Mask
- Add: 0.5 in Around Object

ⓘ Changing these options may affect the appearance of currently applied raster effects.

2. Choose **Effect > Document Raster Effect Settings**. Make sure that the **Resolution** is set to **High**. Click **OK**.

*As you learned in the previous chapter, the Document Raster Effect Settings determine the resolution of any raster effects in your art. This chapter uses the **Texturize** effect, which doesn't look very interesting until you set a ppi of 200 or more and zoom in. If you have an older or slower computer, you may have to wait a few moments for the image to render as you perform each step in the exercise. If waiting is troublesome, you can change the resolution to 200 ppi or lower, but the effect you see onscreen will not match what you see in the text as closely.*

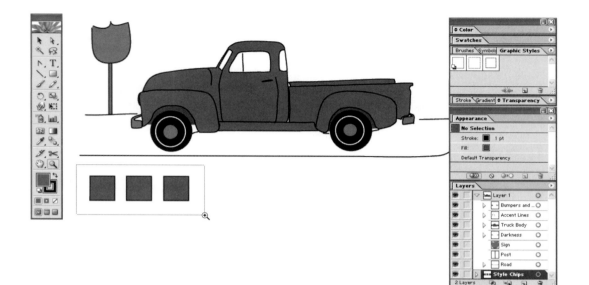

3. With the **Zoom** tool, drag a rectangular marquee to zoom in on the three squares below the truck.

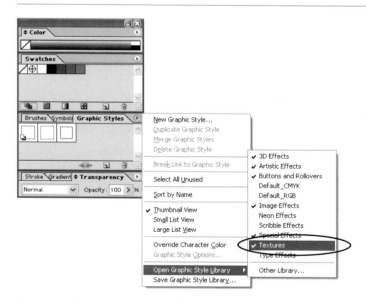

4. Choose **Window > Graphic Styles** to bring the **Graphic Styles** palette forward. It shares a slot with the **Symbols** and **Brushes** palettes by default. Choose **Open Graphic Style Library > Textures** from the **Graphic Styles** palette flyout menu. The **Textures** graphic style library opens on its own palette.

5. Using the **Selection** tool, click the left-most square. Note on the **Appearance** palette that it has a **black Stroke** of **1 pt** and a **medium-blue Fill**.

The other two squares have the same stroke and fill.

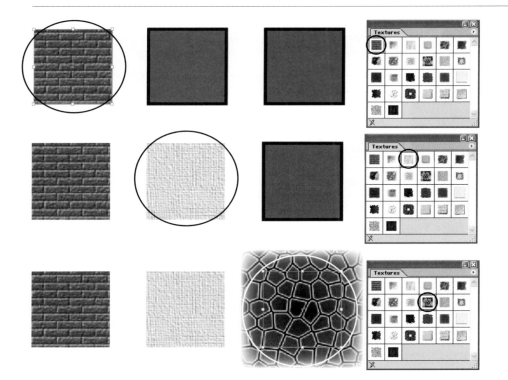

6. Click the graphic style **RGB Brick** to apply it to the left-most square. Click the center square and apply the graphic style **RGB Canvas**. Click the right-most square and apply the graphic style **RGB Cobblestone**. Close the **Textures** floating palette.

That's all you need to do to apply a graphic style to a single object. Select the object you want and then click the graphic style you want applied. The object is then painted with new fills, strokes, and effects.

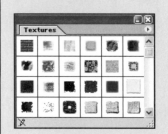

NOTE | Graphic Style Thumbnails

When you open the Textures graphic style library, it may take a moment for all the thumbnail images to appear. The thumbnails for each graphic style are actually squares with that graphic style applied so you can preview what it might look like in your art. Since some of these textures involve multiple raster effects, they may take a few moments to render—yet another reason to make that computer upgrade you've been thinking about!

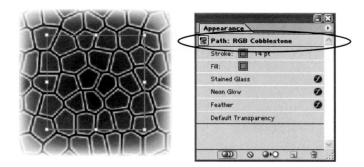

7. With the third square still selected, look at the **Appearance** palette. The object name in the **Appearance** palette—**Path** in this case—has a colon after it and the name of the graphic style in use on that object. The object also has a new stroke color and width and three effects applied to it. The **Stained Glass** effect creates the cobblestone pattern, the **Neon Glow** effect adds the bright edges between the stones, and the **Feather** effect blends the edge of the square into the background. By using the graphic style, you did the work of five steps and three dialog boxes in a single click! Now that's efficiency.

Another use for graphic styles is getting ideas for how to use Illustrator effects. The RGB Cobblestone effect shows how combining a Neon Glow and Stained Glass texture is a really cool idea.

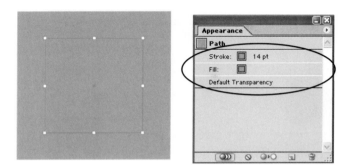

8. Click the **Reduce to Basic Appearance** button on the **Appearance** palette. This button removes all the effects from an object but leaves its stroke and fill intact. The **RGB Cobblestone** graphic style is removed, but the graphic style altered the original stroke and fill on the object. This is an important point with graphic styles: they can change the basic appearance of your art. The only way to get the original colors back is with the undo command or by reapplying them.

NOTE | Default Graphic Style

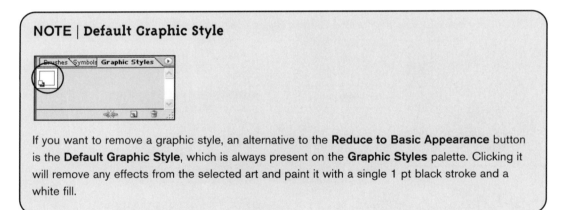

If you want to remove a graphic style, an alternative to the **Reduce to Basic Appearance** button is the **Default Graphic Style**, which is always present on the **Graphic Styles** palette. Clicking it will remove any effects from the selected art and paint it with a single 1 pt black stroke and a white fill.

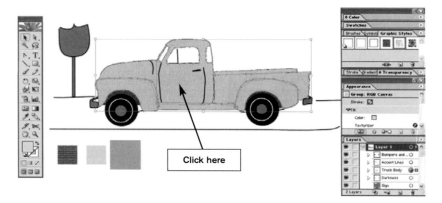

9. Double-click the **Hand** tool to see the entire document. With the **Selection** tool, click the door of the truck to select all the blue truck parts. (They are grouped). On the **Graphic Styles** palette, choose the **RGB Canvas** style to apply to the truck.

When you apply a graphic style from a library, a copy is put on the Graphic Styles palette, so the RGB Canvas graphic style is now on the Graphic Styles palette.

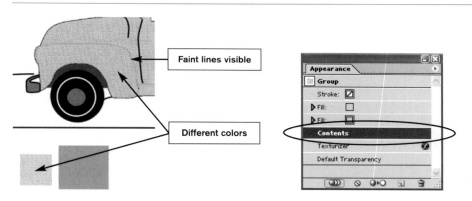

10. Click an empty area of the artboard to deselect the truck. There is a color difference between the **Canvas** of the truck and the square with the same effect applied. There are also faint lines visible through the canvas of the truck. Click the door of the truck again to select it and look on the **Appearance** palette. The effect was applied to the group, not to the objects inside the group. Double-click the **Contents** row on the **Appearance** palette. You may need to scroll down or collapse fill rows to see the **Contents** row.

As you saw in the previous chapter, when you select a group, even though all the objects in that group are selected, the group itself is the target for any effects. This applies to graphic styles, too. Since graphic styles also contain fill and stroke information, the group may get additional fills and strokes, as well as effects. This is why it is very important to know how to target either the group or the contents depending on what final effect you need.

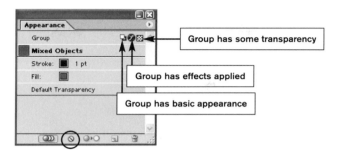

11. Now you can see that the objects in the group still have their **blue Fill** and **black Stroke**. These colors are showing through the partially opaque canvas graphic style. Since the group has color applied, you don't need—and in this case don't want—the objects inside to have color. Click the **Clear Appearance** button to remove the stroke and fill from the objects inside the group. The color is correct now, and the faint lines are gone.

*You know the group has color and effects by the icons to the right of the **Group** row on the **Appearance** palette. They tell you the group has a basic appearance (at least one stroke or fill), the group has effects applied, and that the group has some transparency (is not 100% opaque).*

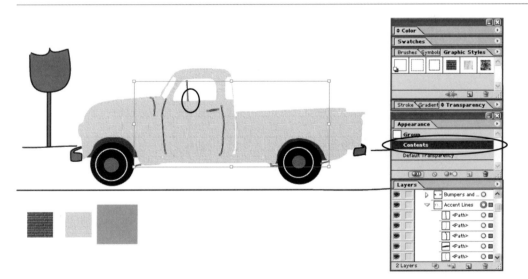

12. As when applying effects, you can select a group and then target the individual objects using the **Appearance** palette. With the **Selection** tool, click the black line in the truck window on the screen. Next, double-click the **Contents** row on the **Appearance** palette. This changes the target from the group to all the objects inside that group.

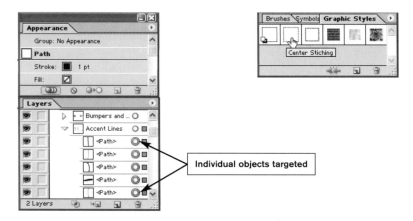

Individual objects targeted

13. Now that the paths are all targeted individually, click the **Center Stitching** style to apply the style.

The Center Stitching style is simply a dashed black stroke with rounded edges. There are no effects in this style. If you had applied this style to the group, the group would have gotten the dashed line, but you would not have seen it because the objects would still have a solid line. The solid line underneath the dashed line would have filled in the gaps between the dashes.

14. Save the file and keep it open for the next exercise.

TIP | Dragging a Graphic Style onto an Object

You can also apply a graphic style by dragging the style from the **Graphic Styles** palette and dropping it on top of an object in your artwork. The target object does not need to be selected for this to work. When you apply a graphic style in this manner, the graphic style is applied to the object you drop the style on rather than any group containing the object. This is a handy shortcut to apply a graphic style to a single object inside a group.

NOTE | Override Character Color

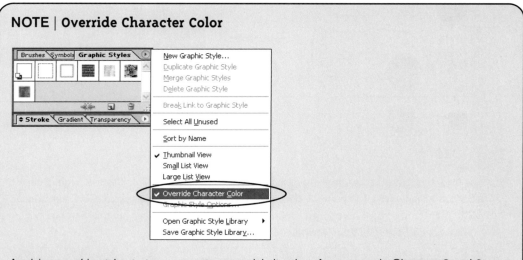

Applying graphic styles to type presents a special situation. As you saw in Chapters 8 and 9, type characters can have one fill (or stroke) color, and the type container can have a different color. This can produce odd and undesirable results when applying graphic styles to type. The default when you apply a graphic style to a type is for any fills or strokes on the characters to be removed and to apply the graphic style to the type container. If the graphic style has a purple fill and you add it to black type, the type turns purple. If you want the type to retain its original color but use the other elements of the graphic style, uncheck the **Override Character Color** option on the **Graphic Styles** flyout menu. This leaves any color on the type characters intact.

2. —————————————Merging Graphic Styles

Sometime you need the elements from two different graphic styles applied together. There are actually several ways to accomplish this, but the simplest is to merge the two styles into one. The result may require a bit of tweaking to get just right.

1. Open the file **styles_truck.ai** or continue from Exercise 1.

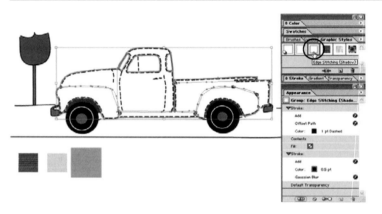

2. Now that the truck has the appearance of cloth, it's time to stitch it to the page. Select the **Selection** tool and click the truck door on the screen to select the group. Click the **Edge Stitching** graphic style to apply it. Unfortunately, an object can only contain one graphic style at a time, so **Edge Stitching** replaces the **RGB Canvas** style.

RGB Canvas: Fills only

Edge Stitching: Stroke only

If you look closely at the two styles, you can see they should work well together. One affects fills only, and the other affects strokes only.

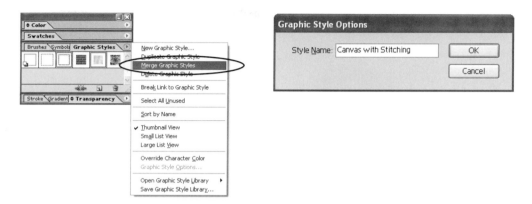

3. Choose **Edit > Undo Graphic Styles** to return the truck to the **RGB Canvas** style. With the truck body still selected, hold down the **Ctrl** key (Windows) or the **Cmd** key (Mac) and click the **Edge Stitching** style. Now both styles are selected on the **Graphic Styles** palette. From the **Graphic Styles** palette flyout menu, choose **Merge Graphic Styles**. Name the merged style **Canvas with Stitching** and click **OK**.

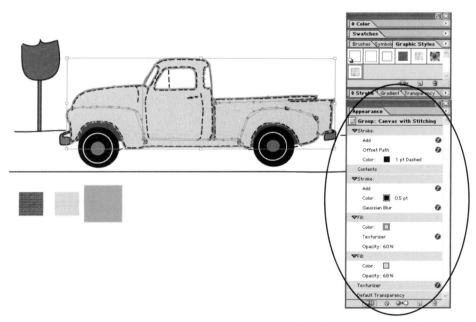

4. The truck now has fills and strokes of both styles combined in a new graphic style called **Canvas with Stitching**. The new graphic style name appears after the word "Group" on the **Appearance** palette.

Merged styles have all the fills and all the strokes of both original styles although some items might be hidden by others. You will learn how to fix this in the next exercise.

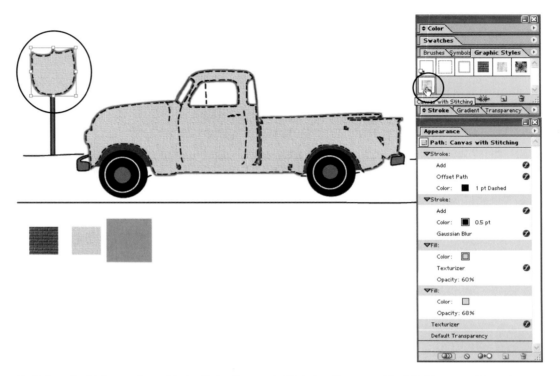

5. Select the highway sign with the **Selection** tool. Click the **Canvas with Stitching** graphic style to apply it to the sign.

You will need the sign to have this graphic style for the next exercise.

6. Save the file and keep it open for the next exercise.

MOVIE | style_stacking.mov

An alternative to merging graphic styles is applying different graphic styles at the object, group, and layer levels. There is even a trick of creating a group containing only one object just so you can apply another graphic style. To see this technique demonstrated, watch the **style_stacking.mov** movie online at **http://www.lynda.com/books/hot/illcs/movies/**.

3. _____Editing Graphic Styles

When you apply a graphic style to an object, you link the object to that graphic style. Any changes to the graphic style appear in all the objects that use that style. This is similar to the linking used by symbols, which you used in Chapter 16, "*Symbols*." When you edit a graphic style, you break the link to that graphic style but you can easily relink, and redefine, the graphic style after the editing is complete.

1. Open the file **styles_truck.ai** or continue from Exercise 2.

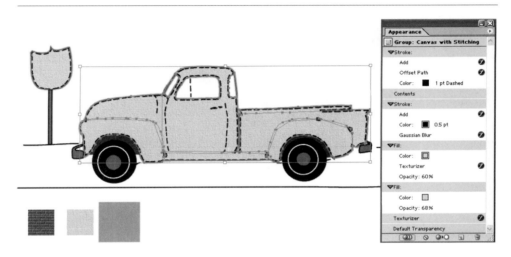

2. With the **Selection** tool, click the cloth body of the truck to select the truck body.

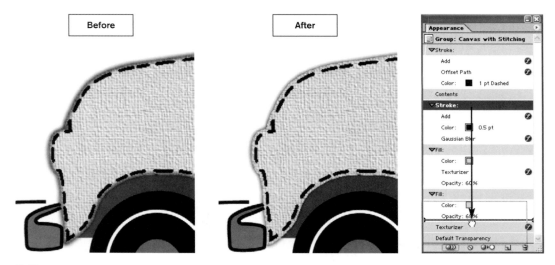

3. The two strokes in this style appear above the two fills on the **Appearance** palette because the strokes came from the **Edge Stitching** graphic style and the fills came from the **RGB Canvas** graphic style. In order to generate the correct look, the order must be the dashed stroke, then both fills, and then the stroke with the **Gaussian Blur**. Drag the stroke row that contains the **Gaussian Blur** below both fills.

*The **Gaussian Blur** was added as part of the **Edge Stitching** graphic style.*

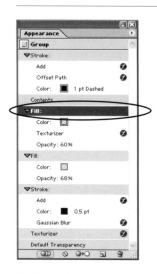

4. The color of the truck came from the **RGB Canvas** graphic style and needs replacing, too. Select the upper **Fill** on the **Appearance** palette. On the **Swatches** palette, click the **Truck Blue** swatch.

*You can select the **Fill** row or the **Color** row on the **Appearance** palette—either has the same effect.*

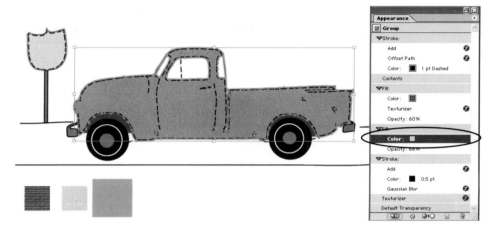

5. The truck is now more teal but not yet what we want because the other fill needs changing, too. Select the second **Fill** (or **Fill Color**) on the **Appearance** palette and click the **Truck Blue** swatch again to change that fill color.

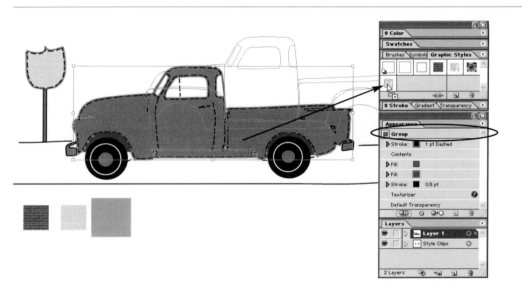

6. The **Appearance** palette now shows the **Group** without the words "Canvas with Stitching." The link to the graphic styles was broken the moment you started editing it in Step 3. The **Canvas with Stitching** graphic style is also no longer highlighted on the **Graphic Styles** palette. Now you can redefine the **Canvas with Stitching** so it reflects the changes you just made and relink it to the truck. Select the **Selection** tool. Hold down the **Alt** key (Windows) or the **Option** key (Mac) and drag the truck body on top of the **Canvas with Stitching** graphic style thumbnail.

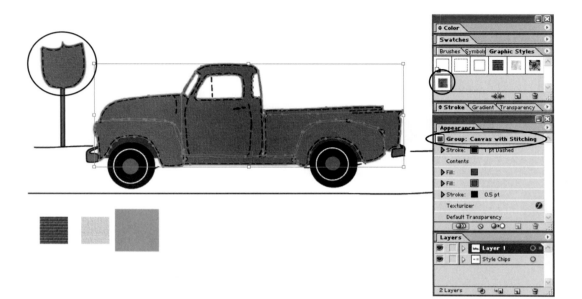

7. The **Appearance** palette shows the graphic style name again, and the graphic style is highlighted on the **Graphic Styles** palette. The highway sign has also changed since it was linked to the **Canvas with Stitching** graphic style.

8. Save and close the file.

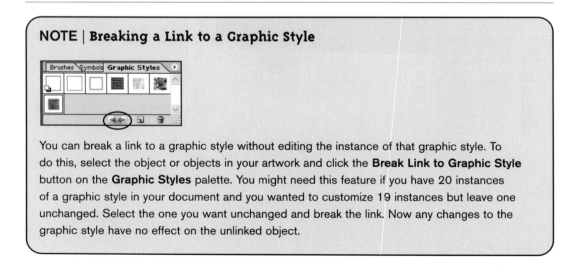

NOTE | Breaking a Link to a Graphic Style

You can break a link to a graphic style without editing the instance of that graphic style. To do this, select the object or objects in your artwork and click the **Break Link to Graphic Style** button on the **Graphic Styles** palette. You might need this feature if you have 20 instances of a graphic style in your document and you wanted to customize 19 instances but leave one unchanged. Select the one you want unchanged and break the link. Now any changes to the graphic style have no effect on the unlinked object.

4. _____Creating and Saving Graphic Styles

Next to creating your own symbols, creating your own graphic styles and building them into libraries is the slickest time- and work-saving technique Illustrator offers. In this exercise, you will create a design you learned back in Chapter 5, "*Fills, Strokes, and Color*," but you will create it as a graphic style you can save to use over and over.

1. Open the file **map_18.ai** from the **chap_18** folder.

2. With the **Zoom** tool, zoom in on the line below the map. Select the line on the screen with the **Selection** tool.

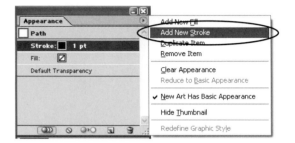

3. On the **Appearance** palette flyout menu, choose **Add New Stroke**.

4. With the new stroke still highlighted on the **Appearance** palette, choose **Effect > Path > Offset Path**. Change the **Offset** value to **2 pt**. Click **OK**.

Offset Path changes the added stroke into a "box" around the original line.

5. On the **Appearance** palette, select the lower **Stroke**. Choose the **Stroke** palette. If it is not expanded to show the **Dashed** line options, choose **Show Options** from the **Stroke** palette flyout menu. Change the **Weight** to **8 pt**, check **Dashed Line**, and set the **dash** value to **2 pt** and the **gap** value to **4 pt**.

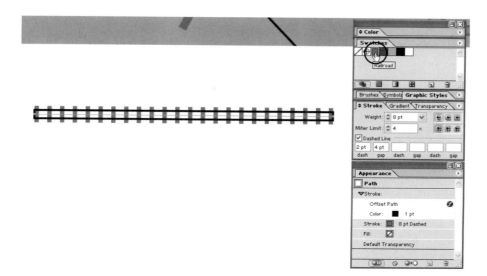

6. Set stroke color for the dashed stroke to the dark brown by clicking the **Railroad** swatch (circled above) on the **Swatches** palette.

7. From the **Graphic Styles** palette flyout menu, choose **New Graphic Style**. Name the graphic style **Railroad** and click **OK**.

*Dragging the styled object to the **Graphic Styles** palette or clicking the **New Graphic Style** button would also create a new graphic style, but it would be named "Graphic Style." Using the command on the flyout menu prompts you to name the graphic style, which helps identify which style is which on the palette. When you are working with several graphic styles with subtle differences, they are hard to distinguish by the thumbnail alone. Since the thumbnail is a preview of the graphic style on a square, if you have a graphic style that is only effects—meaning it does not specify a fill or stroke—then the thumbnail is blank! The only way to distinguish these graphic styles is by their names.*

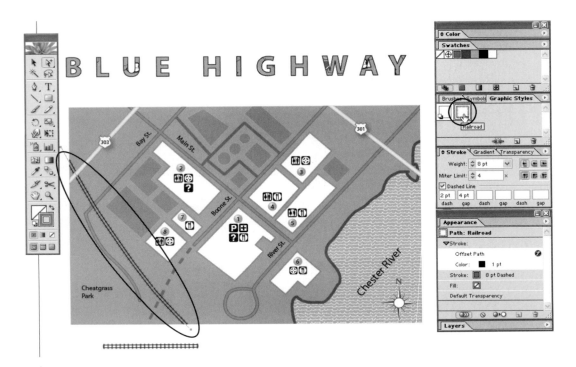

8. Double-click the **Hand** tool to see the entire page. With the **Group Selection** tool, select the path next to the park that should be a railroad. You must use the **Group Selection** tool to select the path, since this path is part of a group inside a clipping mask. Next, click the **Railroad** graphic style on the **Graphic Styles** palette. The path becomes a railroad.

Since the railroad is created with a graphic style, you can edit the path, and the entire railroad effect will change as needed to follow the new path. Using the graphic style is much more versatile than creating the railroad using two separate paths, as you did in Chapter 5, "Fills, Strokes, and Color."

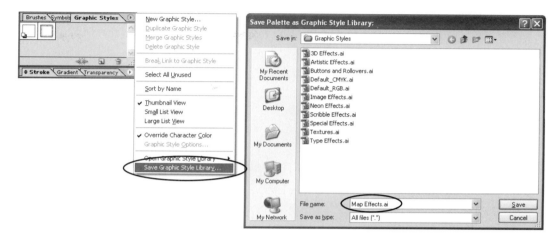

9. If you want to save this graphic style for use in other artwork, choose **Save Graphic Style Library** from the **Graphic Styles** palette flyout menu. Name the library **Map Effects.ai** and click **Save**.

As with other custom libraries you have created, this command will save all the graphic styles on your palette, even those which are not in use. In this case, there are no other graphic styles on the palette, other than the default style, so that is not a problem. The new library will not appear in the list of libraries until you restart Illustrator.

10. Save and close the file.

Spend some time checking out the various graphic styles libraries that ship with Illustrator CS. You will learn a lot about multiple fills and strokes and effects. When you're ready, you can move on to the next chapter to explore a set of brand new Illustrator CS effects: 3D.

19.

3D

| Extrude | Extruding Type |
| Surface Shading and Lighting Angle |
| Bevel | Rotate | Revolve | Revolve with Offset |
| Mapping Art onto 3D Objects |

chap_19

Illustrator CS
H·O·T CD-ROM

Among the most-touted new features of
Illustrator CS are the 3D effects. These
effects are applied to objects just like any
other effect, but they have some visually
astounding results. If you haven't played
with 3D before, this chapter will be a
real treat. The new 3D effects are easy
to use, and they generate results in
just a few clicks. There are lots of
possibilities for the 3D effects, so
this chapter is long. 3D is just too
much fun not to explore in depth.

If you already use 3D drawing tools,
such as Adobe Dimensions, don't
think about these effects as a replacement for the software you currently
use. Instead, they let you create 3D
objects quickly and simply before combining them with traditional Illustrator
tools to create some really cool artwork.

Visualizing 3D

For many people, the biggest obstacle to creating 3D shapes is visualizing the shapes in their minds before seeing them on the screen. All the 3D shapes start as 2D paths that are either extruded or revolved into a third dimension. Some people find the process of visualizing the final product simple, others find it nearly impossible. If you fall into the latter category, don't worry. It comes with practice. The picture above shows the final product of the exercises in this chapter so you have a good idea where each exercise is heading. You might want to refer back to it as you go along. There are five 3D objects in the picture: The snow globe, the mug, the gift box, the table, and the raised type on the front of the table. All the objects are created from very simple paths spun with the 3D effect and some other Illustrator tools you have used in previous chapters.

Warning: 3D effects can take a while to render on screen. More than any other Illustrator CS tool, 3D will make you want a faster computer with more RAM. Hide your credit card while you work these exercises.

I. _____Extrude

The first 3D effect you'll learn is **Extrude & Bevel**. The two functions are related but separate, so you'll start with Extrude. This is the simplest 3D effect to visualize, so it's a great place to start. When you squeeze a toothpaste tube, the toothpaste flows out through a circular hole and becomes a cylinder shaped line of toothpaste. In the same way, when you extrude a circle in Illustrator, you create a cylinder. If you extrude a square, it becomes a block or cube. The further you extrude, it the taller the shape. In this exercise, you will use Extrude to build a solid shape (the table) and a hollow shape (the gift box). Later, in Exercise 3, you'll get a chance to work with Bevel on its own.

1. Copy the **chap_19** folder from the **H·O·T CD-ROM** to your hard drive. Open the file **gift_shop.ai** from the **chap_19** folder.

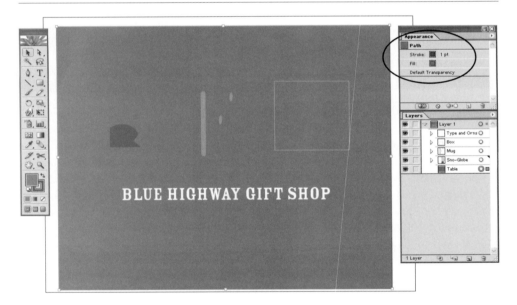

*Believe it or not, these are all the shapes used to create the 3D table, box, mug, and snow globe without the 3D effect applied. The large, solid green (teal) square and the unfilled beige square were drawn with the **Rectangle** tool. The purple ellipses and purple rounded rectangle were drawn with the **Ellipse** and **Rounded Rectangle** tools, respectively. The blue semicircle, brown shape below it, and green ornaments bordering the type were drawn with the **Pen** tool.*

2. Select the **Selection** tool and click the large teal-colored square. Note that this is simply a rectangle with a teal fill and a blue stroke.

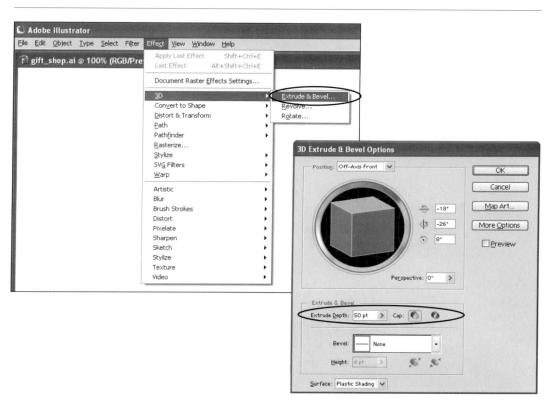

3. Choose **Effect > 3D > Extrude & Bevel**. The default settings are an **Extrude Depth** to **50 pt** and the **Turn Cap on for solid appearance** button selected. Verify that you have these settings.

*3D always opens with the **Preview** box unchecked because 3D effects can take a very long time to render.*

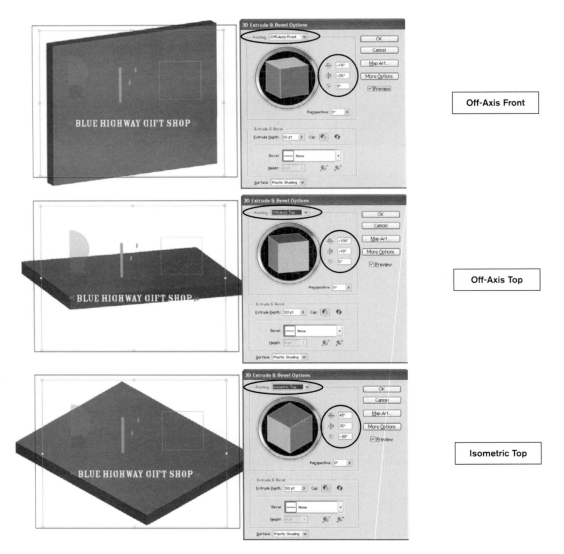

Off-Axis Front

Off-Axis Top

Isometric Top

4. Check the **Preview** check box to see two things happen. First, the extruded shape appears. Second, the shape is rotated to a position where you can see the depth added by the 3D effect. The default position is **Off-Axis Front**. Try various preset positions using the pull-down menu. The 3D effect is easiest to see with the **Off-Axis** and **Isometric** positions. Note as well that the 50 pt deep sides of the shape are the blue color of the stroke and the large flat surface is the teal color of the fill.

*Underneath the **Position** pull-down menu is a cube with one teal face. The teal face represents the original flat artwork. In this case, that is the teal rectangle. As you try different positions, note how the teal rectangle in your artwork and the teal face of the cube in the dialog box always face the same direction.*

5. Choose a position of **Front** from the drop-down menu at the top of the dialog box. The artwork seems flat again because the extrude direction is now directly up out of the page (screen) toward you.

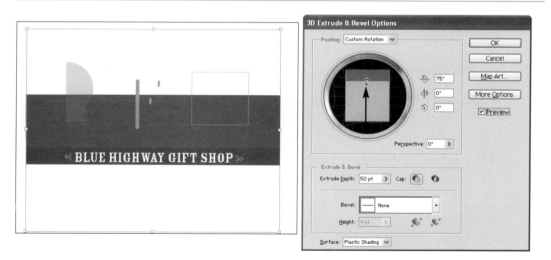

6. Bring your cursor to the bottom center of the cube in the dialog box. Drag upward and the cube will rotate. As long as **Preview** is checked, the artwork will also show the rotation. Rotate the cube in the window to **75°** on the **Red** axis (x-axis). Again, the teal face of the cube and the teal surface in your artwork always face the same direction.

You can rotate 3D art on any axis using the cube in the 3D dialog boxes. You can also grab the ring around the cube and rotate the art as you look at it head-on.

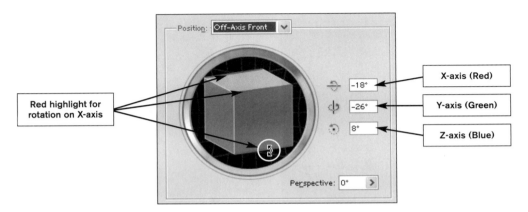

*The amount and direction of rotation for each position is shown to the right of the cube. The three possible axes of rotation are traditionally referred to as the x, y, and z axes. These axes are color-coded in Illustrator to make it easier to see which way you are rotating the cube. When you bring your cursor over an edge of the cube to rotate it, the edges for the axis you are changing highlight in the appropriate color: red for the x-axis, green for the y-axis, and blue for the z-axis. Since the color is easier to visualize than the name x, y, or z, I'll refer to these as the **Red**, **Green**, and **Blue** axes throughout the chapter.*

TIP | Render Repair

If the 3D art on the artboard stops responding to changes you make in the 3D dialog box, uncheck **Preview** and then check it again. The art should re-render correctly. This technique works with any effect that has a Preview check box, not just 3D.

7. The gift shop table is now rotated **75°**, but it does not appear in correct perspective. The end of the table furthest from view should appear smaller since it is further away. Change the **Perspective** to **15°**. Click **OK**.

The perspective setting is similar to choosing a lens for a camera. A low setting (less than 10°) makes the objects look flatter, as if you viewed them through a telephoto lens. A high setting (more than 50°) makes the objects warp as if you saw them through a fish-eye lens. Why use 15° here? I tried other settings and liked the look of 15°. Objects on the table might look better with a higher number depending on the shape of the object. The Perspective slider is a great feature in that you can exaggerate or downplay the perspective to get just the right look, but it does require some tweaking to get just right.

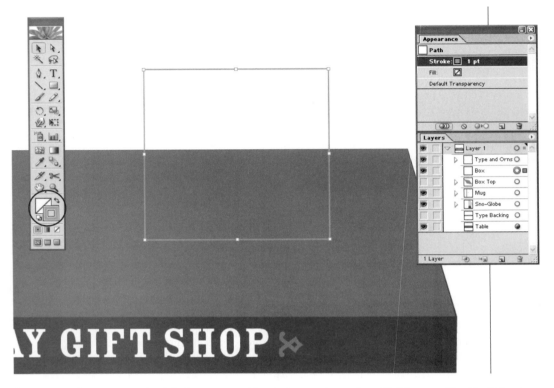

8. With the **Selection** tool, click the square with a beige stroke and no fill. Choose **Effect > Extrude & Bevel**.

*Because **Extrude & Bevel** was the last effect you applied, it appears second from the top of the **Effects** menu.*

9. Check **Preview**. Change the **Position** to **Off-Axis Top**. Because there was no fill, this is a hollow shape. Change the **Extrude Depth** of **170 pt** and rotate the **Blue** axis to a setting of **14°**. The exact rotation numbers should be **Red −110°**, **Green −42°**, and **Blue 14°**. Note the minus signs on the **Red** and **Green** axes! It is very important that you have the correct numbers here, or later exercises will not work correctly. You can also type these numbers in the appropriate fields. As soon as you change the number for the blue axis, the Position changes to Custom Rotation. Set a **Perspective** of **35°**. Click **OK**.

*Since you chose **Effect > Apply Extrude & Bevel** instead of **Effect > 3D > Extrude & Bevel**, the dialog box opened with the settings you used on the table.*

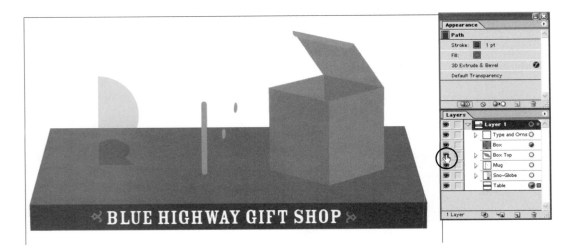

10. On the **Layers** palette, click the **Eye** icon to show the **Box Top** group.

These are just two simple paths to finish the look. As you'll see throughout this chapter, the 3D effect creates most of the look for 3D art, but often you need to add some "flat" art to finish the look.

11. Save the file and keep it open for the next exercise.

2. _____Extruding Type

Type is a lot of fun to extrude. A small extrude can add dimension to type and has many practical possibilities. This exercise also provides a little more practice rotating objects in 3D.

1. Open the file **gift_shop.ai** or continue from Exercise 1.

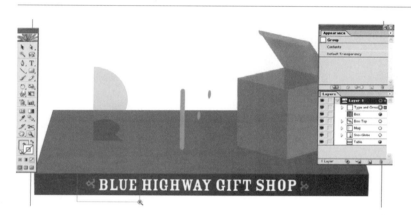

2. Select the **Zoom** tool and zoom in on the green ornament and the word "BLUE" on the front of the table. With the **Selection** tool, click the type to select it and the ornaments on either side. They are grouped, so they will all select at once.

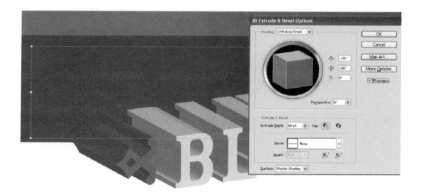

3. Choose **Effect > 3D > Extrude & Bevel**. Check **Preview**. The default **Off-Axis** looks pretty cool, but it's not what we need.

If you choose **Effect > Extrude & Bevel** at the top of the menu, you will get the 170 pt extrude and custom rotation you used for the gift box as the default. If this happens, just change the **Position** back to **Off-Axis Front** and the **Extrude Depth** to **50 pt**.

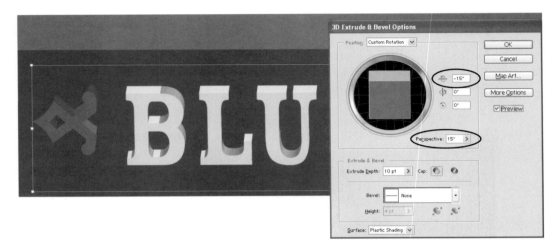

4. Change the **Position** to **Front** and then rotate on the **Red** axis to **–15°**. Set the **Perspective** to **15°** and the **Extrude Depth** to **10 pt**. Click **OK**.

Rotating the type to –15° puts it 90° off from the table top, which was rotated to 75°. This makes the type appear to be on the blue side of the table.

5. Double-click the **Hand** tool to see entire page.

6. Save the file and keep it open for the next exercise.

3. ———————Surface Shading and Lighting Angle

Illustrator achieves its 3D look through a combination of object shape and object shading. The 3D dialog box provides easy control over how objects are shaded and lit. In this exercise, you will adjust the shading and lighting angle from the defaults to settings that better complement your art.

1. Open the file **gift_shop.ai** or continue from Exercise 2.

2. With the **Selection** tool, click the gift box to select it. Double-click the **3D Extrude & Bevel** effect on the **Appearance** palette to edit this instance of the effect. As soon as you edit the effect, the preview of the image disappears. Check **Preview** to view the 3D box in your artwork again.

You can click anywhere on the extruded image to select it, not just the original square. This is a very convenient feature since it can be difficult to see where the original shape is once it's extruded.

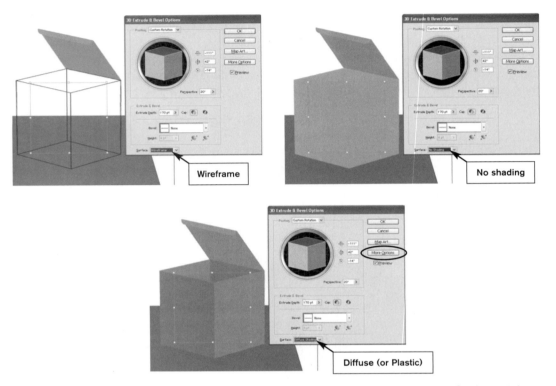

Wireframe

No shading

Diffuse (or Plastic)

3. At the bottom of the **3D Extrude & Bevel Options** dialog box is the setting for the **Surface** of the 3D shape. Change the **Surface** to **Wireframe**, which shows you the shape with none of the surfaces filled in. **Wireframe** is a great view for experimenting with different positions on older, slower computers since it is quicker to render than a filled-in view. It's also helpful for getting the **Perspective** correct since it's easier to see the edges of a shape. Change the **Surface** to **No Shading**, which fills all the surfaces with the original stroke or fill color as appropriate. Since there is no shading with this option, the object appears flat. Change the **Surface** to **Diffuse Shading**, which shades the surfaces to give a 3D effect, but there are no highlights on any surface. The shading makes all the surfaces darker than the original color in varying degrees. There is a fourth setting called **Plastic Shading**, which includes highlights. You will use this shading later. On flat surfaces such as this box, however, **Plastic Shading** and **Diffuse Shading** are identical. With the **Surface** set to **Diffuse Shading**, click **More Options**.

Incidentally, the wireframe surface is a pretty cool looking effect—especially on spheres and type. Consider using it somewhere as art.

4. Near the bottom of the dialog box is a sphere with a white diamond in a black square, which shows the direction light is shining on the 3D object. Drag the **diamond** to the upper left. The shading changes to simulate light from the left rather than the right. Change **Ambient Light** to **75%**. Ambient light is the light shining on the object from every direction, so increasing it makes the darker less dark. (Remember, the shading is normally a darker version of the 3D objects fill and/or stroke color.) If you increased **Ambient Light** to **100%**, there would be no difference between the colors on each side, and the object would appear flat. Click **OK**.

The setting for lighting direction on the shaded sphere is extremely sensitive! Even small changes can have major results on the look of the object. You may have to experiment a bit to get a look similar to the example in this book.

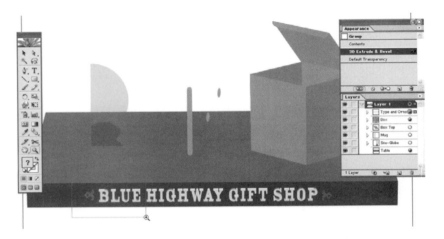

5. Click the word "BLUE" with the **Selection** tool to select the type and ornaments on either side. Select the **Zoom** tool and zoom in on "BLUE."

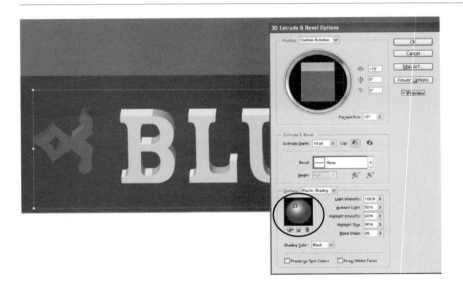

6. Double-click the **3D Extrude & Bevel** effect on the **Appearance** palette to edit it. Once again, the preview image disappears, and you must recheck **Preview** to see the 3D effect in your artwork. Change the lighting angle for the type and ornaments to the upper left to match the box.

*Because the type uses **Plastic Shading**, there are two extra fields: **Highlight Intensity** and **Highlight Size**. You will experiment with these in later exercises. For the moment, leave them with the default settings.*

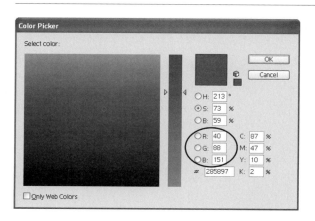

7. The type is filled with white, but it appears gray in 3D. This is because it is shaded with black. Change the **Shading Color** from **Black** to **Custom** on the drop-down menu. When you do, a box appears to the right of the menu. If you have never used this feature before, the box will be red. Double-click the box to open a **Color Picker**.

8. Enter a **RGB** value of **R 40**, **G 88**, and **B 151**. This is the blue used on the border of the table. Click **OK**.

9. Illustrator is now using dark blue for the shading, and the type better matches the background. The ornaments are also shaded with blue, but this looks fine against the blue background. Click **OK**.

*Since the blue is not as dark as the original black, the overall effect also lightens the 3D type. This is why you did not change the **Ambient Light** to **75%**, as you did with the gift box. If you had, it would be too light with the blue shading instead of the black.*

10. Double-click the **Hand** tool to see the entire page. Save the file and keep it open for the next exercise.

4.  Bevel

The Bevel part of the Extrude & Bevel effect shaves off or warps the sides of the extruded object. The beveling happens on the sides that are created by the extrude. In the case of the gift shop table, these are the blue sides.

1. Open the file **gift_shop.ai** or continue from Exercise 3.

2. Click the table with the **Selection** tool. Double-click the **3D Extrude and Bevel** effect in the **Appearance** palette to edit the effect. Check **Preview** to make the effect reappear in your artwork.

Note that when you select the table, the bounding box appears around the original flat shape without the 3D effect applied. You can actually resize and rotate the bounding box, and Illustrator will recalculate and reapply the 3D effect on the transformed shape. This behavior is a bit odd until you get used to it, but it does work.

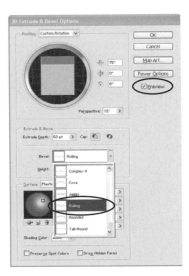

3. Choose a **Bevel** of **Rolling** from the drop-down menu. Check **Preview**.

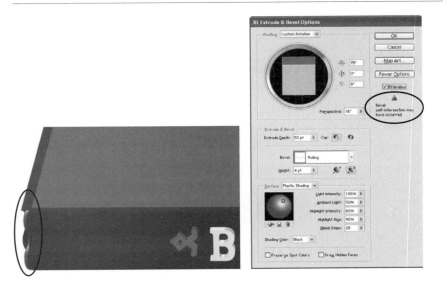

4. Depending on the speed and available memory on your computer, this effect may take some time to render. Once it renders, you will see a warning under the **Preview** check box that a **self-intersection** may have occurred. There is also a problem evident at the corner of the bevel. These two items are related. The next step will fix the corner. For more information on the warning message, see the upcoming sidebar called "Self-Intersection."

5. Change the type of bevel from **Bevel Extent In: Bevel is subtracted from original object** to **Bevel Extent Out: Bevel is added to original object**. This fixes the problem at the corner. Click **OK**.

The unbeveled table had a blue side and a green core that came from the original blue stroke and green fill. When the bevel subtracted from the object, the blue color of the sides was maintained, but the corner showed through to the green center. With objects that have both a stroke and fill color, adding a bevel usually works better than subtracting.

NOTE | Self-Intersection

When you create a 3D object, there is a chance the paths you bevel or rotate will cross, or intersect, themselves. When this happens, Illustrator may or may not render the objects correctly. You are warned so you can find the problem and fix it—if it is causing a problem in your art. With the table, the stroke color is causing the warning, but it isn't a problem as long as you add the bevel rather than subtract it. Revolved art, which you will work with in the next few exercises, may also result in a path crossing itself. This is usually much more serious and often will not render at all. The screen shot on the right was taken while my computer was attempting a rotation of a complex shape. It worked on the problem for 15 minutes before it displayed an out-of-memory error and gave up! I had try a different shape to get the effect I was seeking.

6. Double-click the **Hand** tool to see the entire page. The bevel looks great except where it appears behind the type. On the **Layers** palette, show the hidden object **Type Backing** to add a flat surface for the type and ornaments.

7. On the **Layers** palette, lock the **Table** object.

The table was a square that covered almost the entire page before it was made into a 3D shape. You can still select it, accidentally, by clicking where it used to appear even though that part of your art now looks like empty space. Locking the object prevents this from happening.

8. Save the file and keep it open for the next exercise.

TIP | Custom Bevels

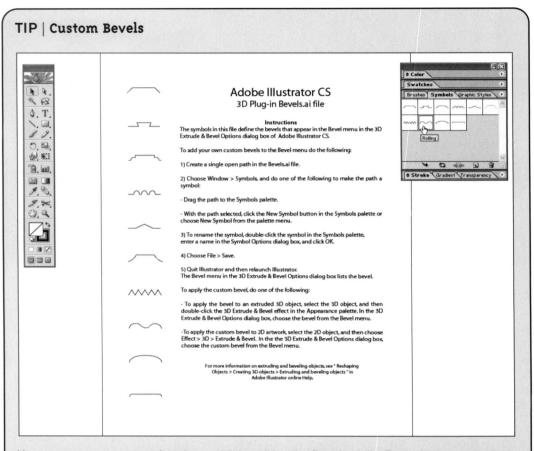

Adobe Illustrator CS
3D Plug-in Bevels.ai file

Instructions

The symbols in this file define the bevels that appear in the Bevel menu in the 3D Extrude & Bevel Options dialog box of Adobe Illustrator CS.

To add your own custom bevels to the Bevel menu do the following:

1) Create a single open path in the Bevels.ai file.

2) Choose Window > Symbols, and do one of the following to make the path a symbol:

- Drag the path to the Symbols palette.

- With the path selected, click the New Symbol button in the Symbols palette or choose New Symbol from the palette menu.

3) To rename the symbol, double-click the symbol in the Symbols palette, enter a name in the Symbol Options dialog box, and click OK.

4) Choose File > Save.

5) Quit Illustrator and then relaunch Illustrator.
The Bevel menu in the 3D Extrude & Bevel Options dialog box lists the bevel.

To apply the custom bevel, do one of the following:

- To apply the bevel to an extruded 3D object, select the 3D object, and then double-click the 3D Extrude & Bevel effect in the Appearance palette. In the 3D Extrude & Bevel Options dialog box, choose the bevel from the Bevel menu.

- To apply the custom bevel to 2D artwork, select the 2D object, and then choose Effect > 3D > Extrude & Bevel. In the the 3D Extrude & Bevel Options dialog box, choose the custom bevel from the Bevel menu.

For more information on extruding and beveling objects, see " Reshaping Objects > Creating 3D objects > Extruding and beveling objects " in Adobe Illustrator online Help.

You can create any custom bevel you wish by editing the **Bevels.ai** file. To do this, open the file **Illustrator CS > Plug-ins > Bevels.ai** and follow the instructions in the file. Each bevel is a simple open path stored as a symbol. Once you add the bevels you want, you must restart Illustrator to use the new bevels.

5. —————————Rotate

Rotate is the simplest of the 3D effects in that it takes a 2D object and rotates it into three dimensions, but it does not add any depth. Since there is no depth, the rotated object does not appear three-dimensional itself. Rotate is perfect for putting an object onto a 3D surface, as you will do in this exercise.

1. Open the file **gift_shop.ai** or continue from Exercise 4.

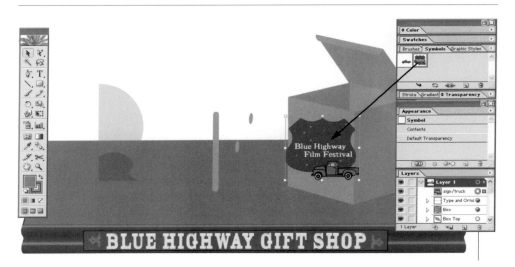

2. Choose **Window > Symbols** to see bring the **Symbols** palette forward. Drag the **sign/truck** symbol from the **Symbols** palette over the box to place an instance of this symbol.

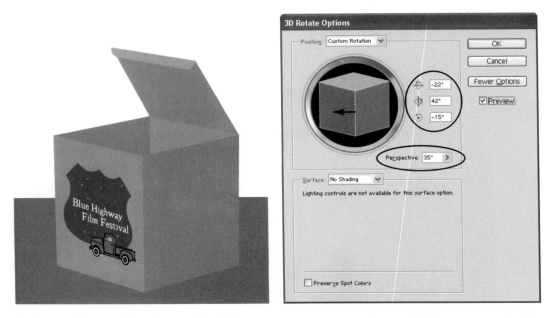

3. Choose **Effect > 3D > Rotate**. Check **Preview** so you can watch the symbol change as you build the effect. Set the **Position** to **Off-Axis Front** and then use the cube to rotate the **Green** axis to **42°**. The final numbers should be **Red –22°, Green 42°,** and **Blue –15°**. Add a **Perspective** of **35°** to match the box. Click **OK**.

4. Double-click the **Hand** tool to see the entire page. Reposition the symbol on the box as necessary.

This technique is useful for creating a "decal" effect that matches the perspective of other 3D objects. As you'll see in a later exercise, there is another way to do this using the 3D effect, but Rotate is a quick way to get the job done and is the only option if the object was drawn in perspective rather than created with the 3D effect.

5. Save the file and keep it open for the next exercise.

NOTE | Scaling 3D Objects

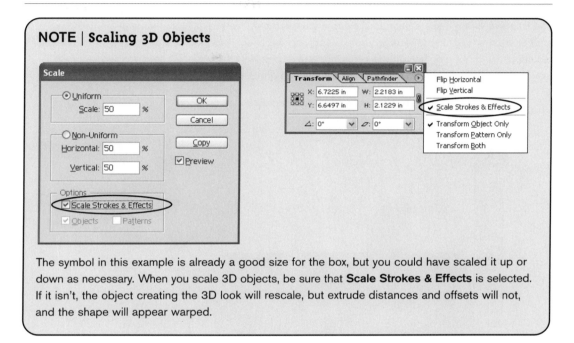

The symbol in this example is already a good size for the box, but you could have scaled it up or down as necessary. When you scale 3D objects, be sure that **Scale Strokes & Effects** is selected. If it isn't, the object creating the 3D look will rescale, but extrude distances and offsets will not, and the shape will appear warped.

6. ——————————Revolve

The **Revolve** effect takes a path and revolves it around the Green axis (y-axis/vertical axis). These effects are the toughest to visualize before applying the effect, but they produce some of the coolest results. Think of the original path as the silhouette or profile of the 3D object. As you will see in this exercise, you may need to revolve multiple paths as a group to get the right final look.

1. Open the file **gift_shop.ai** or continue from Exercise 5.

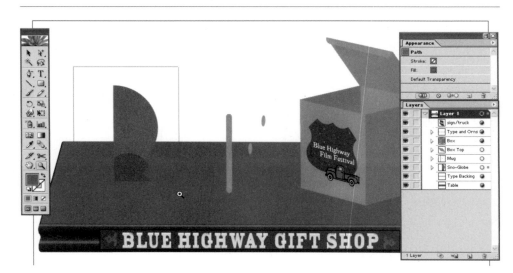

2. Use the **Zoom** tool to drag a rectangular marquee around the semicircle and brown shape on the left side of the table to zoom in on it.

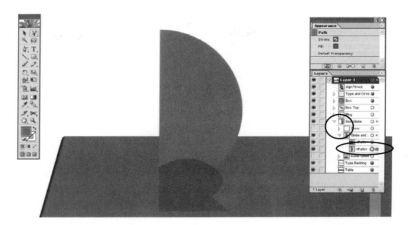

3. Select the **Group Selection** tool and click the blue semicircle to select only that semicircle. On the **Layers** palette, expand the **Sno-Globe** group and the **Globe and Base** group to see the selected path.

*The blue semicircle is grouped with the brown path below it, so you must use the **Group Selection** tool to select only the blue object.*

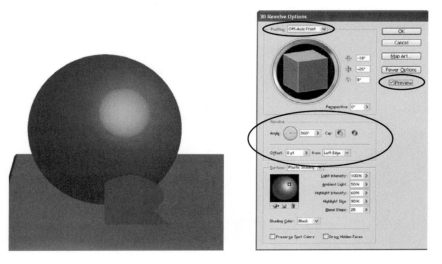

4. Choose **Effect > 3D > Revolve**. Choose a **Position** of **Off-Axis Front** and check the **Preview** check box. The default **Angle** of **360°** and an **Offset** of **0 pt** should create a sphere.

This sphere was created using a filled object with no stroke, but the same shape could have been made using a stroked path with no fill. I find filled objects easier to visualize rotated, but either way works. If the path had both a stroke and a fill, only the stroke color would show since the fill would be "hidden" inside the globe.

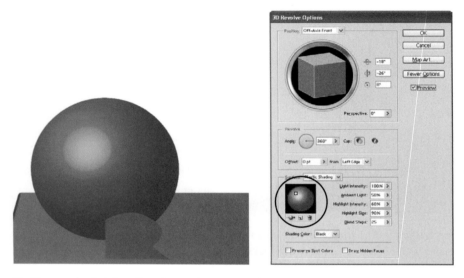

5. Change the lighting direction to the upper left to match the gift box.

Curved surfaces like a sphere really show off the effect of plastic shading. The bright spot on the sphere is the highlight that is only available through plastic shading.

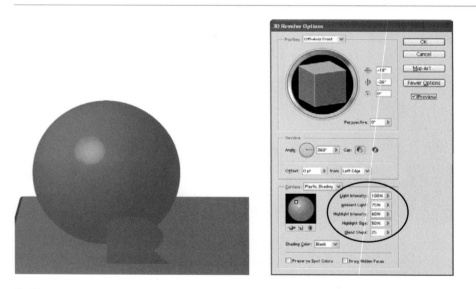

6. Change the lighting to an **Ambient Light** of **75%**. This will lighten the shadowed areas and soften the overall look. Make sure the **Highlight Intensity** is **60%**, and a set a **Highlight Size** of **50%**. The bright spot is now smaller and less pronounced. Click **OK**.

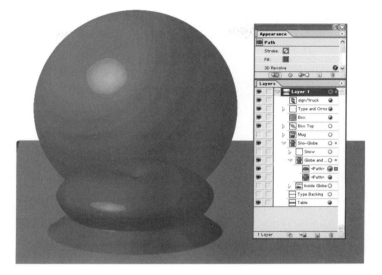

7. Now it's time to add a base for the snow globe. Click the brown shape with the **Group Selection** tool to select it. Choose **Effect > Apply Revolve**.

Apply Revolve uses the same 3D settings you used for the previous Revolve on the sphere, so there is no dialog box.

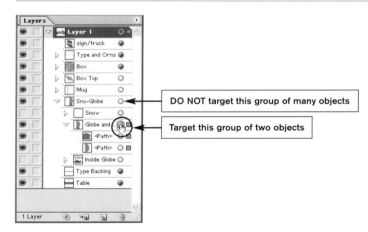

8. Creating the blue sphere and the brown base with separate Revolves creates two cool shapes, but there is no way you can arrange these two objects to put the globe inside the base, which is what we want. Choose **Edit > Undo 3D Effect** to get rid of the 3D Revolve on the base and **Edit > Undo Revolve** to get rid of the 3D Revolve on the sphere. Next, click the **Appearance** button for the **Globe and Base** group on the **Layers** palette to target the group containing both the globe and base paths.

9. Choose **Effect > Apply Revolve**. The Revolve is now applied to both objects as a group, and the globe appears inside the base. Also, all the lighting settings you entered in Steps 5 and 6 are used. How cool is that?

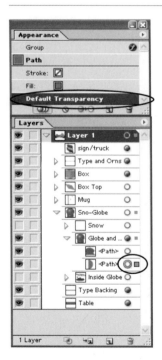

10. On the **Layers** palette, click the **<Path>** for the sphere to select only that path. Next, double-click the **Default Transparency** row on the **Appearance** palette. This opens the **Transparency** palette.

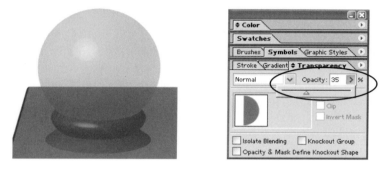

11. On the **Transparency** palette, set the **Opacity** of the sphere to **35%**.

Even though the effect is applied to the group, you can still edit the original objects independently. Another thing you could do while the sphere is selected is move it slightly up or down on the page. It would appear to move up and down in the base. If you move the sphere, be sure to undo the move and return it to the original position before the next step.

12. On the **Layers** palette, show the hidden groups **Snow** and **Inside Globe**.

*As with the top to the gift box, these are flat pieces of artwork added to the 3D effect to get a complete final look. The **Snow** layer is made with several sweeps of a scatter paintbrush in front of the semi-opaque sphere so the snow appears white rather than tinted blue. The other artwork is behind the sphere.*

13. Double-click the **Hand** tool to see the entire page. Save the file and keep it open for the next exercise.

7. —————————Revolve with Offset

Now that you have experience with revolving objects, it's time to bend your mind a bit more with a Revolve with an offset. This is the most difficult 3D effect to visualize before applying it, but it creates some great objects and is an essential part of your 3D repertoire. In addition to revolving with offset, this exercise will demonstrate objects created with Revolves of less than 360 degrees.

1. Open the file **gift_shop.ai** or continue from Exercise 6.

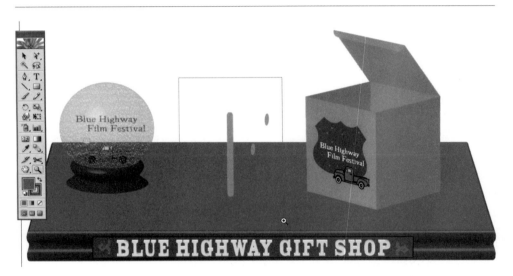

2. With the **Zoom** tool, drag a rectangular marquee centered on the rounded rectangle. This rounded rectangle will be revolved and offset to the left and right, so you want to start with it in the center of your screen.

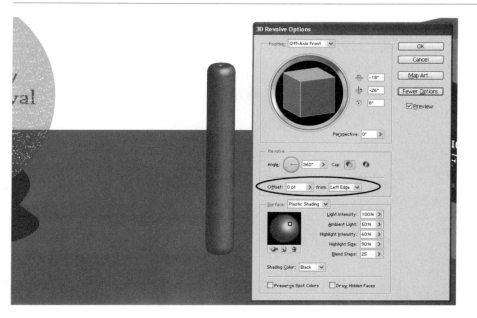

3. Select the **Group Selection** tool. Select the long rounded rectangle. On the **Layers** palette, expand the **Mug** group to make certain only the rounded rectangle is selected.

*Alternately, you could select the path directly using the **Layers** palette.*

4. Choose **Effect > 3D > Revolve**. Check the **Preview** check box to see an **Off-Axis Front** view of the **360°** revolve with an **Offset** of **0 pt** from the **Left Edge**. Note that the revolved object has a "dimple" in the top because the top of the revolved shape is rounded. The center of this dimple is the axis around which the shape is revolved.

*If you are continuing from Exercise 6, you could simply choose **Effect > Apply Revolve**. Since some people are starting this exercise after taking a break, it includes all the steps.*

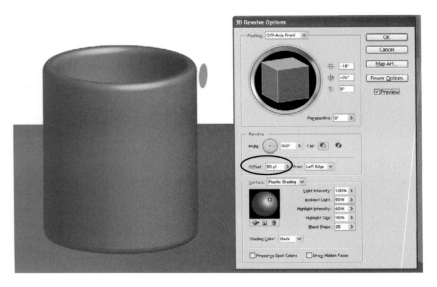

5. Change the **Offset** to **50 pt** from the **Left Edge**. The shape is now a hollow cylinder 100 pt in diameter. It's useful to note that the axis around which the shape is rotated has not moved. Instead, the shape was moved **50 pt** to the right and then revolved around the **Green** axis.

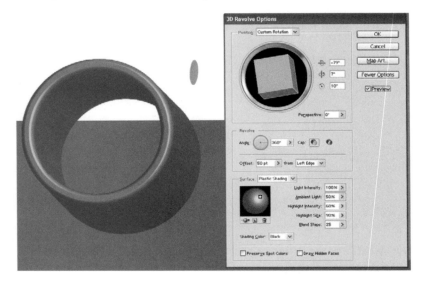

*It might be easier to understand what is happening if you use the cube in the **3D Revolve Options** dialog box to view the shape from different angles. This is a bottomless cup. Return the **Position** to **Off-Axis Front** view if you investigate the shape by rotating it to different positions.*

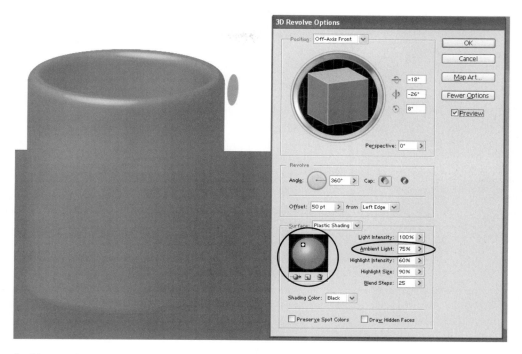

6. Change the lighting angle to the upper left and change the **Ambient Light** to **75%**. Click **OK**.

7. Now it's time to use your virtual potter's wheel. Choose **Effect > Warp > Arc**. Make a **Vertical** arc with a **Bend** of **9%** and a **Vertical Distortion** of **–45%**. Check **Preview** to verify the results. The mug now has a bend to it and is a bit wider at the top than the bottom. Click **OK**.

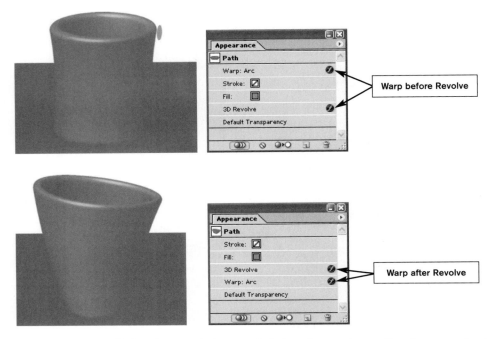

The Warp was applied to the rounded rectangle before the revolve, so the shape was bent with Warp and then that warped shape was revolved. You can also apply an effect after the Revolve. If you dragged the Warp effect down below the 3D Revolve in the Appearance palette, it would asymmetrically warp the cylinder. Mixing 3D with other effects has loads of cool possibilities. If you experiment with moving or changing the warp effect, be sure to undo these changes before continuing with the exercise.

8. On the **Layers** palette, hide the revolved path that makes the mug.

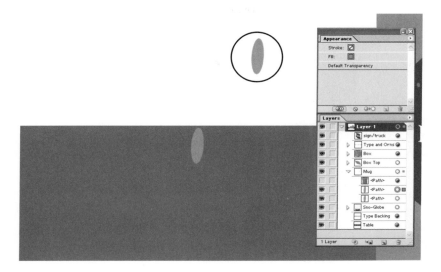

9. With the **Group Selection** tool, select the upper ellipse.

10. Choose **Effect > 3D > Revolve**. Set the **Position** to **Top**, the **Angle** to **145°**, and the **Offset** to **22 pt**. Check **Preview** to verify the results.

Angle sets how far the object is revolved. In this case, it is revolved through only 145° of arc. If it was revolved through 360°, it would appear as a ring.

11. Enter custom rotations of **Red** axis **67°**, **Green** axis **60°**, and **Blue** axis **141°**.

*Again, I got these numbers through trial and error moving the cube in the **3D Revolve Options** dialog box until I saw a look that I liked.*

12. Change the **Surface** to **Diffuse Shading** and the lighting angle to the upper left. Click **OK**.

*This object will become the handle for the mug. With **Diffuse Shading**, the highlight disappears, and the handle becomes less pronounced and appears more in the background.*

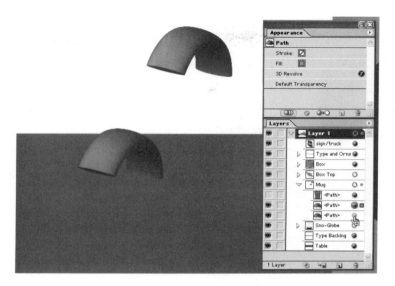

13. Hold down the **Alt** key (Windows) or the **Option** key (Mac). On the **Layers** palette, drag the **Appearance** button from the ellipse you just rotated to the other ellipse. The effect is copied to the second ellipse.

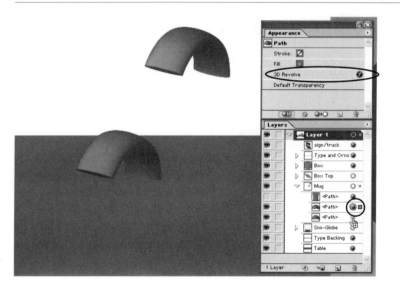

14. On the **Layers** palette, select the second ellipse by clicking the right of the row where the blue box appears. Double-click the **3D Revolve** effect on the **Appearance** palette to edit the effect for that ellipse only.

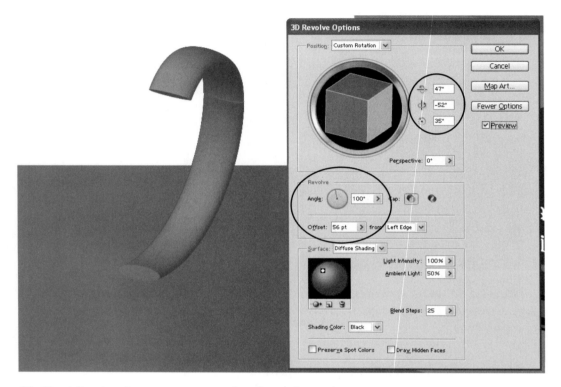

15. Check **Preview** first, so you can see the effects of your changes as you enter them. Enter custom rotations of **Red** axis **47°**, **Green** axis **−52°** (note the minus sign), and **Blue** axis **35°**. Set the **Angle** to **100°** and the **Offset** to **56 pt**. This changes the second object so it is a smaller arc of a larger ring. Click **OK**.

Some tweaking may be needed to get the two objects to line up as they appear above.

16. Unhide the path that creates the mug.

17. Save the file and keep it open for the next exercise.

MOVIE | revolve.mov

To see the steps of this complex exercise performed, watch the movie **revolve.mov** located in the **movies** folder of the **H•O•T CD-ROM**.

NOTE | Large File Size with 3D

You might notice that the **gift_shop.ai** file is getting rather large. The file started at about 500 KB, and the completed file will be over 6 MB. This is especially odd if you think you aren't adding any artwork! All the paths and symbols are included in the original 500 KB file. The size is because Illustrator saves raster images of all the 3D artwork at rather high resolution as part of the file. This allows you to zoom in and out and view different parts of the artwork without constantly waiting for your computer to re-render the art.

8. ————————Mapping Art onto 3D Objects

The Illustrator team included a feature to map artwork onto the surfaces of your 3D objects using symbols. Mapping artwork is easy to do and looks great. The only catch is that you must make your art into a symbol before you map it in 3D space. For more information on symbols, see Chapter 16, "*Symbols.*"

1. Open the file **gift_shop.ai** or continue from Exercise 7.

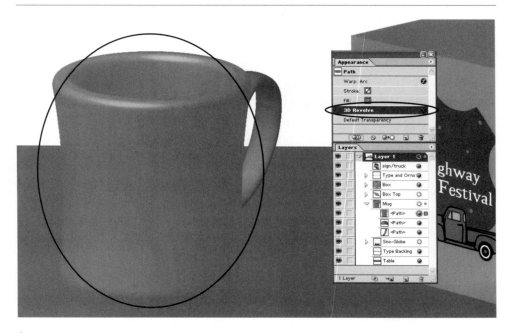

2. Select the **Group Selection** tool and click the body of the mug to select it and not the handle. Double-click the **3D Revolve** effect on the **Appearance** palette to edit it.

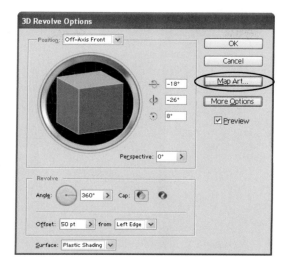

3. Check **Preview** and then click **Map Art**.

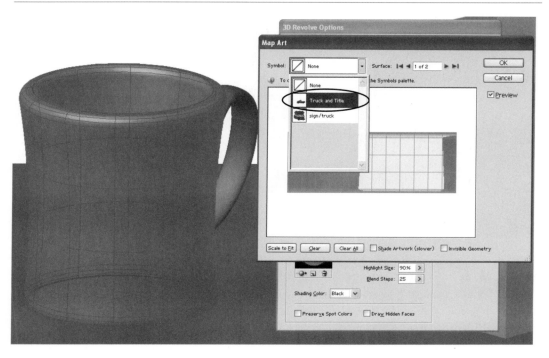

4. The **Map Art** dialog box opens. Make sure the **Surface** is set to **1 of 2**, which is the outside of the mug surface. **Surface 2 of 2** is the inside the mug. Select **Truck and Title** for the **Symbol**.

5. The symbol appears in the white preview area of the **Map Art** dialog box and on the mug. Hold down the **Shift** key and use bounding box in the **Map Art** dialog box to rescale and position the **Truck and Title** symbol over the light gray area, as shown above. The light gray area is the area of the object that is visible. Any part of the symbol extending into the dark area or the white space is not visible in your art. Click **OK** for the **Map Art** dialog box and click **OK** again for the **3D Revolve Options** dialog box.

*There is also a **Scale to Fit** button in the bottom left of the dialog box. This is especially useful when the symbol is initially so large its bounding box cannot be seen.*

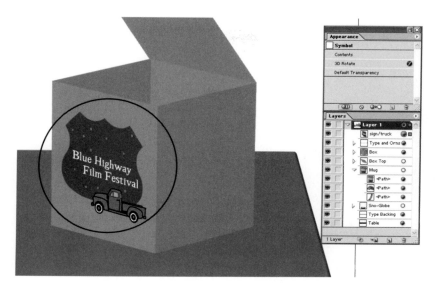

6. Select the **Hand** tool and drag to pan over to the gift box. You used the **Rotate** effect to add art to the gift box, but the map art effect can do it, too, and offers some extra possibilities. Select the **Group Selection** tool and select the **Symbol** on the front of the box. Press **Backspace** or **Delete** on your keyboard to delete it.

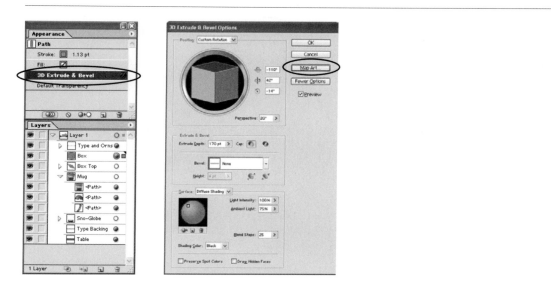

7. Click the body of the box with the **Group Selection** tool to select it and not the lid. Double-click the **3D Extrude & Bevel** effect on the **Appearance** palette to edit the effect. Check **Preview** and click **Map Art**.

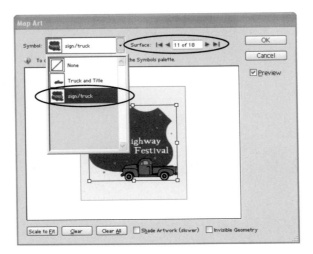

8. Use the **Next Surface** arrows to advance to **Surface 11 of 18**. The selected surface will highlight in red on the box, too. Next, select the **sign/truck** symbol.

Eighteen surfaces? There are obviously four outside sides to the box and four inside sides, but each corner and the top and bottom edges also are available surfaces. These surfaces are only 1 pt wide, however, so mapping art onto them doesn't have much utility.

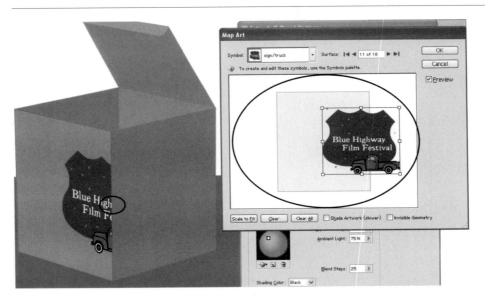

9. Slide the **sign/truck** symbol to the right in the **Map Art** dialog box until the letters "way" from the word "Highway" disappear.

10. Use the **Next Surface** arrows to advance to **Surface 14 of 18**. Next, select the **sign/truck** symbol for this surface.

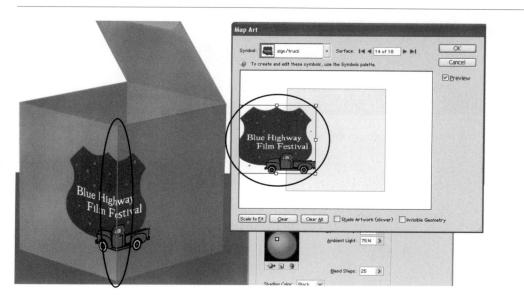

11. Drag the symbol to the left and align it to get the effect of the logo wrapping around the box. Click **OK** for the **Map Art** dialog box and click **OK** again for the **3D Extrude & Bevel Options** dialog box.

> **WARNING | Mapped Art Uses Document Raster Effects Settings**
>
> When you map raster art onto a 3D shape, it is rasterized at your Document Raster Effects Settings rather than the setting for the original art. For example, if you map a 300 ppi photo onto a 3D object, and your Document Raster Effects Settings are set to the default 72 ppi, then the photo is resampled to 72 ppi. You might not notice the change onscreen, but it will be very noticeable when you have the final file printed. For more information on Document Raster Effects Settings and printing, see Appendix C, "*Print Issues*."

12. Double-click the **Hand** tool to see the entire page.

13. Save the file and close it.

TIP | Printing 3D Art

Since 3D is an effect, it is a good idea to expand the appearance of all your 3D objects before sending them out to a printer. This ensures the art will appear correctly when printed. To do this, select the 3D objects and choose **Object > Expand Appearance**. If you have a group that contains multiple 3D effects, selecting the group and choosing **Expand Appearance** will expand all the 3D effects in the group (as well as any other effects). Do not expand your art until you are ready to send it off. Once it expands, it becomes many separate groups, paths, and compound paths (perhaps hundreds of paths on complex art) and is very difficult to edit. For that reason, always keep an un-expanded copy of the art in case you need to edit it later on.

The 3D effect isn't a replacement for a full 3D drawing program like Dimensions, but it is one of the coolest additions to Illustrator CS. Expect the capabilities of this tool to grow dramatically in subsequent versions of Illustrator.

20.

Templates and Actions

| Using Templates | Creating Templates |
| Using Actions | Editing Actions |

chap_20

Illustrator CS
H•O•T CD-ROM

Part of any professional illustrator's work involves tasks that are repetitive and, well, boring. It might be creating an advertisement that is only slightly different from one you have done 10 times before, or it might be a color change in 30 different documents to reflect the new look created by the marketing department. Illustrator can't relieve you of these tasks, but it can make them simpler, quicker, and more error-free.

What's Special About a Template?

If you've worked with computer content for any length of time, you have had the experience of opening up an old document just to get the layout or other design elements you needed for a new document. This technique is always a bit clunky, though—involving deleting a bunch of old information and the possibility of forgetting to save it as a new document and losing the original file. (I'd rather not admit how many times I've done that.) Templates offer a better way and more. Templates allow you to create files with the design elements you need in place and leave placeholder elements that change. Preset elements can include artwork and any swatches, symbols, styles, or other palette items you want. Templates let you set the document setup and print setup options in advance. This is a huge plus if your work requires various color profiles and print configurations. Templates protect your original work by always opening as a copy rather than the original document. This is not only a plus for protecting your work, but it is ideal when many artists are using master templates from a server computer on a network. Finally, templates are essential if you are creating on-the-fly Web images or automated artwork.

NOTE | Template Layers

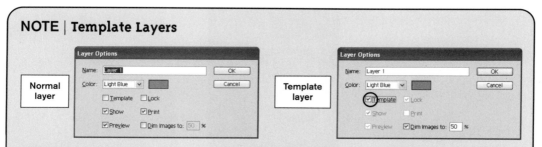

This chapter is about template files; however, the term "template" can apply to a single layer or sublayer on the Layers palette. These layers are locked and do not print. Images on template layers are automatically dimmed. To create a template layer, double-click the **Layer** row in the **Layers** palette to open the **Layer Options** dialog box, and check the **Template** check box. The options for **Lock**, **Show**, and **Preview** will all check and dim, and the option for **Print** will uncheck and dim. The **Dim Images** option will also check and be set to a default of **50%** white, but you can change this setting.

If you do create a template layer, it has a special icon that replaces the **Eye** icon on the **Layers** palette so that you know it's a template. You can still show and hide the layer by clicking on this icon, just as you did with the **Eye** icon. You can also leave the layer as a regular layer and adjust the options for **Lock**, **Print**, and **Dim** separately, which is my preference. Using objects on layers as templates for drawing is discussed in Chapter 11, "*Pencil and Line Segment Tools*."

I. _____Using Templates

Illustrator CS ships with dozens of professionally designed templates for use in business, media and Web production, personal use, and just plain fun. Theses templates are free for you to use as you wish. They can also be a great source of inspiration in designing common projects, such as CD cases or Web banners.

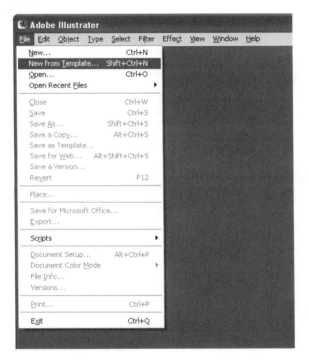

1. Copy the **chap_20** folder from the **H•O•T CD-ROM** to your hard drive. In Illustrator, choose **File > New from Template**.

2. The **Templates** folder opens by default. **Double-click** (Windows) or **single-click** (Mac) the **Cards and Post Cards** directory.

3. Double-click the file **Post Card 5.ait** to open the template file.

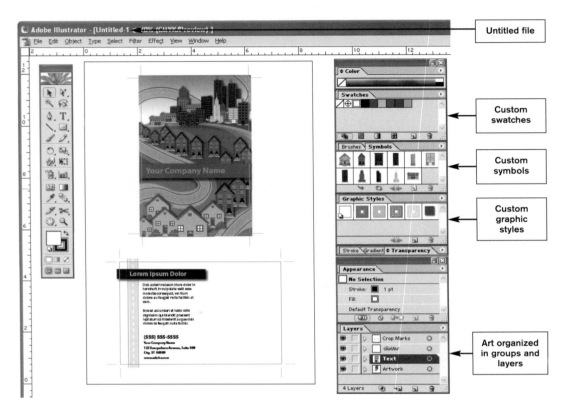

*Rather than open the actual template file, Illustrator opens a copy of the template an in untitled file. The file contains artwork you can customize to meet your needs, as well as custom swatches, symbols, graphic styles, and type styles. The artwork is organized in the **Layers** palette to help you select and edit the art you want.*

*Your **Graphic Styles** palette and **Symbols** palette may not be visible at the same time. They are separated in this picture to better show what the template file contains.*

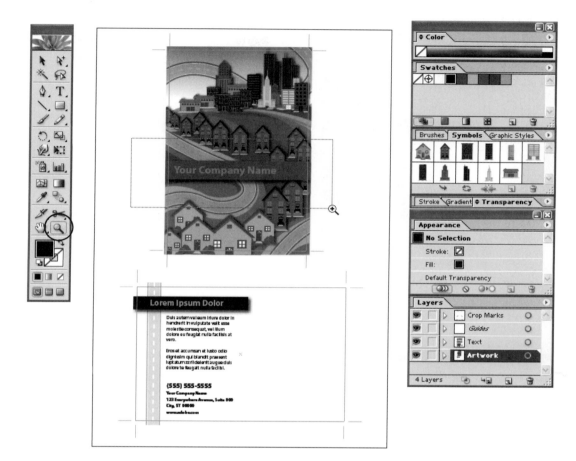

4. Select the **Zoom** tool and zoom in on the text "Your Company Name" on the front of the postcard.

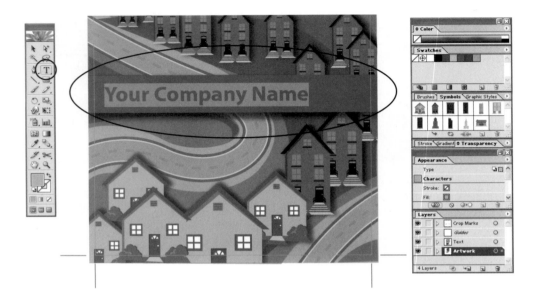

5. Select the **Type** tool. Click three times on "Your" in "Your Company Name" to select the entire line.

6. Type **Blue Highway Film Festival**.

Simply editing the text is the quickest way to customize the template, but all the art is editable, too. You could customize it as much as you wished.

7. Choose **File > Save**. Since the template opened as a copy of the original, this file has never been saved. The default file is usually your **Illustrator CS >Templates** folder. To save the version you've been working on, navigate to the **chap_20** folder on your hard drive, name the file **postcard.ai**, and click **Save**. Click **OK** to accept the default options.

8. Close the file.

MOVIE | startup.mov

When you choose **File > New** to create a new Illustrator document, you are actually opening a template file with nothing on the artboard and a default set of swatches, brushes, symbols, and graphic styles. You can edit these templates and change the default settings for new files. To see how this is done, watch the **startup.mov** movie online at **http://www.lynda.com/ books/hot/illcs/movies/**.

2. ————————Creating Templates

Using the templates that ship with Illustrator is fun, but building your own templates is a more important skill for streamlining your workflow. Templates are great for projects such as magazine ads or business cards, where a single design is populated with varying data. Illustrator can also combine a template design with a database to create dynamic, data-driven graphics. These are commonly used to create Web pages on the fly. In this exercise, you will create a template for a Web page element. This element will appear in the Web page you will work on in the next chapter.

1. Open the file **film_preview_web.ai** from the **chap_20** folder.

Delta Series
Skipped is director
Paul Smith's fifth
documentary for
public television
and his best film
more

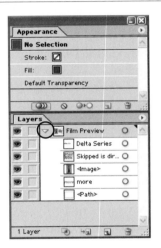

2. Choose **Window > Layers** if the **Layers** palette is not visible. Turn down the expansion triangle for the **Film Preview** layer to see its contents. There are two unlocked type objects, one for the title **Delta Series** and one for the rest of the text. There is also a raster image, the **more** link, and the green border. This is the file as you might have created it for a single Web page element. Now you want to turn it into a template for quickly making similar elements for the Web site.

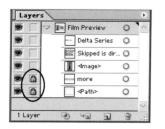

3. Lock the **more** and **<Path>** objects so they are not changed or moved. These two pieces of the template will be the same on all Web elements based on this design.

You could simply save the file as a template now and let anyone using it to create similar art replace the elements to match the example in the template. A more thorough template includes a bit more information and guidance since other people may be designing from this template, or if you might forget exactly which objects you want changed.

4. Since this is a template, you should make sure each object is clearly labeled on the **Layers** palette as to its purpose. This is very important if you are creating data-driven graphics, which use a database to assemble graphics dynamically from a template. The database references objects by their names on the **Layers** palette. Double-click the row **Delta Series** on the **Layers** palette. Change the **Name** to **Series Title**. Click **OK**.

When you create a type object, the name on the Layers palette automatically fills with the text you enter into the type object. Changing the name does not affect the text in your document.

5. Double-click the row **Skipped is...** on the **Layers** palette. Change the **Name** to **Film Info**. Click **OK**.

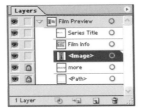

6. Double-click the row **<Image>** on the **Layers** palette. Change the **Name** to **61 x 108 pixels**. Click **OK**.

Putting the file size into the name is an easy way to make sure everyone using the template knows what file size to use.

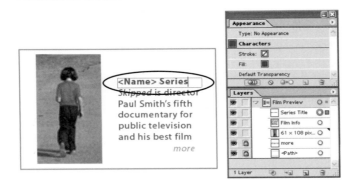

7. Now that you have changed the names on the **Layers** palette, you can put instructions in the file itself. Select the **Type** tool. Triple-click to select the words "Delta Series" on the screen and change the name to **<Name> Series**.

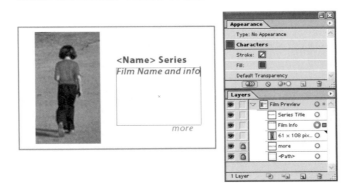

8. Triple-click the word "Skipped" on the screen to select all the remaining text and type **Film Name and info**. All the type will be italicized because "Skipped" was italicized.

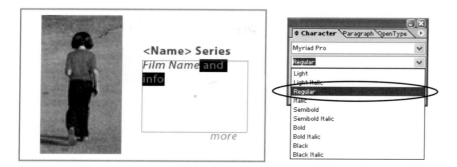

9. Choose **Window > Type > Character** to see the **Character** palette. With the **Type** tool, select the text **and info** and set the format to **Regular**.

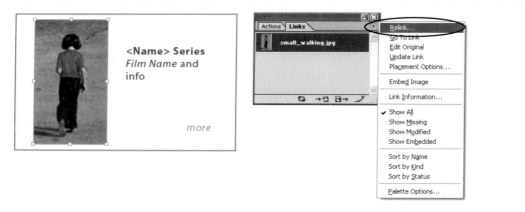

10. Choose the **Selection** tool and select the photo. Choose **Window > Links** to see the **Links** palette. From the **Links** palette flyout menu, choose **Relink**.

As mentioned in Chapter 17, "Filters and Effects," raster images placed in an Illustrator file are linked to the original file rather than embedded in the Illustrator file by default. You manage these links, or choose to embed the raster data, using the Links palette.

11. Choose the file **link_placeholder.gif** from the **chap_20** folder and click **Place**. This GIF file was created in Photoshop specifically as a photo placeholder for this template. It contains the information on what belongs in this space on file and is pretty difficult to overlook for someone using the template.

12. Double-click the **Hand** tool to see the whole page. It's a good idea to create a template so it opens with a view of the full page because different users will have different screen sizes. A template opens with the view it had when it was created, so double-clicking the **Hand** tool is a recommended last step before saving the file.

Also, deleting any swatches, symbols, brushes, and graphic styles not in use will reduce the file size.

13. Choose **File > Save as Template**. The **Save As** dialog box opens with the same file name as the Illustrator file, **film_preview_web** in this case, but the file type is **Illustrator Template (*.AIT)**. Illustrator also automatically goes to the **Templates** folder so the new template is saved with the default ones. This is done simply for organization. You can save the template anywhere you want.

*You could choose the regular **Save As** command and choose **Illustrator Template** as the file type. The only difference is that Illustrator would default to the **chap_20** folder for saving the file.*

14. Create a new folder called **HOT Templates**. On a Mac, the new folder automatically opens, so you can simply click **Save**. On Windows, double-click the new folder or click **Open** and then click **Save** to save your template.

*Now the **film_preview_web** template is available for quickly creating new Web elements that exactly match your initial design. To open the template, choose **File > New from Template**. Open the **HOT Templates** folder and double-click on the file **film_preview_web.ait**. It will open as an untitled Illustrator document.*

15. Close the file.

TIP | Changing the Template

You may wonder how to change the original template when every time you open it a copy opens instead. The answer is: you don't. Open the template as you would to use it normally and make the changes you want. Next, save the file as a template with the same name as the original. Click Yes or OK when asked if you want to replace the original file. The old template is replaced by the new one.

MOVIE | data_driven.mov

Delta Series	**Special Events**	**Latest News**
Skipped is director Paul Smith's fifth documentary for public television and his best film	It's almost here! Getting ready for the festival started about over 300 days ago, and about 14 days before our last event even started. We can't believe it's almost here, either.	11/30 Writing Workshop scheduled for June 1st
		3/26 Fundraiser News
more	*more*	3/15 Schedule Changes

Illustrator's **Variables** palette lets you combine an Illustrator template file with a data set or separate database to create multiple graphics from a single file. To see how you use the **Variables** palette to create data-driven graphics, watch the **data_driven.mov** movie online at **http://www.lynda.com/books/hot/illcs/movies/**.

3. ——————Using Actions

Actions are sets of scripted commands that let Illustrator fly on autopilot. They speed up your workflow by letting you define a task once and then repeat it with a single click. The Illustrator Actions palette comes with several default actions for common tasks, but many of these are one-task actions that help most when working on a batch of files rather than a single document. Single-file actions usually involve simple tasks that involve several annoyingly repetitive steps. For example, before you save custom swatch, brush, symbol, or other libraries, you must select and delete all the unused palette items. An action makes this task a snap, as you will see in this exercise.

1. Open the file **ticket.ai** from the **chap_20** folder.

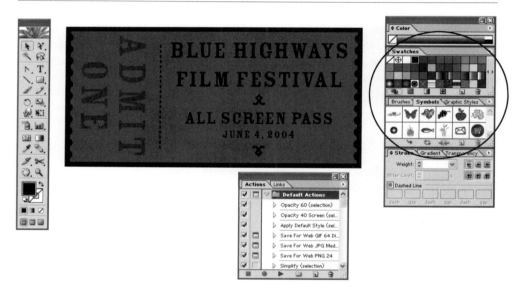

2. Choose **Window > Symbols** to open the **Symbols** palette. Note the unused symbols on the **Symbols** palette and the unused swatches on the **Swatches** palette. There are also unused brushes and graphic styles in the file. Choose **Window > Actions** to open the **Actions** palette.

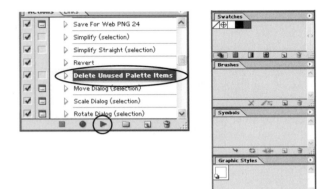

3. On the **Actions** palette, scroll down and select the action **Delete Unused Palette Items**. Press the **Play Current Selection** button on the **Actions** palette. Voila! The unused swatches, symbols, brushes, and graphic styles are all gone with a single click! Accomplishing this same task manually would require at least 12 mouse clicks and pausing at 4 dialog boxes.

If some swatches, symbols, brushes, or graphic styles remain after the action, play it a second time. Actions are sometimes quirky this way. This action sometimes requires a second pass to remove all unused items.

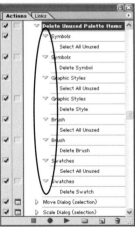

4. Expand the **Delete Unused Palette Items** action if it is not already expanded to see the steps inside it. Expand each of the substeps to see that the action is simply a series of commands. If you could translate this action into plain English, it would say, "On the **Symbols** palette flyout menu, choose **Select All Unused**. On the **Symbols** palette flyout menu, choose **Delete Symbol**. On the **Graphic Styles** palette flyout menu, choose **Select All Unused**…" and so on.

5. Save the file and keep it open for the next exercise.

NOTE | Skipping Steps, Skipping Dialog Boxes

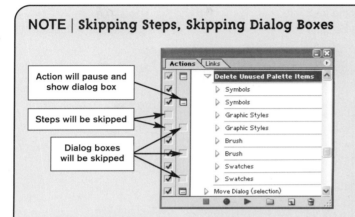

When you play an action, you have the option of skipping any steps in the action by unchecking those rows on the **Action** palette before you play the action. You can also play only part of an action by highlighting that row and pressing the **Play** button. The action will play from that row downward but skip any previous steps. Many Illustrator commands you might include in an action have dialog boxes. You can choose to see or skip these dialog boxes by showing or hiding the **dialog** icon on that row of the **Actions** palette. Some dialog boxes are very simple. In the case of **Delete Unused Palette Items**, the dialog box is only a confirmation that you really want to delete the selected items. Other dialog boxes are more complex, such as all the options for the **Object > Transform > Transform Each** command. If you skip a dialog box, Illustrator uses whatever values were in that dialog box when the action was created.

4. ————————Editing Actions

Now that you can use an action, it's time to create one of your own and see how you might use it in your artwork. In this exercise, you will build an action to create a copy of an Illustrator file with all the type converted to outlines.

1. Open the file **ticket.ai** from the **chap_20** folder or continue from Exercise 4.

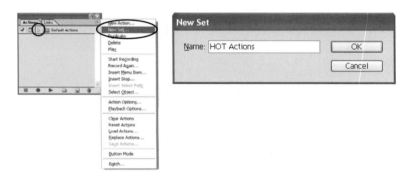

2. Scroll up on the **Actions** palette and collapse the **Default Actions**. From the **Actions** palette flyout menu, choose **New Set**. Name the set **HOT Actions** and click **OK**.

*You can add actions to the **Default Actions** set, if you prefer, but using sets will help you find the action you want in the list.*

3. From the **Actions** palette flyout menu, choose **New Action**. Name the action **Create Outlines** and change the color to **Red**. Click **Record**.

*Since the **HOT Actions** set was highlighted, this action is added to the **HOT Actions** set by default. The red color is a way to find actions quickly in Button mode, described in the upcoming sidebar called "Button Mode."*

4. The **Record** button on the **Actions** palette turns red to indicate that the action is now recording. Choose **Select > Object > Text Objects**. All the text is selected and a command to select all text objects is added to the **Create Outlines** action.

As you record the action, your artwork is also affected by the commands you choose.

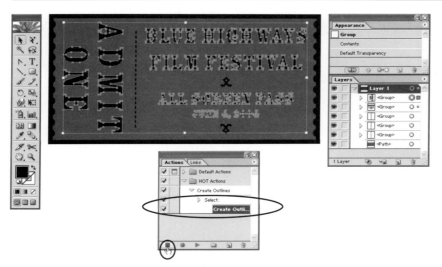

5. Choose **Type > Create Outlines**. All the selected type in the artwork is converted to outlines and the **Create Outlines** command is added under the **Select** row of the action. This indicates that only the objects selected by that select command will be converted to outlines. Click the **Stop Playing/Recording** button to complete recording the action.

6. Suppose you want to add to the action now that the action is recorded? You can simply press the **Begin Recording Action** button and continue recording the action. You can also build an action one command at a time. Choose **Insert Menu Item** from the **Actions** palette flyout menu.

7. When the **Insert Menu Item** dialog box appears, you can type the command name, or you can select the item you want by using Illustrator's menus. Since I can never remember the exact wording of the command, from the **File** menu, choose **File > Save A Copy**. Rather than opening the **Save A Copy** dialog box, the **Save A Copy** command appears in the empty field. Click **OK**.

Action steps added with the Insert Menu Item command are not performed on your artwork.

8. The **Save A Copy** command is now part of the **Create Outlines** action. Since you want the action to leave your original file unchanged, you should add **Revert** to the action as well. While the **Save A Copy** row on the action is still highlighted, click the **Begin Recording Action** button again on the **Actions** palette. Choose **File > Revert**. Click **Revert** when the dialog box opens. **Revert** is added to the action, and the file **ticket.ai** is reverted to its last saved form. Click the **Stop Playing / Recording** button.

9. To test the revised **Create Outlines** action, click the **Create Outlines** row of the action so that the action will play from the beginning. Click the **Play Current Selection** (**Play**) button. The action will play again to select all type and convert it to outlines. Next, the **Save a Copy** dialog box will open.

10. When the **Save a Copy** dialog box opens, click **Save** to save the file as **ticket copy.ai**. Click **OK** to accept the default save options. When the **Revert** dialog box appears, click **OK**. The new **ticket copy.ai** file is saved on your hard drive with all the type converted to outlines, and the original **ticket.ai** is unchanged.

11. Unlike items on the **Swatches** palette, **Brushes** palette, or other art palettes, actions you create in one file are immediately available in all others. Now that you have created the action, you can use it in another file. Close the file **ticket.ai** and open the file **map_20.ai**.

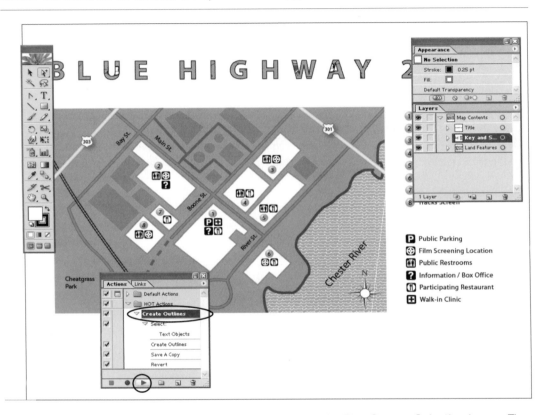

12. Click the top row of the action **Create Outlines** and click the **Play Current Selection** button. The action selects all the type, converts it to outlines, and opens the **Save a Copy** dialog box. Click **Save** to save the copy as **map_20 copy.ai**, and click **OK** to save with the default options. The action continues and reverts the file. Click **Revert**, and the file returns to its original state.

13. Close the file.

NOTE | Button Mode

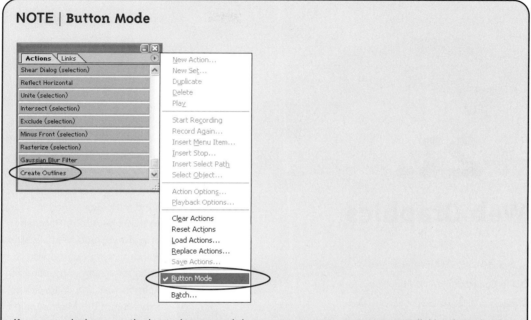

If you are playing a particular action several times, you can save some mouse clicking by selecting **Button Mode** from the **Actions** palette flyout menu. The list of actions changes into buttons with the title of each action on the button. Pressing the button selects and plays the action all at once. If you assigned a color to the action—as you did in Step 3 of this exercise—the button is shaded with that color. If you want to record or edit any actions, you must first exit Button mode.

MOVIE | batch.mov

Actions can be handy when working with a single file, but they are a lifesaver when you have to perform the same task on multiple files. Need to open 40 Illustrator files and save them all as JPEGs? This is no problem with batch actions. To see how to apply an action to a batch of files, watch the **batch.mov** movie online at **http://www.lynda.com/books/hot/illcs/movies/**.

Templates and actions—two great tools to speed up your work flow and cut the boredom of repetitive tasks. Now on to a topic many of you are anxious to read: Illustrator for the Web.

21.

Web Graphics

Web Graphics 101	RGB Mode and Web Color Issues
Slicing and Optimizing	More About Save for Web
Creating a Different Layout	Image Maps
Writing Macromedia Flash Files

chap_21

Illustrator CS
H•O•T CD-ROM

Illustrator began as a tool for creating printed artwork, but it has developed into a powerful tool for creating Web graphics as well. In this chapter, you'll witness the advantages that Illustrator CS offers the Web artist, such as being able to move artwork around more easily than in a raster program like Adobe Photoshop or ImageReady and to scale artwork without losing quality. Add to that tools for slicing and optimizing images, creating image maps, and exporting in the Macromedia Flash format, and you'll soon agree that Illustrator is a great tool for Web graphics.

Web Graphics 101

This is a book about learning to use Illustrator, and not about Web graphics. There are hundreds of books and learning resources related to Web authoring that have the space to go into much greater detail than I have here. A list of learning resources follows this section.

Color Mode was discussed in Chapter 5, "*Fills, Strokes, and Color.*" So far in this book, you've been working primarily in the CMYK color mode, which is appropriate for artwork that is destined to be printed. Web graphics, however, are published to the screen and will be seen in RGB. For this reason, you will learn how to change the color mode to RGB for the exercises in this chapter.

Web colors is a term for colors that are part of a 216-color group that displays reliably between Windows and Mac computers when their color space is limited to 256 colors (8-bit). In the olden days of Web authoring, most computers had older video cards that supported only 256 colors. Today, most computers support millions of colors, so the need to limit your color choices to Web colors is no longer critical for most Web pages. Some cell phone and PDA browsers still use the 256-color palette, however, so Illustrator offers access to this restricted color palette in the event that you want to choose one of these colors.

Optimization is a term used for making Web graphics smaller in file size. Since download speed is an issue for the majority of Web users, it's your job as a responsible Web artist to ensure your file sizes are as small as possible so they will download quickly. In general, graphics that are flat by nature (contain areas of solid color) will be smallest by being saved in the GIF file format. Graphics that are continuous tone in nature (include gradients, photographs, blurs, soft-edges) will be smallest when they're saved in the JPEG format. You will learn how to save in these two formats in this chapter.

Slicing is a process of cutting apart a single image into two or more pieces. Illustrator allows you to do this and puts the pieces back together by reassembling the artwork on export. This reassembly is accomplished through Illustrator CS automatically writing a **table**, HTML code that creates rows, columns, and cells. Why would you want to cut apart an Illustrator graphic only to reassemble it in an HTML table? Some regions of your Web page design might need to be optimized with different settings than others. Slicing is a way to isolate parts of the image that require different types of compression, such as using GIF and JPEG formats within the same document. You also might want to create rollovers in another program, such as Adobe ImageReady. Slices are necessary for certain types of rollovers, but you cannot create rollovers directly from Illustrator CS.

Image maps are artwork on a Web page containing "hot spot" links to an internal or external Web pages. Clicking an internal link would go to a location within my own site. Clicking an external link would go to a location in else's site. You will learn how to create an image maps in an upcoming exercise.

A **Macromedia Flash** file (otherwise known as Macromedia SWF) is a file format, developed by Macromedia, that supports graphics, animation, sound, video, and interactivity. Illustrator CS will write to the Macromedia Flash format, but it supports only images and animation—sound and interactivity are not supported. Illustrator CS is most commonly used for creating vector graphics or animations that are published to the Web as is, or are imported into Macromedia Flash so that interactivity and sound can be added there.

Now that you've familiarized yourself with some of these terms, you'll get to learn more about them through "doing" in the upcoming hands-on exercises!

NOTE | Web Graphics Learning Resources

There are numerous resources from which to learn Web graphics. These are some titles published by lynda.com:

Books

Designing Web Graphics.4 (4th Edition), by Lynda Weinman. ISBN: 0735710791

Photoshop CS/ImageReady CS for the Web Hands-On Training, by Tanya Staples. ISBN: 0321228553

CD-ROM and Online Learning titles

These products contain instruction in QuickTime movie format:

Learning Adobe Photoshop CS for the Web – 5 hours

Learning Macromedia Flash MX 2004 – 18 hours

Learning HTML – 3 hours

Learning XHTML – 3.5 hours

Learning Adobe GoLive – 18 hours

I. _____RGB Mode and Web Color Issues

Since this chapter focuses on Web graphics, you might have questions about color issues. This exercise focuses on three aspects of this issue: converting CMYK to RGB, setting Web color profiles, and picking Web safe colors.

1. Copy **chap_21** from the **exercise_files** folder on the **H•O•T CD-ROM** to your hard drive in a location that you can find again easily. It's especially important that you copy the folder to your hard drive for this chapter. You will need to locate, save to, and open from this folder throughout this chapter.

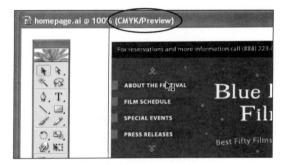

2. Open the file **homepage.ai** from the **chap_21** folder.

The top title bar states this file is in CMYK. Many times you will start with a CMYK file that was created for print, and then decide to take that same artwork to the Web. In order to do so, it's important to switch to RGB mode.

3. Choose **File > Document Color Mode > RGB Color**. This converts the CMYK color to RGB. When you change this setting, you might notice a slight color shift. Don't worry about the shift—this is the way that viewers on the Web will see this artwork, so you might as well view it this same way while you're working!

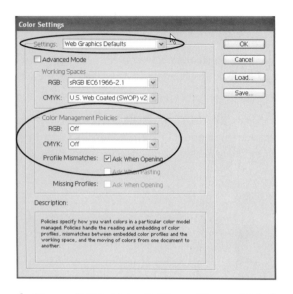

4. Choose **Edit > Color Settings**. Choose **Web Graphics Defaults** from the **Settings** pop-up menu. This setting will turn off RGB color management. Click **OK**.

Color profiles (also known as color management) help ensure the colors in an illustration print the same way you see them onscreen. Since Web browsers don't read color profiles, there is no need to use them in your file. It's best to work without them because they can give you false confidence that your file looks a certain way, when it won't look that way once published to the Web. Choosing the Web Graphic Defaults turns off color management. It is the equivalent of choosing a color profile that turns off color profiles!

5. Next you'll learn how to use Web colors by recoloring the object called **background** in the **Layers** palette. Click the arrow for the **bg** layer to view its sublayers. Scroll to the bottom to locate the layer called **background**. Click the **Lock** icon to turn it off. Click the **Appearance** button to target this layer. A red square will appear next to the circle, and the layer will become selected on the screen.

Double-click here to access the Color Picker

6. With the **background** sublayer selected, double-click the fill color. This will open the **Color Picker**. Check the box on the bottom left called **Only Web Colors**. The color will shift to the closest Web color. Click **OK**.

You just shifted the color from a non-Web color to a Web color. Web colors are no longer essential for Web graphics authoring, but some clients still want you to use them. Now you know how! The process can be repeated for any other object on the screen. Simply select the object first, then double-click its fill color, and click the check box for **Only Web Colors***.*

7. Scroll to the bottom of the **Layers** palette and click inside the **Lock** icon region to activate the **Lock** icon for the **background** object. This will lock the background image so you can move objects around freely in subsequent exercises without bumping the background image out of place.

8. Save the file and leave it open for the next exercise.

NOTE | Image Size Onscreen and Online

One thing to be aware of when creating Web graphics in Illustrator is that their dimensions on the Illustrator artboard and their dimensions in a browser window may not be the same. To get an idea how big an image will appear on the Web, choose **View > Actual Size**. This will be the approximate size of the image on a computer with the same screen resolution and screen size as the one you are working on. This is very rough approximation though since monitor sizes and resolutions vary widely.

A better choice is to decide beforehand how big you want the image to be in pixels. Web graphics are measured in pixels, or dots of color, so you can choose how big you want an image and then draw it that many pixels high and wide or resize it to those dimensions before you export it to a Web format. To change the measurement units in Illustrator to pixels, choose **File > Preferences > Units & Display Performance** (Windows) or **Illustrator > Preferences > Units & Display Performance** (Mac) and choose **Pixels** for the **General** measurement.

2. —————————Slicing and Optimizing

In this exercise, you will learn how to slice the image for optimization purposes. Once finished, the file size will be smaller than if you had not done this process. Then, you'll learn how to output the finished file as HTML and Web graphics.

1. Open the file **homepage.ai** from the **chap_21** folder or continue from Exercise 1.

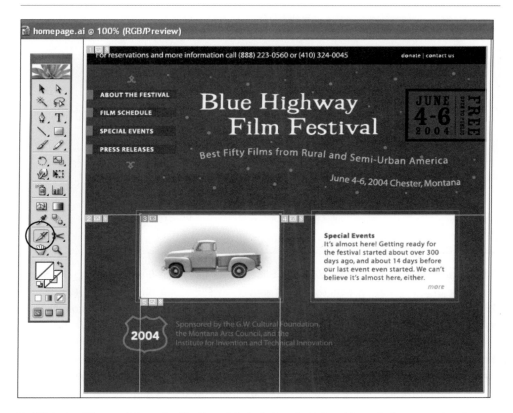

2. Click the **Slice** tool from the **Toolbox** (circled above). Using this tool, drag a rectangle around the white box that contains the truck on your screen. Try to get the rectangle on the edge of the white box as tightly as possible. Immediately after you do this, a series of different slice regions appear on your screen numbered 1 through 5. Even though you cut only one slice, Illustrator created additional slices automatically to create rows and columns for the table that it will write to hold this slice in place once the image is reassembled later in HTML.

The Slice tool draws from the tip of the blade of the icon.

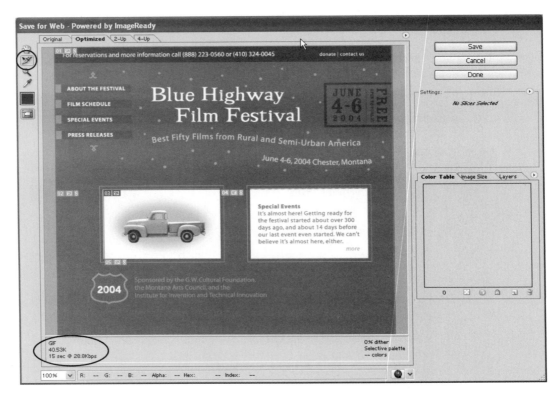

3. Choose **File > Save for Web**. Click the **Slice Select** tool (circled above). Using this tool, click off the image and notice the bottom readout. It should say something similar to **GIF, 40.53K, 15 sec @ 28.8 Kbps**, which reflects the total file size for all the Web graphics. This information may vary on different systems since the Save for Web interface is "sticky," which means it keeps settings from one use to the next. This readout shows the current file type (GIF), how big the current file is (40.53 KB), and that this Web page would load in 15 seconds on a 28.8 modem. (Your file size may be slightly different depending on exactly where you made the slice. Even a one-pixel difference could change the total file size.) Now it's time to optimize the slices in this document to make the overall file size smaller so it will download even faster!

*The entire Web page seems dimmed because the slices are visible. You can toggle slice visibility on and off by pressing **Q** on your keyboard. Make sure the slices are visible and the image looks dimmed out again before performing the next step.*

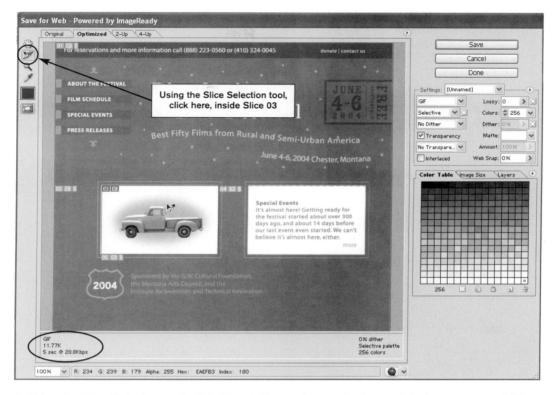

4. Using the **Slice Selection** tool, click **Slice 3**. The readout on the bottom left changes to say **GIF, 11.77k, 5 sec @ 28.8Kbps**. (Again, your file size might be different.) This shows the file size for the graphic contained within this slice.

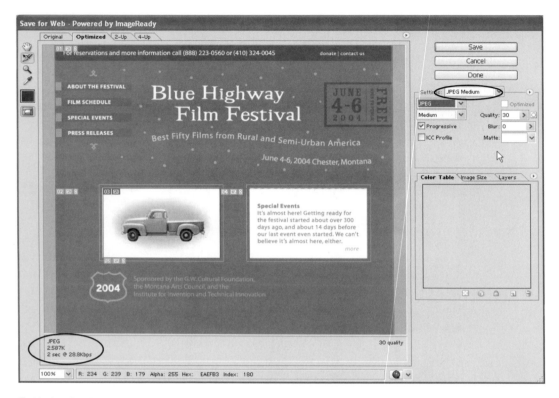

5. Under **Settings** on the right, choose the preset called **JPEG Medium**. This changes the image settings to **JPEG**, **Medium**, **Quality 30**, and **Progressive**. On the bottom left, you can see the file size for this slice has been reduced dramatically. Images like this, with soft edges and gradients, will compress better as JPEG files than GIF files. A thorough chart is located at the end of this section that goes into the JPEG optimization interface in greater depth.

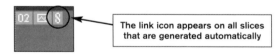

The link icon appears on all slices that are generated automatically

6. Using the **Slice Select** tool, click inside **Slice 1** on the top of the image. This slice has a file size of approximately **15.5 KB** and the default GIF optimization settings. Click inside the other slices (**2**, **4**, and **5**) and note their file sizes and optimization settings.

*There is a **link** icon inside all the slices except for Slice 3. Slice 3 was the slice you created by dragging the Slice tool around the artwork. The other slices were automatically generated. By default, automatic slices all share the same optimization settings, which are indicated by the presence of the link icon.*

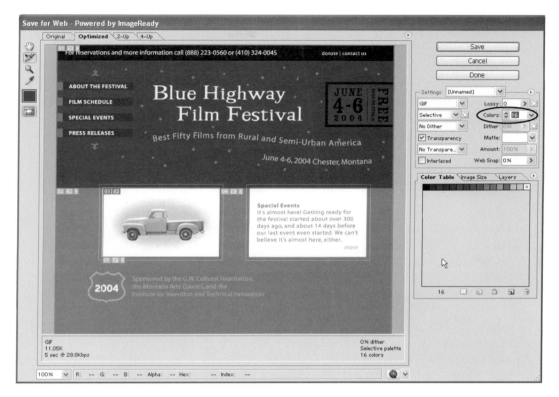

7. Change the **Colors** setting to **16**. The image still looks fine, but the file size was reduced. Click the other linked slices to observe that their file sizes are lowered as well. Changing the settings for one linked slice will change the settings for all of them. A thorough chart is located at the end of this section that goes into the GIF optimization interface in greater depth.

If you feel the reduction to 16 leaves parts of the design too grainy, experiment with larger numbers of colors that look better.

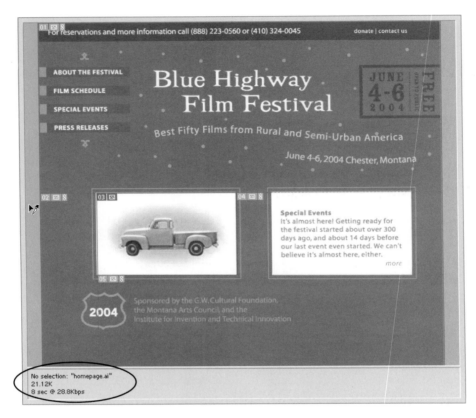

8. Click in the gray area immediately to the left of the image to deselect all slices and note that the overall file size is cut in half from the original file size. That's the advantage to slicing and setting different parts of the graphic to different optimization settings.

9. Click **Save**, and the **Save Optimized As** dialog box will open. Navigate to the **chap_21** folder you copied to your hard drive from the **H•O•T CD-ROM**. The **Save as type: HTML and Images** setting will save the images and write an HTML file for you. The file name automatically entered with an .html extension from the original name of the Illustrator CS document. The **Settings: Default Settings** selection will use all the settings you just created in the **Save for Web** interface. The **Slices: All Slices** setting will write all the slices into a folder on your hard drive. Click **Save**.

10. Locate the **chap_21** folder. Inside, you should find the HTML document Illustrator just created and a folder called **images**. Double-click the **images** folder to look inside.

11. Illustrator wrote five different image files for the five different slices. Note that **homepage_03.jpg** is a JPEG file, and the other four images are GIF files. This matches the settings you created in the **Save for Web** interface earlier in this exercise. Go back to the **chap_21** folder and double-click the **homepage.html** file. It will open in a Web browser.

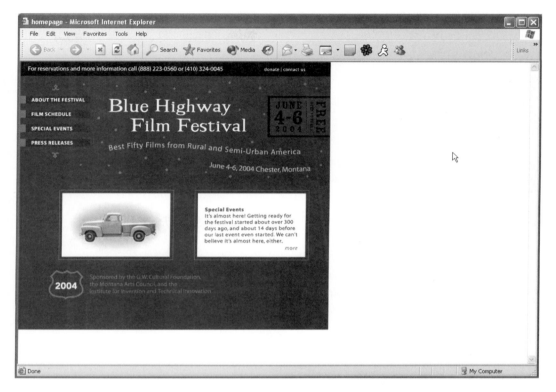

12. You should see the finished result of your labor. You could publish this page to the Web, or you could bring this file into another program such as GoLive or Dreamweaver (see bonus Chapter 22, "*Integration*" on the **H•O•T CD-ROM** for exercises that show this process).

13. Return to Illustrator CS and save the file. Leave it open for the next exercise.

NOTE | More About Slices

You will find more information about slices in the under the **Help** menu of Illustrator CS. Here are a few helpful facts:

- You can make a slice automatically from any object by selecting the object and choosing **Object > Slice > Make**. The benefit to working this way is that if you move or scale the object, the slice will move and/or scale as well.

- You can give your slices custom names, and add alternative text by accessing the Slice Options interface. Select your slice or slices, and choose **Object > Slice > Slice Options** to access this dialog box.

- To show or hide slices, choose **View > Show Slices** or **View > Hide Slices**.

- Aligning and distributing slices is possible if you've set them up using the **Object > Slice** technique. To align or distribute slices, first select the slices you want to adjust using the **Slice Select** tool. (Hold your mouse down on the **Slice** tool, and you will be able to access the **Slice Select** tool.) Choose **Window > Align** and click the align or distribute options.

- To delete a slice, select it with the **Slice Select** tool and press the **Delete** key. To delete all your slices, choose **Object > Slice > Delete All**.

MOVIE | object_slices.mov

Making slices using the **Object > Slice > Make** and **Object > Slice > Create from Selection** options offers some advantages and disadvantages compared to using the **Slice** tool. To see these techniques compared, watch the movie **object_slices.mov** online at **http://www.lynda.com/books/hot/illcs/movies/**.

More About Save for Web

Adobe Illustrator CS uses the same Save for Web interface as other Adobe products. This interface was developed for Adobe ImageReady. It is a powerful mini-program that helps you save Web graphics from many Adobe products. Here is a handy chart to help you understand some of the deeper features of this mini-application.

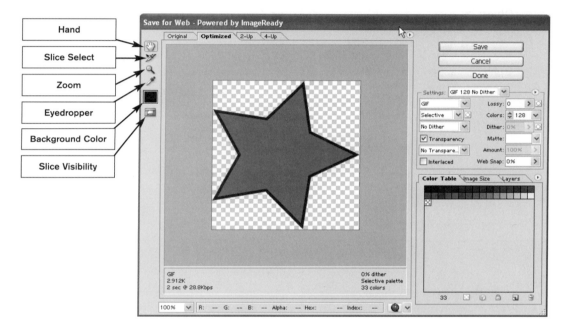

Save for Web Tools	
Tool	**Description**
Hand	The Hand tool allows you to scroll around a large image.
Slice Select	The Slice Select tool allows you to select slices and set their optimization settings.
Zoom	The Zoom tool lets you zoom in and out of your image.
Background Color	You can set a color here for the HTML background color.
Slice Visibility	Click this button to toggle slices on or off.

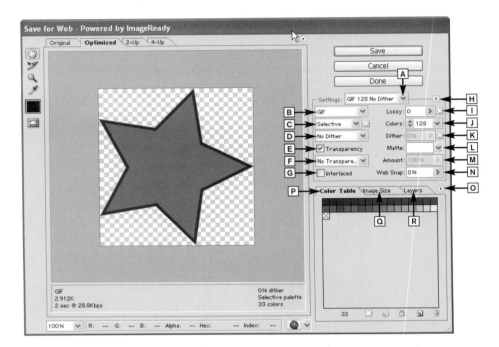

GIF Compression Options

Name	Description
A - Preset pop-up menu	Choose from preset compression values, including settings that ship with Photoshop CS, or your own custom settings.
B - Optimized File Format pop-up menu	Apply JPEG, GIF, or PNG compression to an image.
C - Color Reduction Palette pop-up menu	Choose the best color palette to compress your GIF images. The Adobe engineers give you a lot of options for using different palettes. You should try them out on different images, because there is no best choice until you apply it to a real sample. The alpha channel button to the right of the Color Reduction Palette pop-up menu doesn't work in Illustrator CS.
D - Dither Algorithm pop-up menu	Choose different dither patterns.
E - Transparency check box	Turn this on to activate transparency.

continues on next page

GIF Compression Options *continued*	
Name	**Description**
F - Transparency Dither Algorithm pop-up menu	When transparency is activated, this setting allows you to dither or blend the edges of a transparent image to a background color on a Web page.
G - Interlaced check box	Turns on interlacing. This will make the graphic initially appear chunky, but it is visible to the viewer sooner. It will come into focus as it fully downloads.
H - Optimize menu	Save and load custom settings for the Preset pop-up menu (A).
I - Lossy menu	Lossy compression can reduce file size at the expense of image quality. Try entering a value to see if it makes a difference to the file size savings without making the images appear too noisy.
J - Colors pop-up menu	Set the number of colors for the GIF output. Fewer colors make for a smaller file size, but can compromise image quality.
K - Dither slider	Use this slider or enter numeric values to increase or decrease the amount of dither. Dithering uses fewer colors to simulate the original colors by creating a pattern of colors that blend together to create a color that isn't there. It is really only helpful with photo or gradient images—and these are usually better saved as JPEG images anyway.
L - Matte pop-up menu	Matte color will change the color of transparent pixels (must be used in conjunction with the Transparency check box [E]). This setting will also control the background color of the HTML.
M - Transparency Dither Amount slider	Controls the amount of dither for transparent images.
N - Web Snap pop-up	Allows you to snap non-Web safe colors to the closest Web safe color palette.
O - Color Table menu	Offers several options for controlling the color table in GIF images, including loading and saving custom color tables.
P - Color Table tab	Offers a preview of the colors in the image. This feature works only with GIF compression, not with JPEG.
Q - Image Size tab	You can resize the image with this tab.
R - Layers tab	Allows you to activate CSS (Cascading Style Sheets) for positioning of your graphics.

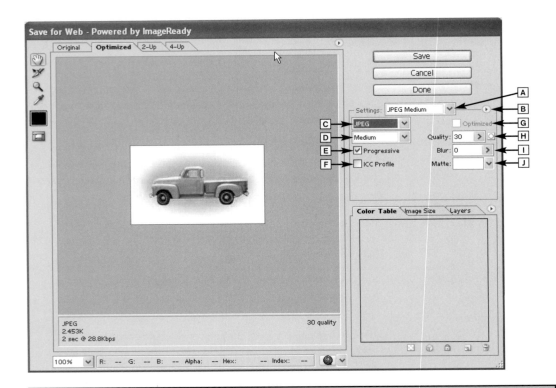

JPEG Compression Options	
Feature	**Description**
A - Preset pop-up menu	Choose from preset compression values, including settings that ship with Illustrator CS, or make your own.
B - Optimize menu	Save and load custom preset settings.
C - Optimized File Format menu	Apply JPEG, GIF, or PNG compression to a document or a slice.
D - Compression Quality pop-up menu	Choose a preset quality. You can choose a preset, or enter values into the Quality setting.
	continues on next page

JPEG Compression Options *continued*

Feature	Description
E - Progressive check box	Turn on the Progressive setting. Progressive JPEGs, like interlaced GIFs, appear chunky and come into focus as they download.
F - ICC Color Profile check box	Turn on ICC (**I**nternational **C**olor **C**onsortium) profiles. ICC profiles work with some printing devices, but not with Web browsers. They add file size to a compressed image, and aren't desirable for Web graphics.
G - Optimize check box	Turn on the optimized settings. This will make the smallest possible JPEG images.
H - Quality slider	Sets the compression quality. You can manually type a value or use the slider. The alpha channel button beside the Quality pop-up menu does not work in Illustrator CS.
I - Blur slider	Choose a blur value. You can manually drag the slider or enter values. Blur can decrease the file size of an image saved as a JPEG but can make the image, well, blurry.
J - Matte pop-up menu	A matte color will replace transparent pixels when an image is saved as a JPEG. This color will also set the background color in the HTML document.

3. ——————Creating a Different Layout

One of the great benefits of working with Illustrator CS for Web design has nothing to do with Web graphics and everything to do with vector objects. When working in a program such as Photoshop or ImageReady, you are primarily editing raster objects. In Illustrator, you can work with raster objects (in the **homepage.ai** file, the layer that contains the truck with the glow is a raster graphic), but most layers are composed of vectors. This means that objects can easily be moved, resized, and manipulated with no loss in quality. This exercise reviews techniques you've learned about in other chapters to demonstrate how flexible Illustrator can be for Web graphics due to its inherent strengths as a vector-based drawing tool.

1. Open the file **homepage.ai** from the **chap_21** folder or continue from Exercise 2.

2. Using the **Selection** tool, click an ornament above or below the navigation items. Both ornaments become selected since they are grouped.

3. On the **Layers** palette, expand the layer called **bg**, and notice that **ornaments** is selected here, too. Turn off visibility for the **ornaments** layer by clicking the **Eye** icon. This keeps the **ornaments** group in the file, but turns off its visibility and deselects it.

4. Select the **Selection** tool. Hold down the **Shift** key and select all four navigation buttons on the screen.

---

5. Choose **Object > Transform > Scale** to open the **Scale** dialog box. Enter the value **110%** into the **Uniform Scale** field. Click **OK**.

6. Click anywhere off the artwork to deselect the navigation buttons. Drag each button into place as you see above. It doesn't matter if the alignment is perfect; you'll fix this next by using the **Align** palette. For this step, just roughly get the objects into place.

7. Hold down the **Shift** key and click each button so all four are selected. Open the **Align** palette by choosing **Window > Align**. Click the **Vertical Align Center** button. This will perfectly center all four buttons along a vertical axis.

8. Next, click the **Horizontal Distribute Center** button. This will evenly distribute the middle two buttons between the two on either end. You're well on your way to an entirely new layout for this Web page!

9. Using the **Selection** tool, click off the currently selected layers to deselect them. Shift+click the **Blue Highway Film Festival** type and the green ticket.

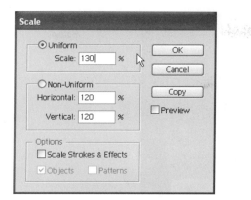

10. Choose **Object > Transform > Scale** to open the **Scale** dialog box. Enter the value **130%** into the **Uniform Scale** field. Click **OK**.

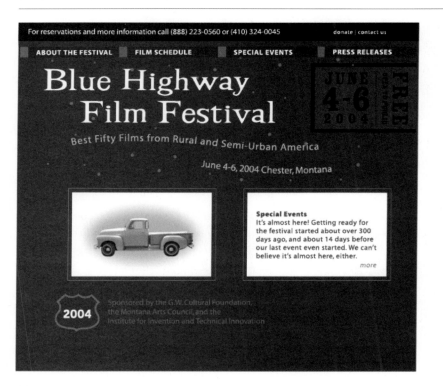

11. Continue to arrange the objects on the screen to match this layout. You will move most items slightly to the left as you do.

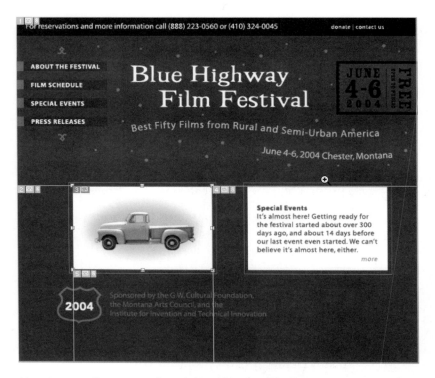

Here is an earlier screen shot of the old layout. You have an entirely different looking Web site now! This is the advantage to working with Illustrator as a Web design layout tool. Because of the vector-artwork, object-oriented nature of the way artwork behaves, many Web publishers prefer designing in Illustrator over raster artwork tools such as Photoshop or ImageReady.

If you wanted to use these files on the Web, you would choose **File > Save for Web**. You could optimize all the graphics again and save HTML and images for an entirely new look than that of Exercise 2.

12. Save and close the file.

4. ———————Image Maps

Image maps allow you to specify areas of the Web page that are "hot" and react when rolled over or clicked. They are a special kind of Web authoring technique that requires both graphics and HTML code in order to work. This exercise will show you how to set up and export image maps from Illustrator CS.

1. Open **imagemap.ai** from the **chap_21** folder.

2. With the **Selection** tool, click the green rectangle around the ticket to select it. On the **Layers** palette, expand the top layer named **Green Borders** to see its contents. Note that this border is a simple path. The other objects that make up this ticket are on the **bg** layer. Open the **Attributes** palette (**Window > Attributes**) and select **Image Map: Rectangle** and type **tickets.html** for the **URL** setting. Clicking this part of the image map would take a visitor to the page tickets.html.

The image map will designate parts of the image to link with particular URLs. When this image map is displayed on a Web page, clicking inside the green rectangle will send the viewer to the Web page **tickets.html**. *Note that you do not need to select all the ticket artwork—in fact, this can cause problems as noted in the upcoming "No Image Maps of Groups" sidebar. You only need to select the object that defines the border of the area you want linked.*

3. Click the oval path to select it. In the **Attributes** panel, choose **Image Map: Polygon**. Type **films.html** into the **URL** setting.

There are three choices in the Image Map menu: None, Rectangle, and Polygon. Anything that isn't a rectangle must be set as a polygon. Because image map shapes can't contain curved lines, an ellipse like this one is approximated by a polygon with several short segments.

4. Click the green highway sign path to select it. In the **Attributes** panel, choose **Image Map: Polygon**. Type **sponsors.html** into the **URL** setting.

WARNING | No Image Maps of Groups

Illustrator will let you select a group with the **Selection** tool and then use the **Attributes** palette to assign an image map link to that group. When you export the file, however, the image map will not work. There is no dialog box to warn you not to do this. This is why I had you note that the paths you selected were simple paths before you assigned the image map URLs. Compound paths and blends also have problems when used for image maps. They will work, but the result is always a rectangle that may not conform to the image shape very well. Envelopes and meshes work just fine for image maps.

If you have several objects in a group and want all of them assigned to the same URL, you can select the group and then double-click the **Contents** row of the **Appearance** palette. This targets all the objects in the group individually. Now if you assign a URL on the **Attributes** palette, Illustrator will create separate polygons for each object, and the image map will function properly.

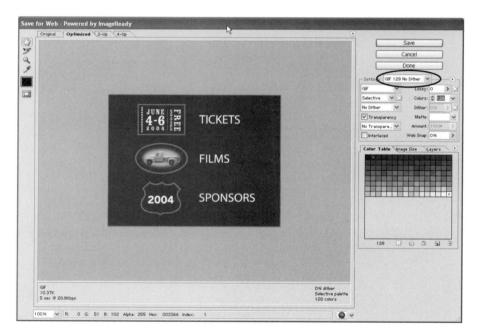

5. Choose **File > Save for Web**. Change the **Settings** to **GIF 128 No Dither**. This setting gives a good balance between image quality and file size. You don't want to be so concerned with file size that your images look distressed! Click **Save**.

*You must save the file using the **Save for Web** command to make the image map graphic. Saving the AI file saves all the settings that you applied in this exercise, which is important if you ever want to reopen and republish this file. However, it won't create any HTML or Web file formats such as GIF or JPEG.*

6. Navigate to the **chap_21** folder on your hard drive. A default file name is already entered since Illustrator CS borrows the name of the AI file and uses the same name for the HTML file and the image files (GIF in this case). Click **Save**.

7. Navigate to the file—called **imagemap.html**—that was just written to the **chap_21** folder. Double-click **imagemap.html** to view the file in a Web browser.

*Illustrator CS automatically put the **imagemap.gif** in the same **images** folder that was created for **homepage.ai** in an earlier exercise. If you wanted to create its own **images** folder, you could choose to save into a custom folder. You'll learn to do this in the next exercise. There is no harm in keeping your images in the **images** folder, as long as you set up the structure identically when you publish this document to the Web. You can also change this structure in an outside program such as Adobe GoLive, Microsoft Front Page, or Macromedia Dreamweaver.*

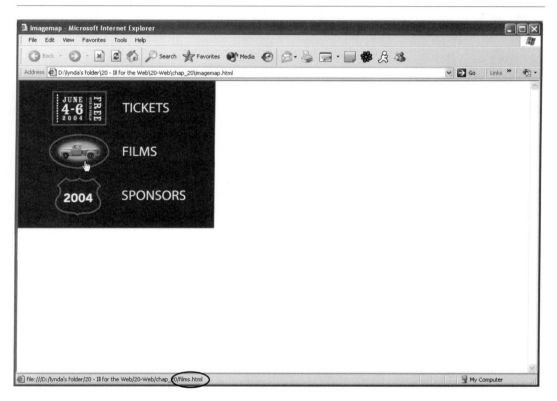

8. Move your mouse over the three buttons. You'll see that the icon changes to a hand symbol once the image map region is rolled over. Also, in the status bar of the Web browser window, the different URLs that you entered will appear with each associated button.

Note: *If you click the image map area, you will get an error message since you have not created real files for **tickets.html**, **films.html**, or **sponsors.html**.*

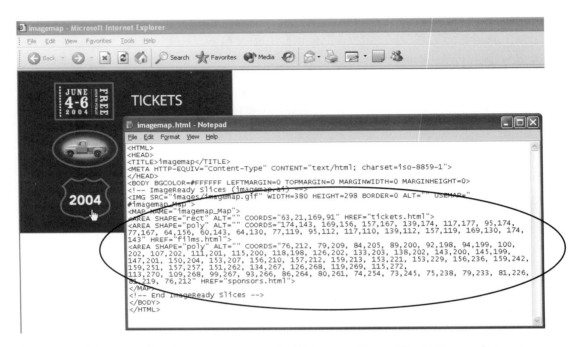

9. In the Web browser, view the source code for the Web page. Choose **View > Source** (Internet Explorer), **View > Page Source** (Netscape), or **View > View Source** (Safari). This shows the raw HTML code including the code for the image map. It shows the **AREA SHAPE** text that specifies the coordinates for the hot regions. Note how the area shape for **ticket.html** is a **"rect"** defined by only two x–y coordinates on the image, whereas the **"poly"** for **sponsors.html** requires dozens of coordinates to approximate the highway sign shape.

10. Close the source code window. Return to Illustrator and save and close this file.

When you save the AI file, all the image map settings are stored for a later date when you reopen it.

5. —————————————Writing Macromedia Flash Files

Adobe Illustrator CS can write files in the Macromedia Flash (Macromedia SWF) file format. The question is, why would you want to do this? Combining Illustrator CS and Macromedia Flash lets you have the best of both worlds: create outstanding vector graphics using a powerful vector editing tool (Adobe Illustrator CS.) and output in a format that offers animation, interactivity, sound, and stand-alone Web publications that don't even need a browser in which to play (Macromedia Flash). Most people export Illustrator files in order to import them to Macromedia Flash so they can add other features to the files. You can learn more about this in the bonus Chapter 22, "*Integration*" on the **H•O•T CD-ROM**. For now, you'll learn how to export a layered Illustrator file to the Macromedia Flash (SWF) format.

1. Open **I_ill_animation2.ai** from the **chap_21** folder.

2. Click on and off the **Eye** icons on the different layers so you can view the artwork on each separate layer. These layers were designed to be frames in a looping animation sequence. The animation runs from the bottom frame to the top, so this animation will display a count-down of 3–2–1.

3. Make sure all the **Eye** icons are turned back on. Choose **File > Export**. Navigate to the **chap_21** folder and create a new folder in this location. Name the folder **flash**. On a Mac, the new folder will open automatically. On a Windows computer, click **Open** to open this new folder.

4. Once you're in the new folder you created, choose a **Save as type** of **Macromedia Flash (*.SWF)**. Click **Save**. The purpose of making this folder is so the graphics and HTML files won't intermix with the other files in the **chap_21** folder. You could let them intermix if you wanted to; this technique simply shows you how to keep them separate.

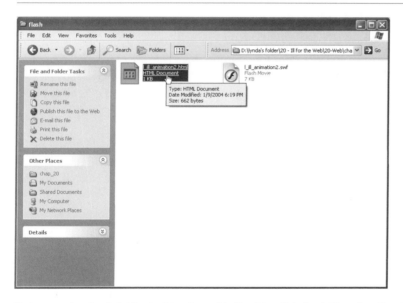

5. Choose **Export As: All Layers to SWF Frames**. Make sure that the **Frame Rate** is set to **2 fps** (frames per second), and that **Looping** and **Generate HTML** are turned on. Click **OK**. A chart describing all the options in this dialog box follows this exercise.

6. Locate the **flash** folder inside **chap_21**. Double-click the **I_III_animation2.html** file. It will open in a Web browser.

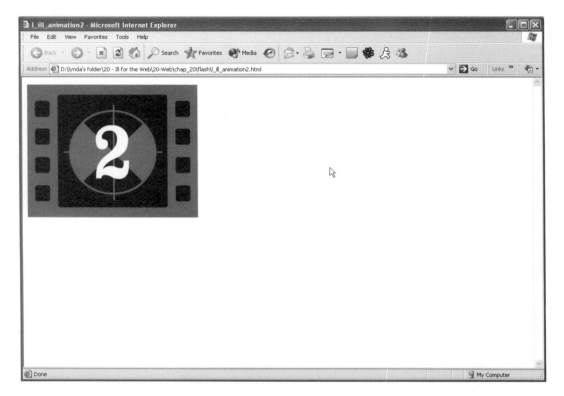

The animation should play right away and loop continuously. This document could be published to the Web as is, or it could be imported into Macromedia Flash to add other features to it, such as interactivity (play it when it's clicked, or to a add a play button), a soundtrack, sound effects, or voice narration. This is a very simple animation, but much more complex animations are possible.

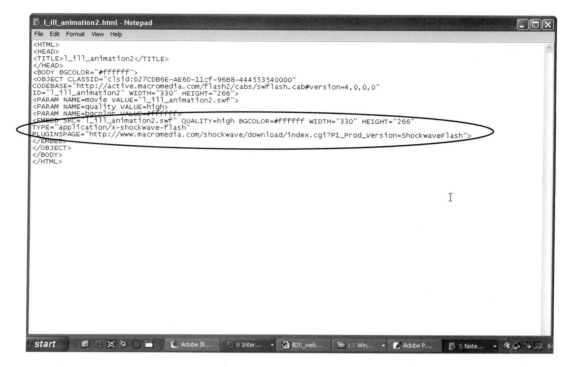

7. In the Web browser, view the source code for the Web page Choose **View > Source** (Internet Explorer), **View > Page Source** (Netscape), or **View > View Source** (Safari). The HTML code written by Illustrator includes a plug-in detection script to send people to the Macromedia Web site if they don't have the Flash plug-in installed.

As I said earlier, most people don't use Illustrator CS as a Flash authoring tool. Instead, they use Illustrator CS to create vector graphics and use the Export features to save a Macromedia SWF file that can then be imported into Macromedia Flash. One key part of learning to save a Macromedia Flash file from Illustrator CS is that instead of using the Save for Web feature, you use the Export command.

Macromedia Flash (SWF) Settings	
Setting	**Description**
Export As	Specifies how to export the Illustrator file. Choosing **AI File to SWF File** will write the entire Illustrator document as a single SWF frame. Choosing **AI Layers to SWF Frames** will export the artwork on each layer as a separate animation frame. Choosing **AI Layers to SWF Files** will export multiple SWF frames as separate SWF files from the layers in the Illustrator document.
Frame Rate	Specifies how many frames per second the animation should play. Note that a computer's processor speed, video card, and number of applications running all affect the actual playback, so this setting is not very reliable.
Looping	Sets an animation file to play over and over again. This option works only if you've chosen **Export As: AI Layers to SWF Frames**.

continues on next page

Macromedia Flash (SWF) Settings *continued*	
Setting	**Description**
Generate HTML	Writes the HTML for the SWF file. It is saved to the same location as the SWF file on your hard drive.
Read Only	Prohibits users from modifying the exported SWF file.
Clip to Artboard Size	Exports the file based on the artboard size, instead of the artwork bounding box itself.
Curve Quality	Sets the accuracy of the Bézier curves. A lower number will create a smaller file size at the expense of image fidelity.
JPEG Quality	Specifies the quality of the resulting JPEG. If you choose a **Lossy** method, you will be able to apply additional optimization.
Resolution	You can set a higher resolution than 72 pixels per inch, but the file size will be larger.

*Congratulations! You have finished not only another chapter, but the entire book! Thank you for your time and attention as we explored the fundamental aspects of Adobe Illustrator. I hope this work has given you the confidence and knowledge to continue the exploration on your own. Even after doing all the exercises in this book, you have seen only a small sample of what is possible with Illustrator. Be sure to check out the bonus chapter on the **H•O•T CD-ROM** for information on using Illustrator in conjunction with other popular graphics and design software.*

I hope you enjoy your Illustrator journey as much as I enjoyed creating this book. Remember, even though Botticelli's Venus no longer appears on the Illustrator splash screen, she is always watching and ready to help as your muse.

A.

Troubleshooting FAQ and Technical Support

| Appendix A |

H•O•T

Illustrator CS

This FAQ is intended to help if you run into any problems while following the exercises in this book. An updated version of this FAQ can be found on this book's companion Web site: **http://www.lynda.com/books/ hot/illcs/**.

Adobe Technical Support on the Web

Adobe offers several support options on its Web site. The main support Web site is

http://www.adobe.com/support/main.html

This page gives you access to downloads, lists of service providers, and training options applicable to all Adobe products.

Support information specific to Illustrator is found at

http://www.adobe.com/support/products/illustrator.html

This page provides Illustrator top issues, FAQs, tutorials, and discussion forums supported by Adobe. The forums are very active and are a great place to ask a question. Many Adobe employees and developers watch the forums and respond with helpful information.

Adobe Person-to-Person Technical Support

Adobe offers a limited period of technical support for new products where you can talk to a real live human being on the phone or via e-mail. Support is only available for problems with installation or product defects, such as recurring software crashes. You must register your copy of Illustrator to receive this service. Here are the numbers to call:

Macintosh   **206-675-6207**
Windows   **206-675-6307**

Adobe also offers what they call "Product Expert Incident Support" for questions and issues involving the use of Illustrator. This support is provided for a fee on a per-call or yearly contract basis. This is the number to call:

Macintosh or Windows   **206-675-6300**

Please note that lynda.com cannot help troubleshoot technical problems with Illustrator.

Peachpit Press

customer_ask@peachpit.com

If your book has a defective CD-ROM, please contact the customer service department at the email address listed here. I do not have extra CDs at lynda.com, so they must be requested directly from the publisher.

lynda.com

http://www.lynda.com/books/hot/illcs/
illcshot@lynda.com

I have created a companion Web site for this book, which can be found at **http://www.lynda.com/books/hot/illcs/**. Any errors in the book will be posted to the Web site, and it's always a good idea to check there for up-to-date information. I encourage and welcome your questions, comments, and error reports to **illcshot@lynda.com**.

Frequently Asked Questions

Q: When I open an Illustrator document sent to me by someone else, I get a message that a font is not available.

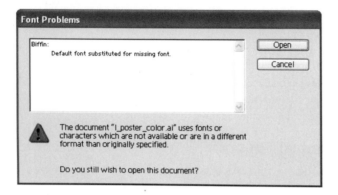

A: The illustrator file uses a font that you do not have installed on your computer, is not compatible with your operating system, or was not embedded in the file itself. By default, Illustrator CS embeds at least the characters in use for every font used in the document. Some fonts are prevented from embedding due to copyright settings added by the font maker. Even if the fonts embed, fonts embedded from a Mac may not work on a Windows computer and vice-versa. If you open the file, the missing font is temporarily replaced with the default system font. You can work on the file and return it to the sender, but the missing font will not appear correctly.

If you want to see the font correctly, you can purchase the font yourself, have the person who created the file send you the font so you can install in on your system, or have the person who created the file convert that type to outlines so it becomes a series of paths. Once the type is converted to outlines, you can no longer edit it as text.

Q: When I open an Illustrator document sent to me by someone else, I get a message that the document's color profile does not match the current working space. What in the world does that mean?

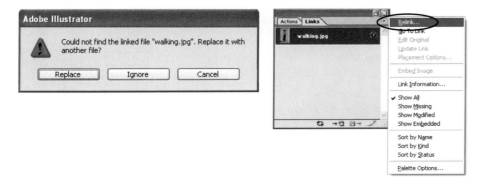

A: Color profiles offer a way of making colors on your monitor better represent the color you would see in other media such as print or film. If you are planning to return the file to the person who sent it, you can ask them if they want you to use his or her embedded profile. If not, the best course of action is usually to discard the embedded profile because it probably is not important to your art to manage color that precisely. Using different profiles may make the same color values appear differently on your monitor.

Q: When I open an Illustrator document I get a message that a linked file cannot be found.

A: Illustrator does not embed placed images in the AI file by default. Instead, it records a link to the location of the placed image. So, if someone sends you a file with a placed image, he or she must also send you the image. If you choose Ignore when you seed the error message about the placed image, you can still open the file and work on it. When the person who sent you the file gets around to sending you the image, you can relink the image by choosing **Relink** on the **Links** palette flyout menu.

Q: When I open an Illustrator document I get a message that the file contains legacy text, and I am asked if I want to update it. What should I do?

A: If you open a file created in Illustrator 10 or earlier containing type, you will see this message. Illustrator CS uses a completely new type engine that is not compatible with previous versions of Illustrator, so you must convert the type to the new format if you wish to edit it. If you never need the file saved in the older format, then updating all the text is a good choice. Once updated, the text is not readable in earlier versions of Illustrator. You can export the file back to a legacy version, but this often creates problems with type. For more information see the end of Chapter 9, "*Type Appearances and Styles.*"

Q: Why does Illustrator CS convert documents that don't contain text? How do I get rid of that [converted] part of the file name?

A: Illustrator CS converts all files created with older versions of Illustrator into a new format. It only asks you about conversion if the file contains text. When you save the file from Illustrator CS, you can no longer reopen it in the older version. So that you don't accidentally delete an older version, Illustrator CS appends [Converted] to the file name. If you want this feature disabled so you can easily replace your older files with converted ones of the same name, go to the **General Preferences (Edit > Preferences > General** [Windows] or **Illustrator > Preferences > General** [Mac]) and uncheck the **Append [Converted] Upon Opening Legacy Files** option.

Q: I can't find a feature that existed in previous versions of Illustrator. What happened?

A: Some features found in previous versions of Illustrator have been removed from Illustrator CS. In most cases, the missing feature has been replaced with a new feature. For example, the **Scribble and Tweak** effect has been replaced with more powerful **Scribble** effect, and **Tweak** has been moved to the **Distort & Transform** submenu. Other features of previous versions of Illustrator have been removed because they have become obsolete, such as the **MM Design (Multiple Master)** palette.

Q: I'm using Illustrator CS on a Mac, and every time I launch Illustrator, it gets to updating the font menu and then unexpectedly quits.

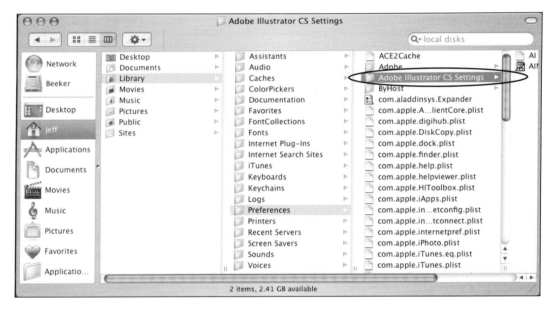

A: The problem is probably a corrupted preference in your user account. (If you know how to create a second user, create one, log in as that user, and launch Illustrator CS. If the problem goes away, then it is a corrupted preference.) If this is the problem, you can usually fix it by going to your user "home" folder (the one that looks like a house) and delete the folder **Library > Preferences > Adobe Illustrator CS Settings**. Empty the **Trash** and relaunch Illustrator.

Q: On the Mac, Illustrator seems to slow down, hang, or quit unexpectedly. The problem seems intermittent and Illustrator works fine for a while after I restart it.

A: There are too many potential reasons for freezes and crashes to document here. There is a common issue on the Mac that is not technically a problem with Illustrator but often affects Illustrator users. Font management on the Mac is often a source of trouble if you have more than 50 or so fonts in use. Mac OS 10.3 (Panther) addresses some of these issues with the introduction of Font Book, but more powerful third-party solutions are available. If you have more than 50 fonts installed on your Mac, consider installing Suitcase X1 from Extensis software. The software comes with a custom plug-in specifically for Illustrator CS. The demo runs for 30 days with all the features enabled and is available as a free download at **http://www.extensis.com/**. If the problems go away with Suitcase running, you can purchase a serial number and activate the software permanently.

Q: When I start up Illustrator CS on my Windows computer, I get a message that it "Could not Complete Operation."

A: You may not have enough free disk space. Try deleting unneeded programs and files. It is also possible you have too many fonts installed. Windows will handle more fonts without problems than the Mac OS, but eventually you may need to create a separate partition on your hard drive to store your fonts. This is usually only a problem if you have literally thousands of fonts.

Q: Will my third-party plug-ins from Illustrator 10 work with Illustrator CS?

A: Maybe. Some Illustrator functions, such as the type engine, are completely changed; others have not changed at all. Try 'em out and see. Regardless of whether they work or don't, it's best to contact the developer(s) for your plug-ins and see if there is an updated version for Illustrator CS.

Q: When I select type and then use the eyedropper to copy a color, nothing happens or the color appears incorrectly.

A: This is one of the most common problems new or upgrading Illustrator users experience. There are actually two issues, either of which can cause this behavior. The first issue is that there is more than one way to select type. If you select type with the Type tool, you select the characters of the type. If you select the type with any of the Selection tools, you select the container for the type. Normally, the *characters* are filled, and the *container* has no stroke or fill. If you select the type container, however, and then use the eyedropper to sample a color, that fill is added to the container rather than replacing the fill on the type characters. Now the type has two fill colors and appears either unchanged or oddly colored. The simple solution is to hold down the **Shift** key when you sample a color you want applied to type. With the **Shift** key depressed, the color is applied to the characters regardless of how you selected the type. For more information and an exercise demonstrating how this all works, see Chapter 9, "*Type Appearances and Styles.*"

Q: The bounding box can be handy, but it makes it hard to see my art. Can I turn it off? How about the dot that is the center of the selected objects?

A: The bounding box can be toggled on and off with the **View > Hide Bounding Box** and **View > Show Bounding Box** command. The center mark for selected objects can be toggled on and off using the **Show Center** and **Don't Show Center** buttons on the **Attributes** palette.

Q: When I make a compound path, sometimes the inner areas are filled and sometimes they are not. The behavior seems completely random.

A: Illustrator uses one of two different algorithms to decide how compound paths are filled. The **Even/Odd** winding rule behaves in a very predictable way in that the same shape always produces the same pattern of filled areas and holes. By default, however, Illustrator uses the **Non-zero** winding rule to fill compound paths. This rule can be frustrating to new users since the same shape can fill in different ways depending on the direction the paths were originally drawn. The rule in use and the direction of any simple path inside a compound path are controlled on the **Attributes** palette. For a detailed explanation of how to use these buttons, watch the **winding_rule.mov** movie online at **http://www.lynda.com/books/hot/illcs/movies/**.

Q: Part of my artwork won't print even though I can see it clearly on the screen.

A: Double-click the layer containing the artwork and make sure the **Print** check box is checked. If the **Print** check box is unchecked and grayed out, make sure the **Template** check box is unchecked.

Q: I want to see a zoomed in view of my art in one window and the entire page in another at the same time. Can I do this?

A: Yes, you can. Set the zoom you want for the first window and then choose **Window > New Window**. A second window opens with the same zoom setting. Set this window to the other zoom level you want. On a Windows computer, you can then choose **Window > Tile** and the two windows will appear side by side. On a Mac, you must arrange them manually. (This is not a slight to Macs. The **Tile** command takes advantage of a feature built into the Windows OS and was not created by Adobe.)

B.

Online Resources

| Appendix B |

The Web is full of great resources for Illustrator users. You have ample choices among a variety of discussion groups, listservs, and third-party Web sites that can really help you get the most out of the new skills you've developed by following the exercises in this book. This appendix lists some of the best resources for learning and extending Illustrator CS.

H•O•T

Illustrator CS

Discussion Groups

Adobe Sponsored forums

http://www.adobe.com/support/forums/main.html

Adobe sponsors a *very* active discussion forum, which is a great place to ask questions. Many Adobe employees and developers watch the forums and respond with helpful information. There are actually two separate forums, one for Windows and one for Mac. This is a bit unfortunate since most issues are actually platform-independent. You might want to post your question on both forums to get the widest audience. You must register to post on the forum. Registration is free and does not result in spam if you uncheck the options to receive free product information.

Mac Design Online forum

http://www.macdesignonline.com/

Don't let the Mac name scare you away if you use Windows. Most of the topics discussed are platform independent. Choose Illustrator from the list of forums on the lower-left side of the page to go to the Illustrator forum.

Listserv

A listserv is different from a newsgroup, and offers another way people can ask questions and get help with Illustrator. Questions and answers are exchanged through the email application of your choice. Sterling Ledet & Associates, an Adobe product training organization (**http://www.ledet.com/**), maintains a useful listserv for Illustrator using Yahoo Groups. You can join at **http://groups.yahoo.com/ group/illstrtr/**. This listserv is less active than the Adobe user-to-user forum, which can get overwhelming at times!

A Few Third-Party Illustrator Web Sites

Adobe Studio

http://studio.adobe.com/tips/main.jsp

Illustrator World

http://www.illustratorworld.com/

Mac Design Online–Illustrator Section

http://www.macdesignonline.com/illustrator.html

TIEM Design

http://tiemdesign.com/HOWTO/Illustrator.htm

Pluginz.com

http://www.pluginz.com/default.php

Adobe Plug-ins

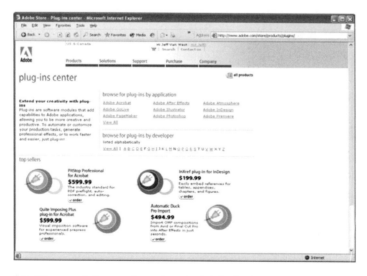

http://www.adobe.com/store/products/plugins/

Rick Johnson/Graffix

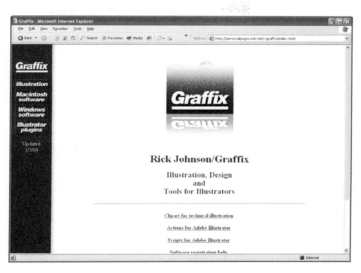

http://personalpages.tds.net/~graffix/index.html

Mordy.com

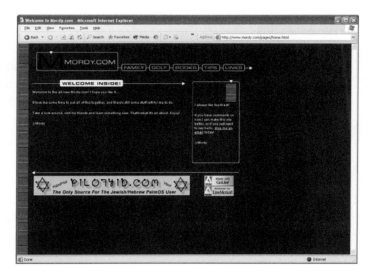

http://www.mordy.com/pages/tips.html

C.

Print Issues

| Appendix C |

H•O•T

Illustrator CS

When you are simply printing an Illustrator document for your own review, you'll probably just choose **File > Print**, click **OK**, and get the result you need. When it comes to printing Illustrator documents professionally, the subject becomes very complex. Because output options and the equipment used varies so widely, the subject is impossible to address in hands-on exercises. This appendix touches on many of the issues and directs you to other resources to learn more about areas beyond the scope of this book. The best advice if you are new to professional printing is to find a good printing service (usually called a service bureau) and ask them to help you get up to speed. The Illustrator discussion forums are also a great place to ask print-related questions and draw on the experience of many people at once.

General Printing

Illustrator CS has a completely new print dialog box, with far more features than ever before. One key feature that you may use when printing proofs from your own laser or inkjet printer is the **Fit to Page** option on the **General** section of the dialog box. This is especially useful for artwork that is an odd size, such as the tabloid-size poster you have been working with throughout this book. When you choose Fit to Page, the artwork appears in a preview window on the left. Bringing your cursor over the window changes the cursor into a Hand tool, which lets you change the position of the scaled artwork on the page by simply dragging.

One other very cool new feature worth noting is the **Save Preset** button. Using this button, you can save sets of print preferences you commonly use and switch between them quickly. This is a great feature when your office or workspace includes multiple printers.

The new Print dialog box also removes the need for the **File > Document Setup** and **File > Separations Setup** commands. The old Document setup options are distributed to several places in the new dialog box, and color separations are now in the Output section.

Service Bureaus

When you take an Illustrator file to an outside service bureau, it's very important to contact the vendor first. Most service bureaus vary in their instructions regarding how to properly prepare your files. It's best to have a discussion before you prep the files, so you can be 100 percent sure that you're doing it to their specifications. Make sure that in addition to the artwork you include linked images and fonts (unless you have converted to outlines, which you learned to do in Chapter 9, "*Type Appearances and Styles*"). Other requirements may involve file flattening, color separating, trapping, cropping, and other terms and concepts described in this appendix.

Important Vocabulary Terms and Concepts

There are many new terms and concepts to learn when you're preparing artwork to go to a professional printer. Here is a brief alphabetical listing of some of the most common topics:

Printing Terms and Concepts	
Term	**Meaning**
Bleed	When the image runs past the cropped area of the printed page so that no white space appears.
Color profiles	Color profiles offer a means to create consistent color between computer screens and printing devices. Using color profiles to ensure consistent color is often called **color management**.
Color separations	Artwork that will be commercially reproduced and that contains more than a single color is printed on separate master plates, one for each color. For example, four plates, one each for cyan, magenta, yellow, and black inks, can be combined to reproduce most colors. This process of separating the colors for use on different printing plates is called color separation.
Flattening	Illustrator artwork containing transparency, blends, or blending modes, is often flattened in order to prepare artwork for service bureaus or formats that don't support transparency.

continues on next page

Printing Terms and Concepts *continued*

Term	Meaning
Preflighting	The word "preflighting" comes from the term that pilots use to make sure everything is working properly before takeoff. For you as an Illustrator user, preflighting is the process of making sure your digital files will appear correctly when they are output to film. It is a troubleshooting process in order to discover problems with files before they ruin a job or incur extra charges for fixing problems on press. Check out the infomania preflight Web site at **http://www.infomania.com/preflight**.
Registration marks	When printing a full-color image using four-color process printing, four plates are produced for each of the four colors: cyan, magenta, yellow, and black. Registration marks help the printer reassemble the plates to perfectly align to each other.
Spot color	Spot color refers to ink colors that aren't mixed in CMYK; they usually involve another color system, such as Pantone Matching System.
Trapping	Trapping is the process of overlapping adjacent colors to avoid color registration problems. Trapping, also called "choke and spread," is necessary in screen printing. You can specify trapping as part of your Illustrator file, or the service bureau can add it. Many service bureaus will automatically add trapping to your file, so talk to them first.

Valuable Techniques

Here are a few tips that often come in handy when printing from Illustrator.

Tiling

You could print a huge poster or billboard from Illustrator, considering that artwork can be scaled to any size without losing quality. Artwork that doesn't fit on a single page can be printed onto multiple sheets of paper for reassembly if you use a technique called **tiling**.

Access the **Tiling** option in the **Setup** section of the **Print** dialog box. The page tiling boundaries will show up if you choose **Tiling > Tile Full Pages** or **Tiling > Tile Imagable Areas**. Once tiling is active, you can drag your artwork preview image around the window on the lower left to change how the art is tiled on the pages. You can also adjust the tiling in your artwork using the Page tool. It shares a tool slot with the Hand tool.

When the artboard is divided into multiple page tiles, page numbers are assigned. These do not print— they are for your reference only so you understand the order in which to reassemble the image.

Cropping

Many times, you'll want to restrict the size of an image through cropping. Unlike in Photoshop, where you use a crop tool to achieve this, Illustrator uses crop marks. The process goes like this: Drag a square or rectangle object over your artwork in the shape of the crop. (Cropping is always square or rectangle because that's the shape of an electronic document.) Once this object is created and selected, choose **Object > Crop Area > Make**. In the **Setup** section of the **Print** dialog box, choose **Crop Artwork to: Crop Marks**.

Only one crop area can be defined per document. If you want to re-create a crop area, choose **Object > Crop Area > Release**. Select the square or rectangle that you originally used, and choose **Object > Crop > Make**. Any previous crop area will be replaced by the new one.

Flattening

Although you can create transparent objects in Illustrator, some printing devices can't print the resulting file. To solve this, flatten your artwork. To preview how your flattened image will look, choose **Window > Flattener Preview** and click the **Refresh** button on the **Flattener Preview** palette. From the **Flattener Preview** palette flyout menu, you can choose **Show Options** and then set different options and view the results. You must click the **Refresh** button each time. To set the flattening features in the printed file, choose **Advanced** from the list on the left of the **Print** dialog box and choose the desired settings from the **Overprint and Transparency Flattener Options**.

Percent Ink

When you create colors using the CMYK method, you are actually specifying how much ink of each color goes on the page on a scale of 0 to 100%. The total amount of ink is the sum of all four individual inks, so if a color is 50% Cyan, 25% Magenta, 25% Yellow, and 30% Black, the total ink is 130% (50+25+25+30=130) Many presses have a limit to how much ink they can apply to the page, usually about 200–300%. Be aware as you create custom colors that you many need to limit the amount of ink you choose.

Font Usage

Whenever you deliver a job to a service bureau, it's best practice to deliver the fonts as well. If you assume that they have the same font, and they don't, a font substitution will be made, and your document might not look as expected. Here are some guidelines for this practice:

- Look at your font license agreement to see if it's acceptable to supply a copy to the printer. (It usually is.)

- Sent both screen and printer fonts if you're using Postscript (Type 1) fonts.

- Avoid mixing TrueType and Postscript fonts in the same document if possible.

- OpenType offers a solution to cross-platform type issues (the same font works on Windows or Mac) but is still a fairly new technology. Check with your print service before sending OpenType fonts.

Sending Images to a Service Bureau

The most common mistake with sending files to a service bureau is not collecting the images (and fonts, which was already addressed), or not preparing the images properly. In general, there are two preferred formats for images: EPS for vector art, or TIFF for high-resolution raster art. Avoid sending GIF, JPEG, WMF, BMP, or PICT images to the printer. Make sure that your raster artwork is in CMYK. The only time to use RGB images is for the screen (Web publishing, CD-ROM interfaces, PowerPoint presentations, and so on). Adobe has a Web page devoted to helping you find a Service Bureau at **http://partners.adobe.com/asn/partnerfinder/printserviceprovider/index.jsp**.

Index

H•O•T

Illustrator CS

Symbols

A

Page numbers beginning with "CD:" refer to bonus Chapter 22, "Integration," found on the H•O•T CD-ROM.

Page numbers beginning with "CD:" refer to bonus Chapter 22, "Integration," found on the H•O•T CD-ROM.

Page numbers beginning with "CD:" refer to bonus Chapter 22, "Integration," found on the H•O•T CD-ROM.

Page numbers beginning with "CD:" refer to bonus Chapter 22, "Integration," found on the H•O•T CD-ROM.

Page numbers beginning with "CD:" refer to bonus Chapter 22, "Integration," found on the H•O•T CD-ROM.

Page numbers beginning with "CD:" refer to bonus Chapter 22, "Integration," found on the H·O·T CD-ROM.

Go Beyond the Book

with lynda.com Training CD-ROMs:

**Learning Adobe
Acrobat 6**

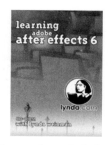

**Learning Adobe
After Effects 6**

**Learning Macromedia
Dreamweaver MX 2004**

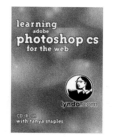

**Learning Adobe
Photoshop CS for the Web**

- Watch industry experts lead you step-by-step.
- Learn by viewing, and then by doing.
- Maximize your learning with high-quality
  tutorial source files.
- Over 33 active titles in our collection.

Visit http://www.lynda.com/videos/

lynda.com

Hands-on Training Books, CDs, & Online Movie Library.

Keep Learning

with More Hands-On Training Books:

Adobe After Effects 6
Hands-On Training

Adobe Photoshop CS &
ImageReady CS Hands-On Training

Adobe Acrobat 6
Hands-On Training

Macromedia Dreamweaver MX
2004 Hands-On Training

- Learn by doing.
- Follow real-world examples.
- Benefit from exercise files and QuickTime movies included on CD-ROM.
- Many other titles to choose from.

Visit http://www.lynda.com/books/

lynda.com™

Hands-on Training Books, CDs, & Online Movie Library.

Learn More for Less

@ the lynda.com Online Movie Library: